CROSS COURT REFLECTIONS

By
Bobby Bayliss

DEMENTI BOOKS

First Printing

Author - Robert Bayliss

Publisher
Wayne Dementi
Dementi Milestone Publishing, Inc.
Manakin-Sabot, VA 23103
www.dementimilestonepublishing.com

Cataloging-in-publication data for this book is available from The Library of Congress.

ISBN: 978-1-7330268-7-1

Cover design: Jayne Hushen

Graphic design by Dianne Dementi

Line art courtesy of Julia Petrozzi

Printed in U.S.A.

A full good faith effort has been made to trace copyright holders and to obtain their permission for the use of copyright material. The publisher apologizes for any omissions or errors and would appreciate notification of any corrections that should be incorporated in future reprints or editions of this book.

Praise For
Cross Court Reflections

"The one and only – Bobby Bayliss! No one has earned more respect from the players fortunate enough to have played under his tutelage, first at Navy (15 years) and then at Notre Dame (26 years). The same is true from his coaching peers, who have witnessed him do his magic with his players for decades.

The uniqueness of a small team like tennis (usually a total of 10-12 players) is that for four years BOTH the athlete and the coach share just about everything in each other's lives. Remember that the 18-22-year old is away from parental influence with new-found freedom for the 1st time. This gives a coach an extremely important role and almost sacred responsibility in the over-all development of each person, off the court as much as on.

There are so many sub-plots taking place on almost a daily basis over the course of each year that life is never dull nor without its challenges. Bobby thrives in these moments, and like cream, continues to rise to the top. I speak as a parent, when I say there is no one I would want there with my young man during these times than Coach Bayliss!

So, buckle up and hold on for a recount of Bobby's final year of coaching – you are promised from start to finish a fast moving, fascinating and exhilarating adventure!!"

Dick Gould
Stanford University, Retired Men's Tennis
Coach; ITA National Coach of the Year and
National Coach of the Decade

"When it comes to optimizing our full potential in the pursuit of any goal or endeavor, a trusted mentor is essential. Having played this incredible sport at every level, I have been blessed to reap the benefits of a few devoted souls. They possess three distinct qualities which permeate everything they do. Firstly, they are faithful. Unwavering in their support irrespective of the number of times you stumble, yet honest with their assessment of what needs to be corrected. Secondly, they are attractive—meaning their values and principles are rightly aligned and they live and demonstrate those values daily through their actions. Faith, family and friends are paramount. And finally, they are humble. Always carrying a modest opinion of themselves, they are willing to learn from others and continually strive to become the best version of themselves. Coach Bayliss embodies each of those characteristics, and to this day continues to be the most significant mentor in my life."

David DiLucia
Notre Dame All American: 1990-1992; ranked #1 in college tennis; recipient of Dan Magill Award; former coach of women's world #1 player Lindsay Davenport

"My two years as Coach Bayliss' assistant were the most memorable of my coaching career. After reading this book I feel like I'm back in the Eck Tennis Pavilion in South Bend. Coach Bayliss' evocative, unparalleled talent for expression gives the reader a behind the scenes look at the college tennis world. Only Coach Bayliss can weave such an indelible collection of anecdotes while striking the perfect balance of wit, humor and sincerity that define this legendary coach. I consider it required reading for all college tennis coaches and players!"

Billy Pate
Princeton University, Head Coach, Men's Tennis; former University of Alabama Head Coach, Men's Tennis; Chair of Men's Tennis Division I Operating Committee

"Having been delighted and charmed by Coach Bayliss' humorous writings over many years, I couldn't wait to read *Cross Court Reflections*. I was not disappointed. Rarely do we get a private glimpse into the way a Hall of Fame coach really thinks...up close and personal. Bobby delivered as promised, with humor and humility. See for yourself why 'Bullet' Bayliss has had such a profound influence on so many players and coaches, including myself, over his illustrious career."

> **David Fish**
> Head of Development of Universal Tennis;
> Retired Harvard Men's Tennis Coach; ITA
> Hall of Fame

"*Cross Court Reflections* is a wonderful mix of fun and insights into the college tennis scene, vividly portrayed by Bobby Bayliss, one of the most successful and highly respected collegiate coaches of our times."

> **David A. Benjamin**
> Princeton University, Head Coach, Men's
> Tennis: 1974 - 2000; Executive Director,
> Intercollegiate Tennis Association: 1978-
> 2015; #1 Player at Harvard; ITA Hall of
> Fame

"Coach Bobby Bayliss has truly captured every element of a college coaching season. It is a must read and will take you on a special journey. Any coach, player or parent, will learn something. I have been fortunate to compete against Bobby's Notre Dame teams. They were always extremely well prepared and competed as champions. Bobby's book highlights the same approach. Bobby Bayliss is a true leader. He sets the standard in collegiate tennis. His passion for tennis, knowledge of the game, and honesty are great assets to the development of our sport. We owe a great deal of our success to Bobby Bayliss' contributions."

> **Craig Tiley**
> CEO Tennis Australia; Tournament Director,
> Australian Open; University of Illinois Head
> Coach, Men's Tennis; National Coach of the
> Year/2003 NCAA Champions

"Reading Bobby Bayliss's *Cross Court Reflections* brought back many great memories of playing college tennis. I've always been proud to have been one of Coach Bayliss's first tennis recruits. He knew exactly what to say to seal the deal for me to attend the Naval Academy. He told my mother he would take care of me. And that is what he did, on and off the court, win or lose, he was always there for his players. This book is a must read for tennis players, coaches, fans and anyone who likes a good heartfelt story."

Craig Dawson
USNA '73; Naval Academy's #1 Player,
1991-93; NCAA selectee

"What a great read! This book will really help you understand what a coach feels in and out of competition."

Mike Brey
Head Basketball Coach, University of Notre Dame; National Coach of the Year

"An inside look at college tennis, where team dynamics can lead to a group of individuals accomplishing more than their individual abilities suggest is possible. Coach Bayliss, a true legend in the game, spent four decades stockpiling wins and losses on the tennis courts. Yet through it all, he never lost sight of the true purpose as a coach...the opportunity to impact the lives of young men and prepare them for life off the tennis courts."

Andy Zurcher
Notre Dame All American; NCAA Doubles Semi-finalist, 1994

"Coach Bayliss is truly one of the all-time greats, whose love for the game is rivaled only by his love for his players. His coaching, guidance and incredible sense of humor positively impacted me and countless others throughout our lives and careers. It's great to see him share his leadership, his legacy and his passion for collegiate tennis with readers."

Chuck Coleman
Notre Dame All American: 1991-1993

"Bobby Bayliss is one of the top three or four coaches in the nation. He does a great job in preparing his teams. He is extremely analytical and thoroughly studies his opposition to find a weakness. Every time you play a Bobby Bayliss-coached team, you know you're in for the fight of your life. He is a great friend off the court, but a highly competitive adversary on the court."

Jerry Simmons
Louisiana State University, Retired Men's Tennis Coach; ITA National Coach of the Year; ITA Hall of Fame

"After reading Bobby Bayliss' *Cross Court Reflections* it is so apparent that college tennis has never looked better. Bayliss does an amazing job of making you feel like you are in the first row of an epic 4-3 dual match. I truly had a hard time putting it down and also appreciated the inside knowledge from the Hall of Fame coach. Thanks, Coach."

Brian J. Kalbas
University of North Carolina, Head Coach, Women's Tennis; ITA National Coach of the Year; Three times coach of the ITA National Team Indoor Championship team

"Coach Bobby Bayliss has been one of the most influential people in my entire life. He is the best coach I have been around – in any sport – and taught me not only how to compete, but also many valuable life lessons which still serve me well many years after playing competitively."

Mike Sprouse
Notre Dame's #1 Player: 1995, 1996; #1 in Midwest college tennis

The La Jolla Beach and Tennis Club. March, 2006. Whenever we could work it into our schedule, we would fly to San Diego for Spring Break and play the Pacific Coast Doubles, followed by a match against UCLA or USC. L. to R., Santiago Montoya, Eric Langenkamp, Andrew Roth, Ryan Keckley, Brett Helgeson, Sheeva Parbhu, Stephen Bass, Barry King, Patrick Buchanan, Coach Todd Doebler, Coach Bayliss.

Tampa, FLA. April, 2008. Big East Championships. After graduating Stephen Bass, Barry King, and Ryan Keckley, I knew that the 2008 season would challenge us. Nonetheless, we captured yet another Big East crown. L. to R., Coach Bobby Bayliss, Stephen Havens, David Anderson, Tyler Davis, Santiago Montoya, Brett Helgeson, Dan Stahl, and Coach Ryan Sachire. Kneeling: seniors Andrew Roth and Sheeva Parbhu.

TABLE OF CONTENTS

Dedication   xiv

Foreword   xvii

Prologue: A Poignant Memory ~ And a Life Lesson   xix

Introduction to Cross Court Reflections   xxv

Chapter One: A Trip Down Memory Lane ~ Looking Back   1

  1. The Crazy Life of a Coach   13
  2. Down Tobacco Road   17
  3. An Unexpected Turn of Events   22
  4. Summer Activities of a Coach   27
  5. Recruiting ~ The Lifeblood of Your Program   32
  6. Togetherness in Recruiting Circles   40
  7. Camaraderie Among Coaches   45
  8. The Importance of Recruiting   54
  9. Another Season Begins   58

Chapter Two: Practicing at the Fitzwilliam Club   67

  1. An Annapolis Connection   71
  2. Taking on the Irish Davis Cuppers   77
  3. Turning a Group of Players into a Team   80

Chapter Three: The Fall Season   85

  1. Resources Available to the Coach   88
  2. College Athletic Leadership Today   92
  3. Fall Competition   98
  4. An Outstanding Fall Competition   101
  5. An Old School Coach   109

Chapter Four: Team Practice   113

  1. Evaluating the Personnel ~ What Needs to be Done 117
  2. The Importance of Doubles   126
  3. Scholarships and Lineups   132
  4. The Relevance of College Athletics   136
  5. Army vs. Navy ~ The Greatest of All Rivalries 139

6. Preparing for Regionals   145
7. The Significance of David Benjamin   150
8. Close, but no Cigar   153
9. Midwest Regionals   156
10. Life Lessons Taught by College Athletics   168
11. Final Fall Event ~ The Tribe Invitational   177

Chapter Five: The Lull Before the Storm   189

1. Old vs. New   194
2. 1971 NCAA Tournament at Notre Dame   198
3. MIT and a Hard Fought Match   202
4. Answering the Bell   205
5. Off and Running ~ The Season Begins   208
6. ITA Kick-Off Weekend   215
7. Bouncing Back and Faith Restored   220
8. On the Road   225
9. A Close One in Lexington   228
10. Why College Sports   235
11. Next Up ~ The Michigan Wolverines   239
12. The Big Picture   243
13. Craig Tiley Builds a Champion and Brad   249
    Dancer Continues the Quest for Excellence

Chapter Six: Spring Break and Beyond   257

1. The Blue Gray National Classic   260
2. A Trip Back to 1994 ~ The Irish Host the NCAAs   262
3. Greg Patton Takes Tennis to Idaho   267
4. Down the Stretch   273

Chapter Seven: Nearing the Finish Line   279

1. Changes in College Sports   285
2. A New Rival Emerges   298
3. Big East Championships   303
4. 2013 NCAA Tournament   311

Chapter Eight: For All of the Marbles   317

1. Practice in Columbus   325
2. "Last Hurrah"   334
3. Comparing the Matchups   340

    4. And Then Came the Rain   351
    5. The Day After   359

Chapter Nine: On to Champaign ~ A Career in Conclusion   363

    1. In Retrospection   368
    2. An Evening to Remember   371
    3. Bayliss Joins Vaunted 300 Club   374
    4. Another Look Back   379

Chapter Ten: Epilogue: Never Saw This Coming   387
    ~ An Unexpected Opportunity

    1. Next Up ~ the Tar Heels and the Wolfpack   394
    2. Another Close One   397
    3. Spring Break ~ Never a Bad Thing   399
    4. Home Cooking is Usually Better   406
    5. The ACC Tournament and Then the Wait   414
    6. Several Days Later   417

DEDICATION ~ FOR PAT

I would like to dedicate this book to my wife, Pat, without whose patience, support, and understanding I would not have been able to launch and sustain a career in college coaching. We have moved three times to very different locations. In each case, I was thrown immediately into the process of building a team. This demanded my time, effort, and attention, all the while introducing me to new friends and requiring me to build new relationships, always with the goal of creating excellence and ensuring that I was engaged and stimulated. She, on the other hand, was forced to leave her friends and support systems, oversee how each transition challenged our children, place our kids in new schools, find new doctors and dentists, and see that our family remained closely connected and happy. These were just a portion of her responsibilities. Team travel and recruiting required me to miss countless weekends. Somehow Pat took all of this in stride......oh, and I forgot to mention that she also needed to deal with the wild swings of emotions of her husband - me - as I reacted to the wins and losses that shaped my career.

I would also like to include each of our children in this dedication. I am more proud of my family than of any coaching achievements in my life. Our daughter, Jackie, and each of our sons, Rob, Brendan, and Patrick, have been highly successful in their own right, and our eight grandchildren have been gifts from God. This book is a testimony to the patience and love they continue to show us and each other. Thank you, Jackie, Rob, Brendan, and Patrick, as I know I missed many sports contests, school productions, and even some graduations. I could only do this because of the exemplary lives you led and continue to lead. I am so very proud of the adults you have become: mother, fathers, and caring people.

So, Pat, thank you for your love and also the assistance you have provided me on this work. You made it all possible, and I so very much appreciate your selfless assistance, albeit proofreading, suggested changes, or seeing my thoughts through a different prism. You have been my greatest gift and blessing, as shown in my moments of "reflection."

Lou Holtz is one of America's most successful, well known, and popular football coaches, in addition to being a successful author, motivational and in-demand speaker and TV commentator. Born in Follansbee, WV he attended Kent State University on a football scholarship, graduated and began one of the great coaching careers of all time. He served as head coach at William and Mary, North Carolina State, the New York Jets, Arkansas, Minnesota, and Notre Dame [where he won a national championship]. After a career as a TV commentator on ESPN, he became the head coach at South Carolina. At every stop along the way, he sent his team to at least one bowl game.

Lou Holtz is in great demand as a motivational speaker and has authored books on the same subject. His "Dr. Lou" skits on ESPN became nationally famous. A statue in his honor looks over the Notre Dame Stadium, where he was particularly beloved by his players. He is a 2008 inductee to the College Football Hall of Fame.

FOREWORD

When Bobby Bayliss contacted me to write the Foreword for his book, it brought back many fond memories of my eleven seasons at Notre Dame, and the friendships made during that time. Obviously, fans think primarily about what kind of success a coach can deliver in wins and losses; I understand that, but my feelings for the University of Notre Dame go far beyond games won or lost. Certainly, we experienced some success, but my recollections primarily involve people, not championships. One of the things that comes through loud and clear in Bobby's book is his love for Our Lady's University. On this, and many other things, we are in agreement. One of my fond non-football memories is that I served – at Bobby's request – as the speaker for the 1994 NCAA Tennis Championship banquet. It was a great evening!

When I arrived at Notre Dame, the football fortunes were not in a good place. While the job of rebuilding was certainly arduous, I felt a special purpose in this task, something difficult to put into words. I wanted success for Notre Dame and was inspired to give the task my best effort. I arrived at a special time, because, shortly after we won the 1989 national championship, good things began to happen in other sports as well. Not only did Bobby take his tennis team to the NCAA team championship final and remain nationally competitive for many years, but positive things also began to happen in soccer, women's basketball, baseball, lacrosse, and other sports. It truly seems like a magical time, as I look back and sort through memories.

Bobby takes the reader through his last season coaching at Notre Dame. He effectively uses this as a vehicle to segue back to many stories he has to tell you about his players, teams, and inter-actions with other coaches. He inserts the reader into these stories, allows you to feel his pain and anguish, excitement and elation, and you understand that the moment has produced a life lesson that the reader can incorporate into daily living. It is apparent that Bobby strongly believes, as do I, that sports can teach life lessons and provide participants with experiences which form values and influence people in positive ways. The confidence a young man or woman gains through the process of commitment, hard work, and overcoming obstacles can be life-altering and becomes a part of that athlete's very persona, allowing it to provide inspiration and self-assurance in other areas of that person's life.

It is interesting that Bobby feels that his years at the US Naval Academy prepared him for the bigger stage onto which his national success projected him. He believes that the Academy's reinforcement of values such as integrity and accountability became ingrained in his core and remained a part of his decision-making and his ability to handle the stress of competition. These values, combined with the spirituality and sense of community that both he and I found compelling at Notre Dame, allowed him to operate and perform daily tasks with the comfort that comes from knowing you are doing the right thing. I personally can understand the love and loyalty he has for his former players, because we both value relationships over fame and fortune. This is something that most successful coaches incorporate into their daily lives.

I hope you enjoy this book as much as I did. It just might leave you knowing why athletics can be such a strong and effective tool to shape and influence lives, especially at the important ages of 18-22 years. You likely will look at coaches differently and be able to understand what motivates and guides them, especially during the heat of competition. In an era where we all too frequently see sports teams and other valuable school activities being eliminated in cost-containment measures, it is especially important that we hold dear the values that are derived from them.

GO IRISH!

Lou Holtz

PROLOGUE

A Poignant Memory ~ And A Life Lesson

The beauty of coaching is that
you get to touch lives.

Morgan Wooten

Most of us over the age of thirty can vividly recall where they were and what they were doing when they heard the news of the terrorist attacks on the World Trade Centers on September 11, 2001. It is one of those indelible life experiences, much like the Kennedy assassination is for people over 65. In my case I was attending a meeting of the head coaches at Notre Dame, conducted by our Director of Athletics, Kevin White. At some point during the meeting, Kevin's secretary interrupted him for a private moment, after which he dismissed the meeting, telling us that "something crazy is happening in New York City now and we need to take up this agenda at a later time." I walked back to our offices at the Eck Tennis Pavilion with our women's coach, Jay Louderback, wondering just what could be going on back in New York. I entered my office and turned on the television to see what was transpiring, only to learn about - and view live - the horror that we now commonly refer to as "Nine-Eleven." My assistant coach, Billy Pate, and I found our eyes glued to the screen in disbelief, not really comprehending the disaster taking place in real time, wondering things like "Who?' and "Why?"

Shortly thereafter my office telephone rang and I reached to pick it up, not expecting the clamor of loud and tumultuous sounds which came blaring out from the handset. My first reaction was that I had a bad connection, but before I started to hang up I began to notice recognizable sounds and understand that my connection was very good indeed and that what I was hearing were the chaotic sounds of screaming, sirens, screeching tires, and various other indications of that tragedy. Soon I discerned a faint voice which I recognized over the din. It was my former team captain of the 1998 Notre Dame tennis team, Danny Rothschild, and he was straining to be heard over the background noise. "Coach, are you there? It's Danny. I got out! I'm safe! I can't talk long. We are sharing a cell phone and reception is terrible and the battery is low. The guys will want to know about me and I'm sure they'll call you. Let them know I made it out safely. Got to run!" Sure enough, the calls began to arrive and I was able to reassure Danny's teammates of his safety, but the impact of his call resonates deeply with me even today. Danny was concerned for his teammates…..enough to make the call to his coach to ensure that the word reached them. At a critical and defining moment in his life, he had remembered the very same men with whom he had battled, scratched and clawed, and shared so many of life's experiences -- sufficiently so as to make an effort to let them know of his safety.

That's one thing you learn in sports. You don't give up; you fight to the finish.

Louis Zamperini
['Unbreakable']

If ever there had been any doubt about the validity of my life's work of teaching, mentoring, and coaching young men from 18-22 years of age, it ended right then and there. As a coach we all hope that we are imparting life lessons and doing everything we can to provide the environment that will allow our players to become better people, but it is difficult to keep our eyes on that ball while we are in the throes of competing and concerned about our respective team's won-loss record, ranking, and post-season finish. Not a day goes by without my realizing some situation I could have handled in a better manner, but all of us in this crazy profession need to believe that our efforts to produce victories also embody positive mentoring. The call from Danny Rothschild told me that I was not a failure and that his feelings for his coaches and teammates were so strong that they had compelled him to reach out to us in the middle of a true life and death crisis and spoke to his own core values and desire to do the right thing.

Obviously the impact of "Nine-Eleven" far overshadows my brief recounting of it - something that took only seconds and did nothing to save lives or change the world. Nonetheless, I can still hear Danny's voice today, as well as the many dreadful sounds in the background. I have told this story many times, to both individuals and audiences, and it never gets old for me. It is an affirmation for me that not only is my profession engaging, challenging, and, honestly, lots of fun, but it also impacts lives. This impact can be for the better or worse, and it is my obligation and challenge that it be a positive one.

Bobby Baylis

~ Cross Court Reflection ~

Your ability to win games is one thing, but your ability to create athletes of good character--that should be your first responsibility!

Herman Edwards

BOBBY

1968 coached Thomas Jefferson HS, Richmond, VA to the State Championship

1969-84 coached the US Naval Academy (248-80)

1980 US PTA National Coach of the Year

1980-87 Head Tennis Professional, Wellesley Country Club

1984-87 Tennis and squash Coach at MIT (43-23)

1987-2013 Men's Tennis Coach, Univ. of Notre Dame (474-236)

1992 Wilson National Coach of the Year

1991 Coach of US Tennis Team at World University Games, Sheffield, England (Gold Medal)

2003 Coach of US All Star Team vs. Japanese All Stars

BAYLISS

COACHING
FACTS

1994 Winner Rolex Meritorious Service Award

14 time conference Coach of the Year

Halls of Fame: Univ. of Richmond Athletic Hall of Fame, Thomas Jefferson HS Athletic Hall of Fame, Richmond Tennis Association Hall of Fame, Blue Gray National Classic Hall of Fame, Intercollegiate Tennis Association Hall of Fame

Intercollegiate Tennis Association Board of Directors 1988-2013

"Wimbledon is such a special experience.....beautiful grass courts, strawberries and cream, terrific tennis. What's not to like?"

Bobby Bayliss

Introduction to
Cross Court Reflections

*'Coach' is one of the greatest titles
anybody can have. They impact
kids' lives in a way that no
other teacher does.*

Phil Knight

My pathway to the college coaching ranks was far from ordinary. Perhaps it could best be said that I stumbled there, as I certainly never remember having any such goal or plan. Unquestionably, it was something that I would have signed on to join, but without a road-map for achieving a career in coaching, I simply was clueless about how to navigate the process and make it happen. As a young boy I was really taken with sports and moved from one to another in my efforts to become a great and famous athlete, but at just a smidgeon over five feet tall entering high school and weighing perhaps one hundred pounds dripping wet, my options were, shall we say, limited. I was always throwing and catching a ball and had two younger brothers who were recruited as college basketball players, but tennis came later to me, having learned that it might be my last and best resort.

Attending a large public high school with a strong athletic tradition made it more difficult for me to stand out, and I made the varsity basketball team only as a senior. Had I been a better basketball player, tennis might never have become my sport of choice and love. In talking to friends from those days I now realize that, while my physical talents seemed pretty ordinary to them, almost all remember that I worked very hard and seemed to be extremely driven. I remember only that I never felt like practicing was work. It was what I did for fun. I was fortunate that in Richmond, VA, my hometown, there was a large public park (Byrd Park) that had a highly unusual tradition and collection of very strong tennis players. Being around "the Park" exposed me to a level of tennis that is not normally available outside of outstanding country club programs or, in today's world, tennis academies. Sam Woods, a man who devoted his life to tennis and youth, was the pied piper who made Byrd Park a tennis mecca and opened the door for me and many others. The competitive atmosphere around "the Park" forced me to gain both much needed determination and a love for competition, something that fueled me and kept me working hard to improve.

Persistence is the mortar that holds the bricks together when the high winds blow.

Seth Davis

I chose the University of Richmond as my college and loved every minute of my four years there. While tennis became my greatest priority as an undergraduate, I was also active in fraternity and social life, intramurals, and student government, among other things, and also became a dean's list student. Interestingly, it was the advice of my college basketball coach, Lewis Mills, that steered me towards tennis. Perhaps it was his way to get rid of me, as I was so dedicated that cutting me would have been difficult. Richmond was the perfect place for me, as it provided a D-I program, yet fielded a sufficiently weak, non-scholarship team when I arrived that I was able to make the squad and play in every match beginning as a sophomore. (Freshmen were ineligible in all sports in those days and played on freshman teams.)

> *Success is falling down nine times and get-*
> *ting back up ten.*
>
> Jon Bon Jovi

Let's make one thing clear: Richmond was no tennis powerhouse when I began there and, in fact, we went 0-12 my first year playing . Add to that my personal record of 0-12 at #5 and #6 singles[11 of the 12 matches went to a third set], and my best guess is that I was likely the worst college player in the United States.I could hit the ball somewhat modestly, but figuring out how to win escaped me. Nonetheless,it was this combination of opportunity and the considerably stronger and talented base of players who arrived one class behind me[thank you, Sandy, Butch, and John] that allowed me to develop into a decent college player as a senior. This beginning allowed me to transition to a much higher level in the coming years. The patience of my college coach, Leonard McNeal, with a young player trying to find his way, was no small factor, either. Thanks, Coach, for caring. You were right. You don't have to hit every ball as hard as you can and ridiculously close to the line every time in order to become good. Combining this with the exposure to even better players as I also worked as an assistant tennis professional at the nearby Country Club of Virginia, some of whom played "the tour," took me to a greater and greater level and pointed me toward a future in tennis..... more on this later.

The thought of writing a book has always intrigued me, perhaps because I have both an undergraduate and Master's degree in English, and wanted to put them to use. I decided early on that I did not want to write something just to be able to say that I had. I wanted to be able to add to the current state of scholarship, and was unsure of just how to accomplish that.

There's nothing to writing. All you have to do is sit at a typewriter and open a vein.

Red Smith

I have found too few books on tennis that I thoroughly enjoyed reading and hope to change this. Gordon Forbes's "A Handful of Summers" is, to me, the greatest book on tennis around. It would have been fun to recount my numerous significant tennis exploits, as he did, except that my playing highlights were, in comparison, not very significant and even less interesting. My best tennis came, in fact, after I began coaching at the Naval Academy. After some reflection I realized that my career in coaching, particularly as it pertains to what I have both enjoyed and observed, was indeed interesting and included incidents that were dramatic, humorous, and begged telling. It is important to me that I somehow convey to you why I believe that coaching is not only important, but even more necessary in today's world, and that it leaves behind a legacy of life lessons. To have the responsibility of mentorship thrust upon me was both daunting and invigorating. Whenever I doubted my abilities, I was able to remember a comment or note from a former player telling me that I had made a difference in his life, perhaps the greatest compliment any coach can receive. I also want you to feel my passion as a big match approaches. I want you to understand the tremendous elation in winning an important victory. I hope that I can also convey to you the feeling of great disappointment and angst that seemed to crush me as our team fell to a rival, or lost in the NCAA tournament. Most of all, I will try to convey the sense of responsibility that I always felt that somehow, someway, I might have touched each life and left it even just a little bit better. To use the immortal words of Grantland Rice:

> *When the one great scorer comes to write*
> *against your name....*
> *He writes not if you won or lost, but how*
> *you played the game.*

The most remarkable thing about my own career, you see, is that it even happened at all. When asked in 1968 by the Athletic Director of the US Naval Academy if I had an interest in becoming the next Navy tennis coach, my reply was "Do you mean the varsity team?"I can still hear his laughter today - 51 years later. It began as on-the-job training. Everything came unscripted and unplanned, but I have loved every day of it and want to use this forum as a way to encourage others to chase and follow their dreams, because, as I have found, they can indeed come true. So jump on board and let's take this ride together. It might be many things, but dull is not one of them.

> *The reason why people give up so fast is that*
> *they tend to look at how far they still have to*
> *go instead of how far they have gotten.*

Muhammed Ali

Notre Dame players celebrate upset victory over #1 USC in NCAA semi-final match with University of Georgia. May, 1992. Athens, GA . L to R - Chris Wojtalik, Andy Zurcher, David Dilucia, Will Forsyth, Mark Schmidt, Coach Bobby Bayliss. *Photo courtesy of University of Georgia Sports Information*

CHAPTER ONE

A Trip Down Memory Lane

*A coach will have more impact
in a year than most people
do in a lifetime.*

Billy Graham

Looking back

May 17, 2012. As I drive east on Rt. 316 leading to Athens, Georgia, a flood of memories cascades from the recesses of my mind and heart. You see, Athens is the Mecca of collegiate tennis and its high priest is the venerable and dynamic giant in our world, Dan Magill. Magill had a vision long ago that Athens would become just what it is today - the home of the NCAA Tennis Championships. Even though the powers that control the sport have long since mandated that the tournament rotate annually to other spots [Palm Springs, California; South Bend, Indiana; College Station, Texas; Tulsa, Oklahoma; Palo Alto, California; Winston Salem, North Carolina; and Waco, Texas] due to the enormous home-court advantage held by the host Georgia Bulldogs, the tournament is coming home - back to the land of giant magnolia trees and pretty girls wearing lipstick, speaking with a soft Southern accent so thick you could cut it with a dull butter knife. The goal for most of us fortunate enough to coach this sport is, first and foremost, to make it to Athens where the top sixteen men's and women's teams will assemble to compete for the national title. Making it to the Sweet Sixteen validates your season. Arriving here means that you have been successful and that your players are in for a wonderful experience. Because I know that I am going to step down a year from now I am excited to once again experience the sights and sounds of Athens and ante bellum southern hospitality at its best.

When I took over at Notre Dame, my goal was to bring our team here and achieve something special. To be sure, the event had been dominated by the perennial tennis powers- UCLA, USC, Stanford, and Georgia, among the most successful. My job description - head coach with no assistant while teaching physical education courses and directing the newly finished Eck Tennis Pavilion - did not lend itself toward instant success. It all crystallized for us in 1992, my fifth season, when our squad from up north scratched, clawed, and fought our way to the NCAA Finals, becoming the lowest [10th] seed and first non-sunbelt team ever to make it to the Championship match. Led by the skinny, but charismatic David DiLucia, our Irish squad overcame the smart money and overwhelming odds and narrowly defeated a very talented Mississippi State team laden with Frenchmen to get the opportunity to face the #3 Georgia Bulldogs in the quarterfinals. The match with Mississippi State was challenging, to say the least. Led by Daniel Courcol, a future French Open main draw participant, and tennis-savvy Coach Andy Jackson, State pushed us to the limit before we snuck out a hard fought 5-3 win in the round of 16. It was anything but easy, as Jackson's Frenchmen were fast, competitive, and went for their shots with conviction. By the time the match ended under the lights I was exhausted and relieved. Survive and advance is the theme. We would live to fight another day!

Next up were the talented and highly favored Georgia Bulldogs. Beating Georgia at home in the NCAA tournament is not impossible, but it certainly qualifies as heavy lifting. Georgia had previously demonstrated that they were capable of winning it all and attracted a full house of 5,000 plus fans for virtually all of their home NCAA contests. The Bulldog fans do not cheer; rather, they bark - loudly and often, ramping the decibels to levels few experience in tennis. This creates an atmosphere in which it is truly difficult not to be intimidated. Their beloved Bulldogs had, time and again, won matches they had no business winning, particularly so on these same courts. We played brilliantly at times, winning four of the six singles and somehow escaped with a 5-4 victory capped by the 7-6,7-6 win at #2 doubles led by juniors Andy Zurcher and Will Forsyth. At a key point in the second set tiebreaker one of the Georgia players had cracked the racket he was using and incurred a code violation [point penalty] at a critical juncture in the match. Georgia assistant coach Peter Daub quickly asked the umpire if the penalty point would have been assigned had the racket not cracked. The umpire indicated that breaking the frame was what forced the code violation. Coach Daub told the player, Nirav Patel, to reach back and continue with his old racket, but the umpire would not allow it, eliciting a loud chorus of boos and elevating the drama. Shortly thereafter, Patel netted a return of serve from Forsyth and the match ended abruptly, giving us the upset win as Zurcher and Forsyth hugged each other ferociously. I remember walking to the media tent for the post-match press conference feeling like a 500 pound weight had been lifted from my shoulders, such was the burden that the Georgia fans brought to the opposition. I had watched many a match like this over the years and they all seemed to go Georgia's way. We needed to take a few moments to enjoy this one, but the turn-around time between matches allowed very little opportunity for such reflection, as we faced an even more daunting task in less than 24 hours. I made it a point to mention to the media that we had been honored to compete against the Bulldog crowd and that they really knew their tennis. I was hoping for this to give them a reason to root for us the next day, as our task seemed close to impossible.

———

We would accomplish many more things if we did not think of them as impossible.

Vince Lombardi

———

The next day we faced the #1 seed and defending national champion Trojans of Southern California who had beaten Dennis

Emery's SEC Champion Kentucky Wildcats while we were battling Georgia. USC had begun a four year stretch that saw them
lose only once in 15 NCAA tournament matches from 1991-4,
winning three NCAA titles during that time span. We knew we
were underdogs and, in fact, had lost 6-3 to the Trojans the previous fall in a match played indoors before 850 fans in South Bend
the evening before the Notre Dame/USC football game.

True courage is facing danger when you are
afraid.

J M Barrie

Despite the prognosticators who agreed, we had little
chance for victory. Our guys were loose and comfortable, due
mostly to the confidence and swagger they had gained the day
before. We also knew we would not have to face anything like yesterday's crowd. As we began the pre-match warm-up, Northwestern's popular coach, Paul Torricelli, walked onto the courts to wish
me luck and noticed right away that I was much more relaxed.
Heck, we were playing with house money, and I hoped those same
Bulldog fans might today be cheering for us. They were! Nonetheless, the stars really needed to be in perfect alignment for us to
beat USC, and boy were they ever! The Trojans' #4 player, Wayne
Black, was undefeated and had fashioned a 25-0 record going into
our match. Black would later be ranked #1 in the ATP tour rankings in doubles. USC's #1 player, Brian Macphie, had perhaps the
best serve in college tennis and had beaten our #1, David DiLucia,
the previous year right here on the same court in our round of 16
match. Their #2, David Eckerot, was ranked among the nation's
top 10 and Coach Dick Leach's son Jon had experienced a tremendous year at #3. They had swept the doubles against us at our place
in the fall, so where were we going to get our points?

Our #6, reliable Ronnie Rosas, got us started with a straight set dismantling of his opponent. Ronnie's groundstrokes were like lasers that afternoon, and his win gave us more hope. At #2, Zurcher unexpectedly made quick work of Eckerot 6-2, 6-2 in an athletic display of serving and volleying that pinned the Trojan behind the baseline all day. Andy did not hit with great pace, but his athleticism was on full display as he dove for Eckerot's passing shots, more often than not feathering a delicate touch volley just out of the reach of the scrambling Trojan. After splitting the first two sets at #3, Chuck Coleman, who possessed the greatest return of serve I have ever seen at the college level, confided to me that his hamstring was tightening, and he had concerns about being able to finish the match. In an effort to give him some kind of workable plan at such an inopportune time, I advised him to go for bigger shots on his groundstrokes in order to keep the points short and limiting his running. He responded courageously, hitting winner after winner, to take the third set, putting us up 3-1 and the crowd began to buzz with excitement. Back to Colemen's returns…. I will always remember the match point in a doubles match Coleman and DiLucia played against Jonathan Stark and Jared Palmer of Stanford. Chuck took the first serve of Stark [one of the biggest in the college game] and hit it so hard that it flew past Palmer - clearly within his reach - without his making any move toward it to give us a huge upset win. Over the years I had found that, in telling a player to be more aggressive, you take both pressure and responsibility off his shoulders, and he is more likely to be successful. If he misses, he is only following orders and the fault is yours. This removes fear and responsibility from the equation and allows him to hit out with impunity. Coleman painted the lines from his baseline position that day and gave us yet another point. We were beginning to take control and make an upset feasible.

At #4, Forsyth had fallen behind to the previously unbeaten Black 4-1 in the third set. Black's undefeated year loomed large at that point, but something came alive in Will as he began clubbing winners and miraculously fought back to take the last five games in a row to win 6-4 in the third set, giving us a 4-1 lead with the #1 match hanging in the balance. When Will found his competitive groove, he could beat anyone at the college level, and this was the perfect time for his trip into "the zone." That left the match in the small but capable hands of DiLucia, who was himself undefeated in dual matches for the season and, coming into the NCAAs, the top ranked player in collegiate tennis. You could hear the buzz from the crowd as the impossible became more than a hope and a prayer. As DiLucia broke the serve of Macphie - no easy feat, for Macphie had a nasty lefty delivery - he walked toward the bench knowing that if he held serve we would claim the biggest upset in the long and hallowed history of the NCAA tournament. The pressure of having played many of the country's best players this year had prepared him for this moment. As the nation's top-ranked college player, he had won plenty of big matches, but he had also lost a few and benefitted from the experience. He was ready today. Last year's loss to the same player had prepared him.

—◦—

Winning is great, sure, but if you are really going to do something in life, the secret is learning how to lose. Nobody goes undefeated all the time. If you can pick up after a crushing defeat, and go on to win again, you are going to be a champion someday.

Wilma Rudolph

—◦—

I understandably was searching for something to say to David on the changeover, hoping to relax him, as his anxiety at that point was pretty evident. Experience had taught me that when a player is stressed there are two emotions that can make him forget the enormity of his task: anger or laughter. I had to figure out quickly which to use. I took a big chance. As David sat down next to me, I pulled my hotel key from my pocket and placed it on the bench between the two of us. He looked with annoyance at

the key, back at me, and then back to the key. Irritated, he asked
"What the heck is that?" Without blinking I replied "See the pretty
girl in the red top in the third row over there? She gave it to me
and told me that if you win this game she will be waiting for you in
room #312." Without a word, David glanced at me and the pretty
Georgia co-ed, and grinned knowingly before walking out on the
court to serve out a love game and clinch the match for us, but not
before some drama occurred. At 15-love Macphie made a half-
hearted effort returning David's first serve, simply bumping it back
to him in an indication that he had heard it clip the net for a let.
DiLucia moved up to the ball and similarly nudged the ball into the
open court, as Macphie had not made a call. The umpire promptly
called out "thirty-love"and Macphie quickly asked for a correction.
The umpire immediately asked David "Mr. DiLucia, did you hear
a let?" David's reply was "No, I did not, but I trust Brian." The
umpire then explained that two of the three people involved had to
hear the let for it to be valid. The point stood. Macphie looked at
David, saying "You don't want to win this way." David looked to
me for help. I froze and remained quiet, as I had not heard a let either. Deep inside I was ready to burst out "NO. NO. Don't give up
this point," but of course remained silent. DiLucia handled the situation incredibly well, winning the next two points aggressively to
clinch the win. I will never forget the next few moments as David
dropped down to his knees with clinched fists and screamed to the
crowd before being mobbed by his teammates and engulfed by the
thunderous applause that one can only find in Athens. We had done
the unthinkable. We had beaten the nation's #1 team on the site of
the sport's greatest venue. I must add that I was glad David did not
later knock on the door of Room 312, as I would have answered
the door, much to his disappointment.

The photo of the team celebrating our win on the court
appeared on the cover of the 1993 Notre Dame tennis guide. Few
people noticed that DiLucia had changed his shirt and was now
wearing a t-shirt that included a drawing of Bart Simpson looking
at a girl. The inscription below it said "Drink 'til she's cute!" Fortunately our sports information contact, Jim Daves, had air-brushed

the picture from David's shirt. Wearing a non-institutional shirt at the facility was an NCAA no-no. I find it interesting that I still remember this twenty-six years later.

———◦◦◦———

Impossible is just a word thrown around by small men who find it easier to live in the world they have been given, than to explore the power to change it. Impossible is not a fact. It's an opinion. Impossible is potential. Impossible is temporary. Impossible is nothing.

Muhammad Ali

———◦◦◦———

If this story had been written by the Brothers Grimm, we would most certainly have won the next day to capture the national championship, but, alas, history records that Notre Dame lost to Stanford giving the Cardinal's Dick Gould his umpteenth NCAA title [he won 17 in a 24 year span]. I had the chance to see how Cinderella felt as the clock struck midnight. Gould is a legend in our ranks, and for good reason. He is simply the best ever in our sport, or perhaps any sport. He always says and does the right thing. He recruits the best players, coaches them to an even better level, and represents college tennis with class and dignity. Predictably, I received a handwritten note from Dick as soon as we returned to campus. He tried to congratulate me on such a historic season and extolled my virtues, etc. He could not have been nicer. He mentioned that he knew just how I felt; that one never knows when or if they will ever get back to a championship match and, to be that close to winning a national championship had to be frustrating for me. I wrote him back, trying to call on humor, and told him that I actually was feeling great until I got his letter, knowing that we could laugh about it later.

It is memories like this, and so many others that grab me as I make the turn onto Broad Street and check into the Holiday Inn. I know that this is my last such trip to Athens as a coach, for I decided several years ago to retire after the 2013 season. Next year's NCAAs - and my last as a coach - will be held in Champaign, Illinois, hosted by the University of Illinois. Because this is very much on my mind I consciously allow myself to reflect on some of the great things I have experienced here, both in the team and individual portions of the NCAA Championships. Our team would not be playing here this year, as we had lost a hard fought second round NCAA match to Ty Tucker's Buckeyes of the Ohio State University in Columbus after defeating Vanderbilt in the first round. The "drive vs. fly" policy employed in sending the various 64 NCAA-bound teams to their respective first and second round destinations has pretty much required our presence in Columbus four of the last five years. Ohio State's 200 plus home match winning streak has left our dreams behind on the Ohio State campus on those years.

The disappointment of not being able to bring my team back to Athens was palpable. In my dreams we played my last match in the NCAA finals, this time winning and allowing me to ride off into the sunset in a fully loaded Lexus with our greatest achievement in hand. History does not allow us to write our own scripts and see them through to fruition. While there was much to celebrate as I began my last year as an active coach, I would not have another "Athens moment" to ponder. Yes, we had our top singles player, Greg Andrews, in the individual man 64 player draw, as well as our top doubles team, Niall Fitzgerald and Casey Watt. To win two rounds in either the singles or doubles would bring a player All American honors, something that any player seeks and something to highlight the school's resume and enhance recruiting for future classes. However, to me and to most coaches, the goals we set are primarily team goals, and it is disappointing to view the team matches here in Athens in the role of spectator. It is hard not to notice the difference in crowd responses to the team championships when contrasted with that of the individual ones in singles and doubles. Hamburger does not taste nearly as good after a steady diet of filet mignon.

This is my frame of mind as I arrive. There is a lot going on at the NCAA Championships for me, as I am a member of the Board of Directors of the ITA - the Intercollegiate Tennis Association. Board meetings, the general membership meeting, committee and awards selection meetings are scheduled at various times during the fortnight. This event offers the greatest opportunities for our coaches to get together and personally discuss the issues of the day - dual match format change, no-ad scoring, and the manner in which the format of this event might change. I will be busy. I have also agreed to appear as part of a panel of coaches and tennis professionals sponsored by the USTA - the United States Tennis Association, the governing body of tennis in the U.S. The panel will be attended by prospects [the NCAA term for recruited student-athletes] and their parents. The panelists will try to inform them about what to expect during the recruiting process: admissions strategies, official visits, how coaches determine scholarships, etc.

In addition to the assets of the city of Athens, I believe that one reason that the USTA has chosen Athens and this tournament to host this workshop is because nearby Atlanta is perhaps America's top tennis town and the NCAAs always draws tons of spectators. It will be special for those attending. Because of my involvement in these events my more-than-capable associate head coach, Ryan Sachire, will handle many of the practice sessions for our individual tournament participants, something that is common practice with many head coaches. Ryan is a rising star in the coaching ranks. The USTA has appointed him to work with the top college players who will play, as amateurs, in USTA professional tournaments this summer as part of the USTA/ITA Summer All Star Team. It is a tremendous honor and one he will more than capably fulfill. I have been blessed to have had many great assistants and to see them move to head coaching positions: Billy Pate - Alabama and Princeton, Todd Doebler - Penn State and Amherst, Brian Kalbas - North Carolina, Mike Morgan - Middlebury, Ryan Keckley at San Diego, Bob Detrich at West Point, and many others over a 44 year career as a head coach. I am especially excited to be involved in seeing that Ryan become my replacement. I have discussed this at length with Notre Dame's athletic leaders Missy Conboy and Jack Swarbrick. Ryan is ambitious, hard-working, knowledgeable, and absolutely passionate about Notre Dame and college tennis. His father was a coach and his mother is a teacher. It is in his genes and he appears to be right out of central casting. He became a three-time All American at Notre Dame and the ITA Senior Player of the Year. He had a successful professional career as a player. It is a perfect match and I am going to be his biggest fan. I can't wait to see him in action. He has the drive to push players to the next level. More on this to come.

———◇———

"Come to the edge," he said. They said, "We are afraid." "Come to the edge," he said. They came. He pushed them. And they flew.

Guillame Apollin-aire

———◇———

The best part of the nearly two week stay at the NCAA Championships for me is being around and able to interact with the other coaches. These guys are the only people in the world who have "walked a mile in my moccasins." There is no such thing as a stereotypical tennis coach. We are an eclectic breed. We come in all shapes, sizes and personalities, but we all have three things in common: a passion for our sport, a desire to help young men and women, and a deep competitiveness that drives us to work very hard. While we are constantly trying to best each other, on the court and in recruiting, we have tremendous empathy for our colleagues. We have watched some of them get fired, sometimes because we beat them too often, and we understand the frustrations involved in our profession. We talk openly to each other about our families, marriages, bosses, and health. It is odd, I know, but in many ways I feel like many of my best friends are scattered all over the country and coach college teams. We get together in large numbers several times per year: at the NCAAs, our ITA Coaches Convention in December in Naples, FL, at the largest junior tournaments where we are involved in evaluating talent and coercing it to attend our respective universities, and at collegiate events held during the school year such as the Blue Gray National Classic, the National Team Indoors, and others. We are brothers-in-arms. I have had coaches speak in confidence to me about intimate family issues and I believe it is because I know the frustrations and pressures they face, the time demands, and the issues of being away from family. We are constantly monitoring the progress of each other's teams. The internet has made it impossible to be uninformed. In short, we understand each other.

Notre Dame Tennis at Aviva Stadium, Dublin, Ireland. Left to right: Pat Bayliss, Billy Pecor, Coach Bobby Bayliss, Quentin Monaghan, Ken Sabacinski, Blas Moros, Nico Montoya, Alex Lawson, Michael Fredericka, Coach Ryan Sachire, Dougie Barnard, Greg Andrews, Wyatt McCoy, Spencer Talmadge, Matt Dooley, Ryan Bandy, and Bianca Fox.

The Crazy Life of a Coach

The life of a coach is crazy. We depend far too much on our own successes to bring happiness into our lives. It is virtually impossible to explain what I feel during the season because so much depends on whether we win or lose. We would all be better served if we had the ability to step back from our emotions and consuming schedules and reflectively take stock of things in order to bring focus and clear thinking into play. I am not stupid. I know better. Nonetheless, I continually allow my emotions to dictate how I handle things. I can promise you that when I return from a weekend of successful away matches I am absolutely giddy. This is the best time to ask me for money, a favor, or most anything else. I can't wait to get on the internet to see how the other schools have done. I send congratulatory emails to other coaches who have had similar results. Life is good!! Nothing can bother me. However, when we lose, particularly if we have squandered a great opportunity, I am absolutely miserable. I am numb. Nothing else matters. I could learn that I have inherited a million dollars and I would not care. I just want to be alone and feel sorry for myself. I don't want to receive telephone calls. Distraught is perhaps not a sufficiently strong word to describe my emotional state on such occasions. How crazy can this be? While I understand intellectually that more than 99% of the people in our country will never know or care what our team does, it is of little consolation to me. It seems crazy to tie your happiness to the whims and performances of a group of 18-to-22 year old young men. The latest loss could be due to a key player's receiving a "dear John" letter from his girlfriend, flunking a test, concern for a sick family member, or worrying that his girlfriend might be pregnant. And on top of this, I might never know what is going on and might be the cause of his problems, or even that he has them. Despair is the closest word I can come up with to try to explain how we all feel after a poor [i.e., losing] performance. Inevitably, at these times I try to envision the ramifications of each loss on our post-season opportunities and search for possible future wins that could right the sinking ship.

A good illustration for the futility we frequently face because of events in the lives of our players occurred to me in 1975 when I was a young coach at Navy. One of my favorite all-time players there was Bobby Phillips, now Admiral Bob Phillips. For Bobby, having grown up in South Carolina without a great deal of family money, coming to Annapolis was a dream come true. Bobby was one of the truly elite competitors it has been my pleasure to coach. He was our team captain [and future flag officer] and we were playing one of the weakest teams on our schedule, but what I did not know was that on that day Bobby's father was undergoing a serious surgical operation. He had requested permission to fly home, but was discouraged from the trip by his mother and the Commandant of Midshipmen. In the middle of the match Bobby began to miss his shots and lose his temper uncharacteristically. At that point I walked on to his court, not knowing about his concerns, and reprimanded him, warning that another outburst would cost him the match. Sure enough, that outburst happened quickly and I walked on to the court to stop the match, awarding a default to his opponent. Bobby went ballistic and I quickly told him to go to our locker room and wait for me there. I told his close friend and teammate, Kevin Miller, that he needed to follow him and calm him down.

—◦—

A coach is someone who tells you what you don't want to hear, has you see what you don't want to see, so you can be who you've always known you could be.

Tom Landry

—◦—

14

I arrived, as quickly as I could, in our tennis center several minutes later. Our locker room was in shambles, as pieces of Bobby's wooden Spalding racket were scattered and several lockers had been turned over. Tennis shoes, rackets, towels, and jock straps littered the floor. The room looked like a bomb had just exploded. I walked into this scenario and immediately became afraid of a physical altercation. Because Bobby had been a Golden Gloves boxer in Charleston, I knew that I might be in trouble. Bobby came at me, only to throw his arms around me sobbing uncontrollably. As he composed himself he explained why he had behaved as he had and everything became clear. I felt remorse for having defaulted him and we sat down and talked things out. He called home to learn that his father had made it through surgery and would be fine. All was better immediately. I missed much of the match, but nothing else mattered at that point. I tell you this because we all have similar life stories and time and space keep me from recounting many more others like it. I never knew the challenges awaiting me every day when I walked into my office. The life of a college coach is similar to that described by the mother of Forrest Gump. It is "like a box of chocolates; you never know what you're going to get."

I know that God will never give me more than I can handle. I just wish he didn't trust me so much.

Mother Theresa

Try to understand what drives us. We know all too well the impact of a particular loss and how it might affect our NCAA and conference tournament opportunities. By all rights, I should no longer feel pressure. I am one of only two men's coaches in the country at this writing [Manny Diaz of Georgia is the other] to have taken his team to the NCAA Tournament for 22 of the last 23 years at the same institution. Some of these appearances came when the NCAA allowed only 20 teams to advance to participate in the NCAA Championships and at-large bids were truly scarce. We are all competing for the same thing: a strong finish at the year's end. To most of us this means the conference and NCAA tournaments. What is necessary to achieve this? We position ourselves best for success by being seeded in the best position in these end-of-the-year events, hence the importance of regular season results. We know all too well that the seeding committee will look at each loss in a particular way. Did it occur at home or on the road? Was the score close? Did both teams have all starters available for play? The higher our ranking, the better our chances for a higher seed, thus enabling us to advance deep into the tournament. It is as if we all had a calculator in our heads to analyze the many possibilities each win or loss brings. Welcome to my world!

Stephen Bass crushes a backhand down the line for a winner in the Big East Championship match against Virginia Tech. April, 2004. *Photo courtesy of Miami Athletics Department.*

Down Tobacco Road

I remember a particular crazy weekend in 2006 when we flew to North Carolina to play UNC and Duke on back-to-back days. Both were ranked in or near the top ten. We were only a few spots below each of them, but in the same general range. One win would boost us in the rankings, particularly because the ITA rankings reward highly ranked wins and offer less penalty for "good" losses. I knew the matches would both be close. We were healthy and playing with confidence. It would not be a stretch to take both. I felt good karma. Ours was a team that would later advance to the "sweet 16s" held at Stanford, but I did not know that yet, obviously. The first match was against North Carolina in Chapel Hill. It was ridiculously close. They had a great crowd. We fought very hard, but lost 4-3. Everything came down to our #1 singles player, Stephen Bass, who lost his match in a third set tie-breaker. While he lost the match, he did not fail. He was simply in the process of building a better resume, something difficult to acknowledge at the time, but one of the special things about sports.

A man may fall down many times, but he is not a failure until he says that someone pushed him.

Elmer G. Letterman

Stephen was crushed. I realized, more than our players, that this loss could really come back to bite us, but because we were to play Duke the next day, I had to put a good spin on things and told the team how proud I was of the effort we had expended. What I felt, and what I expressed to our squad, were not necessarily the same thing. We had experienced a tough break. One of our top players, Brett Helgeson, began to cramp in the middle of the first set and could not continue, forfeiting his match and leaving us in a difficult position. He was one of our strongest players and had a two-handed backhand that he could hit with both power and accuracy and I knew he was on his way to becoming one of the better baseline players in the country. It was the only such occurrence that happened to Brett in his entire four year career, but as one of my Navy players, Dave Andrews, often said, "Life's a b*#*h and then you die." So, after the match we returned to the hotel, showered, and ate, turning in early for a good night's rest, ready for the opportunity that Duke presented the next day as soon as I exchanged notes about Duke with UNC assistant coach Don Johnson.

What happened the next day is still hard to talk about. Duke is a natural rival for Notre Dame. Both schools have tremendous athletic traditions. Both fall into the private and elite academic category. Both have a national presence and strong athletic brands, Duke's largely due to its basketball tradition and ours certainly attributable to its iconic football past and present. We compete for many of the same players. As the match began we came out strong and were locked in and fighting hard on every court against another good team on the road. Once more the match twisted and turned until it was tied 3-3 and everything was again in the hands of Bass, playing Duke's French star Ludovig Walter. Bass went up a break late in the deciding set and served for the match, only to have his own serve broken and forcing yet another tiebreaker to decide the match.

As the third set unfolded, I began to think that surely we would not lose in a similar manner on consecutive days. The tennis gods would certainly think twice before throwing that much on my plate. Heck, I had gone to Mass earlier that morning and things were going to fall our way this time....NOT! Yes, Stephen served for the match, but could not hold. He found himself in yet another third set tiebreaker and dropped it once again. After losing, Stephen lost all control, shouting at the top of his lungs "I never want to be in this position again. I don't want to have to decide the match ever again." Naturally, I could not let this continue and began to shout back at him and in front of the spectators… "Yes, you will. I want you out there when it matters. I want this again for you. Next time you will win." The crowd gaped at the ongoing scene with open mouths. It was surreal. But I wanted him to know that this was the way a player grew. A player has to crawl out on the proverbial limb because that is where the fruit is. He had to go through the painful stages in order to learn and compete at the highest level. Less than one month later in Montgomery, AL we found ourselves locked in yet another battle, this time against Fresno State in the opening round of the Blue Gray National Collegiate Tennis Classic. As Stephen began the third set under the lights I reminded him of that earlier weekend and told him that he was better prepared for this responsibility. He had paid his dues in full. He won 6-2 in the third that evening to clinch for us. Lesson learned. Game over!

———◦———

Failure is nature's plan to prepare you for greater responsibilities.

Napoleon Hill

———◦———

That was Stephen's junior year. The next year he defeated Tulsa's Arnaud Bruges [later ATP top 100], Georgia's John Isner [ATP top 10] and Illinois's Kevin Anderson [ATP top 10], all in very exciting matches. He reached #4 in the ITA rankings and led our team to a ranking of #4 nationally in April. One of the truly interesting things about coaching DI college tennis is seeing the players who played against your team succeed on the ATP Tour, and I have enjoyed watching both Anderson and Isner on the TV in our family room. We won the Blue Gray that year and fared well in the National Team Indoors and NCAAs. Stephen was named the MVP of the Blue Gray and won the ITA Von Nostrand Award given annually [with a stipend] to an outstanding graduating senior who was going to play professionally. It probably could not have happened had he not gone through the painful process of facing the responsibility of having to play for all of the marbles with the team match hanging in the balance. It is a nerve-wracking experience. It is only through the white hot heat applied to iron to soften it that it eventually hardens and becomes steel. The competitive process is a similar one.

———◦◦———

I have learned over the years that when one's mind is made, this diminishes fear. Knowing what must be done does away with fear.

Rosa Parks

———◦◦———

Welcome, once again, to my world! A college tennis coach is more than someone who hits balls with his players and advises them on tactics and strategy. We, at times, serve as academic advisors, love-life counselors, psychiatrists, bus drivers, dieticians, job placement analysts, health experts, equipment analysts, budget directors, travel agents, family counselors, athletic trainers, and fitness experts. We have, on average, a dozen or so players on our teams. Each is unique. All of them are different in many ways. Many are alike in certain areas. All come with expectations of playing time, scholarships, after graduation plans which affect scheduling for them, health and emotional issues, and hopes and dreams.

The coach needs to be at least aware of all of these things. He will write letters of recommendation to prospective employers or graduate schools. When I coached at Navy, I taught Freshman English for five years [I have a Master's degree in English Literature] until I took over the squash team as well and could not afford the missed class time. We run summer camps. We, in some cases, solicit funds from donors. We reach out to alumni. We promote our matches. We are in constant touch with the team's academic advisors and athletic trainers. We have our players in our homes for team cookouts and dinners. We hold "secret Santa" parties for our teams. I even wrote a poem each year for this occasion. We plan team bonding affairs. Heck, there is not much I have not done in my years of coaching. Now that you have had a small taste of it I will take you through my final year as a Division I college coach. It will begin and run chronologically, but much of what I cover will be in anecdotal stories and my own philosophical meanderings on various topics that make up the collegiate athletic experience. I will even sprinkle in some quotes that you might enjoy. An example:

—◦—

You are never too old to set another goal or dream a new dream.

CS Lewis

—◦—

An Unexpected Turn Of Events

The mediocre teacher tells. The good teacher explains. The superior teacher demonstrates. The great teacher inspires.

William A. Ward

My own journey into the coaching profession now seems much more driven by happenstance than design. As a young boy I was always attracted to sports. I practiced more and worked harder at them than most boys my age. My initial serious commitment was to basketball. That same commitment later was transferred to tennis when I realized that the dream of an NBA career was not to be. I can honestly say that while an undergraduate I never considered coaching as a career choice. In fact, it seems that I did not have any real plan for my post-graduation life. Keep in mind that I, like all other healthy males over the age of 18 in 1966, faced the inevitability of the military draft waiting for me upon graduation. Rather than electing to serve as an officer through Officer Candidate School or the ROTC program on the campus at the University of Richmond, I had decided to allow myself to be drafted because the commitment was for only two years, as opposed to the longer terms required for an officer. Looking back, this most likely would have ended in a tour in Vietnam, but for the diagnosis of my irregular heartbeat which eventually precluded any military duty whatsoever. I learned that I had failed the Army's draft physical shortly before I was to graduate. I had assumed that I would pass the physical, given that I had played both basketball [my freshman year] and tennis [all four years] in college, all of which required passing a medical exam. I had guessed that the Army would take most of the summer to process and send me orders to report for duty, so I had planned to play as much tournament tennis as possible until that time. After that I would have a two year wait while serving in the Army in which to decide what I wanted to do with the rest of my life when discharged. Thoughts of law or graduate school were among the options I was considering, especially because the GI Bill would finance most of the tuition costs. My life, it seems, was about to present me some different plans.

As I learned that my options were now wide open, one of the first people I turned to was my college tennis coach, Leonard McNeal, as I began to contemplate what I might do when I grew up. Coach McNeal told me that he had an idea for me, but he needed to check out something and asked me to come back the next day to see him. When I returned a day later he told me that he had the next two years of my life figured out. He wanted to take a sabbatical leave of absence for a year and had arranged for me to coach the Richmond team in his absence. In return, I would attend the University's Graduate School in English Literature, my major, with all expenses covered for two years. I secured a position as the assistant tennis professional at the prestigious Country Club of Virginia less than a mile away and quickly found myself on a path that continued to open opportunities to me for the next fifty years. The head tennis professional at CCV was Fred Koechlein, a towering figure in Mid-Atlantic tennis circles and a man from whom I would learn much. His guidance and example became pivotal as I began my career.

The next year began my love affair with what I consider the greatest of livelihoods. Coaching that Richmond team in 1966-7 was unlike anything that came after it, as the team members were, and remain, some of my closest friends, so it was more like "hanging with my guys" than coaching. But things changed quickly, or as the saying goes, "Man plans and God laughs." Late in the next summer as I was preparing to return to finish the remaining requirements for my master's degree I received a telephone call from Mr. William Brock, the principal at my secondary school alma mater, Thomas Jefferson High School. He had kept up with my whereabouts and knew that I was only six credit hours and a thesis away from my M.A. and graduation and presented me with a proposition: come back to TJHS to teach English and coach tennis and assist with basketball. I could leave TJHS right after lunch and drive to the U of R for a class and return in plenty of time for practice. I would still graduate in June as expected, but I would have some money in the bank and a year's experience under my belt. I thought things through and decided to take advantage of his offer. My coaching career was launched! On top of it all I have never spent a happier year working than that 1967-8 school year. I was able to live at home to conserve money. My wife-to-be, Pat, was committed to a one year fellowship for a master's degree at Ohio State and we planned to be married the following summer. Things had fallen into place. My friends have since convinced me that being away from Pat that year kept her from learning more about me and calling off our wedding. Lucky for me!

The year at Thomas Jefferson was magical for me and cemented any plans I might have had that did not include coaching tennis. I inherited a terrific team that went undefeated in Virginia High School League play and won the state championship. We even beat some college teams, including Penn State, in a match played at TJHS. Looking back now, it seems as if life was leading me in the direction of working with young men.

Perhaps the biggest reason that I found my way into the coaching world involved my interaction with a young man I had never met. In 1968 the Richmond schools had been recently integrated, as Richmond was just coming out of the segregated South era. In one of my English classes was a likeable young African-American boy of perhaps sixteen years of age, Wyatt Kingston. Wyatt not only seemed to show little interest in English, but he arrived perhaps fifteen minutes late the first several days, claiming that he became lost in his new settings. After perhaps the fourth day in a row of this tardiness I warned Wyatt that I would not tolerate any more tardiness, only to hear him mutter something to the effect that if this class were about basketball he would certainly be on time. English, it seemed, held no interest for Wyatt. Because I was upset and believed that he had challenged my authority, I snapped off a challenge to him in front of the class, telling him that I would meet him in the gym immediately after school and play him one-on-one in basketball. If he won, I insisted, he could come and go as he pleased, but if I won he would be on time, pay attention, and give his best effort. Looking back now, I realize how foolish this was, but having some experience at college basketball I must have believed in my ability to handle the situation. To cut to the chase, I met Wyatt and beat him that afternoon in front of a crowd that had gathered as word of our contest crept out. Rather than pout about losing, he became an instantly changed young man and we became very close. I am still in touch with him today and am very proud of the man he has become. He has interacted with disadvantaged youth for many years and teaches them how to start their own businesses, from growing and selling produce to mowing lawns. He has become a surrogate father to countless boys and continues his work-ministry even today in his late sixties, far eclipsing anything that I have achieved. Wyatt told me that I had become a father figure to him, adding "You gave me attention and provided a role model for me at a time that I, who had no father, desperately needed both." This was how I learned about the power of sports and the importance of setting a good example for others. I tell this story, not to make myself look good, but to make you understand how important an example you can become to others. This validated my instinct to make a career of coaching. I spoke to Wyatt only last week about his efforts to bring tennis to some of Richmond's poorer neighborhoods. He is continuing his efforts to help those who need it.

Despite my love of teaching and coaching at Thomas Jefferson, an unanticipated telephone call threw my plans into change mode once again. As I have said many times, "Man plans. God laughs." Suddenly, a new chapter now appeared on my life's horizon. Several days before I was to fly to St. Louis to be married in July 1968, I received a call from the Director of Athletics at the US Naval Academy in Annapolis, MD, Captain J.O. Coppedge, wondering if I had an interest in becoming the head coach at the US Naval Academy. The decision was an easy one, despite my love for TJHS, and in 1969 at age 24 I was named the head men's tennis coach at Navy, one of the great undergraduate institutions in the world and a place that would shape me for the better, as I was surrounded and inspired by accountability, integrity, and highly motivated and outstanding young men for the next 15 years of my life.

At Navy, I came into contact with military careers that helped shape the world. My former Navy players have become Blue Angels, captains and admirals, novelists, and even the Supreme Allied Commander of NATO. I will forever owe them and the Academy a debt of gratitude for shaping my life. I left with a veritable PhD in excellence and leadership. Midshipmen who graduate from the US Naval Academy know how to think and act under pressure, know right from wrong, and have acquired the integrity needed to guide them through the rest of their days. It is almost impossible not to have some of that rub off on those of us fortunate enough to have shared their experiences. Character shapes all.

~ Cross Court Reflection ~

Men of genius are admired. Men of wealth are envied. Men of power are feared, but only men of character are trusted.

Zig Ziglar

Summary Activities of a Coach

You've got to get to the stage in life where going for it is more important than winning or losing.

Arthur Ashe

It has been interesting to look back on my earliest years coaching tennis at the Naval Academy and contrast them with the current era. Much has changed. College tennis has a new dual match format. A match in the previous format could take five hours easily. The NCAA has dramatically reduced the number of contests and length of playing seasons in all sports. We see the influence of television and marketing. There is a distinct feel to both the fall season and the second semester, which is devoted entirely to dual match play. Recruiting in today's world of high-tech IT is vastly different from that of the 1960's and 1970's. There have been tremendous advances in sports medicine and strength and conditioning training. Diet has taken on a new importance: changes in equipment (racket, strings) have introduced more physicality into dynamic stroke making. The advent of social media has made recruiting a 24/7/365 operation and is only getting worse. I used to finish my scheduling for the coming year in the summer, but that ship has sailed. We are now well more than a year or two out in scheduling. One similarity between the old and new is that summer provides a brief [and becoming even more brief] respite from the rigors of competition.

Two things come to mind as summer nears: recruiting and summer tennis camp. Many coaches run very lucrative summer camps and earn significant revenue to supplement their salaries. This is true in almost all sports. At Notre Dame we have a branch of the athletic department which oversees and promotes all athletic camps. We [athletics] compete with various other campus departments for dormitory space, meals served in the dining hall, and the use of all things non-athletic on campus that might provide entertainment for our campers. There is a period of approximately two weeks between returning from the NCAAs and the beginning of camp. To be sure, there are camp responsibilities that need to be taken care of promptly, but for many, this is the time a coach feels that he can finally come up for air. Summer school has not yet begun, and the feeling of release that the season's end provides gives us more relaxed hours and perhaps even a short family vacation. Typically, the entire athletic department pauses for a deep breath in early June. I very much looked forward to this time because I could sleep later, come home earlier, and we could do things as a family that were not possible during the school year. Vacations need to be planned between camp and recruiting responsibilities. While recruiting can be smothering and never really stops, there is a brief respite from most other responsibilities. This period, along with part of the Christmas break, allowed me to catch my breath.

Recruiting has taken me in various directions and to many places, perhaps to evaluate one particular player, often to observe the strongest competition, and sometimes even internationally. I have been to Dublin, Ireland for the Irish National Junior Championships seven times, as there is a connection between Notre Dame and the Irish. Most years I attend the US Open Juniors, held concurrently with the US Open in New York. I have attended sectional events in June in Los Angeles [Southern Cal Juniors], Richmond, VA [Mid-Atlantic Juniors], Indianapolis [Midwest Closed Juniors], Boston [New England Juniors], and London [Wimbledon Juniors], to name a few. This carousel is always spinning. There was never a shortage of places to go to gain exposure for your program. Staying put was never an option, nor was waiting for a crisis. There is always an event I could attend that showcases junior tennis players. Additionally, once you have completed the recruitment of the current year's class, there is another, and another. Planning for the future never stops.

—◦—

It wasn't raining when Noah built the Ark.

Howard Ruff

—◦—

The holiday ends when tennis camp begins. Let me be clear about one thing: coaches run summer camps for one reason - to supplement their incomes. Summer tennis camp exists in its own world. Try tackling all of these problems at once: dormitory roommate assignments, placing players in the proper skill groups, homesickness, monitoring the raging hormones of 16 and 17 year old boys and girls at night, finding off-court activities that appeal to everyone, ensuring security, hiring the right number of staff to complement the number of campers [and thus turn a profit], dining hall food, seeing that dormitory turf wars with other sports camps are kept to a minimum, being on time for meals, and transportation to and from the dorms in thunderstorms and tornado watches. All of this has been trumped more recently by the Jerry Sandusky-focused attention on child abuse that has swept through all campuses. The hiring of staff has become much more complicated, as all staff are now subjected to a security investigation/search that takes weeks and sometimes seems as tough as the security clearance for entering the White House.

Every coach can give you his/her camp horror stories, but several come immediately to mind for me. It is every coach's nightmare that a camper might sneak out of the dorm after curfew to rendezvous with another of the opposite sex. Notre Dame still operates single sex dorms and the good Fathers here take this issue very seriously. I remember going to the emergency room several times in one week with a 17 year old girl camper having night time anxiety attacks and driving her three hours to her home in Indianapolis at 6:00 AM to meet meet her mother. I also remember at checkout on the last day of camp a distraught mother approaching us with the news that her daughter had disappeared and could not be found. She was quite disturbed and assured us that her daughter ALWAYS followed the rules, hence something MUST have happened to her Because of this, she said, she was certain that her daughter might have been abducted. Jay Louderback, our women's coach, and I raced to her dorm, only to find her relaxing on the second story balcony enjoying the pretty view of our campus, clueless to the uproar that her mother had caused. We were only too happy to bring her back to her mother.

Then there was the time in 1991 when I placed a 12 year old girl camper on her flight home to Puerto Rico when camp was over. After she connected in Chicago she flew from there to San Juan, but no one was there to pick her up. American Airlines called me at home that evening to tell me that they were going to fly her back to South Bend. At this point camp had ended and there were no dorm beds for her, so she came home with me and slept in our house with our family that night. Her parents had not gotten to the airport to meet her due to car trouble; they lived an hour away. Keep in mind that this was before cell phones, email, etc. After dropping her at the airport once again the next day I got another call from American Airlines, telling me that her parents were, as happened the day before, nowhere to be found. I was put on hold, wondering what to do next. Tennis camp does not come with an owner's manual. Soon the agent came back on the line with the news that her parents had just arrived and I could now relax and go home. Coach Louderback has said more than once that his two favorite days of the year are Christmas and the last day of camp.

Occasionally camp can bring pleasant surprises. This past June [2013] I was able to reconnect with Rick Forzano, the former head football coach of the Detroit Lions. Rick and I were coaching at Navy at the same time when I began my career. He had done a tremendous job bringing the Navy program back to respectability before leaving for the NFL. His grandson attended camp and he stopped in my office for a long chat and trip down memory lane. It was great to see Rick and talk about the "good old days." He has since passed and I now treasure that meeting.

When I arrived at Notre Dame I had been given the green light to start up a tennis camp. I had never been involved in anything like what we were about to do and I needed some assistance. Fortunately, I connected with Charlie Hoeveler, formerly one of Dartmouth's best-ever tennis players. He had started an organization called US Sports Camps which evolved into today's Nike Tennis Camps. Partly because of Charlie's likeability and partly because it made good business sense I contracted with him to handle our camp. He would promote and fill the camp, supplying us with t-shirts, prizes, evaluation forms, and everything we would need. All I had to do was hire the staff and run the camp. It worked very well for us and we were very successful, at times averaging more than 100 campers for each of the six weeks of camp. All went well until the late 1990s when Notre Dame signed its first-ever school contract with adidas. This presented an insurmountable problem. Nike, having bid on the Notre Dame contract and lost, did not want an adidas presence in its system. Adidas certainly did not want a Nike camp on the Notre Dame campus. With no other solution in sight Charlie and I agreed to part ways, but have remained friends to this day, reconnecting often at the NCAA Championships, the US Open, or some other tennis event. It was important that we create a way to part as friends.

Life is what happens to you when you are busy making other plans.

John Lennon

Recruiting...
The Lifeblood of your Program

The other item that occupies much of a coach's time in summers is recruiting, or, as I call it, the "R" word. I learned pretty quickly that there were limits as to how much better most players can get. In order to beat better teams, you need better players. The only way to ensure a consistent flow of talented players is to go out and get them. I, and many of my colleagues, place a high value on the teaching and mentoring portion of my responsibilities, but my competitive nature drives me to recruit better players each and every year. I never had a mentor in this area and had to figure things out for myself. Suddenly, at age 24, I found myself a head college tennis coach at the US Naval Academy with no one to teach me what to do. The world in 1969 was vastly different from today's. When I began coaching there were few rules limiting the contacting of prospects. Imagine no internet, no cell phones, no social media. All recruitment was either face-to-face, via telephone, or by letter. There were no agencies like www.tennisrecruiting. net, among many others, that exist today. The Universal Tennis Ratings [UTR] had not yet been conceived. Recruiting was hard work. It requires that you stay on top of it every day. The will to win required making recruiting a priority.

It's not the will to win that matters. Everybody has that. It's the will to prepare to win that matters.

Bear Bryant

At Navy, an incoming student paid nothing to attend and was, in fact, given a salary while attending, as he was technically enlisted in the Navy. Therefore, I felt I had 4,300 scholarships at my disposal, since that was the size of the Brigade of Midshipmen. I used a telephone credit card and spent several hours every day and evening calling prospects. There were no restrictions on the number of calls per week, whom could be called, or anything like what is in place today. It was like the wild, wild, west. I was calling at the height of the Viet Nam war and not everyone was receptive to my military sales pitch. Additionally I had no assistant and we had a plebe [freshman] team that matriculated every year in late June. They were allowed to practice a sport almost daily in the summer, so I also needed to be there with them in the afternoons. Because we fielded both a plebe team and varsity one I knew that I could recruit in larger numbers than my civilian counterparts, but gathering the names and addresses of prospects was the most difficult challenge. The USTA published a list of the top 75 nationally ranked players in the 16-and-under and 18-and-under age groups, but that list didn't get you very far, given that hundreds of other colleges wanted the same players. I would then write every USTA section [i.e. Midwest, Mid-Atlantic, Southern, Texas, etc. - 17 in all] for the contact info for their players. A few would reply to my request. Most would send me a list of players and hometowns, but without enough information to see that a letter actually made it to the player. I did the same with districts within sections [i.e. Northeast Ohio, Central Michigan, etc.]. This gave me a large list of players, but not many complete addresses. It was a challenge that needed a solution.

As I expanded my contacts within the USTA I found a friend who worked in the USTA office in New York who would allow me to use their data base to find addresses. He was not allowed do it for me. I also was able to get tickets to the US Open from him, and suddenly a plan popped into my mind. I assembled all of the names and hometowns that I had received and put them in alphabetical order. I called five of my friends who would want to attend the Open. We left Annapolis, Maryland, at 5:00 AM, arriving at the USTA offices at 51 E. 42nd Street at 9:00 AM. We were immediately ushered into the data base area where [remember that this is 1970 or thereabouts] there were computer generated sheets separated alphabetically in large, heavy groups. We divided ourselves into three groups: A-G, H-P,and Q-Z. In each group of two one person would read out the name and hometown while the other would look for it on the appropriate sheet. For example I would call out the name-Jonathan Adams, Hopewell,Virginia. My partner would find it, and I would write down #16 Oak Street and the zip code. We would then go to the next name on the list until we had every name and address of any player ranked nationally, sectionally, or by district, as all ranked players needed to be USTA members. For many of these young men, mine was the only recruiting letter they would receive. After we finished I would take my friends to the US Open for a day of spectating, followed by a leisurely drive back to Annapolis that evening. There were no night matches at that time. The Open was then held on the grass at Forest Hills. I am pretty sure that I contacted far more prospects than any other coach in the country, normally reaching out to over 700 16 and 17 year old prospects. By 1971, only a year later, my Navy team was pretty good, finishing 21st at the NCAAs held that year at, of all places, Notre Dame.

Any resemblance to recruiting today is negligible. Today's world includes personal and professionally made dvds mailed to the coach, different recruiting services, more tournaments and expos for college coaches to attend to meet and evaluate players, the involvement of private, personal coaches. much greater participation by parents, recruiting showcase events, ITF tournaments to supplement the USTA events, USTA Futures [professional tournaments], lots of home visits by the coach, a limit of five official visits per prospect, dead periods when no contact is allowed, official and unofficial visits galore, UTR ratings for a more accurate assessment of a player's ability, and on and on. Not many days go by without the arrival of a video highlighting the strokes and virtues of the next would-be phenom. As coaches, we are looking for any advantage. Let me tell you one quick, true story. Around the beginning of this century I was involved in the recruitment of a good Midwestern player named Ryan Heller. He was interested in a good academic school with a strong tennis program. We were a good fit, I thought. There was just one snag. Ryan was Jewish and Notre Dame is a Catholic school. I remember one conversation we had. It went something like this:

Coach: "Ryan, you seem to want the things Notre Dame offers. What are you thinking?"

Heller: "You are right about the tennis/academic combination, Coach, but I'm not sure I am comfortable about the Catholic part of Notre Dame. "

Coach: "Relax, Ryan. Here's how it will work. You'll go to the dining hall to have lunch with your friends. As you sit down to eat, one of them recites the Jewish blessing in Hebrew" (At this point I recited the Jewish blessing, very much to his astonishment!)

Heller: "Wow! How did you do that?"

Coach: "In the two summers between my sophomore and senior years in college I was a tennis instructor in an all-Jewish overnight camp. I was almost the only Gentile there. I simply paid attention and tried to absorb everything that I could of the culture."

Heller: "How did that work out for you?"

Coach: "Wonderfully. It was a great and broadening experience for me". (At this point I was feeling pretty confident that my message was going to work.)

Heller: "Nice try, Coach, but I'm going to Michigan."

Sometimes even your best line won't work. That really happened. And there are so many more that I could tell you.

In one of my early years at Notre Dame I flew to make a home visit to meet with a junior player from the Boston area. Per the norm, I watched him practice with his tennis professional/ coach and then moved into a private room with the player, his parents, and the pro where we could discuss any thoughts or questions about Notre Dame. His father began with a question and followed up with two more, at which point the prospect said "Shut up, Dad. He is here to talk to me!" Without saying anything I made an instantaneous decision. This guy would not ever be on one of my teams. If he is disrespectful to his father, he will certainly not hesitate to treat me the same way. I followed his career at another top tennis school, where he led a team insurrection that resulted in the firing of his coach. I had learned that character trumps talent in recruiting. It was a valuable lesson.

Another recruiting story: my father died on January 5, 1988. Our family arrived at home that evening from a week at Disney World. No more than five minutes laater, I received a telephone call from my brother Billy in Richmond, Virginia, telling me of Daddy's passing. I was crushed and slept very poorly that night, knowing I needed to pack the next morning and travel to Richmond for the funeral and all that went with it. His death was unexpected, and it made it even tougher to take.

The next morning as I was packing my suitcase, I answered the phone. It was Tony DiLucia, the father of David DiLucia, the top prospect in the current national recruiting class. As he identified himself, nothing registered with me. I was so distressed that I did not recognize who he was. My mental and emotional state was such that I would not have understood anything he said. He told me that they had picked a weekend for David's official visit [just getting him to visit was a real coup] and they would arrive in several weeks, waiting for me to provide instructions as how we would provide David's airfare, etc., Not even realizing who he was, I simply replied in an off-the-cuff manner that he should let me know when he was on campus and come by to say hello- and nothing else! There was a very pregnant pause. Tony did not expect my confused words and I was still in deep denial of my father's death.

Understand that David had been a semi- finalist in the US Open Junior Championships a few months earlier in Flushing Meadows, New York. Yes, THAT US Open. Many thought he should consider bypassing college for the professional ranks. He was, in fact, a "franchise player." I had just blown off his father. Suddenly my mind began to clear, and it dawned on me what I had done. I tried to figure out how to dig my way out of the hole I had created.

Not knowing what to do, I simply told Tony what was going on in my life, hoping he would understand and not hold it against me or cancel the visit. What happened next is still hard for me to believe. Tony, whom I hardly knew, began to tell me that he had also lost his own father a year earlier, almost to the day, and that he understood my grief. He then walked me through what would happen in the coming days and months, much as a minister or grief counselor would do. The more we talked the better I was able to come to grips with my emotions. He had become my unwitting therapist and that day a bond between us was forged. We still speak every few months and he still sends me a wonderful Christmas gift every year, even though David graduated more than 25 years ago. That we were able to convince David to commit to Notre Dame later was the recruiting coup of the year in college tennis and I have to believe that the friendship that began that day had something to do with it. Tony flew to Illinois in 2013 for my ITA Hall of Fame induction.

I was never completely comfortable in my role as a college recruiter. While I wanted and needed the best players I could get, I wrestled continually with the image of a slick encyclopedia salesman in my conversations. The temptation was always there to say what the prospects wanted to hear, but then I might face recriminations if I had in any way been misleading. Conversations revolved around our schedule, facilities, and program. The South Bend weather [First prize - an all expenses one week trip to South Bend, IN. Second prize- a two week all expenses trip to South Bend, IN….you get the idea.] was also a topic of discussion. Many players wanted sun belt tennis. I had to sell cold winters and lots of studying, not always something the top players wanted to hear, as many wanted a light academic load and had no plans to graduate. At Navy I had to broach the topic of Vietnam, also an unpopular discussion, so this part of the problem was not new for me. I quickly decided that honesty and candor had to be my message, so I usually brought up the most unpleasant aspects of my product first and got them out in the open.

At Navy, I sold the challenge of being a Midshipman. At Notre Dame I sold the total package-an extraordinary institution, great education, and difficult team schedule. To David I sold the idea of being the cornerstone of a new dynasty - the guy who made others come. It was effective. Heck, I certainly could not sell the current product, as the team I had inherited was not a strong one. In the previous year, my first, we lost to Kalamazoo College, a DIII school. That was the longest one hour van drive back that I have ever taken. Little did I know that in my fifth year, David's senior year, we would play for the national championship on the last day of the season. I had to get him to trust me that we would, indeed, be very good and would play a very strong schedule. Thank goodness he did. His signing made all of the other top players who came after him at least take a look at us. We also were able to add both UCLA and USC to the next year's schedule.

One more recruiting story for you. At Navy I began recruiting a player named David Geatz from Grand Forks, ND. In case you haven't guessed, there are no ATP players from Grand Forks. It gets really cold there. Hockey reigns supreme and tennis is an afterthought. He needed a scholarship in order to attend college, as his financial resources were very lacking. The Naval Academy covered all expenses and was a dream come true. David was a bright young man who would later earn his PhD and coach at both Minnesota, Cornell, and Pennsylvania, but the Academy required a higher math SAT score for admission than he had achieved. He re-took the SAT .When his score came in it was not sufficient for the rigorous Navy standards, so I had to place a difficult telephone call to give him the bad news. David began to cry as I told him Annapolis was not to be. When he told me he would not be able to go to college I knew there was a solution, but it would be tough for me to swallow. I asked him if he would consider Army in West Point, New York. He said that he would, of course, consider the US Military Academy, but that they had not expressed any interest. Now, try to understand that Navy and Army do not try to build up each other's programs. Theirs is perhaps the country's fiercest rivalry. Coaches were hired and fired for their ability to beat the other. Nonetheless, I was sufficiently moved to call Ron Holmberg, the Army coach, and recommend David to him. The decision was difficult, but I had done the right thing. I knew David would become Army's #1 player and was hoping that the good Lord would somehow reward me for my kind gesture. He did.

Because David won the North Dakota state high school championship without the loss of a single game - every match was 6-0,6-0 - he was named to *Sports Illustrated's* "Faces In The Crowd" for his achievement at about this time. Sight unseen, the tennis coach at New Mexico State called and offered him a full scholarship. Due to the more lengthy admissions process at West Point David accepted the NMSU offer and became their #1 player as a freshman. He later transferred to New Mexico and made the NCAA tournament before playing professionally for a bit. He is now one of college tennis's better coaches, having won Big Ten titles at Minnesota and now moving to Pennsylvania in the Ivy League. I had dodged a bullet and my undefeated record against Army [I finished 15-0] stayed intact. My goal was still in place.

~ Cross Court Reflection ~

A goal without a plan is just a wish.

Antoine de Saint-Exupery

Togetherness in Recruiting Circles

The man who is afraid to risk failure
seldom has to face success.

John Wooden

Summers provide college tennis coaches with the greatest opportunities for recruiting. There are numerous tournaments where we can attend for the purposes of meeting and evaluating top players. Sectional tournaments are held in June. July offers, among many others, the National Junior Claycourts. The Claycourts were held for many years in Louisville, KY, a hotbed of junior tennis, but moved in the last decade to Del Ray Beach, FL where they remain. Shortly thereafter follow the US National Junior Team Championships, formerly held as the National Junior Davis Cup at the University of South Carolina in Columbia, SC, but now in Champaign, IL. Immediately next, usually in early August is the crown jewel of junior tennis, the US Nationals Boys 16 and 18 Championships held annually for more than a half century in Kalamazoo, MI. These events are referred to by all as the Claycourts, the Team Championships, and, simply, Kalamazoo, just as the All England Club's tournament is called Wimbledon.

The Claycourts is the first of the elite national events and is certainly on the radar of most college coaches. For many of us it is the first time we have seen each other since the NCAAs and the chemistry amongst coaches is good. We are no longer competing [at least on the court] against each other and most of us enjoy our mutual company. We exchange gossip. Matches from conference or NCAA play are discussed, as are the recruiting interests and scholarship availability of each coach. The NCAA limits prospects to only five NCAA official visits [visits where the institution provides expenses for travel, meals, lodging, etc.] It is important for each of us to secure these coveted visits from the top players and this is the time when many players are making the final decisions as to which schools will receive their five official visits. This is the time when each coach needs to secure the top visits possible. Getting a prospect on your campus to hang out with your players is a must in order to gain a commitment. This event and Kalamazoo sponsor what have come to be called "Expos" which take place the day before play officially begins.

Behind every young child who believes in himself is a parent who believed first.

Matthew Jacobson

Players typically arrive a few days ahead to practice on the surface on which they will play and most attend these recruiting events where each school that has signed up and paid for a booth can meet with prospects, parents, and coaches to discuss mutual interest, scholarship or roster availability, etc. There is clearly the chance to see which coaches have been actively recruiting or are simply desirable in the recruiting process by the size of the lines at each booth. In recent years it has become the norm for many coaches to set up meetings privately before play, thus negating the need for the Expo, but for many coaches the Expo is a must. This is a time for feeling out by both parties. In some cases the recruiting process has ended and commitments have already been made. In recent years the recruiting process has accelerated and non-binding commitments during the junior year are common. Commitments are only verbal, however, and no coach can fully relax until his prospect has a signed grant-in-aid and letter-of-intent. This cannot be done before the "early" signing period in November of the prospect's senior year. Not all schools give athletic scholarships and many rely on merit and/or need-based aid to attract their prospects. Some offer both. Some are highly selective in the admissions process while others require only the NCAA minimum standards. We are not all playing by the same rules in this regard. All of us, though, are trying to figure out just how each prospect will fare in our respective programs. That is the big question.

You never know how a horse will pull until you hook him to a heavy load.

Bear Bryant

I remember well being at the Claycourt Expo in July, 2004. A skinny Indian young man and his father worked their way to the front of my line. They seemed interested, but I knew almost nothing about him. This is where things get tricky. You don't want to spend lots of time with a player that you don't think is very good. He may keep others from lining up at your booth and, if he is not a good player, it might not represent what you are seeking and encourage others to look elsewhere. Likewise it is never a good thing to be rude to anyone, so this was a situation I wanted to avoid. He was from Omaha, NE, not a city that spits out many Wimbledon champions, and he and his father asked question after question to me. As some top players in my line grew impatient and left to line up at another school's booth my patience was being tested, but I knew that good manners were always right. I bit the bullet and showed him and his father the courtesy they deserved. Little did I know that this skinny, little boy would not only attend Notre Dame, but become an All American in his sophomore year, reaching the quarter-finals of the NCAA singles. He is now Dr. Sheeva Parbhu and I attended his wedding last summer back in Omaha. He is one of the best competitors I ever coached and was often the last match on in a 4-3 win. Thank goodness that I was not rude that day.

While recruiting is ever ongoing at these events, all of us are aware of the NCAA rules which limit contact during the tournament as long as the player is still in the event. Once he has lost you can talk to him and even sit down for a lengthy chat. However, a coach is only allowed three contacts and four evaluations. A contact is any face-to-face meeting when conversation is exchanged. You are allowed "normal civility" such as "Nice match" or "See you tomorrow." Unanticipated meetings like this do not count as contacts. This is where the rubber meets the road and a number of coaches try to stretch these regulations by extending "Nice match" to "Nice match and we have your visit all set up Here is your flight information." This would be a clear violation of NCAA policies.

Sometime during the 1990's when the NCAA passed the rule limiting contacts during the course of competition I faced a dilemma. I did not want prospects and parents to take my adherence to the rules as a sign that I no longer had any interest. I knew that some coaches would abuse the rule and, accordingly, I had small cards printed that explained the rule. I then wrote on that same card that I was certain that no parent would want his or her son to commit to a coach who willfully broke the rule. Pretty soon I got some dirty looks and even a few comments from those who were pushing the envelope. That is turning a negative situation into a positive one.

A fortunate circumstance for Notre Dame is our location and proximity to Kalamazoo which is just over an hour's drive from our campus. Hence, we are able to arrange to meet with prospects and show them around if they are willing to make the trek to South Bend. Typically we try to encourage folks to stop here on their way from Champaign to Kalamazoo or to stop by before or after Kalamazoo ends for them. The University of Michigan enjoys a similar advantage. I mentioned that four evaluations are allowed, but this applies only during the school year, so summer evals are unlimited. Once the school year begins a coach can only evaluate a prospect four times. There has been a concerted effort to streamline these rules, as one needs an NCAA manual on his person in order to be sure. There were limits on telephone calls[one per week], texting, and other social media [IM, etc.]. Many of these just changed and may change again, the reason being the difficulty in proper enforcement. It seems that the rules governing recruiting are tweaked almost annually, so coaches have to stay updated at all times. In fact, coaches were required to take and pass an NCAA administered test annually during the summers.

Reunited. Former Notre Dame great Barry King with his coaches Ryan Sachire and Bobby Bayliss prior to the match between Irish Davis Cuppers and Notre Dame. August 1, 2012. *Photo by Cindy Sachire.*

Camaraderie Among Coaches

*Go for the moon. If you don't
hit it, you'll still be
heading for a star.*

Willis Reed

Camaraderie between coaches is on full display during recruiting events. Many of us room together, share meals, and find comfort in the company of our peers. Perhaps a decade or so ago I invited a group of coaches to my home for an evening of "burgers, banter, and beer." The drive between Kalamazoo and my home is just over an hour in length, as I previously mentioned. As the day ended a dozen or more coaches piled into cars and trekked to Granger, IN and my home where we talked about all of the usual things, most of which involved tennis, and everyone had to shuck their own ears of corn. There are lots of stories within our group and it is difficult to separate the truth from legend, but at a certain point we called each other out to test the veracity of a story we had heard.

With us that evening was Jerry Simmons, the veteran LSU coach, reputed to be one of the toughest of all competitors. Legend had passed on a story that concerned Jerry, whose hatred of losing was well-founded. The story was that after a particularly difficult and long loss to a bitter SEC rival, Simmons threw all of the players into the team van and began the long drive home - sans showers and a meal. As the drive continued the team captain made his way to the "shotgun" seat of the van to ask Coach Simmons if they could stop for dinner. Simmons assured the captain that indeed they would pull into a place to eat shortly. A few minutes later the van pulled into a rest area - not a restaurant - and Simmons passed a large paper bag back to the players. The players, afraid to say anything contrary to their grizzled coach, found 8 opened cans of Alpo dog food there, each sporting its own plastic spoon. "You played like dogs; you'll eat like dogs!" growled Simmons. Now for the moment of truth. One of us said, "Now, Jerry, you didn't really do this, did you?" He laughed, "Yes I did, but we stopped a little later for a real meal."

This led to a "Chuck Kriese story" and we asked him to confirm several of these. Kriese is the charismatic man who overturned the ACC applecart as he burst onto the scene in the 1970's at Clemson where he developed a dynasty based on an indefatigable work ethic and passionate approach to coaching. The main story we had heard that was screaming for verification involved Chuck [the Clemson coach at the time] during a match at Kentucky. Reportedly Kriese was in the middle of an intense contest in Lexington and the Kentucky crowd was brutal. Kriese suddenly raced to the middle of the courts and bellowed to all: "Stop the match! Timeout!" The referee came running over to the Clemson coach and said, "Coach, you can't do that. There are no timeouts in tennis." Kriese looked at him in disbelief and replied, "There must be timeouts in tennis! We have them in football, baseball, and basketball." The crowd was incredulous and had stopped their cheering and intimidation of the Clemson players, waiting to hear what would happen. The referee confirmed the lack of timeouts and while the crowd was silent Kriese yelled to his players, "All right you Clemson Tigers, I am really proud of the effort you are giving! Don't let these redneck, idiot fans get to you"....or words to that effect, thereby insulting the very spectators who were right in front of him. The crowd suddenly turned its attention and vitriol on the coach, hammering him with insults, which was exactly what he wanted. He had gotten them to leave his players alone and direct their disdain at him, giving the players a better chance to win. Kriese confirmed the story and all of us realized that there was plenty of wisdom in what he had done, as well as a police escort out of town.

Eventually I was asked to verify a story, and I did. It involved our team in 1993 when we played LSU in Baton Rouge. Both teams were in the top ten at the time and Coach Simmons was pretty tough to beat, especially at home. It was my first trip to Baton Rouge and I was anxious to see firsthand whether the stories about the Tiger fans were true. Trust me, they were! LSU had a layout in which all six courts ran in a row. The covered bleachers were right behind the baselines and ran the length of the facility. The roof over the bleachers served both to shield the fans from sun and rain, but also to channel their insults and add volume to them. As we began the match I realized that this might even rival Georgia in home court advantage and our players were really getting an earful. One fan, in particular, ran back and forth between courts yelling in the loudest voice I have ever heard. LSU won the match and we went back immediately to the hotel for showers, dinner, and an early night's rest.

The next morning was Easter Sunday and I had our team put on their coats and ties to accompany me to Mass at the local parish church where the priest, a young, wholesome looking man, looked at me and said, "You must be the Notre Dame tennis team." I confirmed his suspicions, but asked him how he knew who we were. He replied, "I was one of those rednecks yelling at you yesterday. I love my Tigers." He then gave us a quick tour and led us to the front to be seated. As Mass began the priest said, "We have some special guests at Mass with us today." He then gestured towards us and said, "It is appropriate that on this Resurrection Sunday we salute them as they try to resurrect their season after the whuppin' our Tigers gave them yesterday." Talk about home court advantage! Baton Rouge is a difficult place to go when looking for an easy match. Nonetheless, I have learned that playing pressure matches during the season is the most useful preparation for post-season play. A team needs to play difficult opponents to reach its potential.

—◦—

I've missed more than 9,000 shots in my career. I've lost almost 300 games. Twenty-six times I've been trusted to take the game-winning shot and missed. I've failed over and over again in my life. And that is why I succeed.

Michael Jordan

—◦—

Jerry Simmons was so driven that he never stopped competing and was always thinking about what he could do to make his LSU team better. I vividly remember receiving a call from Jerry one year early on Christmas morning. After wishing each other a Merry Christmas I asked him what had prompted this morning's call as my kids continued opening their Christmas presents and my wife glared at me to get off the phone. He got right to the point and wanted to understand why our Notre Dame teams had experienced so much success against one of his SEC rivals, Mississippi State. As I looked at my wife's pained expression wondering why Jerry had called and why I would not hang up, I shrugged off the question with an honest, "I don't have a clue. Just luck, I guess." That was not enough for him and he pressed for a logical answer to an illogical question. Finally, I thought of a way to end the call. "Jerry" I said, "Where you go wrong in your approach to playing Mississippi State is that you are so competitive and gruff that those guys, who are mostly older players from France, come in more motivated against your team than ours. We don't want to wake them up. We know how talented they are and treat them with great respect. Since they are more experienced than our guys we go out of our way to defer to them and avoid giving them any extra motivation. You, on the other hand, have them extra-motivated for your matches." "You are right!" shouted Simmons. "That is the key. Thanks!" as he hung up the phone.

I returned to my family and quickly forgot the entire conversation. That May we once again drew #5 ranked Mississippi State in the NCAA round of 16. Before the match I exchanged pleasantries with Bulldogs coach Andy Jackson, one of the top coaches in the college game. I asked him how things were going for him and he replied, "You won't believe this, but Coach Simmons has become really nice. I actually enjoyed our time together before our match. He is a changed man." I could only chuckle at the comment.

———

Lose as if you like it; win as if you are used to it.

Tommy Hitchcock

———

It is things like this that cement the relationships between coaches. We have all lost difficult matches and have all been turned down at the last possible moment when a top prospect changes his mind and signs with someone else. Some of us have been fired for not meeting the expectations of our athletic directors. We respect and appreciate each other. We have all enjoyed varying degrees of success. There will always be that bond. To be sure, there are some rivalries that preclude a good relationship, but for the most part we coaches enjoy each other's company. I truly value my relationship with my fellow coaches. When I was coaching Navy I found that I needed to supplement my coaching income. I mentioned this to Harvard's coach Dave Fish and within a few days he had the Wellesley Country Club in Boston contact me to investigate my interest in their head professional/director of tennis summer position. Within a few weeks I had landed the position and Dave told me I could live with his family for five weeks until school let out in Annapolis and I could bring my family to Wellesley to a home I rented there. I did this for five consecutive summers before we moved to Wellesley and I took over at MIT. As I look back on this gesture, I believe that it allowed me to stay in coaching during a difficult financial time. With four children and college tuitions approaching I simply could not have been able to handle the expenses I was facing.

I have stayed close to Trinity's Paul Assaiante for 40 years, despite our meeting as the head coaches at Army and Navy, respectfully. I have enjoyed his recent ride of success as he has captured 13 consecutive national championships in squash [17 in a 20 year period] and set the record for consecutive victories in any collegiate sport at well over 200. After Notre Dame had contacted me about its upcoming coaching vacancy, I almost removed my name from consideration, fearing that I would not make the cut. It was Paul who gave me a much needed pep talk and convinced me to apply for the position which I wound up holding for 26 years.

I will always be thankful for the opportunity to begin my college coaching career in the environment of the service academies. Paul agrees. A special example of this was during the time I prepared to join the Catholic Church in 1979. I was told that I needed a sponsor, or godfather. The man I selected was my then team captain at Navy - Gene Miller - who after graduation went on to become a Navy jet fighter pilot. Gene still calls me at times to see where I am spiritually. He once asked me how long it had been since my last confession. He got very upset with me when I jokingly told him that I had not sinned. He takes that responsibility very seriously.

———⊙———

There is nothing on this earth more to be prized than true friendship.

Thomas Aquinas

———⊙———

It is encouraging to see the dinners together, the ultimate frisbee games, and the overall camaraderie that bonds coaches together on our various summer recruiting travels. We understand each other. We know how important it is for a coach to be physically present watching a top prospect play, even though he already knows everything he needs to about him and should probably head out to view other players, but feels the need to "babysit" that particular player on that day, as mom and dad are there and will notice which coaches seem interested. We exchange information freely, hoping to stay on top of the latest rumor about where a particular player has given his verbal commitment, if for no other reason than to avoid wasting time on someone who has already decided to go elsewhere. Interestingly, we get to know the players well and feel we have invested much in the recruitment of each. When they decide to go to a different school we know that we will see them again, soon enough, wearing the colors of their chosen university. I try to keep my sense of humor throughout and frequently joke with players about their choices. If a player chooses a school that has orange as one of its colors [Tennessee, Virginia, or Clemson come to mind] I am quick to tell him how much I envy his opportunity to wear that shade of orange and how fortunate he is to be able to wear the same shirt on consecutive days - to the football game on Saturday, hunting with his buddies on Sunday, and to his job - picking up trash on the highway - on Monday. We all need a good laugh once in a while.

While it is still summer, we know that for most prospects the decision to attend the school of their choice needs to be made by early November in time for the early NCAA signing period. Commitments can be made at any time. Rumors abound about how much scholarship aid a particular prospect has been promised. The boys are in a system that allows only 4 and ½ scholarships at any time per team. Girls, on the other hand, are given 8 scholarships, or grants-in-aid. The women's scholarships are 8 "head count" grants, meaning that at any one time there can only be 8 women on a team receiving athletic aid. Men's scholarships can be split into pieces and there is no limit as to how many players are receiving athletic aid; all that matters is that the sum of that aid can never go above 4 and ½ total scholarships. For this reason it is not uncommon for a men's squad to carry more players than most women's teams. This really affects the way we recruit. For some, the amount, or percentage, of a scholarship is important for ego's sake. For this reason it is necessary for men's coaches to work with a larger base of prospects. The amount, or percentage, of scholarship offered might well be the difference between your landing or losing your top prospect.

~ Cross Court Reflection ~

The only limits to the possibilities in your life tomorrow are the 'buts' we use today.

Les Brown

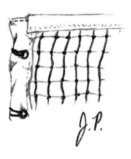

52

Media Praise for 1992 Team. A collage of media commentary during the 1992 season.

The Importance of Recruiting

In this lifetime, you don't have to prove nothin' to nobody but yourself. After what you've gone through, if you haven't done that by now, it ain't gonna happen.

"Rudy," the movie

In the mid 1990s, I was recruiting a young man who later became an All American at another school. He was exceptionally bright and I told him that he had an excellent chance to apply for and win one of the "Joyce" scholarships given on the basis of academic - not athletic - performance. I was also recruiting Ryan Sachire [the current Notre Dame coach]. Both boys lived in Ohio and I believed that I could land both, due to the Joyce scholarship. The other boy did, in fact, receive the Joyce offer and it was better than an athletic scholarship because it included an additional allowance for clothing and travel which were not allowed in an athletic scholarship. After receiving this great offer he turned it down, mostly because I had chosen Ryan over him for the athletic grant. Ryan, of course was a three-time All American and one of the truly great players in the history of Notre Dame tennis, but I will always feel that another player's ego got in the way of our team's opportunity to become extraordinary.

As the National Junior Championships in Kalamazoo ends, thoughts turn to the upcoming school year and our current teams. Certainly, there are a few other events that some of us will attend to scout for talent, such as the US Open Juniors at Flushing Meadow and some ITF [International Tennis Federation] events, but school begins for most of us shortly after Kalamazoo. Recruiting now consists of getting commitments from prospects to make our school one of the five "official" visits and lining up the flights and plans for those visits. For each of us this is our chance to make the best impression possible. Much planning goes into which of our players will "host" each prospect, what type of entertainment will take place, and whom the prospect will meet on his visit [academic advisor, strength coach, sports psychologist, athletic administrator, etc.]. This is when you need to count on your best team player salesman to work his magic. Most of this will take place while you are not present and you need to be able to trust your entire team to do a great job. This also creates a dilemma for the "host" player, as the recruit being influenced to join us might, in fact, take his place in the starting lineup. It is a true test of character and loyalty.

When I first arrived at Notre Dame, I was extremely fortunate to have as our best player a junior named Brian Kalbas. In addition to playing #1 on our team, Brian was our hardest worker and best leader. As I mentioned earlier, I made no bones about the fact that I was going to try to land the country's top recruit, David DiLucia. I wanted Brian to be his host. It gets tricky here because I was asking Brian to recruit the player who would push him down from his perch in our lineup. David could have his pick of the best tennis and academic schools in the country because of his ability. He had reached the semi-finals of the US Open Juniors in September, an event that included all of the best 17 and 18 year old tennis players in the world. How could I expect Brian to take on this task, knowing that his reward would be to surrender the #1 spot in our lineup to a freshman? I counted on two things: Brian's character and his love for Notre Dame. He did everything with David that weekend, even enlisting him to play for his dorm in an intramural "broomball" contest. I was right and Brian was the biggest reason David chose Notre Dame.

I was most afraid of SMU, a perennial tennis power coached by Dennis Ralston, one of the greatest players in US tennis history. Heck, I would have given anything to be coached by

Ralston. Also in the hunt was newcomer-to-the-top ten Georgia Tech. We put on the full court press. Our athletic director, Dick Rosenthal, got involved and spent significant time with David and his parents during his official visit. Missy Conboy, Dick's #2, became part of the group. John Heisler, our extraordinary director of sports information met with the DiLucias with Tim Brown's recently won Heisman trophy sitting on his desk. I certainly called upon my limited powers of persuasion, but when the dust had cleared and David was wearing blue and gold it was Brian who had had the greatest impact. Not only did Brian selflessly influence David, but later that spring he similarly worked his magic on a transfer student, Walter Dolhare, who became our #2, pushing Brian to #3. This story, though, has a happy ending for Brian. After graduating in 1989 he became my first assistant coach at Notre Dame and was a very big part of our meteoric rise to the 1992 NCAA finals. His ability to get the most out of our players and to find just the right thing to say on court in the heat of battle was immeasurable. He left us in the fall of 1993 to become the head women's coach at William and Mary, guiding the Tribe to the NCAA's elite eight in 1998 and was named the ITA National Coach of the Year. He has since moved to Chapel Hill, NC where his 2014 team was also a national runner-up and he garnered yet another National Coach of the Year award, in addition to three National Team Indoors titles. He is one of the truly great coaches in our sport. David has referred to him as an older brother and still values his counsel. Brian had more than a little to do with our run to the 1992 NCAA finals. Brian had both discipline and commitment in ample quantities. He remains to this day someone I admire very much.

Tie discipline to commitment and it becomes an irreversible decision that you will do today what most people won't so that you can have tomorrow what most people can't.

Zig Ziglar

Landing David was the catalyst to an outstanding recruiting class the next year. While he might not have been able to change the minds of all of our other prospects, what he did was to make the best players we recruited the next year stop and at least take a look, such was his influence. No less a spokesman than Arthur Ashe came out in some national publications with the comment that David's decision to join us was significant for tennis. I spent such a great amount of time on this to point out the importance of recruiting in college sports. While "coaching players up" is possible, it is certainly a lot easier to be great when you have more talent.

As the summer ends and the school year begins the next chapter in the life of a coach is upon us. Now it is time to earn your salary and take anywhere from ten to fifteen individual players and turn them into one cohesive unit. This is where we earn our reputations. And I will be able to focus more on my coaching ideas knowing that Ryan wants to handle most of the recruiting responsibilities. Coaching college tennis without worrying about recruiting is like eating ice cream without worrying about the calories. My final season is going to be fun.

US Open 2017. Coach Bobby Bayliss and his wife Pat at the US Open, August 2017.

Another Season Begins

Life consists not in holding good cards,
but in playing those you hold well.

Eugene Hare

Every coach feels the excitement of a new school year. Returning players are back. Everyone is in a good mood. Excitement filters its way throughout the campus. All players get a fresh start. Football season is ready to kick off. And for a coach, it is a time of optimism and big plans. My close friend and former assistant at the Naval Academy, John McGinty, said it best. "Seeing the newly recruited players out on the courts for the first time, hitting balls with your team, is like opening your Christmas presents." Visions of "what ifs" and "why nots" bounce in and out of your thought process. We are all undefeated at this time. There are no real team morale issues. Life seems pretty darn good. The fall season is a different animal from spring. There are no events with team scoring, thanks to a decades-old NCAA edict. It is time to build your program, to shape your vision out of the clay that is your squad. To be sure, there will be team and individual issues, but none carrying the stress of the regular season when a lineup change can mean the difference between a win and a loss. Add to this the absence of no overdue term papers, no mid-term exams, and the fact that everyone on campus feels the same sense of joie de vivre. It is matched only by the period right after exams end in the spring, as your team readies itself for the NCAAs without any academic pressure. The fall season allows each player to realize his/her potential and find out what they can do.

Far too many people have no idea of what they can do because all they have been told is what they can't do.

Zig Ziglar

This year, my last, is special for all of us. Something that I have always tried to do is to schedule matches and events that offer our players something they won't find anywhere else. We have taken foreign tours to London, Paris, Rome, Vienna, Salzburg, and Dublin at various times. The NCAA allows an institution to make such a trip, usually in the summer, to international spots because of the cultural and educational benefits they offer. Such an adventure can only be taken once every four years. I have approached alumni for donations to fund these trips and they have always responded. In fact, when I sent letters to tennis alumni in 2001 to assist with one such venture the first two, and largest, checks came from two of the all time greatest players in Notre Dame tennis history: David DiLucia and Ryan Sachire. Our guys have been fortunate to see Wimbledon, practice on the "tiere battu" [red clay] courts at Paris's Roland Garros, play a French club team on red clay, an Austrian team on a similar surface, cross Dublin's Liffey River on Ha'Penny Bridge, discover London, admire the Blue Danube in Vienna, and visit the Vatican, just to name a few stops we have made at various times. On a spring break in 1994 we played five matches in Hawaii. These trips have been a luxury I don't take lightly and have left me with many fond memories. I am indeed fortunate that the spin of the dice somehow pointed me to South Bend, a place where leadership can make a big difference.

Leadership is something you earn, something you're chosen for. You can't come in yelling 'I'm your leader.'

Ben Rothlisberger

59

This year we have a different opportunity. Our football team opens its season in Dublin, Ireland against the US Naval Academy. My goodness, the stars are aligned in such a way that I just had to be a part of this! To combine my 15 year Navy career with my 26 year Notre Dame tenure in a place that the Notre Dame faithful looks on as a second home is a can't miss opportunity. I have been going to Dublin to look at prospects play tennis since 2004 and I know many of the tennis crowd there well. The Irish Junior Nationals are held annually at the Fitzwilliam Club, Ireland's answer to Wimbledon's All England Club. History and tradition drip from its walls. In August, 2011 I asked the tennis professional at Fitzwilliam, Jimmy McDonough, if he thought that there would be any interest on their part to stage a match between Notre Dame and the Irish Davis Cup players. He seemed excited about the idea and I left Dublin sufficiently encouraged to try to put something together.

My first contact was with Barry King, one of my all-time favorite Notre Dame players and a current member of the Irish Davis Cup squad. Between him and Jimmy things progressed rapidly and before I knew it we had a genuinely festive event planned. We cleared this with the NCAA, which did not call it a foreign tour, but rather "playing on foreign soil" since school had already begun. I was able to fund the trip using a "restricted fund" that we had kept to which many tennis alumni had long been contributing. We would take all 13 players. It would take place during the second week of school and we would miss three days of class, something the Notre Dame leadership tracked very carefully. We would fly to Dublin on Wednesday August 29th, arriving on the morning of the 30th. We would take a brief tour of Dublin, grab a bite to eat, and head to the Fitzwilliam Club to practice on the "Irish grass", a synthetic surface similar to Field Turf used here in the US. The surface would be tricky for our players. This was a common surface in Ireland due to the frequency of rain there. Adjusting would not be easy, but that mattered little. It played similarly to real grass, rewarding slice serves and approach shots as well as drop shots and volleys. The next day {Friday} we would play the match. There would be ample food for spectators [a pig roasted on a spit], live

Irish music, and great competition, followed by a banquet for both teams. On Saturday we would get up for a hearty Irish breakfast and walk from our hotel to watch the Navy vs. Notre Dame football game in Dublin's Aviva Stadium. The next morning [Sunday] we would fly back to Chicago and bus back to campus. Not a bad opening trip for our four freshmen in their second week of school!

The beginning of the school year holds many mandatory housekeeping chores for coaches. Before any of our players can begin competition they need to be certified eligible for NCAA purposes by our Office of Compliance. Freshmen have to be cleared by the NCAA Clearinghouse. While somewhat perfunctory, this involves monitoring things like satisfactory progress towards graduation, something that almost never presents a problem at a school like ours. In my 26 years as a head coach at Notre Dame all of our players have graduated on time, with their class, with only one exception- a young man who changed majors after his sophomore year and had to go back to take mandatory sophomore classes in the Mendoza School of Business, adding a year to his tenure. I have been congratulated on this by several of my colleagues, but it is pretty normal - and expected - here. Additionally, all players have to be cleared medically by our Sports Medicine staff. There are a few other house cleaning chores to cover, but by the end of the week most teams have been cleared to practice and compete. The tennis year now begins in earnest.

It is week two and we are ready to leave for Dublin, but suddenly there is sadness in our camp. The NCAA has determined that Eric Schnurrenberger, one of our entering freshmen, will not be cleared for travel and competition in time to join us. The NCAA Clearinghouse is following a protocol established in conjunction with each country to determine whether a prospect's high school transcript is sufficient for eligibility. Eric is a special and unusual case. He entered a program in Switzerland for "talented and gifted" students that took five years for its participants, rather than the standard four years. Because some international players have come to the US either much older than normal or ill-prepared for the academic rigors of college the Clearinghouse has been created to regulate such things. Its problem, like those in any bureaucracy, is that "the devil is in the details." In Eric's case his extraordinary academic achievements have set off a red flag.

The frustration many coaches feel in dealing with the NCAA is a frequent topic of conversation, but the organization has a thankless job. It was created by our colleges and universities to provide direction, guidance, and to be an arbiter in cases like Eric's. Eric will carry a 3.9 GPA into his senior year at Notre Dame, but his unusual path has cost him a year of eligibility. It is an example of why I sometimes refer to the NCAA acronym as standing for "No Clue About Athletics." An example of this occurred in the 1990's when many of the smaller schools, in an effort to cut costs, lobbied the NCAA to pass a rule that outlawed multi-color stationery, so I had to order new, one-color stationery for the next year, only to see the rule rescinded the following year. Go figure! I feel for Eric, but admire his stoicism as he wishes us all good luck and safe travels. One of my biggest regrets this year will be that he was not allowed to travel and compete with us. He demonstrates his great character by continuing to practice hard and show improvement every day. Nonetheless, I will always regret that I did not have the opportunity to coach him in competition.

———⊙——

You can't force your will on people. If you want them to act differently, you need to inspire them to change themselves.

Phil Jackson

———⊙——

We assemble bright and early at the Eck Tennis Pavilion on the morning of August 29th, excited about the adventure ahead. Adidas has provided us with some great looking clothes in Irish green that give our team a feeling of uniformity and a sharp appearance. The bus ride to Chicago's O'Hare airport goes smoothly and we quickly say goodbye to our driver and file into the line for the initial flight to New York's Kennedy airport.

Suddenly we have a problem. The woman checking passports has indicated that the passport of freshman Quentin Monaghan is invalid because it has begun to delaminate, the result of having an earlier encounter with water that has long since dried. I become flustered, wondering what to do. Technically she is correct, but there is little doubt that Quentin is one of us and certainly not a terror threat. Still, she will not budge. Here I stand with a 17 year old freshman, wondering what recourse I have. The chartered bus has already left and it will be problematic to get him back to campus. The lady tells me that he can simply go to the passport office downtown and get a new one, but we have no transportation and my best option seems to be to have him take a bus back to South Bend and miss the trip. Miraculously another woman appears, a supervisor, who stood aside watching our dilemma play out. She pulls me aside telling me that she might allow Quentin to travel, but fears that he might have the same problem in New York and be stranded there. After conferring with Quentin I call his mother who approves of his coming with us. She has a sister in New York, she says, who will pick up Quentin, if necessary, and arrange his transportation back to South Bend. The woman from American Airlines agrees and we quickly pass through security with Quentin in the middle of our line, holding his passport where it delaminated so that he is cleared by security. This is but one example of what can go wrong when escorting a dozen or so young men in their team travel adventures.

The flight to Kennedy goes smoothly, but we run into another problem there. Because we are flying to Dublin on Aer Lingus we need to leave the terminal to catch a shuttle to the proper terminal. We then will need to re-enter and once again pass through security. The shuttle is late and, as I look at my watch, I realize that we are in danger of missing our connection. This is very problematic because over 30,000 Notre Dame fans are flying over for the game and most flights have been booked for months. Should we miss this flight it is doubtful that we would be able to get on another. We now begin to re-enter security clearance and make our way to the gate. I ensure that Quentin once again is in the middle of our group, all similarly attired. He passes muster and we now sprint [my wife and I are quickly passed by our players] to our gate hoping to make the flight. As we rush to the gate, I am reminded that our players now can run much faster than I, a concession to my approaching 69th birthday. Somehow we make it and are the last people allowed to board. For the first time in hours I breathe a sigh of relief. As I have said before and will say again, welcome to my world! The logistics of team travel and recruiting are two of the things I will not miss when I retire.

The flight arrives on time in Dublin and once again I need to be in charge. Our travel has been arranged expertly by John Anthony, president of Anthony Travel, the agency that handles all of Notre Dame's travel, as well as that of many other colleges. John has once again proven his expertise, as we are immediately greeted by an Anthony Travel representative after we are cleared through customs and reunited with our luggage. We have been assigned a mini-bus and driver who will remain with us throughout the weekend. I am immediately relieved. Most of our players have never flown to Europe and are processing the feeling of both excitement and exhaustion now at 7:30 AM Dublin time. I remind them that their own body clocks are still set at 2:30AM and to grab some coffee to assist them.

———⊙———

If you have been here, no explanation is necessary. If you haven't, no explanation will suffice."

Lou Holtz, referring to the University of Notre Dame

———⊙———

As we load our bags into the storage compartment of the bus our driver cheerfully greets us all and I begin to relax, as the rest of the trip has been scripted so there should be no more scares. My wife, Pat, joins me on the bus and the team settles in for the scenic drive through lots of green fields and into Dublin. As we arrive at our hotel, the Herbert Park, I once again remind myself to thank John Anthony, as it is perfect. A full Irish breakfast awaits us and we have some time to check into our rooms and orient ourselves before heading to the Fitzwilliam courts for our only practice on the slippery Irish synthetic grass playing surface. Pat and I have time for a brief rest and I feel a sense of relief that things have gone well, forgetting the stress and travails that began almost 18 hours ago. We have a wonderful suite with a great view. We are in Dublin and life could not be better.....

~ Cross Court Reflection ~

When you feel in your gut what
you are and then dynamically
pursue it - don't back down
and don't give up - then
you are going to mystify
a lot of folks.

Bob Dylan

NOTRE DAME MENS TENNIS TEAM
Vs
FITZWILLIAM DAVIS CUP SELECTION

WARM UP FOR
THE FOOTBALL GAME
Notre Dame V Navy Aviva 1st September

FITZWILLIAM LAWN TENNIS CLUB
Friday 31st August 2012

TIME
2pm With Singles Followed By Doubles
ENTERTAINMENT
Live Irish Music, Notre Dame Cheerleaders
Food and Drink Served All Afternoon
Tickets €10 Available on The Door

Tennis Will Host A Free Clinic For Juniors At 12 Followed By A Q&A Session With Coaches and Play

CHAPTER TWO

Practicing at the Fitzwilliam Club

If you think the secret to taking your game to the next level is new information, trick plays, or the latest technique, then you're wrong."

Rene' Vidal

Before we left and as we were giving out the new uniforms, shoes, etc. for our trip I noticed that the shoes we were issued for training, not tennis, had pebbled soles and resembled the shoes now created for play on grass courts. Remembering the slippery nature of the synthetic grass courts I asked each player to bring his training shoes on this trip in case they were a more suitable complement to the grass. It might have been one of my better observations, as our guys slipped and fell whenever they tried to change direction. I quickly asked them to get out the trainers and give them a try. They were much better and our practice became much more productive. The uncertainty of whether or not you may lose your footing is one of the worst feelings a tennis player can have. It affects you in more ways than simple movement. Without

Left: Advertisement for the Notre Dame vs Ireland Davis Cup Team. August 31, 2012. The match was played at the Fitzwilliam Lawn Tennis Club, Dublin, Ireland.

the confidence that solid traction gives you, everything is affected, much like a hard court player experiences when he/she first plays on a clay court without knowing how to slide. Whenever we get to a new place, especially one as different as these courts played, I try to allow the players to begin to warm up and hit without much structure, as some may need more time than others to acclimate. Ryan and I joined our manager, Bianca Fox, as we sought to find Jimmy McDonough to check with him. Bianca accompanies us on all our trips, handling much of the logistics, money, etc. Notre Dame has had a program for student managers in place for many years, rewarding those who stick it out all four years with a generous tuition reimbursement for their senior year.

We found Jimmy and the club manager and exchanged gifts with them. I had brought team warm-ups and a few other items and they seemed especially grateful. They also presented each of us with the official membership tie of the Fitzwilliam Club and a commemorative book covering the club's history. Jimmy explained the format for the next day's matches. We would play singles matches first, followed by doubles, reversing the ITA format we use in our college matches. The Fitzwilliam group would include many of its Davis Cup Team members, including Conor Niland, the ATP star and former All American at Cal-Berkeley. Niland would play against our own Greg Andrews, a strong player who would narrowly miss his own All American chances during the spring. Niland had qualified for both the US Open and Wimbledon the year before, losing to Novak Djokovic in New York. He had learned to overcome failure.

Notice the difference between what happens when a man says to himself, 'I have failed three times.' and what happens when he says, 'I am a failure.'

S.I. Hayakawa

Barry King would also play, this time against his alma mater. Barry had clinched Ireland's last Davis Cup win as an ATP professional and had been contemplating retirement soon and working in the financial industry. Perhaps my biggest surprise was seeing Irackli Akhvlediani at the club. Irackli and Barry were two of only a few international players that had played for me at Notre Dame. He was from Vienna, but came to help Barry and to assist in coaching the Irish guys and it was great to catch up. At Notre Dame I had been outspoken in the college tennis community that college coaches should not over-recruit foreign players to the point where we took away the opportunities from our own American players, but I really liked both Irackli and Barry. When Irackli arrived I played a little joke on him, telling him that in America we often used nicknames, citing Billy for William, Bobby for Robert, etc. He indicated that it was also done in his culture. I asked him if he knew the American nickname for Irackli and told him that it was "Bubba." He went around campus for weeks introducing himself as "Bubba" Akhvlediani and still contacts me with that name. He recently treated Pat and me to a wonderful dinner in London.

After hitting for an hour or so we took the team on a better tour of Dublin and gave them some time to shop and look around on their own. We hit the high spots: the Post Office on O'Connell St., Trinity College, Temple Bar, etc. Seeing the still remaining bullet holes in the outer walls of the Post Office Building provided an instant and graphic reminder that the Irish struggle for independence was not unlike our own. By the time we met up at 3:00 PM they were falling asleep. We went back to the hotel for an early dinner and bed. We had a full day or two ahead of us. If we expect to play well tomorrow we will need some rest and forego any tourist-oriented activities and prepare for the upcoming match. This is a small price to pay for being ready to compete tomorrow.

Players do not differ in how much they say they want to win. They differ in the price they are willing to pay to win.

Gary Curneen

Seeing how uncomfortable our players were on the synthetic grass made me realize how one dimensional today's players are. Today's matches, even at the highest professional level, are glaringly one dimensional. Coming to the net seems like an afterthought to most. Many of today's current players play from way over on the left side of the court [assuming they are right-handed], and battle to control play with their respective forehands. It is a cookie-cutter approach, one taught ad nauseum in clubs and tennis academies worldwide. One of the reasons is that the grass court season is short and many players skip that part of their development which includes coming forward. Another is that today's equipment allows them to hit a more dynamic ball with added topspin for control, and use more of the court for creating angles heretofore thought too difficult to attempt. Today's 'poly' strings hold the ball longer and allow players to generate more topspin. Add in superior training methods and better nutritional habits and the result is longer points. Passing shots are easier to hit, and that slows down forays to the net even more, as it is more difficult to discern whether the opponent's shot is a topspin lob or passing shot. Top players are using smaller grips, something not possible in the wooden-racket days, as the rackets were too heavy to facilitate smaller grips. At times today's matches become battles of attrition, rather than skill. Pardon the "old school" way I view tennis.

An Annapolis Connection

The next day arrived early. The air of excitement was easy to notice as we met for another great Irish breakfast. A quick ride to the Fitzwilliam Club left us with plenty of time to warm up and be ready to go. As I arrived I ran into a former Navy player of mine who came over to greet me. Cutler Dawson, now Admiral Cutler Dawson, retired and the president of the Navy Federal Credit Union, the world's largest credit union, came over to say hello. He, obviously, was in Dublin to see Navy play in tomorrow's football game, but told me that his brother Craig, also a former Navy player of mine and one of the greatest in Navy history, was, in fact, at the Fitzwilliam Club where inside the club's squash courts his squash team [Craig had become Navy's squash coach] was playing against the squash team of the Fitzwilliam Club. What a wonderful coincidence! Craig had been the best overall player for the length of his entire career that I had coached at Navy. He was also one of the best competitors I had ever coached. I was able to run inside and briefly catch up with him as his team was playing. There is never a bad time to catch up with a former player, and my relationship with Craig meant a great deal to me.

Seeing Cutler brought back one of my fondest memories. When I was hired at Navy in 1969, the vacancy I filled was created partially because of Army's success in tennis against us. They had won almost every match for the last decade, and, in the context of that rivalry, it was unthinkable for Navy to allow this trend to continue. I learned quickly that the Army-Navy rivalry is unique in both its intensity and its mutual respect. I had sat next to Army's Bob Knight, who coached Army basketball prior to becoming a coaching legend at Indiana, at one of the Army-Navy winter sports banquets and realized early how important it was for each Academy to beat the other. Coaches at Army and Navy are perhaps best known for their records against their complement. We also root for each other in just about every other contest.

To say that I was overwhelmed with a sense of responsibility for my first Army Navy match would be an understatement.

I knew that Army had beaten Navy the year before in a close match, but realized that my new Navy team had graduated its top two players from the previous year and we went into my first Army-Navy match as a sound underdog. We had lost to Harvard 9-0. Army had beaten them. We had lost 5-4 to several Ivy League teams that Army had beaten 9-0. It certainly did not look good for our chances. One thing that I had found in our Navy guys was that they would never quit. We had worked hard all year and were in terrific shape. This would not matter, though, unless we played well enough to extend the match, but if we could, the heat and humidity of Annapolis in June would likely take a toll. There are three Army-Navy sports weekends each year - fall, winter, and spring. With the exception of football, where all Cadets and Midshipmen travel to Philadelphia for the football game and both schools close up shop for the weekend, each of the schools hosts certain sports on the same weekend, where there is an overall winner. The winner of the weekend series gives liberty [a free pass] to its students for the evening.

The person who says it cannot be done should not interrupt the person who is doing it.

Chinese proverb

Tennis does not offer upsets as often as many sports, because there are essentially six individual singles matches and three in doubles. If a key player has a bad day or is injured it only costs the team that individual point, whereas in football or basketball, poor play by a quarterback or point guard can doom the entire team. Our 1970 Navy tennis team had endured a lot. When we travelled to play the Ivy League schools we faced protests because of the Vietnam War. For me the greatest such story happened in Providence, RI against Brown. We had won the match and went back to the locker room on their campus to shower. When we came out of the locker room to get into our Navy station wagons we found ourselves surrounded by literally hundreds of irate Brown students and anti-war activists protesting our involvement in Viet Nam. Taunts like "Warmongers!" and "Fascist Pigs!" were shouted at us. As we got into our vehicles it got worse. One bearded man yelled at the top of his lungs, "What do you have to say for yourselves?" I was terrified. They began to rock our cars, and I thought I was about to become a part of Walter Cronkite and the 6:00 PM CBS News. I had never been this afraid for my very life. Once more came the booming voice, "What do you have to say for yourselves?"

We had a player on our team from Alabama, Clay Stiles, who was chock full of personality. Clay told me to roll down the window so he could answer the man's question. I was afraid to lower the tailgate in the back where Clay sat, but he insisted, saying "Just crack the window, Coach. I can talk to these folks!" I took a chance and lowered the window. Clay placed his mouth near the opening to answer the man's question. He waved to the angry mob and began to reply. Suddenly the crowd quieted, remarkably. Clay began…. "Y'all want to know what we have to say for ourselves. Is that right?" "Yes!" yelled the growing crowd. Clay then slowly and patiently shouted "Well, war is our business…...AND BUSINESS IS BOOMING! Hit it, Coach." I slowly put the car into gear, and it lurched slightly. Suddenly the crowd backed away, as some were laughing at Clay's comment. I saw the opening and drove out of there a quickly as I could with our other vehicle following closely. We had averted a serious problem. Leadership is a valuable commodity, and Clay Stiles had provided it for us that day. He is not a big, imposing man, but his words packed just the right punch.

I am not afraid of an army of lions led by a sheep. I am afraid of an army of sheep led by a lion.

Alexander the Great

Back to the present….. Cutler Dawson was in that car with us that day and he also played a pivotal role in our Army-Navy match. He played a tenacious lefty named Joe Reeder. They had played against one another the previous year in the Army-Navy match at West Point and Reeder had won in straight sets. They had similar styles of play, as both preferred to hit forehands and each would run around his backhand to get a forehand whenever possible, leaving lots of court space open. Because each played over in the court for forehands and one was left handed while the other was right handed it placed both players on the same side of the court, each hoping for a forehand from which he could take the offensive. Cutler understood that Reeder was physically stronger and was willing to swallow his ego and began to roll topspin lobs deep to the Reeder backhand. At just the right moment he would sneak into the net for a forehand volley or overhead which he could put away. Face it, neither of these guys was going to be mistaken for Pete Sampras or Roger Federer with their respective styles of play. The match was not pretty. If you were looking for style points you should have watched another match. Yet the display of effort and raw courage was right there for all to see. Somehow, though, Cutler was willing to be very patient and wait for just the right ball to thwart the physically stronger player on guts and mental toughness alone. I watched that match in awe of the determination on display and understood that while neither had a career in professional tennis ahead of him, the leadership of our country was in tremendous hands.

———◇◇◇———

It's not about how you win. It's about how well you're able to come back when you're down.

Serena Williams

———◇◇◇———

History reveals that Admiral Dawson rose to the very top of the leadership chain of the Navy and Mr. Reeder was also very successful, later becoming Undersecretary of the Army as a civilian. It was an honor to watch that day, as sophomore Gordon Perry beat senior Bill Malkemes in three tough sets at #1 singles, serving and volleying often behind a high kicking twist serve that gave him time to sneak into the net, diving for everything as he finished with bloody knees and elbows. At #2, Bob Custer straight setted Jack Stevenson with his crisp and flat groundstrokes and our Alabama hero, Clay Stiles, also won. We defeated a very good Army team in a match nobody [myself included] expected us to win, as Dawson and Perry clinched for us at #1 doubles. I had won my first Army-Navy match 6-3. It was the first of 15 straight. I began to understand the enormity of its significance as I watched our superintendent, Adm. James Calvert and athletic director, Bo Coppedge both hurdle the fence next to court #1 and join in our post-match celebration. A difficult first season, complete with more than its share of challenges, ended in spectacular fashion because our guys had grown and rebounded from the earlier adversity we had faced. The hours of hard work had paid off. Yet another life lesson provided by the world of sports.

~ Cross Court Reflection ~

The strongest foundations are built from adversity. Lay your foundation and don't forget to thank everyone for the materials.

David Brinkley

Navy and Notre Dame meet in football. Coach Bobby Bayliss with former Navy player Admiral Cutler Dawson[center] prior to kickoff. Admiral Dawson, then President of the Navy Federal Credit Union, played a major role when Navy upset Army in the 1970 Army Navy tennis match, the first of 15 consecutive wins in that historic rivalry.

Taking on the Irish Davis Cuppers

Now back to Dublin. Remember, I told you there would be flashbacks, as I have so many wonderful stories to tell and need to find proper segues from one to another.

Our match against the Irish Davis Cuppers went pretty much as expected. They were good and deep and most had been, and some were still, playing professional tennis. Greg Andrews, our top player, had his hands full against Niland, who is now the Captain of the Irish Davis Cup Team. Greg has a monster forehand, hit with plenty of topspin, but he lacks the same confidence in his backhand. Niland played a similar, but more evenly balanced, style and was simply too tough. In a very physical display of athleticism and solid all court tennis, Niland showed the form that had qualified him for the previous Wimbledon and US Open draws[he had played Novak Djokovic at the US Open], rarely making an unforced error while hitting blistering forehands to all corners of the court. All of the Irish players are somewhat comfortable on the synthetic grass. A great number of these courts can be found in Ireland because of the rainy climate. I was surprised to see that play does not stop there when it begins to rain because the surface allows for a consistent bounce and the players are both used to the conditions and wear shoes that enhance footing. The courts did not allow Andrews the time and space he needed to get into position to hit his usual forehands to dominate, as the ball rarely bounced high enough to give Greg the time he needed for this normally dominant shot. Niland took everything thrown at him and came back for more, sliding across the grass like he was born on it[he was]. It was a great learning experience for Greg.

While we were able to win some of the matches, the Irish were better, almost as though they wanted to show us just who the

"Fighting Irish" really were. Another interesting match took place between Niall Fitzgerald, our co-captain the previous year, now playing Davis Cup for his native Ireland, against our Wyatt Mc-Coy. Wyatt is always the fastest guy on the court, but today he had trouble with his footing and the strength of Niall's overall game. It had been a pleasure to coach Niall and see him grow from a young but unfinished and talented player with lots of promise, though lacking in poise and presence, into a solid, dependable player whose ability to do many things made him a difficult matchup for most college players. It was especially nice to see the proud parents of both Barry and Niall there watching their sons play. I will always have a soft spot in my heart for the Emerald Isle and its people. This trip just cemented what I already believed. The wonderful dinner after the match was a perfect ending to a great day. The Irish team gave us Fitzwilliam hats. Stories were told. Fun and fellowship was had by all. No one can tell stories and entertain you like the Irish. It was yet another of the great experiences that college tennis affords its number. Our guys went to bed with full stomachs and an experience to cherish, knowing that they had given their best collective effort.

If you don't go after what you want, you'll never have it. If you don't ask, the answer is always no. If you don't step forward, you'll always be in the same place.

Nora Roberts

Dublin went all out for the Notre Dame-Navy football game. Banners celebrating the occasion were hanging over streets and all of the celebratory events were well attended. There was an outdoor mass early the next morning that attracted thousands. Scott Malpass, the personable University Vice President who brilliantly oversees Notre Dame's endowment, rented a local pub, the Foggy Dew, and invited hundreds of us to an extraordinary cultural and gastronomic affair with admission by invitation only. The next morning we enjoyed another great Irish breakfast, complete with sausages, fried tomatoes, and blood pudding, among other delicacies. Now it was time for us to be tourists. We walked to the game, a 51-10 Irish victory over Navy and returned for dinner. There exists great mutual respect between these two extraordinary institutions, as the Navy had saved Notre Dame during World War II by moving some of its training programs to the campus, enabling Notre Dame to remain open. There were some droopy eyes the next morning as we boarded our bus to the airport, as I suspect that some of our guys sampled the Dublin nightlife. Fortunately, Quentin Monaghan did not face any scrutiny in the security and boarding process and we made the long trek back to South Bend while many in our group slept on the flight. It was special for me to have my wife Pat accompany us and enjoy all that went on.

One of the beautiful things about taking the entire team on an early trip like this one is that they are summarily forced to become a TEAM. By eating, sleeping, competing, and travelling together immediately there is a bond that develops far more quickly than it might normally take.

Turning a Group of Players into a Team

Perhaps the greatest challenge faced by any coach is ensuring that all of his players somehow become a real team - a group of people united in a common bond to achieve success together. Perhaps the best explanation of this that I have ever heard or read lies in the following quote by New York Yankee great Don Mattingly who said:

> Then at one point in my career something wonderful happened. I don't know why or how, but I came to understand what 'team' meant. It meant that although I didn't get a hit or make a great defensive play, I could impact the team in an incredible and consistent way. I learned that I could impact my team by caring first and foremost about the TEAM's success, not my own. I don't mean by rooting like a typical fan; fans are fickle. I mean CARE, really CARE about the team…….about US. I became less selfish, less lazy, less sensitive to negative comments when I gave up ME. I became more and more a captain, a leader, a better person and I came to understand that life is a team game. And you know what? I've found that most people aren't team players. They don't realize that life is the only game in town. Someone should tell them. It has made all the difference in the world to me.

It is a life lesson college tennis players, who have been involved in the sport mostly on an individual level, must quickly learn. In today's world of frequent home-schooling to allow for more tennis exposure, young players are increasingly unaware of the importance of working with others to attain collective goals. Establishing a true team culture needs to be an important priority for any aspiring college coach. It can be difficult to understand for a young man who, until now, had measured his success only by his personal accomplishments. Many college players find that they are working in a team environment for the first time in their lives, unlike those in other sports.

Whenever I attend any type of team reunion it is especially rewarding to see the true outpouring of emotions as former teammates once again discover that the ties that had bound them are still very much intact. In a matter of minutes everyone is 21 years old again. Conversations turn immediately to a game, meet, or match that took place decades ago. Grins change to laughter. Handshakes become hugs. And before long the group realizes that they are, indeed, still very much a TEAM. Immediately conversations turn to those who could not make it. Concerns are expressed for teammates experiencing a difficult time in life. It is not happenstance. It happens because of the many shared experiences that involved shared effort, failures, and successes, all the while knowing that these things could not have been possible without the contributions of everyone.

You need to work as hard to be a great teammate as you do to be a great player.

Jon Gordon

One of the things that can ensure a great team culture is senior leadership. In most of the teams that I have coached I found strong leadership from at least one of the seniors. In the others the leadership came from another player, but his influence was no less impactful. Similarly, coaches know that a lack of leadership can be a killer. My theory on this is that there is a limit to how much players can take from a coach before it begins to go in one ear and

out of the other. You only have so many silver bullets in your proverbial gun and you need to pick and choose when you use them.
A strong captain takes charge and handles many of the team's little
problems and keeps them from even reaching the coach. Without
this filter, the coach finds himself correcting certain things that
might not carry great importance. Suddenly, when a team crisis
arises and the coach needs to step in, his authority and equity has
been compromised. The message he passes on lacks the authority it
should have carried because of the many and unnecessary previous
interventions. I try not to use profanity around my teams, but when
I really want to convey a strong message and decide to employ
some alternate words, I find that they have greater meaning and effect if I enlarge my vocabulary appropriately.

——◦◦◦——

Leadership isn't a difference maker. It is
THE difference-maker.

Urban Meyer

——◦◦◦——

Tennis, as a collegiate sport, presents special challenges to
its coaches in the area of teamwork and team culture. Throughout
their junior careers, tennis players are individuals, and not part
of any team. They have competed individually and been coached
primarily in the same way. In recruiting, I believed it to be a bonus
for a prospect to have also played a team sport. Football, basketball, baseball, and soccer players grew up understanding that they
could not excel without the aid and cooperation of teammates.
They all needed someone to block and screen for them, not to mention passing the ball their way. Athletes in team sports blend more
naturally into a team culture. Frequently in college tennis, a new
player may spend more time than wanted on understanding the
dynamics of being part of something greater than himself/herself.
Selfishness needs to give way to a spirit of cooperation and pride
in the exploits of others. As a former basketball player in both high
school and college I had absorbed those lessons well and had little

patience for those who had not. I simply was never going to coach my team as if it was comprised of a group of all-stars. Looking back, I believe that establishing a team culture was a significant building block in the success we experienced. As I retired many of the notes I received thanked me for establishing such a culture. It certainly made the transition to marriage and employment an easier one.

This was a challenge I found when I arrived at Notre Dame. The returning players had been recruited for, and played in, a program with different goals than those I brought with me. I knew immediately that I needed to change the culture when, in a team meeting, one of the seniors told me that he preferred to miss our ITA Regionals because it conflicted with our home football game with Alabama. I also had to understand that this group was recruited with a smaller budget, fewer scholarships, and a different vision than mine. Fortunately for me, several of the freshmen, Paul Odland, Dave Kuhlman and Ryan Wenger, I inherited were on board with my goals, as were a nucleus of upperclassmen led by Brian Kalbas and Dave Reiter. That made my job easier.

~ Cross Court Reflection ~

A great culture can make a mediocre strategy successful, but a weak culture will always undermine even the best strategy.

Urban Meyer

US Open at Flushing Meadow, NY. August, 2009. Notre Dame Coach Bobby Bayliss assists Wayne Bryan in a clinic during a brief rain delay at the US Open.
Photo courtesy of Wilson Sporting Goods

CHAPTER THREE

The Fall Season

Everyone thinks that greatness is sexy.
It is not. It is dirty, hard work.

Ben Hogan

College tennis is amorphous. The fall season is one of player development, experimentation, and tournament match play, as opposed to the spring term which is dominated by the greater pressure of dual match play, leading to post-season play [conference and NCAA tournaments]. It is also the time for a coach to establish his/her team culture. In the fall we try to determine who is likely to be starting in both singles and doubles roles by intrasquad competition as well as competition in several tournaments that vary depending on the needs of the program in any specific year. It is also the time to improve biomechanics and add changes both tactically and strategically. For a mostly veteran team the fall might be about exposing your players to the highest level of individual play that they can handle, giving each player the opportunity for ranked wins which will eventually qualify him/her for the NCAA Singles and Doubles tournaments. For a younger team the priority might be to have the players enter events which will demonstrate which players will become starters and which ones will "ride the pine," or serve in reserve roles. You learn quickly that everyone wants to play, to be a starter who puts it on the line in every match. Most want to play as high as they can, either from pride or a genuine desire to help the team and win big matches, but there are always a few who are more comfortable playing in the lower lineup spots where victories are easier to achieve. Intra- squad matches and practice sets carry more meaning during the fall when the coaches are trying to determine which players will become starters or make the travel roster. During the second semester everything is focused on winning the next team match and the pressure to win is serious. This means practicing on the surface nearest to that of the next foe, replicating the coming opponent's game style in practice[practicing against a left-hander or a particular playing style], or adjusting from indoors to outdoor play, no easy feat. It is also the time that we must take these individual players and turn them into a team. Each coach needs to plant the seeds of his/her team culture now.

———⊲∘⊳———

It's not just about working hard. It's about working together. You have to care more about the team than about yourself.

John Calipari

———⊲∘⊳———

Every team and player is allowed 25 playing dates by the NCAA. When I first broke into coaching there were no restrictions on the number of matches in which a team or individual could compete and fall play was much more relaxed. At some point in the 1970's a limit of 35 dates of competition was placed on each team and player by the NCAA in order to cut down on missed class time and travelling expenses, as a few coaches had begun to over-schedule and had limited their players' academic opportuni-ties. That number was reduced to 30 dates in the 1980's and further cut back to 25 - the current quota - as we approached 2000. On top of this all play and practice must be limited to 144 days over the course of the school year, to be divided by each school so that they decide how many dates to use in the fall and spring. Most teams use somewhere around six weeks in the fall, saving all of the rest for the second semester. This is where coaches need to be creative in order to get the maximum mileage from those 25 dates. By the time you read this, it is possible that the NCAA regulations might have changed slightly, as has frequently happened.

There is no team scoring allowed during the fall, hence the plethora of fall singles and doubles events as well as "hidden duals," tournaments in which a virtual match is played, yet no team score is kept or published while individual results count and can build each player's resume. Each of us is left to our own ingenuity and creativity to find a fall schedule that is both challenging and still allows all of the supporting players to see significant action, as the coach needs to know what his lineup will be before the season begins and be able to use real data to the non-starters in explaining why their roles will be mostly supportive come second semester. It is up to each coach to determine how many of the precious playing dates he will use in the fall and how many he will save for spring. Only dual matches played after Jan.1 can be counted for team NCAA qualification and ITA ranking, while individual results for the entire year are countable. I always tried to challenge my team in the fall by sending them to as many national events as our class-miss policy and budget would allow. Exposing them to new venues and better competition is a carrot leading to improved play. Being a part of something bigger than themselves is the glue that keeps them coming back.

~ Cross Court Reflection ~

If we treat people as they are, we make them worse. If we treat them as they ought to be, we make them what they are capable of becoming.

Johann Wolfgang Goethe

Resources Available to the Coach

Typically, each team emphasizes strength and conditioning much more in the fall. At the more significant athletic schools with greater resources, each team is assigned a strength coach who works with the tennis coach to design a program to fill the needs of each player and team. In smaller schools this might be a chore the coach handles. In my early career strength coaches were not normally available to tennis coaches, as well as to most "Olympic" sports. Today the "Power Five" schools all supply strength coaches to each program and team. For me, this was a learning experience, as it was not available to most schools when I began coaching at Navy. I learned, over time, that I had to trust the strength coach in his knowledge and understanding of what was best for tennis, as opposed to football. I eventually learned how important these folks were to my team. For us, the primary benefit to be gained was in injury prevention, with adding strength in the proper body areas, a secondary benefit. Certainly, though, I came to realize the importance of having and utilizing a good strength coach. Not only were our guys suffering fewer injuries, but I could see that they were moving better and hitting the ball harder. They had greater flexibility which influenced injury prevention. We were a better team because of the knowledge and skill of our strength coach.

At Notre Dame, we have added two dieticians who also work with our players on adopting an intelligent eating regimen. We have access to a sports psychologist, Dr. Mick Franco, and he has helped many of our players in their ability to handle stress, set performance goals, and feel better about themselves in and out of competition. Mick and I have enjoyed many experiences together, as we watch our guys battle and compete for wins. I work with one specific travel agent from Anthony Travel, the company that handles the needs of all Notre Dame teams. Additionally we are assigned someone for our team from the office of NCAA Compliance. This is the person who will oversee our ability to steer clear of NCAA violations, both in recruiting, and team eligibility issues. When we were with adidas, they assigned two people to work here on campus and meet with coaches to best supply us with shoes and clothing.

You can see that I have a full complement of experts to assist Ryan and me as we navigate the waters of putting out the best product possible. On my first Navy team in 1970 I had to handle all of these things by myself and, obviously, my ability to provide everything my team needed has been greatly enhanced. Because the dual matches are held in the spring, we use the fall to integrate all of these specialists into our team agenda. We normally lift [use the strength coach in our Guglielmino Center] three days per week in the fall. Emphasis is on lighter weights and greater reps until November when competition ends and we try to gain strength and some bulk[heavier weights]. Dr. Franco tries to get to know our guys with some group sessions [stress management, relaxation techniques, etc.] in the fall, laying the groundwork for an individual player relationship that becomes year-round. One of the things I notice is that after working with Mick, our guys stop making excuses for their mistakes. He builds his own relationships with our players and they are free to consult with Mick as their time and schedules allow.

Never ruin an apology with an excuse.

Ben Franklin

Our trainer, Tony Sutton, works with our players to similarly build a relationship of trust which will allow the player to confide in him about any injury or ailment. As he knows our players better, he is able to anticipate many of their individual needs and take steps to prevent team-killing injuries. The hope is that by January, when the players return from Christmas vacation, they will all have a fully functional support staff in place to aid them in eating, competing, and everything else they need to maximize their success. In some conferences the team trainer travels with the team to away matches. We do this on a more limited basis. Tony needs to work in concert with the strength coach to best minimize the chance for injury in the weight room, as after a specific injury, Tony might want to cut out one or two of the weight routines we do for that player. A final addition to the team's support is our academic advisor. I was fortunate enough to have several terrific people handle this role for our squad over the years. He/she works individually with each player to navigate with him the path to academic success, sometimes pointing out to me when a specific semester will be particularly demanding for a player and, at times, suggesting to me that a day off to catch up academically might be wise. Part of experiencing success in the fall lies in how a coach can best utilize all of these assets and ensuring that his players understand and are receptive to each of these members of the support staff. I have come to trust Tony and rely on his opinions.

Additionally, every team has an athletic administrator to which the head coach reports. I have had some truly outstanding people serve as my sport administrator, none more so than Missy Conboy, now the #2 person to Director of Athletics Jack Swarbrick. I was an usher in Missy's wedding more than 25 years ago, as she married Bill Mountford, the captain of my 1983 Navy team, who had come by to visit me when he got out of the Navy. I introduced him to her as I showed him around the campus in the summer of 1989. As we arrived back in our tennis facility our receptionist was holding the phone for me. As I joined Missy on the call, she said "Bob Bayliss, don't you ever bring an adonis like that into my office without some notice so that I can make myself presentable. "I asked her to join us for lunch. After 15 minutes together, I noticed I was pretty much excluded from the conversation and realized that some fast acting chemistry had been manufactured and, as they say, the rest is history. Three children later they are still very much in love and I am the godfather to their oldest daughter, Darby, a 2016 Notre Dame alum and member of the women's tennis team. Her character sets her apart from many of her peers.

~ Cross Court Reflection ~

Your character is what you really are, while your reputation is merely what others think you are.

John Wooden

College Athletic Leadership Today

While I am on the subject of athletic administration, it might be prudent for me to pass on my observation on athletic leadership, and how I have seen it change. I have been fortunate to work for some truly great people- athletic directors and administrators who helped shape my life. When I first broke into coaching it appeared that almost all directors of athletics, hereafter known as ADs, were former coaches who were promoted into their positions, usually after a successful run on the field or court. These former coaches understood the pain of an unexpected loss and the ecstasy of seeing your team perform at its highest and upset a higher ranked opponent. They, themselves, had gone through most everything that we faced. They could feel our pain and appreciate what went on in a typical season. That is no longer a given, and in fact it is now unusual. Today's ADs come, for the most part, with law degrees, MBAs, and even successful careers in the corporate world. Some have never worked for an athletic department or college. Many have ridden the train through the ranks of intern, assistant AD, etc. Nowadays it is unusual to find an AD at a major university who came up through the coaching ranks, as the challenges are different. I have been blessed to the extent that I have never been forced to work for an athletic director whom I did not like and respect. This, however, is not something that many coaches today can say, judging from comments I hear from coaches at other schools. I was recruited to Notre Dame by Gene Corrigan, who had been an SID [sports information director], had coached, and had also worked at a small college[Washington & Lee] and a large one[Virginia]. I sensed immediately that he was a man of character and that thought was promptly reinforced during the hiring process.

After a search, I was offered the position of head men's tennis coach at Notre Dame. While I wanted very much to accept the position, I was disappointed in the salary and respectfully requested more. Gene seemed to understand and told me that he would approach his superior to see what could be done, but he asked me to tell him what my current financial arrangement was. I explained that I was not only the head tennis and squash coach at MIT, but the head tennis professional at the Wellesley Country Club in Boston. Both parties knew and understood my responsibilities to the other and allowed me to handle the duties of each. This afforded me a six figure income, which in 1986-7, was certainly one of the largest incomes in college tennis. Gene was genuinely surprised and began to counsel me to forget about Notre Dame and stay in Boston, as that was significantly more than I could earn at Notre Dame. I was looking ahead and thinking of Notre Dame's free tuition for dependents of faculty and staff, and he indicated that he would try to get permission to offer me more money and get back to me. I knew that Notre Dame presented me with an opportunity that I could not ignore. I knew that it would be worth it to take this risk and that I would later regret it if I did not.

Regret for the things we did can be tempered by time. It is regret for the things we did not do that is inconsolable.

Sydney J. Harris

The next day my phone rang, and Gene let me know that he had secured the raise I sought. I answered quickly and said, "Well, you have just hired a new tennis coach," accepting his offer. "No" he replied. "Here is what you are going to do. I want you to pretend that you have accepted this offer and think it through as you go through the rest of this week. Look at the beautiful New England scenery as you drive home. Think about how fortunate you are to have such a great combination of jobs. While I really want you to come here, I have to be honest and tell you that I think you are crazy to give all of that up. Take your time and think it through and call me next week. If you have come to your senses and want to stay where you are, we will walk away friends. If not, I will know I have hired a great coach."

The following Monday I called Gene to tell him that I would be joining him at Notre Dame. He told me that he still thought that I was crazy but was happy to have me on board. Things worked out well for me here, as I was able to start a tennis camp and all of my children, four of them, have degrees from Notre Dame. Yet it was his integrity that really sold me on Notre Dame and made me appreciate that there is only one way - the right way - to do things. I don't know how many ADs would have handled the situation in a similar manner. One thing I remember about this process is that he asked me for one good reason to give up what I had in Boston. As I searched for a proper response I came up with "I am tired of being the dumbest guy in the van [at MIT]." We both enjoyed a good laugh over my comment. Gene is what I call an "old school" AD.

Failure is simply the opportunity to begin again more intelligently.

Henry Ford

Corrigan was a good friend of the Naval Academy's AD, Captain "Bo" Coppedge, and it was Captain Coppedge who told him to contact me. I learned, throughout my Navy tenure, to trust Captain Coppedge with everything. I still vividly remember sitting in his home trying to tell him that I needed to take advantage of the lucrative offer in Boston [Tennis professional at the Wellesley Country Club/tennis and squash coach at MIT] and leave the Academy after 15 wonderful years. As my voice cracked and I began to cry, he told me that he understood everything and wanted to work with me to make the transition as seamless as possible. I knew that he always "had my back."

Yet another story about ADs. Shortly after Kevin White left Notre Dame for Duke, I ran into him at the NCAA tennis championships held, at the time, in College Station, TX. Kevin was an exceptional leader and all of the coaches at Notre Dame enjoyed working for him. He spotted me and came quickly over to exchange greetings. I was feeling pretty down-in-the-mouth over my team's recent loss and perhaps Kevin sensed it. He immediately asked me if he could have a few minutes of my time and I agreed to meet him the next day at the courts. When I met with him I asked ''Well, what can I do for you?" "No" he answered. "This is about what I can do for you." He knew that our team had been eliminated early and could tell that I was feeling more than a little sorry for myself. He then proceeded to give me a 15 minute pep talk about what I meant to Notre Dame and to college tennis and my family. By the time he finished I was carrying myself in a totally different way and was ready to run through a wall. Now that is leadership! Kevin no longer worked for Notre Dame, yet he went out of his way, meeting me in a separate place and "coached me up" to a better place. It is no wonder to me that he continues to be highly successful today. The coaches at Duke today have affirmed that same feeling to me. Kevin, too, is "old school."

In another experience I can cite leadership at its finest. Leaving the Naval Academy was extremely painful for me because of the quality of the people with whom I interacted. One such person was Carl Ullrich. Carl had arrived at Navy as its crew coach, but his character, integrity, and other admirable traits pushed him into the Associate AD position. He eventually left to become the AD at Western Michigan and moved from there to a similar post at the United States Military Academy at West Point. My final chore at Navy before leaving was the Army Navy tennis match, one which garnered more than its share of publicity, as my Army Navy record stood at 14-0 going into the match. The Washington Post ran a story about the match and whether or not I could continue my unmatched streak. As the starting lineups were introduced, there was a pause and out of the stands came Carl. He had driven down for a presentation for me and presented me with a beautifully framed picture of the crests of both schools aligned with the block monogram of each as well. He gave a short speech about me to the surprised crowd, listing my achievements, and then got right back into his car for the five hour trek back to West Point. His gesture was overwhelming. That beautiful, framed picture still hangs in my office today.

I can give you yet another interesting story about leadership today in college athletics. I made the decision to retire in 2013, several years in advance of that date. I would turn 69 just after the 2013 season ended and, for many reasons, I thought that it would be the right time for me. I was tired of being asked by recruits how long I expected to coach. The first thing I had done was to be assured that my more-than-able and dynamic assistant, Ryan Sachire, would be my successor. After everything had been put in place, our very capable Senior Associate AD, Missy Conboy, called me in for a private meeting. She wanted to be certain that I had not changed my mind and told me that I was certainly welcome to continue. She did this twice more before I finally met with her and our AD, Jack Swarbrick, to discuss the timing of an announcement, etc. Missy clearly was thinking of what would be best for me and created a position for me as Director of Tennis Facilities which allowed me to retire from coaching, but gave me something to occupy some of my time and allow me to segue into retirement, rather than jump into it cold with both feet. It has worked out extremely well. Missy then had me appointed to the NCAA Tennis Committee, an experience I have thoroughly enjoyed. I kept my position on the ITA's board of directors, as well. This thoughtful process has allowed me to retire incrementally, yet still stay involved. No recruiting, no team travel nightmares, no upsetting losses, and very few problems or stress. Missy's knowledge of what made me tick and Jack's willingness to go along with the idea to create a new position in an era when all athletic expenses were closely questioned made a difference in my life. Yet this was made possible by two administrators who had no background in coaching. I joked to her that after giving Notre Dame some of the best years of my life, I would now give her some of the worst.

Irish Great Returns to Campus. Former Notre Dame All American David DiLucia returns to campus to meet with Coach Bobby Bayliss. As a collegian, DiLucia was ranked #1 in college tennis his senior year.

Fall Competition

*The more successful you become,
the longer the yardstick people
have to measure you by.*

Tom Landry

Over the years my scheduling philosophy included several things. One was my relationship with the other coach or person running the event. Next was the level of competition involved. Additionally there was the venue - was it a special place our team would enjoy? Finally I needed to consider the cost involved, as I was supposed to stick within my budget at year's end. Ideally I would try to include all factors. I took our team many times to fall tournaments at both William & Mary and Harvard, as I am very close to both coaches - Peter Daub at W & M and Dave Fish at Harvard. I enjoyed going to both places. Pat and I honeymooned in Williamsburg, VA, so the William & Mary campus was familiar. I grew up in nearby Richmond. Lots of draws for me. I had also lived in Boston when I spent three years coaching tennis and squash at MIT in between stints at Navy and Notre Dame, and I had been the tennis professional at the Wellesley Country Club in Boston for the five summers before we moved up there. Both schools had great facilities. Both tournaments invited other good teams there for great competition. So it is easy to see why we made more than a few trips to those events.

I got to know Peter Daub under unusual circumstances. When I was coaching at Navy he became the coach at

Temple in Philadelphia. He wanted to bring his team to Navy to play us and I agreed, based on his strong reputation as a developer of talented 18-and-under players. The Temple team arrived as rain began. I told Peter that, while we had indoor backup courts in our Halsey Field House, they were multi-purpose and the environment became a bit of a zoo in the afternoons when the match would be played inside a curtain that dropped down to encircle the courts and keep balls from rolling on to the track. Peter agreed to play indoors, but had a problem with one of our three courts. It was somewhat near the broad jump pit used in track and field, but I assured him that in over ten years of practices and matches no one had ever been injured. Peter was less than thrilled with the arrangement and initially refused to allow a match to be played there. I told him that if he refused to use that court we would have to cancel the match, as it would take too long to complete on just two courts.

Sensing resistance and hoping to avoid a clumsy impasse, I invited Peter to walk downtown with me for a cup of hot chocolate so we could get to know one another better and give his team time to get used to our courts. He grudgingly agreed and, sure enough, we spent a quality hour together and returned to Halsey Field House to meet with his team. As we arrived I saw two of his players carrying his #1 player into our training room for medical attention. The Temple player had broken his ankle on the very same court about which Peter had protested. He missed the rest of the season. It was an awkward beginning to what would become a great friendship that has lasted to this day. Daub's consistent work ethic continues to impress me even today and is the biggest reason for his success in coaching.

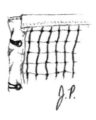

~ Cross Court Reflection ~

Success doesn't come from what you do occasionally. It comes from what you do consistently.

Styrling Strother

Irish take on Austrian Squad on red clay in Vienna. The 2006-7 Notre Dame squad played a match in Vienna against a group of European professional players. Notre Dame squad, left to right, first row: "Bubba" Akhvlediani, Stephen Bass, Santiago Montoya, and Brett Helgeson. Second row: Ryan Keckley, Sheeva Parbhu, and Eric Langenkamp. Third row: Brandon Pierpont, Barry King, and Coach Bobby Bayliss. *Photo by Pat Bayliss.*

An Outstanding Fall Competition

During my last few years at Notre Dame, we had participated in a great fall event held at the famous Olympia Fields Country Club about 20 miles south of Chicago. It was inspired/begun by Illinois's innovative coach Brad Dancer, who realized that a disproportionate slice of the membership at OFCC was comprised of graduates of both Notre Dame and Illinois. Brad also reached out to teams like Texas, Kentucky, Duke, Georgia, California, Pepperdine, and others to provide great competition for our guys. This past fall [2012] we also went to a USTA sponsored event in Napa Valley, CA that included good college teams and several of the best USTA junior players in the country . Former Michigan coach Bruce Berque had some very strong events in Ann Arbor that we played. There were college Grand Slam events in the fall, but they were for elite players and most schools selected to participate brought only one or two players. I would frequently send one group of players to an event with Ryan while I would take another group to a different venue. What you can probably see, though, is that the fall was more relaxed, as team results did not count during the fall semester.

One interesting tradition started right here at Notre Dame. Because fall events did not count for team ranking it usually made more sense to utilize your dates in the fall to multi-day events in which your players got to play more matches, as NCAA rules allowed a multi-day event that included no team scoring to count as only one playing date. This is just one example why some coaches feel that "NCAA" is an acronym for "No Clue About Athletics." However, in the fall of 1989 we did something special. In talking with USC assistant [later head coach at SMU] Carl Neufeld we thought it would be a good idea to take advantage of the Notre

Dame/Southern Cal football rivalry and create an event for our tennis teams that piggy-backed on the football weekend. Cost was a concern, but we agreed to split the costs and charge admission to defray them. And so was born the football/tennis tradition that worked so well for both teams. USC was always contending for an NCAA title and we were finally building a potent lineup so we agreed to play USC in our new Eck Tennis Pavilion on the Friday evening before the football game. We charged $5 per person [that would be about $12 in today's dollars] and filled the place. We had 750 paid spectators and a standing room only crowd. No one left feeling they did not get their money's worth. USC beat us 5-4, but that night Notre Dame tennis arrived. The Trojans, on the other hand, became NCAA champions in 1991, 1993, and 1994. The fact that we were able to beat them in the 1992 NCAA semi-final was enhanced by the familiarity we had with them which came from two such fall matches.

Future ATP Tour pros David DiLucia and Byron Black went at it at #1 singles and the other matches were equally attractive and fiercely battled. It worked so well that USC coach Dick Leach and later Peter Smith came back several times to do it again. We supplemented those matches with teams like Stanford, Baylor, and Oklahoma in other years when they played us in football and the USC football team was playing Notre Dame in Los Angeles. It gave our guys the chance to compete in front of a great crowd against those great opponents in an electric environment that can only be created by a college football weekend. It was win-win! Note that every one of those schools, including ourselves, has won an NCAA title or been the runner-up. I still remember leaving the football stadium in 1990 and finding Stanford's Jonathan Stark and Jared Palmer asleep under a tree waiting for the game to end. They had left the stadium when Notre Dame had a big lead and missed a miraculous Stanford comeback. Both of those guys reached #1 in ATP Tour doubles after leaving Stanford. I was the first person to let them know that Stanford had won the football game. It appeared that they had enjoyed themselves a little too much the evening before following our match.

Advice is what we ask for when we know the answer, but wish we didn't.

Erica Jong

Having just played a match against the Irish Davis Cup players, we looked forward to the remaining fall matches and tournaments. We had two weeks before our next competition. We would take advantage of being allowed to compete in two different events the same weekend. Ryan would take one group of players to nearby Western Michigan University to compete in their invitational event while I would take most of the top group to Chicago's Olympia Fields Country Club to lock horns with players from Kentucky, Pepperdine, California, Illinois, and Texas, all national powers. Our players are housed by host families, while coaches are each assigned a private home, or 'cottage' on site that is theirs through Sunday when the tournament concludes. We eat most meals on site at the club, so this is a tournament that has it all: great competition, terrific housing, entertainment, very good food, and, for me, a group of coaches I really enjoy.

The teams arrive at different times on Thursday, some early and others just in time for the clinic that is arranged for OFCC members and their kids. Getting used to the well-manicured clay courts at Olympia Fields is important, as clay is a surface that college teams almost never use. The art of "sliding" on the clay quickly comes back to most players. Without it they will slip often and find elbows and knees bloody at the end of a tough match. Just before dinner we have all players and coaches out on the courts hitting balls with the members and making sure that everyone has a good time. As we finish and file into the dining room for a great meal I find the first of many tributes to me in my final year awaiting me. Brad has arranged that on each table placing is a placemat with my picture, bio, and some interesting and flattering facts about my career. I have known Dancer since I tried unsuccessfully to recruit him and watched him develop into a very smart All Big

Ten player. He has climbed quickly in the coaching ranks and has already taken his Illini squad to the NCAA finals. They are always one of the country's better teams.

During dessert, he and the club manager presented me with speeches and a beautiful plaque. It is now that I realize the imminent finality of my career. It is an act that will be re-created at various stops throughout the season and I can honestly say that I am really touched tonight at being honored in such a way. I appreciate the effort it took to do this and know that Ryan was involved as well. As I leave the dining area to go to my "cottage" for the evening I vow to enjoy this year in a way that I have never been able to do and to cherish each stop along the way. There will be many "lasts" ahead, as in my last match in Columbus [Ohio State], last Midwest Regionals, last spring break trip, last Blue Gray, last Big East championship, and last NCAA tournament. As the late Dan Magill used to say "that horse has left the barn," meaning that there is no turning back on my decision to retire. 'Tomorrow' has suddenly become today.

Tomorrow belongs to those who can hear it coming.

David Bowie

The next morning the courts are full of enthusiastic players and emotions run high. While we are not exposed to clay often our guys seem ready to take on all comers as the pairings are announced and the first group of matches begins. I am counting on Greg Andrews to anchor our team, so I look for a strong effort from him. Greg grew up in nearby Kalamazoo and has one of the country's best and biggest forehands. He hits a very dynamic ball, loaded with heavy topspin, from that side and tries to run around backhands when time allows and end points with his favorite shot. His opponent today is Campbell Johnson, from Cal- Berkeley, who transferred from Georgia. Johnson plays a similar style. Both find the clay court allows them more time and the ability to dominate with forehands. Initially I am happy with this match-up, as Greg rarely loses to a similar style player, such is the strength of his howitzer-like forehand, one of the better shots in college tennis. Yet, as the match progresses I am surprised at Johnson's ability to trade big forehands with him. We are expecting big things from Greg, so seeing him drop the first set in a close tie-breaker is unsettling. I try to advise Greg to move up in the court to take away Johnson's time and ability to get forehands. He is initially reluctant to abandon a style that has served him well throughout his junior career, but quickly makes the adjustment and takes the second set 6-3. Now I feel he is back on track and move to another court to try to help out there. It is difficult to anticipate what will happen and, therefore, equally tough to know which court you should join, but I need to be open to what each player is feeling before overloading them with advice.

If you want to change the way people respond to you, change the way you respond to people.

Timothy Leary

Unlike most tournament tennis, college tennis allows coaching to take place at any time, as long as it does not interrupt the flow of a match, allowing you to pass on advice to your player. The dilemma involves knowing when and how much to say and it varies with each player and set of circumstances. Ignoring the player can leave him feeling abandoned and unsupported, but smothering him with instructions and advice will cause "paralysis by analysis." There is a fine line in this communication that is usually reached through trial and error. Greg and I had a "come to Jesus" moment when he was a freshman. We were knotted in an extremely close first round match in the NCAA tournament against East Tennessee State, a very dangerous "floater" in the draw. It was Greg's first NCAA match and his opponent, Charles Bottoni, matched up well against him. Bottoni was a lefty with a big forehand of his own. Left-handers are tough for Greg and other right-handers who look to run around to get forehands because the natural spin on a lefty serve takes the ball out to a righty's backhand, making it difficult to maneuver for forehands. As the team match developed we unexpectedly found ourselves knotted at 3-3 with the entire match depending on whether our freshman [Greg] could beat a strong veteran. Late in the match, failure appeared imminent.

Unless you are willing to have a go, fail miserably, and have another go, success won't happen.

Phillip Adams

When Greg lost his serve and fell behind 4-3 in the final set, Bottoni had only to hold his wicked lefty serve twice and ETSU could go back to Johnson City with one of the bigger upsets in the tournament. Greg dug in, however, and eventually found himself in possession of a break point which, if he converted, would even the match and give him some all-important momentum. When Bottoni missed his first serve I told Greg to stand all the way over in the ad court. In fact I forced him to stand with both feet wide of the doubles alley near the side fence, giving Bottoni a very easy play if he could only hit his second serve anywhere near the center service line and virtually daring him to go for it. Greg did not want to do this, but reluctantly followed my instructions. I told him that if it did not work it would be my fault and not his. You could have driven a truck down the middle of the service box and Greg could not have touched it with his racket. I knew that most lefties are very hesitant to aim for the "T" on a second serve and was hoping for a double fault. Greg's court position was forcing Bottoni to go for the "T," challenging his manhood. After pausing for deliberation and hoping a quick burst of now-lacking confidence he went for the "T" and hit the ball beyond the baseline, missing his target by over 30 feet. Greg immediately looked at me with a smile of gratitude and relief. It had worked! The match was now tied at four games apiece. From that moment forward Greg held the upper hand and won 7-5 in the third set. A big factor was that Bottoni began to roll in first serves in the ad court, abandoning his big delivery so that he would not have to hit any second serves there. We had advanced into the second round and Greg was our hero. From that day thereafter I believe that Greg saw me differently. I had thrown him the rope he needed to climb out of a big hole and, henceforth, he took my advice more seriously. It was a watershed moment for the two of us.

⎯⎯◦◦⎯⎯

Outstanding leaders go out of their way to boost the self-esteem of their personnel. If people believe in themselves, it is amazing what they can accomplish.

Sam Walton

⎯⎯◦◦⎯⎯

Back to Olympia Fields. This time Greg was not as fortunate. He dropped the third set, but had firmly given his best. What remained to be done in practice was to develop the ability to play up more in the court and trust his backhand, thus limiting the options of his opponent. It was something we would work on frequently in the practices ahead. The other matches that day were less dramatic and we pretty much held our own, but lacked a single signature win. The following day we did a better job. Greg beat the Illini's Faris Gosea and Texas's David Holiner in convincing straight set fashions and then upset Kentucky's Tom Jomby in a great match 6-4 in the third set. Jomby, at 6' 4", was a tremendous athlete with a booming serve and would become an All American in May. Greg's win would boost his national ranking, something that fall play offered without the pressure of dual matches. Billy Pecor won two of his three matches, finishing with a straight set victory over Cal's Andrew Scholnick. Wyatt McCoy came back to beat Illinois's Brian Page and Cal's Johnson while showing off his tremendous speed and ability to get to seemingly everything. Alex Lawson, one of our new freshmen topped players from both Illinois and Pepperdine, while Quentin Monaghan showed glimpses of the All American he would later become. It had been a good weekend for us. Lots of long matches against a national field provided the competition we needed to become a better team. The fall format provides competition for the players and the ability to build resumes that might qualify them for post-season play. It also gives coaches a chance to compare notes and catch up on the recruiting rumors that were floating around. I appreciated spending time with Pepperdine's Adam Steinberg, a well-liked and success- ful coach who would, two years later, take over at Michigan. Adam had played collegiately for Penn State against my Navy team and become one of the country's better coaches over the years, winning an NCAA title in 2006. This also gives me a natural segue into one of my funnier coaching stories.

~ Cross Court Reflection ~

*I've never encountered a person
who achieved anything who did
not, on his path, need to overcome
obstacles.*

Lou Holtz

An Old School Coach

Adam played for the late Holmes Cathrall at Penn State. Holmes was one of my all-time favorite college coaches. If you look up the phrase "old school" in the dictionary, you might find Cathrall's picture there. He is in two very funny stories that I must tell you. One involved the Penn State team of Virgil Christian and Lee Sponaugle, who had qualified in doubles for the NCAA Doubles Championships. At the end of the NCAA Team Championships, the individual singles and doubles events are played. Penn State was not an elite team, but Coach Cathrall turned every one of his players into good competitors. He seemed to be one of those coaches who, when handed a lemon, could make lemonade. In the mid-1980's Christian and Sponaugle were slated to play a heavily favored Stanford team led by All American Danny Goldie in the round of 32. The match was scheduled for 2:00 PM in Athens, GA and the Nittany Lion team was chomping at the bit for the opportunity to take on Stanford, the gold[some say "Gould"] standard in the collegiate game. Cardinal coach Dick Gould by then had established a dynasty in Palo Alto and had become very successful in Athens. Gould won 17 NCAA titles in 24 years. Beating anyone from Stanford was difficult and momentous.

After a thorough morning hit and lunch the Penn State duo agreed to rest and be out in front of the Athens Holiday Inn at 1:00 where Coach Cathrall would pick them up to drive to the courts. They came down at 1:00, as requested, but after waiting awhile could not find their coach. After calling his room the players did not know what to do and continued to wait until, out of desperation, they began to walk and hitch-hike to the courts. Try to picture them running and frantically trying to flag down a ride to the most important match of their lives. They were picked up by a stranger and taken to the courts, but arrived late. Imagine their frustration, as they had waited all year for this opportunity. For their tardiness they were forced to walk right on court and begin the match against the waiting Stanford duo without having hit one ball to warm up. Obviously playing with nothing to lose, both players played a great match and somehow went on to record a stunning upset, noting that Cathrall, who had fallen asleep and slept through his hotel wakeup call arrived mid-way through the second set.

Now for my second Holmes Cathrall story. As I mentioned earlier, Cathrall refused to allow a very limited travel budget to be an excuse for a lack of good competition, and in the 1970's began the practice of making his players find their own lodging at various places where they played. Steinberg, Christian, and others found out that as freshmen Cathrall would pull into the campus where the team was to play the next day, drop off the players, and tell them what time to meet him in the morning. Incredulously, he would then drive away. Somehow, someway, the Penn State players were able to find lodging and used this as a competitive edge in the next day's match. Anyone reading this is not likely to believe it, but just ask those players about their travel adventures. Times have certainly changed. I might add that any coach doing this today would likely be terminated. Social media can be very unkind.

I can personally verify to its truth because in 1966 I was the senior team captain of the University of Richmond men's tennis team and saw it in action. Immediately after we finished our team match against Penn State, Coach Cathrall, whom I did not know, came up to me to tell me how well I had played and what a pretty game I had. I was both easily fooled and flattered, and our conversation continued. He then asked me what special event was going on in Richmond. I did not know of any such event and told him that. He then added that he assumed there would be hotel rooms to be had, but that he had tirelessly searched and could not find a single one.

Gullible, but flattered, I told him that we had couches in my fraternity lodge and that his players were welcome to use them that evening, as there was nothing going on at the lodge that night.

He thanked me and then asked for directions. I was one of only two people who actually lived in the lodge and was able to see that the Penn State players could sleep there that evening. Now, fast forward ten years. I was coaching at Navy. My assistant, David Snidow, had also played at Richmond and was also a Lambda Chi[my fraternity]. He told me that every year after the Penn State-Richmond tennis match the players from Penn State would show up at the Lambda Chi Lodge, acting as though they had been invited….and sleep there for the evening. Imagine such a thing in today's world of Facebook, et. al. Even today, Coach Cathrall's Penn State players display great pride and bond together like brothers. Out of that group have come Dwayne Hultquist [Head coach at Florida State], Steinberg[Head coach at Michigan and former NCAA champion and National Coach of the Year at Pepperdine], and Virgil Christian, USTA guru and 2014 Tennis Industry Man of the Year, to name just a few. All of them played against my teams at Navy.

Pardon yet another segue, but as I take you through this current calendar year I plan to continue to slip these asides and some philosophical musings into the conversation when appropriate. It is the only way to relate things that I have observed and still maintain the continuity of the calendar year in college tennis.

~ Cross Court Reflection ~

The winner isn't always the one holding the trophy at the end of the tournament; sometimes it's the champion that once again captures our imaginations and inspires us all.

Justin Gimelstob

Notre Dame NCAA Round of 16 match versus Georgia. Georgia defeated Notre Dame 4-3. Coach Bobby Bayliss (right) talks with #1 doubles team and All Americans Andy Zurcher and Todd Wilson (center). Zurcher and Wilson won the match. May 21, 1994. *Photo courtesy of Mike Bennett.*

CHAPTER FOUR

Team Practice

Winning is important, yes. But HOW and WHY you win are equally - if not more - important. Because without meaning, even your most important victories will ring hollow.

Tony Dungy

Following the great event held by Olympia Fields Country Club it was time to get back to basics. We had competed in two events already. The freshmen had been given an opportunity to show what they could do. The returning players had all shown progress from the previous spring. We could easily assess where we were as a team and what needed to be done. It was now time to go to work. For me, practice is something I treasure. As a coach I have the opportunity to work with each player and develop their games to the highest level possible, but it is also a special challenge. If I attempt to make changes in a stroke or grip I must have the trust and cooperation of the player involved. For without this belief and trust it is difficult to make effective changes.

Imagine yourself in the shoes of a new freshman who had been coached most of his life by a local tennis professional. For him to learn that part of his repertoire needs to be changed is not an easy thing to have to face. In my early years I was too quick to point out a problem and suggest a solution. I learned the hard way that changing a player's stroke was difficult. That player had hit thousands and thousands of balls in a certain manner with a certain backswing, grip, and follow through, not to mention footwork, in order to have confidence in the stroke. In other instances a player had experienced success with his game and it was all he knew. For me to jump in and suggest a change might break down the player's confidence quickly. I had three tasks here: first, to assess the state of his present game correctly, second, to convince him to trust me; and third, to show him how to make the change in a way that made sense to him. I needed to understand that most players have been coached by a tennis professional who might not agree with me. I also had to demonstrate the reason for change and the expected outcome. Finally, this had to be done at a time where the player would not be competing. Without tons of successful reps it is difficult for the desired change to take hold. It is difficult to achieve anything that you are afraid of doing.

Everything you've always wanted is on the other side of fear.

George Adair

At Navy I had a player, Bayly Taff, who competed at a very high level and loved the battle. He played an attacking style that had brought him much success as a junior player and earned him the #2 ranking in the USTA Southern Section of the US. He liked to get to the net and could volley effectively there and hit overhead smashes like they came out of a cannon. Bayly played with a continental grip on his forehand which allowed him good transitional opportunities, but I had even bigger plans for him. I knew that at the next level Bayly would need more stability and consistency from the backcourt, for at a higher college level he would not be able to serve and volley all of the time. This was complicated by the fact that his coach at home, Bill Tym, is both successful and well known….and someone I liked and respected. Tym had known Bayly's penchant for the serve and volley and had given him the tools to use for it. We discussed a change. He was adamant in his desire to stick with his game and "dance with who brung 'ya." At the end of the fall I asked him to give me ten days to prove I could make his forehand better and pointed out that I needed his trust and full cooperation. I said that after that time period he could then make up his mind what to do and that I would support that decision. To Bayly's credit, he gave it his best shot, but throughout the first six days told me that I was an idiot to try this. On day #7 he shut up and the stroke began to settle into his comfort zone. By day #10 he was the proud owner of a solid forehand that was between an Eastern and semi-Western grip[more of his hand behind the grip] and went on to become a terrific player and team captain. His success was directly tied to his trust and willingness to make the change work. Not every freshman is amenable to this type of change.

Success seems to be largely a matter of hanging on after others have let go.

William Feather

As I look back on changes I tried to make in the games of various players, I see varying degrees of success, but overall I believe that player development was a strength of our program, especially at Notre Dame. Players like Mike Sprouse, Andy Zurcher, Todd Wilson, Casey Smith, Javier Taborga and Stephen Bass all began their careers in the bottom half of the lineup and, in the cases of Mike, Todd, and Javier, were not in the starting six. In fact Todd's backhand, when he arrived at Notre Dame was nicknamed "the black hole" because if you hit the ball there it never came back. All but Mike became All Americans and Mike missed that distinction by the slimmest of threads. Sometimes the problem had nothing to do with strokes, but rather encompassed playing style. Ryan Sachire arrived as a 6'6" freshman who could pound near-winners from the backcourt, but was a step slow. Eventually, I knew, players would start running down his howitzers and float back simple returns because Ryan rarely ventured to the net. While he was far from an accomplished volleyer, Ryan needed to add the threat that he might follow in behind a great shot to force counter-punchers to take more risks when on defense. Ryan might have been the easiest player to coach that I have had. Both parents were school teachers and his father was a coach who had given him good fundamentals. The result: a healthy respect for authority and the willingness to trust the coach.

So the factors I need to consider are the ability of the player to win with what he has, his athletic ability, and his willingness to be open to change. David DiLucia, however, was very fundamentally sound, but, as a freshman, sometimes overhit on short balls. It took awhile to get him to understand that his volleying and presence at the net had already eclipsed that of most professional players. It made no sense for him to risk an error on an approach shot when he had the goods to finish consistently coming forward. Add to that his recent success in national junior events [Easter Bowl winner and US Open Junior semi-finalist] and you can understand why he was initially resistant to change. Additionally, his coach was Nick Saviano, one of the top developers of junior talent in the world and a former ATP top 50 player in his own right. I decided to contact Nick and that conversation helped immensely.

Evaluating the Personnel...
What Needs to be Done

As practice settles into a good routine, this is one of the things that I must consider: who needs developmental change and how difficult might it be. Looking over our new freshmen at practice today, I can see that Quentin Monaghan will be rock solid, but will need to add a bit more punch and aggressiveness to his game. He, too, has to plant the fear of finishing at the net to keep an opponent from simply running down his shots and floating back returns. He will also need to make his forehand better by flattening it out somewhat. The spin he employs gives him control, but denies him the chance to finish the point. Classmate Alex Lawson is a tremendous athlete and has doubles instincts well beyond those of a normal freshman, but gets lost at times playing singles, looking like he lost his directions and needing help finding his way home. It will be a shame if we can't eventually turn him into a solid singles player. Another freshman, Kenny Sabacinski, needs elevator shoes to reach 5'7," but he is a pretty good mover and has a very versatile game. All he will need is some improvement in his serve to challenge for a starting spot in the lineup because he is not afraid to finish at the net. Their classmate Nico Montoya is versatile and has nice touch around the net. We should be able to get him to hit a little bigger from the backcourt and challenge for serious playing time. Being left-handed never hurts, either. Jay Louderback, our well regarded women's coach, told me once that he believes that lefties should lose not serve more than once per semester. I want all of our lefties to own the "can opener', the wide serve in the ad court that pulls the right-hander way off the court.

The real question is Eric Schnurrenberger, the Swiss freshman whom the NCAA has deemed ineligible for competition this year. Since Eric will not be competing in 2012-13, this is a year when he could make any necessary changes. His game, though, is well rounded and nothing jumps out at me now that needs fixing, other than adding some power, as his speed is not a strength. This, though, will happen as a result of our strength and conditioning program. Off-court and weight room workouts figure far more prominently in today's tennis that they did in my playing career. I will need to pay special attention to Eric as the year moves on, as he will not have the added motivation that match play provides. Somehow we need to see his development move positively despite this disadvantage.

In the returning group Greg Andrews looks to be hitting bigger than ever off the forehand side, but is also transitioning into the backhand better. His return of serve, once a weakness on the backhand, has become a strength, as it has now become more compact and allows him to cut into the court as he hits it. It is important for me to see Greg make All American honors before he graduates. No one works harder. Having a 3.9 GPA in Accounting will also make it easy for him to have a job waiting for him at graduation. Give me six of him and I'll promise you an NCAA title in May. His brother was an All American swimmer at Stanford and Greg wants to achieve a similar goal at Notre Dame. On the next court, Ryan Bandy has shown improvement and it looks as though he will challenge for playing time after a year "riding the pine." He has a pretty good foundation, but needs more punch and aggressiveness. He will become an important cog in our lineup and win his match when we play defending NCAA champion USC at our place in March. While he doesn't yet know it, Ryan is going to experience great success this spring.

Success is like anything worthwhile. It has a price. You have to pay the price to win and you have to pay the price to get to the point where success is possible. Most importantly, you have to pay the price to stay there.

Vince Lombardi

Wyatt McCoy seems to be more ready to play this year. I expected him to start when we recruited him, but he lacked sufficient punch last year and, although close, did not see much playing time as a freshman. Normally a freshman entering college with a junior ranking of top 10-15 in the country will make the lineup here, so this is a year in which I hope Wyatt makes a jump and adds strength there. He is as fast as anyone in college tennis, but has always depended on his speed and ability to counterpunch to get him out of trouble. I refer to this as defensive speed. At this - the next level - Wyatt has found that his opponents from junior days have gotten bigger and stronger and he needs more pace and depth on his ball to keep them from attacking him. Effectively, the court has shrunk for his opponents. Wyatt's instincts have been defensive and for good reason. Junior players got frustrated as he seemingly got to everything and defended very well against someone who came forward. He needs to use his speed offensively and cut in when moving wide to take the time away from his opponent and hurt him with time pressure. This, and being able to hit through the ball on his forehand side, will make him very tough to beat in a lower lineup position. Once more, I need to ask a very good player, Wyatt, to change what has always made him successful in order to continue his growth. This requires trust and I hope Wyatt will grant me a large portion of it.

The trick to getting ahead is to give the same effort you give to getting even.

Robert Brault

As for the other players, I am happy to see Billy Pecor moving well and hitting an imposing ball. Billy has a ton of ability, but spent his freshman year on the sidelines as arthritic knees kept him off the courts. Billy hits the ball as big as anyone at the college level and would be a great practice partner for those in the professional ranks, as his ball is both penetrating and heavy. My job is to convince him to move up in the court once he establishes dominance in the rally. It will be easy then for him to transition to the net and finish points there. He is ALMOST talented enough to simply continue to try win the point from deeper in the backcourt, but "almost" is a big word in this case. After that we need to improve his court presence and begin to get him to think more positively after losing a point, as he has a tendency to hang his head after missing, something he needs to eliminate.

Just beyond Billy is Michael Moore, a big, strong guy who similarly needs more of a net presence and more self-confidence. Michael is capable of dominating from the baseline, but similarly needs to possess the threat that coming to the net will bring balance to his game. One of my big regrets with Michael is that he ran into a very good counterpuncher from William & Mary in his first-ever dual match as a freshman. He lost 7-6 in the third set because too many of his offensive salvos came back and he lacked the ability to cut some of them off in the air. There are times I think that setback still haunts him. Michael will attend medical school at the University of Illinois next year, although he will not hear of his admissions status until spring. My hope is that being accepted will lift a psychological load off his shoulders and that he will be inspired to play his greatest tennis.

It is so refreshing to see Blas Moros with us again, this time as team captain. Blas is simply one of those guys who always does the right thing, a natural leader. Always positive, Blas has moved from the #5-6 level in our lineup to the point where he might play as high as #2. He arrived as a strong baseline player who NEVER came to the net. He worked diligently to learn these skills, but then needed to understand when to move forward. He now is a complete player and is a consistently good serve away from being a truly elite player. We will rely heavily on Blas this year and he will deliver. He shows up every day.

80% of success is showing up.

Woody Allen

Hitting next to Blas is Spencer Talmadge. The big Californian has a tremendous feel for doubles and has posted big wins for us there. My goal for "the Bear" this year is for him to slim down a bit and become a mainstay in singles. To motivate him toward this goal I kid him often about wanting him to stand beside me in our team picture, so that I won't appear overweight. He is as quiet as others are loud and getting him to speak for more than a sentence or two on any subject is a challenge. Yet the big, quiet guy with the great serve can really take you to school on the doubles court, with instincts much like freshman Alex Lawson.

On the far court I see Dougie Barnard warming up with Michael Frederica. Michael has power to spare and harnessing it is his challenge. He hits through the backhand as well as anyone, but struggles keeping his forehand under control. He has become a better volleyer, but still needs to work on his transitional skills. He will attend law school after graduation, as will Dougie, who always arrives with a smile on his face and a song in his heart. Dougie knows the game well. He was well coached as a junior player by PA Nilhagen in Indianapolis and is one of the rare freshmen who arrives in college already knowing how to play doubles. Because of his slender build, he needs to add some punch and I am hoping that this is the year he really embraces tennis and makes us better. Dougie is bright and wants to take in all that Notre Dame offers. It is difficult for me to fault him for this, but a greater commitment to excellence on the court is also the thing keeping him out of the lineup. Herein lies a familiar dilemma for me. If I recruit a young man and tell him what a great place Notre Dame is, then is it fair to tell him not to sample it? I promise myself to have a sit -down conversation with Dougie soon to let him know that he is close to the doubles lineup and a greater commitment - and bigger second serve- is likely to make him a starter.

One court away is Matt Dooley. Matt took a chance coming to Notre Dame because his junior record was a bit behind our other players, but he has made the decision a good one by working hard each and every day. I believe he can move into the doubles lineup this year. If his consistency improves, he will help us there. Matt is one year away from making a big decision. As a senior he will come out as an openly gay player and I could not be prouder of the way Notre Dame and Ryan, in his first year as a head coach, handled everything. Matt joined former Arkansas All American Bobby Blair in a made -for-TV documentary "Hiding Behind The Baseline." This year, though, Matt's secret will remain with him and will exact a price. He also will attend medical school and excel there. Because he has put forth great effort I am going to push him hard to become a starter in doubles.

———◦———

If you think you are one of your team's top players and leaders, you are going to have to be receptive to being pushed and coached harder than others.

Tom Crean

———◦———

This is my challenge - to take this group of 14 tennis players and mold them into a cohesive unit. For this to happen they will need to stay motivated throughout the year. Every college coach faces the same challenge: how to best utilize his assets[players] in order to achieve the highest level of success. It is easy to get up for the big matches and do all the right things in preparation for them, but the real challenge is making the most of all of the extra practice days when the motivation of an upcoming match is far away. It is one of our biggest challenges in coaching. True greatness lies in what you do when nobody is watching. Everyone works hard when the big stage beckons, but few are able to maintain that same focus during downtime. Any coach needs to depend on his players to continue to work hard and train all throughout the year. A team culture of continually striving to improve is imperative. Peer pressure to do one's best will do more than I can in this regard. It is imperative that our players think 'team' before themselves.

Make sure you love the sport. There will be a lot of tough moments throughout your career, but that love will get you through it all, and it's the days that you do not want to do anything that separate the good from the great.

Noah Rubin

We will play a formidable schedule that includes ten teams that will be ranked in the nation's top 25 at some point, including defending NCAA Champion Southern California. Somehow, out of this group of players with varying strengths and weaknesses, I need to weave a tapestry integrating their abilities in a productive way. I also need to be a part of their growth off the court, as many of them have plans including medical school, law school, or important work in the private sector. We need to work hard, but also to have fun. ["The most wasted of days is one without laughter." EE Cumings]. We need to be able to depend on each other to be there when needed. All need to embrace their respective roles with enthusiasm and dedication. I need to be ready to explain the disappointment of not making the lineup to several, all the while knowing that we will continue to need their productive efforts in practice daily in order to achieve our potential. This is the time - the fall - I need to build us into the best team that we can become. Practice may not sound exciting, but it is my job to make it so. I have to understand that hard work alone will not be enough. Those who are not likely to gain playing time also need to be encouraged, as a bitter role player can become a cancer to a team. As someone once said "If all it took was hard work, then by now 50 mules would have won the Kentucky Derby." Fortunately for me, Ryan Sachire is as committed to excellence as anyone I've known and that makes my job much easier. One of the challenges all coaches face is maintaining a high level of motivation during the first semester. Because there are no countable team results, it is easy for some players to put things in cruise control, waiting for the dual match season to begin in January. Those who consistently produce great effort in this, their "off" season will carry the torch for others. This is where team culture intervenes and ensures success.

One of the biggest impacts a coach at the college level can have occurs in doubles. Almost all college freshmen arrive without much of a clue as to how to play good doubles. Doubles, of course, involves the coordination of two players and getting them to synch with each other and take advantage of the other's strengths is a challenge. Today's tennis has evolved, in singles, into a cookie-cutter style in which both players play predominantly from the backcourt looking for a forehand they can crush, normally in an inside-out direction. To do this successfully, the player needs time to run around any middle-of-the-court balls, something that requires time. To allow for this extra time, most players play back in the court. This instinctively conflicts with conventional doubles instincts, which require players to take balls out of the air and move quickly to the net where they can finish points and pressure the receiving team into mistakes. Entering freshmen have little practical experience playing doubles and even those who excelled as junior players usually have done so because they are simply better tennis players and not because of their doubles skills and instincts. They rarely poach [move early to intercept a ball in mid-flight and end the point with an aggressive volley], don't know where to position themselves, and are clueless in their understanding of formations that accentuate their positives and hide their negatives. When their partner serves, most stand far too near the sideline, as if saying to their partner "Hey, you. Go play singles against these guys." I remember my own formative days playing doubles at the University of Richmond when my partner, Sandy Tucker, had to show me where to stand at the net when he served, and this makes me realize that my own patience is important here.

1994 NCAA Tournament on the Notre Dame campus. Notre Dame All Americans Andy Zurcher and Todd Wilson defeated Georgia's #1 team to clinch the doubles point. In the individual event Zurcher and Wilson reached the semi-finals, as well. May, 1994. *Photo by Mike Bennett.*

The Importance of Doubles

The current dual match format begins with one set of doubles being played simultaneously on three courts. Whichever team wins two of the three doubles sets wins the "doubles point" and takes a 1-0 lead going into singles. Some coaches put little time into teaching good doubles, figuring that it only counts for one seventh of the team score, and focus mostly on singles. To me, this is a big mistake because that one point carries tremendous momentum with it. The winner of the doubles point understands that it has only to split the six singles matches to clinch a team victory. Over the years I have come to respect certain coaches whose teams ALWAYS play great doubles. The phrase "Singles is recruiting, but doubles reflects coaching" is an accurate one. Thus you will see my teams spend significant time in practices working on the finer points of doubles: poaching, faking, reading the return of serve, knowing where to stand, move, and knowing when to change formations. They have to understand that a "body forehand" or "body backhand" can only be "pulled" and move slightly to be in the best position to intercept it as soon as they recognize its location. The difference in some of our best wins has been our ability to start the match with the doubles point in hand. Coaches like Peter Smith, Brian Boland, and Ty Tucker have demonstrated that different styles can be successful and they have built unorthodox formations into their doubles teams that take advantage of special skills possessed by their players and hide similar weaknesses. Some of these include the server staying back on serve, almost unheard of decades ago, but today's equipment allows players to pass and create angles that simply did not exist when I was playing college tennis. Using the "I" or Australian formation in the ad court[for right-handers] is an easy way to force the opponent to hit to your forehand, for example. Our players need to learn which formations, or variations thereof, are best suited to their own individual strengths and hide their weaknesses. This will continue to evolve throughout the season. Our players need to be challenged daily.

―――⟨∘⟩―――

Challenges are what makes life interesting and overcoming them is what makes life meaningful.

Joshua J. Marine

―――⟨∘⟩―――

To me, the key to effective practices lies in dividing up the activities and things I want to do on that particular day. When doing technique work it is best to be fresh and open to achieving the goal. If we need to key on strategy and tactics I add competitiveness into the mix. Frequently, with this goal in mind, I will have the team spread out, two players to a court, and begin to play competitive points.The drill is called "outhouse to penthouse'" as players move up or down according to their successes. I call "time/rotate" at various points in the workout and the winners move appropriately up to the next court while the losers move down. Most people are competitive enough to want to finish on the top court, or as near to it as possible. At each rotation I change the drill by adding a bonus point for achieving a certain goal, such as finishing a winning point at the net or successfully attacking a second serve. By changing the goals I am incorporating tactical elements into the scoring system. At a certain point I add serving into the mix and we continue, almost always giving a bonus point to a player who wins the point aggressively when returning. This creates incentive for players to take risks that they might not have made for fear of criticism, much like what the three point shot brought to basketball. Teddy Roosevelt had this to say about critics:

"It is not the critic who counts: not the man who points out how the strong man stumbles or where the doer of deeds could have done them better. The credit belongs to the man who is actually in the arena, whose face is marred by dust and sweat and blood, who strives valiantly, who errs and comes up short again and again, because there is no effort without error or shortcoming, but who knows the great enthusiasms, the great devotions, who spends himself in a worthy cause; who, at the best, knows, in the end, the triumph of high achievement, and who, at the worst, if he fails, at least he fails while daring greatly, so that his place will never be with those cold and timid souls who knew neither victory nor defeat."

We coaches are continually learning from each other. Some of the drills I use are pirated from others. Some are the product of my own ingenuity. Some of the most effective came from necessity. In planning a drill to teach or emphasize something unique to my team or player I have stumbled onto a number of drills and practice routines that lend themselves to multiple uses and variations. As opposed to ATP and WTA professionals, I have found that for college players, each drill has a shelf life of from five to fifteen minutes during which I can count on desired attentiveness. There is a fine art to having practices achieve what is needed for player development and match preparation while at the same time trying to keep things challenging and fun. Professional players are much more likely to stick to a plan ad nauseum until they get it right. Their careers depend on it. College players sometimes need some stimulation when a drill becomes too repetitive.

It's supposed to be hard. If it wasn't hard, everyone would do it. The 'hard' is what makes it great.

Tom Hanks in
"A League of Their
Own"

128

Typically, at some point Ryan and I end up with anywhere from one to several players on our respective courts, working on skills like approaching the net and volleying, etc. while the rest compete. At practice's end I want to be sure that each player has competed, worked on specific skills, and slowly improved in at least one area. In my early days at the Naval Academy I ran very structured practices, but as my knowledge of what is needed increased I found it more effective to allow the flow of practice to dictate when and what we covered. At a school like Notre Dame I need to be sympathetic to the academic demands of any particular day. For example, during mid-terms I tried to keep the practices shorter and avoided competitive drills, knowing, as the saying goes, that you can't squeeze blood out of a turnip. Players lacking sleep have a shorter practice shelf-life.

Team practice allows you to separate yourself from other coaches with innovative ideas, but also to know when a particular drill has run its course. I pride myself with knowing how to teach technique and what changes might best be instituted for each player. Today's game, even at the professional level, has become somewhat repetitive and limited in the playing styles of most players. As I said earlier, conformity to a 'cookie cutter' approach is prevalent in the modern game.

Conformity is the jailer of freedom and the enemy of growth.

John F. Kennedy

Many are deficient in volleying and the slice backhand. I expect this to change soon, as competitiveness forces players out of their limited shells, and soon I expect to see more professional players making their respective ways to the net more often. Poly strings have allowed players to do more from the backcourt, increasing the amount of heavier topspin to create a more dynamic ball, but there is a limit to how aggressive you can be without making mistakes and more net play seems a logical next step in the developmental process.

Having Ryan on court every day with me is a bonus for me because he likely can still beat all of our players and they respect that in him and try to rise to the occasion when on his court. This is a time for coach/player relationships to form and morale to grow. Everything is geared to getting our guys ready for the second semester, when any single loss might derail your post season fortunes. At various tournaments and venues where players from many teams were circulating and talking to each other I tried to listen and overhear conversations between players as they discussed their own coaches and how they did things. This gave me ideas as to whose brain I would next try to pick when we coaches got together socially. My best teams needed less structure in their practices. The less successful ones were more demanding to coach. I have found that humor can go a long way toward motivation. For example, after observing an errant backhand fly out I would often say "Stephen, that is absolutely the worst backhand I have ever seen hit in my 44 years as a head coach." Then after observing another poor backhand from another player on an adjacent court I would say, in a voice loud enough to be heard by all "Sorry, Stephen." Benign, humorous sarcasm has a place with today's athlete. Just don't make it personal. All coaches want to be liked by their players, but it is far more important to be respected than liked. Once you pander to the players' levels it is difficult to re-establish the fine line that can never be crossed. Excellence then becomes elusive.

~ Cross Court Reflection ~

Excellence is the gradual result of always striving to be better.

Pat Riley

During one of its "foreign tours" the men's tennis team visited the world famous Notre Dame Cathedral in Paris, France. Left to right are: Missy Conboy, Brian Harris, Ron Mencias, Jason Pun, Mike Sprouse, JJ O'Brien, Horst Dziura, Coach Bobby Bayliss, Ryan Simme, Steve Flanigan, and Jakub Pietrowski. August, 1995. Photo by Pat Bayliss.

Scholarships and Lineups

The two most difficult challenges I have always faced were allocating scholarship amounts and deciding who played where in the lineup. Face it, we try to recruit confident players because they will be better in match play. This means that most may believe that they either deserve a larger scholarship or should be playing in a higher lineup position than they currently occupy. One thing I learned to do was to periodically give each of our players a printed sheet of paper that served as a ballot. They were asked to list the playing lineup in the order that each believed most accurately depicted each individual player's position, numbers one through thirteen, for example. In another alphabetical column they were asked to similarly rate each team member in doubles. Finally, I asked for a short comment that each felt was appropriate about their teammates. I wanted this to be constructive, rather than to cause division. Armed with this information, I quickly found that my own assessment was pretty close to what the team felt about almost all of our guys. I kept these sheets, which were completed anonymously, in my desk. Whenever a player requested a meeting with me to discuss his status I was able to access them and show him, anonymously of course, when necessary, that his teammates did not agree with his own self-evaluation. This also gave me ammunition to counter the rare argument from a disgruntled parent that his/her son was not being treated fairly and deserved a larger scholarship.

In women's tennis, the "head count" rule is applied. This meant that there were no partial scholarships. Only eight players could receive athletic aid. Men's tennis, on the other hand, was only allocated four and one-half scholarships. The reason for this is the requirement to balance the total number of men's vs. women's scholarships to become compliant with Title IX demands. The 85 scholarships given in football make it impossible to achieve equity without short-changing the various men's sports. When the decisions are made to offer scholarships of varying amounts they are based on the abilities and potential that each tennis player had demonstrated up to that point. By the time junior year rolled around these amounts no longer represented a fair evaluation of the contributions of some of the players, as in most cases one or two players had made significant improvements and passed another player receiving a greater scholarship. There is no simple solution for this, as the coach needs to consistently bring in an annual class that adds to the team's strength.

A good example of this to me is provided by Mike Sprouse, who captained our 1996 team and received the ITA National Arthur Ashe Award given to the player who best exemplifies the virtues of leadership and sportsmanship in all of college tennis. Mike was selected for this from a field that included all college tennis players. When I recruited Mike he had not reached his full potential and, even though he was ranked #1 in New England, found himself ranked #93 nationally. What I could not anticipate was Mike's determination to become a great college player and willingness to continue to do whatever it took to get him there. As a freshman he worked his way from about #10 in our lineup to #6 by season's end, and ours was a team that reached the Elite Eight in the NCAA championships and finished with a top ten ranking and a Blue Gray National Classic championship, beating three top ten teams in that 1993 event. He improved on this as a sophomore and played #3 on the Irish team that hosted the 1994 NCAA Championships, losing 4-3 to Georgia in the round of sixteen. Not surprisingly, Mike finished as our #1 player and was the top ranked singles player in the Midwest ITA rankings which included all Big Ten schools, among others. In the 1996 National Indoor Singles, he defeated the #1 ranked player in the country, North Carolina's David Caldwell, among other good wins, yet when he graduated his scholarship amounted to something close to 30% of the cost of attending Notre Dame. The reason: once I had allocated scholarship awards to others who did not achieve what Mike had, I was uncomfortable taking that money away. Furthermore, I needed to bring in great recruiting classes the next two years to fill the gaps left by our class of 1993. Fortunately for me Mike's parents were very understanding and did not cause problems, but this story has been told often with a different and unhappy conclusion. Every men's coach has faced the same dilemma. This provides even more necessity to the fact that we need to foster good relationships with our players.

There have been many highlights for me in my coaching career: the 1994 Rolex Meritorious Service Award[a Rolex watch], team runner-up in the 1992 NCAA Championships, two national coach-of-the-year awards, having different players ranked #1 and #2 in college tennis, as well as #1 in doubles, coaching the US team to a gold medal in the World University Games in Sheffield, England, going 15-0 against Army while at Navy, winnning the New England Intercollegiates at MIT, and coaching the college allstars to wins in Tokyo in 2003, among them. Yet none of that really matters in the greater scheme of things. What counts most is the player-coach relationship. The greatest thrill for me is the telephone call or email from a former player asking about how I am doing. Knowing that I have made a difference in someone's life far exceeds trophies or awards and only someone in my position can understand this. A constant reminder for me is the framed picture of David DiLucia that he sent me showing him in action at Wimbledon. In the lower right-hand corner is an inscription that reads "Bullet, your guidance and inspiration have been a gift. Keep the boys focused on that NCAA title. Your former #1, David."

This is something that fuels me because none of us knows when we have said or done something that will have a lasting and positive influence over another. I am frequently flabbergasted to receive a flattering note from a former player thanking me for something I said or did that I don't even remember. One of the most rewarding things about the public announcement that I was entering my final season was that it triggered many such expressions of gratitude. Here is an example in an email from John Dace, a senior on my 1983 Navy team that arrived unannounced in my inbox this year: "Coach...you helped me more than you can imagine. I was a brat and you helped me understand that team, service, and commitment are more than one person. When asked in interviews, in life, or in general who are the most important influences in my life, you are always at the top of the list. Thank you again." My memories of John mostly involve trying to keep him calm in competition. The answer was easy for others to see, but not for him. Often the player himself cannot see what is obvious to others.

Life is too short to chase unicorns. It is too precious to rely on a rabbit's foot. The real solutions we seek are almost always hiding in plain sight.

Gary Keller

Because those who compete in sports at a high level place such a high value on its importance, we who coach find ourselves in the precarious position of knowing that our influence is palpable. This causes me to reflect before taking any action that might have life lesson consequences. Our athletes care deeply about their teammates and want to produce efforts that become part of the solution rather than part of the problem. Most want to view their role on a varsity team as positive and significant. The bond between teammates as well as their coaches is lasting. Their mission to push and prod each other for greater team success is the glue that holds them together many years later. Their mutual quest for excellence provides a forum to perpetuate the memories from matches and practices that took place decades before. One of the great rewards in coaching is seeing former players unite for a reunion. Once they are together it is like letting the genie out of the bottle. Everyone is 20 years old once again. There is simply no pretense. All have been through so much together and have seen each other succeed and fail that current successes, financial or otherwise, hold little or no importance when they are once again together. To see them so excited to be back together again fills me with great pride.

The Relevance of College Athletics

The lasting value of college athletics and its importance as a teaching tool was brought home to me one summer morning in 1988. As I picked up my copy of USA Today to peruse, the headline jumped at me for more than one reason. I saw that a US battleship stationed in the Persian Gulf had mistakenly shot down an Iranian airliner on July 3rd, killing all 294 innocent civilians aboard. Reading further I noted the name of the ship - the USS Vincennes. Immediately I remembered that the captain of my 1983 Navy team, Bill Mountford, was, in fact, stationed on the Vincennes and my thoughts went out immediately to him. I will save you the circumstances because they were complicated. The Vincennes made every effort to contact the airliner, but its pilot had shifted his radio to the wrong frequency and never received any warning. Their speed and trajectory were similar to that of an enemy aircraft. Radar doesn't show a picture of the airplane, so those in charge of the Vincennes had no way of knowing the airplane was not an enemy in attack mode. The USS Cole had earlier been the victim of a terrorist attack that killed 17 US Navy sailors. The senior officers were immediately assembled to come to a decision and all except one decided that the circumstances required that they shoot down the aircraft. That one dissenting vote belonged to Lt. Bill Mountford. This tragedy justifiably caused a firestorm resulting in investigations and Congressional hearings. Many involved were called to testify. After the hearings I received a letter [remember that email had not yet been invented] from Bill. I have saved it and I quote from it:

"I haven't had an opportunity to write earlier with all the happenings that have been going on around here. I obviously can't tell you much in detail, but I can tell you that the pressure around here since 3 July has been something like that of an Army Navy match with the score tied at 3-3 after the singles. I testified two days ago and it was probably the most intense 30-40 minutes of my life. There was all this high brass asking all kinds of questions, with everyone talking into microphones and lawyers everywhere. Not much fun! I will say that my sports[more specifically tennis] background has helped me tremendously in how I deal with this whole affair. Even though this entire thing is much more of a crisis than trying to win a tennis match, the pressure I felt is remarkably similar to how I felt after letting down the team. It is all how you perceive things in your mind, and you and I both know that I was always capable of creating and building up pressure on myself. I am doing well, though; this is something that all will always have to live with, and some will have more trouble than others in dealing with this event." I knew that he was now in a better place when he asked if I had seen his pictures in Time and Newsweek. He closed the letter with "Good luck with the coming season, Coach, and with the future of Notre Dame tennis. I'll be watching, reading, and cheering for you. Take care, and give my best to the family."

Wow! To hear that Bill's experience playing college tennis for me at Navy had prepared him well for the pressure involved in handling a life and death crisis, was very humbling for me and validated what I was doing for a living. As fate would have it, Bill drove cross-country later that summer, as he had resigned his commission in the Navy to pursue an MBA. He stopped and stayed a few days with us. As I was showing him around I introduced him to his future wife, Missy Conboy, as I noted in an earlier chapter. I am now the godfather to his oldest child, Darby, who will graduate from Notre Dame in May. While he pursued his MBA at Notre Dame he served as my volunteer assistant coach. In addition to his "real job" he coaches the girls' team at nearby St. Joseph High School and, now retired, I am his volunteer assistant. His team won the state high school championship several years ago. He was always a cerebral player and carries that trait into his coaching role.

The Lord gave us two ends- one to sit on and the other to think with. Success depends on which one we use the most.

Ann Landers

As I mentioned earlier, I began my college coaching career at the US Naval Academy. It was a fortuitous beginning for me, as I found myself surrounded daily by intelligent and highly motivated athletes. It also threw me right into the greatest rivalry in college sports. The Army Navy rivalry cannot be easily explained. I have been around and observed many great rivalries: Michigan-Ohio State, USC-UCLA, Stanford-CAl, Alabama-Auburn, Harvard-Yale, and many more. The difference between it and others is the combination of both hatred and mutual respect. To people in that contained world, winning the Army Navy battle is everything….and then more. In fact, I was hired at Navy because the midshipmen had experienced little, if any, success over the cadets in tennis for over a decade. I understood that this contest was important, but I was clueless in trying to understand the importance of success when these two great institutions competed against one another. I arrived at the Naval Academy as a young and idealistic boy/man of 24 years. I was thrilled to be given such an opportunity. To me, this was the "big time." Within a few weeks of my arrival I was invited to a dinner given by the athletic department in honor of the department's chaplain who was about to begin a tour of duty in Viet Nam. The dinner was held in the Officer's and Faculty Club and the room was decorated with blue and gold ribbons and streamers, among other celebratory mementoes. When Army or Navy do something like this, they do it well. Tradition oozes from the walls. Think Patton, Nimitz, Eisenhower, and John Paul Jones!

Army vs. Navy ~
the Greatest of all Rivalries

*Enter every activity without giving
giving recognition to the
possibility of defeat.*

Paul J. Meyer

As a young and very impressionable coach I was in awe of my surroundings. Seated across from me were Al Cantello, former world record holder in the javelin, Ed Peery, NCAA Coach of the Year in wrestling, and Glenn Warner, former US Olympic coach, among many other coaches I had quickly come to admire. Peery was undefeated as a collegiate wrestler for all three years - NCAA champion each year. After a few too many drinks, Cantello got my attention. He could see that I was awed by the setting and tradition in attendance. He wanted to pull my chain a bit and asked me if I was impressed with the affair. He said something like "Pretty impressive, isn't it, Bobby? Blue and gold, rah,rah, rah!" I agreed and then watched as he followed up his remarks with "But you gotta pay the rent, Bobby. You gotta beat Army!" At that moment I realized what was my most important job. All of a sudden I felt very uneasy, suddenly burdened with a new responsibility. It was something that I carried around with me there every day. I now understood that I could no longer be afraid to "put it on the line" daily, win or lose.

If you want to increase your success rate,
double your failure rate.

Thomas Watson, Sr.

My 15 years in Annapolis were wonderful. I could not have begun my career at a better place. Navy and Army were members of the Eastern Intercollegiate Tennis Association, along with the eight Ivy League Schools, so I found myself competing with some older and well known foes. Men like Jack Barnaby at Harvard, John Skillman at Yale, John Conroy at Princeton, Eddie Moylan at Cornell, Al Molloy at Pennsylvania, Butch Seewagen at Columbia and John Kenfield at Dartmouth were very well known. Most had written books and were speakers at various conferences, etc. Some had excelled as players. Molloy became a mentor to me and was someone for whose advice I called throughout my career. I had never been on an IVY League campus, yet before long I knew my way around them all. Yet it was West Point that impressed me the most. Built adjacent to the famous Hudson River, it stood like the fortress it had once been, beautiful in spring, foreboding in winter. It seemed like I could recreate scenes from "The Legend of Sleepy Hollow" or "The Last of the Mohicans" each time I glanced toward the Hudson. The varsity courts, called the Library Courts, since replaced, were directly across from the cadet library and included a large statue of Gen. George Patton holding his binoculars, apparently surveying the scene of an imminent battle. Bill Cullen was the Army coach in 1970, and we became friends immediately. He was a good player and we hit balls together often. He knew the game and was insightful with his scouting reports. Despite the Army Navy rivalry I enjoyed his company.

The annual Army Navy match was held during June Week, now known as Commissioning Week. There were three Army Navy weekends, periods in which each school's teams met either in West Point or Annapolis to compete for the athletic supremacy of the fall, winter, or spring. There were five Army Navy contests held each spring: tennis, baseball, track and field, golf, and lacrosse. Two would be in one location while the other three would be held in the other. Army had beaten Navy the previous year at West Point, so at least we would be on our home courts for my first such encounter. They would be the clear favorite and I saw no reason to feel differently as they consistently defeated teams that beat us during my first season. Nonetheless, I was determined to produce a squad that improved as the season developed and would, at the very least, make the Black Knights earn their victory.

June arrived and soon it was time to play Army. While we had a couple of matchups I liked, most leaned toward Army. As the match began I had no inkling that I was about to be a part of something very special - one of only two or three college matches in my career that I would remember in specific and indelible detail as long as I would live. At both #2 and #5 singles we came out of the blocks on fire and Bob Custer and classmate Clay Stiles won their matches in straight sets, while we lost badly at #6 and fell behind at #3. Third singles was a surprise to me because our senior captain, George Galdorisi, was very good in the biggest matches, but unfortunately came up just short today. Gordon Perry was at his best at #1, sliding all over the clay while hitting winners and attacking boldly. He finally secured a victory over Bill Malkemes late in the third set after over three hours of fighting, but we were less fortunate at #3, as newcomer Ray Federici of Army topped Galdorisi in an extremely hard-fought match. All heads then turned to court #4 where senior Cutler Dawson upset Joe Reeder in one of the most courageous displays of will that I have ever seen, and described in detail in an earlier chapter. With four singles in hand we clinched the upset at #1 doubles, as Dawson-Perry simply outcompeted their Army counterparts.

When the match ended I joined the throng of Navy folks celebrating the win, and watched as our director of athletics, Captain J. O. Coppedge and the Academy's Superintendent, Adm. James Calvert, acting like twelve year olds, hopped our short fence in front of the bleachers of court #1 to join in the celebration, as I also described in an earlier chapter. This memory stays with me and whenever I have a free moment to return to it I feel that time has stopped. The next day, as part of June [graduation] Week our team assembled to ring the ceremonial bell in front of Bancroft Hall together before a crowd of thousands of cheering fans and midshipmen. This bell only rings to signify a win over Army, and the many thousands of spectators gathered in celebration cheered loudly as each of our players and coaches took his turn. The statue of the Indian warrior Tecumseh, clad in battle paint [only done on Army Navy weekends] looked on. Each team member would later receive a sixteen carat gold charm, made in Philadelphia by the renowned jeweler Bailey, Banks, and Biddle. The charm's front shows the seal of the Naval Academy with crossed rackets behind it. On the charm's back is the player[or coach's] name, the date, and the score of the match. This is done in all sports at Army and Navy. Pat has a special charm bracelet with all 15 of the charms I won, as I finished my Navy career 15-0 against Army. Our players made a believer out of me.

⊰•⊱

If you have dreams, don't give up. Belief is the most common word to me, even more than hope. For one to achieve his dreams he must truly believe in them.

Novak Djokovic

⊰•⊱

While we are talking about West Point and the Army Navy match, I have a funny story to relate. As we continued to experience success in that rivalry I found that I was often asked what the key to our success had been. The most important key, obviously, was to have better players, but that answer never seemed to satisfy people. Once, when joking with a few of the new Navy plebes [freshmen], the topic resurfaced and several of them asked why we had been able to win all of our rivalry matches. I thought I would have some fun with them and made up a story. In front of the barracks at West Point [like Navy, all cadets live in Washington Hall] is a magnificent statue of George Washington on horseback. It faces the beautiful parade grounds and cuts a majestic figure. I told our plebes that the evening before every Army Navy match at West Point, the plebes on our team sneak out and climb the statue of Washington, where they paint one of the horse's testicles blue and the other gold. That tradition, I would tell them, has been the key to Navy's string of victories. Obviously this is a total falsehood and something I would never encourage, but for a brief period, until they figure out that the story is a hoax, we have some pretty intimidated plebes. Eventually, they figure it out and realize that such a daunting chore does not await them.

Fast forward to May, 1979. Our team is once again in West Point at the Thayer Hotel, ready to take on the Cadets in yet another hard fought match. At 2:00 AM I was awakened by a knock on my door. I got out of bed and opened the door to find plebe Dave Andrews with his face blackened and wearing a camouflage outfit with a request for me. "Coach, can you give me the keys to the car. If I can use it I think I can pull this off. Otherwise The MP's [military police] will catch me." Scared to death and happy that Dave had not been caught, I explained to him that the story was phony and that there was no such tradition. At first he resisted, telling me he did not want to break the tradition, until I convinced him that it was all a big joke. Had he followed through with his plan, he, no doubt, would have been arrested and not been able to play the next day for us. I would hate to think what would have happened had he not come to my room. I really dodged a bullet that evening. Interestingly, Dave was recently inducted into the Hawaii Tennis Hall of Fame and I was asked to say a few words about him for the occasion. I related this story and found that it was indeed well received. Dave never failed in Army Navy competition.

~ Cross Court Reflection ~

Because a fellow has failed once or twice, or a dozen times, you don't want to set him down as a failure 'till he's dead or loses his courage- and that's the same thing.

George Horace Lorimer

Irish Tennis honored at football game. It is always a special feeling to be honored in front of 80,000 fans when the team has done something extraordinary. One of many such honors occurred in 2005. Kneeling [l to r] Brent D'Amico, Andrew Roth, "The Leprechaun," Stephen Bass, and Kaitlyn Redding. Second row: Dr. Hugh Page, Coach Todd Doebler,Ryan Keckley, Patrick Buchanan, "Bubba" Akhvlediani, Yuichi Uda, and Coach Bobby Bayliss. Top row: Sheeva Parbhu, Barry King, Nick Chimerakis, Eric Langenkamp, Jimmy Bass, Brandon Pierpont, and Peter Graham. *Photo by Mike Bennett.*

Preparing for Regionals

You can't hire someone to do
your push-ups for you.

Jim Rohn

Now back to our main story. As my Notre Dame team returned from the clay courts of Olympia Fields, our attention turned immediately to the ITA Regionals, this year held at Michigan State. Additionally we were sending our top player, Greg Andrews, to the ITA All American Championships before the Regionals. Having practiced for a week before on the clay courts at nearby Lakeland Racket Club in order to be ready for the same surface at Olympia Fields, we needed to get back on some hard courts and acclimate for the quicker pace of the courts at Michigan State where play shifted to their indoor courts. While it might not sound like much of an adjustment, the reality is that moving from clay courts to hard can be tricky, especially when play moves indoors. Clay allows a tennis ball to grab and dig into the surface, creating a higher initial bounce and slower pace. It favors patience while faster hard courts reward more aggressive play, especially indoors where the ball moves quickly through the air in a relative vacuum. Outdoor clay courts give the player a chance to use more variety and require more patience because it is far easier to run down good shots and turn from defense to offense. Because Greg would be taking advantage of the opportunity to travel to Tulsa to play in college tennis' premier fall event, the ITA All American Championships, I asked Ryan to prepare him for that. This meant that, on occasion,

Greg would practice outside while I took most of our guys inside to more closely simulate the faster play of Michigan State's indoor facility. One thing I have learned over the years is that you can overcome conditions with a positive attitude.

Life is 10% what happens to me and 90% how I react to it.

Charles Swindoll

Because Notre Dame had already agreed to having Ryan succeed me as the head men's coach I decided early on to see that most of the duties he would need to handle next year would be familiar ones. As the members of the current recruiting class would not play under me I wanted Ryan to have the final say in who they would be. He made all decisions on whom to recruit and which players would be given scholarships. It was what he wanted and what I would have wanted, had I been in his place. As Bill Parcells once said about his position in New England with the Patriots football team, "If I am going to cook the meal, I ought to be able to shop for some of the groceries." Ryan would, in fact, pick all of those groceries.

You can feel uncertain and be ready. You can be afraid and do it anyway. You can feel rejection and still go for it.

Mel Robbins

Beginning back in the summer when both of us went to tournaments like the Clay Courts or Kalamazoo I told Ryan to decide which players he wanted me to watch at those events. He had been very involved with the recruitment of our current freshmen [Monaghan, Lawson, Schnurrenberger, Sabacinski, and Montoya] and had the final say on the group entering next fall. By this time we had received verbal commitments from several top junior players and I was more than satisfied that Notre Dame would continue to field strong teams moving forward. We were, in my words, trading in a 69 year old car[me] for one 34 years old[Ryan]. I had been very open about my decision for several years with prospects so that there could be no misunderstanding. Coaching my last season was infinitely more enjoyable because, for me, there was no recruiting responsibility.

Recruiting never ends. As soon as you have a new class signed and committed, the next one - and beyond - show up in your rear view mirror. Coaches are allowed one telephone call per week and there is the fear that, if you don't call each of your prospects every week, they might feel unloved and switch commitments to another school. Throw into the equation all of social media and the changing NCAA rules governing them and you have a 24/7 equation without any good solution. Unlike many jobs that have components with some closure and relief, recruiting comes with no days off. It is the single thing that I will miss least when I hang up my clipboard and whistle. For me, recruiting weighed on me in an omnipresent and suffocating way. There will always be more calls to make and letters/e-mails to write, no matter how diligent you are. I felt guilty on vacations when I was not calling, almost like not having your homework ready to hand in during my high school days. Whenever I thought I had some free time and wanted to relax I began to think about whom I should be able to call, making it difficult to relax without the feeling that I was neglecting something. And I knew that other coaches were working while I vacationed. The nature of the prospect has changed greatly since I began this in 1969. Lou Holtz once said to me that "Recruits now want only to know about their rights and privileges. 25 years ago they wanted to know their responsibilities and obligations."

I always tried to coach people like I would like to be coached; positively and encouragingly, rather than with criticism and fear.

Tony Dungy

Don't get me wrong. There have been many things about recruiting that I enjoy. Early in my Notre Dame career I asked some of our coaches for help or advice. Digger Phelps was always willing to talk to recruits for me. On top of that he truly believed in the product, as did Lou, who used to tell prospects "You are not making a four year decision to attend Notre Dame. You are making a 40 year one." In the fall of 1989 I knew that the top player in the country, Jonathan Stark, had a sincere interest in Notre Dame. He narrowed his field to three schools; Stanford, UCLA, and Notre Dame. He obviously had his pick. We flew him in for an official visit in late November when we had a home football and basketball game on the same Saturday. Jonathan was a starter on his high school's basketball team in Medford, OR, so I went to Digger to ask him if he would speak with Jonathan during the visit. He agreed to do it and we began to discuss the date and time. Digger suggested that I bring him out on the basketball floor as the team came out to do layups and warm up immediately prior to their game. I told him that it was too much to ask, but Digger insisted. After the football game ended I walked with Jonathan to the JACC for our basketball game, telling him something about Notre Dame's basketball tradition. We entered and made our way toward the basketball court just as the team ran on to the floor. As we neared the bench Digger saw me and winked, shouting at the top of his voice "Hey Jonathan….Jonathan Stark...yeah, you!" Jonathan's eyes got bigger than the basketball bouncing nearby and he giddily ran on the court where Digger spoke with him for a good ten minutes. I have no idea what they discussed, but Jonathan was really captivated. Unfortunately not quite enough, as he chose to attend

Stanford, but we were very close, I am sure. Years later I was at the US Open and noticed Jonathan practicing with Boris Becker. I wiggled my way through the crowd to the front row to watch. He saw me and opened the gate so that I could sit on the court and talk as he practiced. The first question he asked was "How is Digger Phelps doing?"

~ Cross Court Reflection ~

Twenty years from now you will be more disappointed by the things you didn't do than by the ones you did do. So throw off the bowlines. Sail away from the safe harbor. Catch the trade winds in your sails. Explore. Dream. Discover.

Mark Twain

The Significance of David Benjamin

Back to preparing our team for Regionals. The concept of regional singles and doubles play is the brainchild of David Benjamin. Benjamin captained the Harvard team as an undergrad in 1966, before earning his PhD from Cambridge in English Literature. He is also the smartest person I have ever met and became the Princeton men's tennis coach beginning in the fall of 1974. Much like me, he found the college landscape rudderless. Unlike me, he decided to take responsibility for changing it. He quickly became president, and later the executive director, of the Intercollegiate Tennis Coaches Association and went to work. The ITCA shortly became the ITA [Intercollegiate Tennis Association]. He raised literally millions of dollars in sponsorships from companies like Volvo and Rolex and created:

The ITA Singles and Doubles Ranking

The ITA Team Rankings

The ITA All American Singles and Doubles Championships[fall]

The ITA Indoor Singles and Doubles Championships

The ITA Regional Singles and Doubles Championships[winners and others feed into the national event]

The ITA Kick Off Weekend[16 winners move to the national event]

The ITA Coaches Convention[currently in Naples, FL in December]

A working partnership with the USTA

Inclusion of women into the ITA

The ITA National Clay Court Championships[no longer in place]

The ITA Men's Tennis Hall of Fame in Athens, GA

The ITA Women's Tennis Hall of Fame in Williamsburg, VA

And I am just getting started. Benjamin created the ITA Summer circuit, numerous awards for coaches, players, and college tennis alumni. He gained the support of former players like Arthur Ashe and Stan Smith and their support for college tennis.Our own Chuck Coleman won the first ITA/Tennis Magazine Arthur Ashe Leadership and Sportsmanship Award in 1993 and another of our players, Mike Sprouse, won it in 1995.He was also involved the great tradition at the US Open, Arthur Ashe Kids Day. Thanks to David I can look at my Wilson/ITA National Coach of the Year Award on my office wall, as well as the Rolex watch I have worn since winning the Rolex Meritorious Service Award in 1994.

I am leaving out some of what David achieved, but there can be no doubt that he created and shaped college tennis today. For many years he brainstormed with Georgia's Dan Magill to build on the tennis boom of the 1970's and create the landscape of today's college tennis. He retired in 2015 and our coaches association sent him to Paris with his wife Martine as a token gift for all he has done for college tennis. I still serve as the chair of the ITA Ethics and Infractions Committee, another of his creations. He and Magill together made the NCAA Tennis Championships into a hitherto unimagined event that stayed in Athens, GA for 15 years before the NCAA decided to rotate the tournament to share the opportunity with other schools. Standing room only crowds of 6,000 loyal and robust Georgia tennis fans turn this into a must-see iconic event on a par with any of sports' best offerings.The other thing I have failed to mention is David's ability to coach college tennis players. He created great teams at Princeton, where he coached from 1974- 2005. His 1979 squad was a clear challenger for the NCAA title, but a severe ankle injury to college tennis's #1 player, Jay Lapidus, in the team's quarter-final win over Arkansas limited the Tigers in their semi-final loss to Stanford. I saw that he was never afraid to do what he felt was right, even when it meant suspending a player. It is an important trait for a coach, as you are going to be second-guessed often.

~ Cross Court Reflection ~

He who listens to the fans soon sits with them.

Kevin Sundlin

Close, But No Cigar

It was against this Princeton juggernaut that my own Navy team played perhaps its finest match in 1979 in Annapolis. Princeton arrived at the Naval Academy with a deep and talented team with aspirations of an NCAA title. Lapidus, their top player and future ATP star, was a big, strong left handed player with the most unorthodox, yet brilliant, shot in college tennis, a one handed backhand hit with an extreme grip that penetrated and drove through the court with a heaviness rarely seen in the college or professional ranks. Ranked #1 in college tennis, he turned professional at the end of that summer after reaching the final at Orange [the biggest of the pre-US Open tournaments] where he lost 6-4 in the third set to John McEnroe. The Tigers' #2, Leif Shiras, was a semi-finalist in the season-ending NCAA Singles Championship and became a strong player on the ATP Tour, later reaching the finals at Queen's Club [the tournament preceding Wimbledon]. Both players reached the top 30 in the ATP singles rankings as professionals. Not far behind was Steve Meister, another player who also went on to a successful ATP Career. At #4 Princeton played Jim Zimmerman. He had won the Princeton Invitational earlier that year over a field that included Lapidus, Shiras, and Michael Pernfors, among many other strong players. At #5 Benjamin depended on the all-court game of Adam Cioth who had come to Princeton as the top ranked junior out of Southern California. Finally, at #6 was John Low, formerly Texas's # 1 junior player, who had also been highly recruited. No one, including me, expected the match to be close, but my respect for our players grew enormously as the match unfolded.

Lapidus, as expected, was too much for our #1, freshman [plebe] Dave Andrews, and won in straight sets, but that was the only routine score of the day in singles. Navy team captain Gene

Miller played an inspired match against Shiras, losing in three tough sets. And then the fun began. Craig Morrison downed Meister at third singles, using his big, lefty forehand to dictate play. Craig later moved to the top spot in our lineup and qualified for the NCAA singles tournament, winning his first round match there in Athens. Navy #4, Curt Dashiell bested Zimmerman by somehow handling his pace and moving him all over the court to exploit his advantage in movement. At #5 our Jon Wall, the team's best athlete, was at his best as he aggressively took care of Cioth in straight sets. Navy's diminutive Randy Kasamoto used his unusual combination of touch and aggressive serve-and-volley play to down Low. With a 4-2 lead going into doubles [college tennis began playing doubles first in 1993] our chances for the upset of the year seemed bright, but this is why I consider Benjamin one of the most underrated coaches in history. Somehow he got his players to believe that they were going to sweep the doubles and they came out firing on all cylinders. Lapidus-Shiras were ranked #1 in college tennis, so their straight win at first doubles came as no surprise. Jay's booming lefty serve and Leif's backhand volley were perhaps the best shots owned by any college tennis players. Yet we still only needed to win one of the two remaining doubles matches and we felt that we could play at least evenly with anyone in doubles.

The match, however, went right down to the wire and both doubles matches went to tie-breakers to decide the outcome. At that time college tennis employed the nine point breaker and both matches went down to the ninth point, creating drama I had never experienced. Theoretically both teams could face match point at once. As Princeton won the ninth and final point of the #2 match, all eyes shifted to #3 where we served for the match at 4-4 in the breaker - simultaneous team match point. The winner of this point would be celebrating raucously in seconds. Tension hung in the air. Just as we had rehearsed countless times we made an aggressive first serve to the 'T' in the deuce court, as Low had chosen to receive the team match point there. The serve burrowed itself deep in the backhand corner by the "T" and Navy's Curt Dashiell drifted toward the middle from his net position to cover the anticipated return, just as we always practiced, but Low never hesitated and drove his extended backhand return behind Dashiell into the alley for a winner, a risky, but highly intuitive shot. It was simply not meant to be for us!

As the Princeton players celebrated an amazing come from behind win, our guys looked at each other incredulously before congratulating Benjamin's players. It was one of those very rare days in which we had played our best, only to find that our best was not quite good enough. Looking back, there is little I would change if given the opportunity. There are times when life does not seem fair. I took the time to recount this match because it is one of the four most exciting matches of which I have ever been a part. The others are my previously reported first Army Navy match, Notre Dame's quarterfinal upset of Georgia in the 1992 NCAAs, and our improbable upset of #1 USC in the next day's semi-finals. I also wanted it known that David Benjamin was not only the architect of modern college tennis, but one of its best coaches as well. He proved that the Ivy League could play with the big boys. He achieved what many coaches thought was impossible.

~ Cross Court Reflection ~

The greatest pleasure in life is

doing what people say you cannot do.

Walter Bagehot

Midwest Regionals

If you do the bare minimum, expect bare minimum results. If you want to be great, work to be great. Nothing just happens.

JJ Watt

As you may have noted, the fall semester of the school year is dedicated primarily to individual tournament play. The reason for this is that players and coaches can focus their undivided attention to team activity during the second semester. As part of David Benjamin's original master plan, the ITA National Indoor Singles and Doubles was traditionally held in early February. Because it was such a big event in importance there was a disconnect for teams. Each coach had to leave that weekend open in his/her schedule in case a player qualified for Indoors. Yet, if no one qualified, this became a wasted weekend, as it would be highly unlikely to find a suitable opponent on such short notice. Additionally, there was the player-driven conflict of how to handle an injury. To rest a player for a lingering injury so that he could be ready for an individual event was a potential source of team conflict. Teammates wanted every player to make team events a higher priority than individual ones.

For this reason the 12 ITA regions throughout the country now are scheduled in mid-October. The 12 winners, along with at-large and wild card entries meet now at the USTA Billie Jean King National Tennis Center in Flushing Meadows, NY in November to play for the National Indoor Singles and Doubles titles. The stakes at Regionals are high. Everyone in the country wants one of these coveted spots in the draw. Virtually everyone playing there in New York is highly ranked, so opportunities for big wins abound. Heck, if a player excels at this event and the ITA All American, he has pretty much punched his ticket to the NCAAs in May. Opportunities such as this one presents are very rare.

A negative mind will never give you a positive life.

Lee M. Jenkins

It is with this mindset that our team prepares for this year's Midwest Regionals in East Lansing, MI. The October midwest weather hints that outdoor play has a short shelf life. Our #1 player, Greg Andrews, is clearly someone capable of winning an event of this magnitude. Being from nearby Kalamazoo, Greg will also have the opportunity to play in front of his parents and some friends. Doubles matches here are pro sets, so many teams are capable of winning and advancing to New York. The Michigan State indoor courts are fast, and reward aggressive play. The facility is beautiful and well maintained. Although my teams have not lost in East Lansing since 1988 we have had several matches come down to the wire.

This year's draw is loaded with strong, national level players. Among the best are Ohio State's Blaz Rola and Chase Buchanan, Michigan's Evan King, Illinois's Jared Hiltzik, and Andrews. One year from now, Rola will be playing in the main draw of the Australian Open, after qualifying for that event. All will play professionally. Additionally there are more than a few dangerous "floaters" in the draw, players who are capable of beating anyone there on a given day. There will be 56 of the midwest's top players selected by the tournament committee entered in the main draw, while 64 additional players are playing in the qualifying event, the last eight added to the main draw. I am part of the regional tournament committee and we have the responsibility for a fair and just selection process. All coaches normally want as many of their players selected and and the committee annually wrestles with the decision of whether to select a lower player from one of the top teams or a top player from one of the weaker teams and there is no simple answer. Most of us feel that a lower lineup player from Ohio State, for example, will beat the top player from most of the weaker schools. The conference call for selections is, as usual, an arduous one, but selections are made and the tournament begins.

Because we have six players in the "qualies," Ryan leaves earlier in the week with those players while I run practice here in our own facility with our top six. We use new balls exclusively to replicate the faster pace of the Michigan State courts. I am a stickler for this type of thing and have even resorted to practicing with earplugs here just before flying south for outdoor play, as one of the adjustments needed when first moving outdoors involves hearing. Indoors the sound of ball meeting strings echoes crisply and it is easier to process the sound and know how hard the ball has been hit, thus aiding your effort to be in the right place at the right time. Outdoors the sound dissipates and it is more difficult for the indoor-trained ear to properly evaluate exactly when and where the ball will land. Additionally, because your ball doesn't sound as big to you, there is a tendency to swing harder than necessary to replicate the sound familiar to you. My "anally retentive" methods like this might be a bit over the top, but I am always seeking that extra edge.

―――――⊸◉⊶―――――

Only he who can see the invisible can do the impossible.

Frank L. Gaines

―――――⊸◉⊶―――――

It will be interesting to see how our newcomers fare in East Lansing. Each will want to prove that he belongs with the starters and this type of competitiveness is healthy for our team. I am frequently torn when making final decisions as to which players start or travel with us when we play away from South Bend. If you are trying to impress the coaching staff, a strong showing at Regionals is a good place to do it. The field includes the better Big Ten teams as well as the top players from the MAC and other conferences. Each of our players needs to be motivated for his best performance. It is time for us to play big-boy tennis.

─◦○◦─

Let others lead small lives, but not you. Let others argue over small things, but not you.

Let others cry over small hurts, but not you. Let others leave their futures in someone else's hands, but not you"

Jim Rohn

─◦○◦─

In our final practices we focus on serve and return work as well as seeing that some newly formed doubles teams know their respective responsibilities. Ryan has updated me on the players he has taken to the qualies [qualifying rounds]. Freshman Nico Montoya and senior Michael Moore have advanced, each winning the requisite three matches, and we will join them for Friday's singles matches.

From a coach's perspective the Regionals are a challenge. We have eight different players entered in the main draw of singles and five doubles teams. Each player/doubles team needs to be fed, taken to warm-up courts, and dropped at the main site to await being called to play each round at a time that allows them the greatest chance for success. We are fortunate to have a manager with us and she will earn her stripes all weekend, but there are times when either Ryan or I must leave a match in which we are coaching and drive a different player back to the hotel to shower and grab a bite to eat before playing again. I had to set my alarm for 5:30 this morning in order to get ready and finish breakfast so that I can drive the players assigned to me to the courts. There are times when I sit on court with various matches non-stop and have food brought to me, because our eight players are scheduled randomly and we have no control over this schedule. I will be coach, chauffer, dietician, and strategist for several days. It is a big commitment, but one I have always welcomed.

⸺◦⸺

Commitment means staying loyal to what you said you were going to do long after the mood you said it in has left you.

European mantra

⸺◦⸺

I join sophomore Wyatt McCoy this morning as he readies to play Michigan's Evan King. King is one of the favorites to win the singles crown and has an imposing game. He will play professionally after graduation. He is tall and left handed and uses this to his advantage, sliding his serve in the ad court out wide to move Wyatt a good 5-7 feet beyond the doubles alley on returns. Wyatt and I discuss a game plan that requires him to cut in on his returns in the ad court to avoid getting pulled too wide to effectively recover and compete for the point. This is tough for McCoy. He is as fast as almost anyone in all of tennis, including those in the professional ranks. He has used this speed defensively while in the junior ranks, but now finds that, as the players have grown bigger and stronger, the court has shrunk. Wyatt's instincts are defensive, based on years of beating top junior players with his legs and uncanny ability to counter an aggressive move to the net. However today's players are older,bigger,and stronger than they were when he was in high school and more capable of throwing a knockout punch. I will work all year to ask Wyatt to use his great speed offensively and take the ball earlier to take away the opponent's time.

As the match begins I see that there is a path to a possible McCoy victory because King has a big take-back on his forehand and needs time to be effective. If I can convince Wyatt to stand in and use time pressure to the King forehand, he will need to back up and give Wyatt more time to do what he does best. After falling a break of serve behind, McCoy begins to disarm King with his court coverage and breaks back to 3-2. The dilemma for Wyatt is to continue to cut in moving for balls, but it is something that is in conflict with his instincts. Just as I feared, he gradually retreats and is reluctant to hold his ground. Before long, the die is cast and Wyatt comes to the net to shake hands with King, having lost 6-3, 6-2. As our manager leads Wyatt to the car for a shower at the hotel I quickly move to Greg Andrews' court, as he takes on Wisconsin's Alex Robles, a tall, thin player with an aggressive game whose best chance to upset Greg is clearly on a court like this one. But while Robles has a big serve and can get to the net, Andrews is too much for him today. Greg's forehand is the biggest weapon on the court and he hits winner after winner from the left corner of the court. As soon as Greg breaks serve in the second set, having already won the first, I know that you can stick a fork in Robles. He is done! Greg will not let up. I now move quickly to where the draw is posted to see if we have another player competing on another court.

———⋘∘⋙———

You can never let off the gas. You have to keep going and pursuing being the best you can everyday.

Brad Stephens

———⋘∘⋙———

Not far away, I spot Quentin Monaghan engaged in a battle of groundstrokes with Michigan State's Drew Lied. I know Lied from previous battles. He could be a tough matchup for Monaghan, as both players are good competitors and prefer to grind out long points from the baseline. Lied is on his home courts and has a crowd of followers cheering him on. Monaghan is a rock from the backcourt, but his forehand is still developing and he will leave it short at times. This allows Lied to gain control of the point, so I quickly ask Quentin to add some height to his groundies. Both players are better from the backhand side and this one looks like it could take a while. Late in the first set Monaghan realizes that Lied is reluctant to come to the net and take high floating balls out of the air. This proves to be the key to winning. Whenever Quentin is forced deep or wide in the court he simply puts some air under the ball, giving him time to get back in position. He takes the match in straight sets, a harbinger of things to come. Nobody knows it, but as a junior Quentin will reach the semi-finals of the NCAA singles tournament and become another of Notre Dame's All Americans. He shows glimpses of his mental toughness today in his refusal to make unforced errors.

Mental toughness is faith dressed in sweat equity and staying power.

Rene' Vidal

By now it is late in the afternoon and I am starving. One of our players runs a sandwich out to me on court because it is time for Billy Pecor to take the court and Ryan is otherwise engaged with a different player. I take the sandwich with me and discuss a plan with Billy. He is playing a young freshman from Illinois, Ross Guignon, another lefty whose quickness, competitiveness, and ability to think on the court are his weapons. It is a stark contrast in styles. Pecor is big and strong, but lacks speed ["The Lord giveth; the Lord taketh away. The Lord is an Indian-giver!"]. The freshman Guignon looks like he should still be in the tenth grade, but looks can be deceiving. This guy competes like very few. He will use his wide lefty serve in the ad court to set up points and sneak into the net when you least expect it. When in the backcourt he refuses to miss and can drive an impatient player crazy hanging over on the right side of the court looking for a forehand. Still, all things considered, I like Billy's chances. He has groundstrokes that can rip the cover off the ball and a backhand that can hang with those of the best professionals. All of his shots have a heaviness that pushes most opponents back too far to hurt him. Billy hits such a big ball that he makes you feel like you need to replicate his pace to stay even, but if you fall into that trap you are going to be toast. As the match begins I can see what needs to be done. Billy is dictating play and moving Guignon all over the court, but Ross seems to be getting to balls that even I thought were winners. Before long, Billy makes the cardinal mistake of trying to hit his booming groundies even harder and closer to the lines instead of moving up in the court as he takes control of the rally so that he can take an occasional ball out of the air to finish the point with a simple volley.

Herein lies a teaching/coaching moment. I know - because I have seen this type of match unfold thousands of times - that Billy needs to follow my advice to win. Similarly, I know that he wants to follow his own instincts, stay in the backcourt, and slug it out. This was successful for him as a junior player. My dilemma is how far to push. If my coaching advice forces Billy so far out of his comfort zone that he doubts his ability to execute the plan, I stand the chance of "losing" him, making it difficult for him to want to follow my advice in the future, or even be open to such consideration. If I simply tell him what he wants to hear I will be denying him the best opportunity to win, develop as a complete player, and advance. His fragile emotions at this time do not leave him in an objective place. In junior events Billy's firepower from the backcourt was usually enough, but he is now playing on a bigger stage against better players and the rules of engagement have changed. Many coaches choose to back off at this juncture for fear of alienating the player. They choose to allow the player to lose and live to fight this battle another day, avoiding possible conflict. Always a teacher, I choose to stand my ground and try to find a way to get Billy to see the light, knowing that if he does this he will have taken a tremendous step toward elevating himself to potential future greatness. It is a risk, but one I feel might make a tremendous difference in how good Billy can become.

Somewhat predictably, my choice fails. Billy becomes frustrated with my asking him to move out of his comfort zone and his emotions take over. His instinct to keep going for big shots no longer is effective, especially since I have framed the plan in a manner uncomfortable to him. He begins to hang his head after errors. Frustration develops and he comes unravelled. I realize that he is confused and that my knowledge is useless until I can present it in a manner that allows him to feel secure in its execution. What was needed was more reps in practice that emphasized this point. This happens often to many players and does not mean that they - or Billy - are not good people, only that they are conflicted about which tactic to employ. In fact, his desire to win, in the short term, is causing the biggest problem. I am fully aware that by pushing too hard I share plenty of responsibility. It is always easier to take the path of least resistance, but a true teacher is not afraid to hold to principle. To do less than this, in my mind, denies Billy the opportunity to become as good as he can possibly be. This is what I signed on for when I made the decision to come to Notre Dame. It can get lonely in positions of authority.

Good players want to be coached. Great players want to be told the truth.

Doc Rivers

This is now a "to be continued" moment and I sadly realize that we need to better replicate these conditions in practice and drill them until he finds the confidence to risk trusting me next time. Moments like this are truly what all coaches experience, and it is the ability to find a way to empower a player like Billy in such moments that will determine just how successful I can be. When given the choice between taking a player out of his comfort zone in order to better his chance for victory, and telling him what I know he wants to hear, I always opt for the teaching option, yet know that this choice could leave the athlete feeling that I cost him that day's match. I know that, in the same situation, I would prefer being told what to do, even if it made me uncomfortable. I want to give our players the best chance possible for success, while fearing that a negative experience might make it even more difficult for future credibility. If good intentions always produced positive results, my job would certainly be an easier one. My intentions and wishes are good, but as a friend once told me…."If wishes were horses, beggars would ride."

I am a great believer in luck, and I find the harder I work, the more I have of it.

Thomas Jefferson

By the time Billy's match finishes it is long past dinner time. As has frequently been the case in the past I sit down on my bed at roughly 10:00 PM with a pasta dish from "Noodles" as my dinner and eat it watching Sports Center point out tomorrow's interesting football games. If any aspiring coach could see me now and feel what I am feeling, he/she might look for different employment. As I request a wake-up call from the front desk, I realize that this crazy lifestyle will soon come to an end. Dinners will be eaten at dinner time. There is something a little bit sad, and at the same time happy, about this realization. As I put my head on the pillow I begin to think about tomorrow's matchups for us, knowing that the 5:45 AM wake-up call will hit me like a Mack truck.

Sure enough, my wake-up call arrives at "zero dark thirty" and every instinct in my aching body tells me to roll over and go back to sleep. Knowing this is not an option I bound from bed and turn on the shower. Soon I am dressed and meet the players assigned to me to play consolation matches at an alternate facility, the Michigan Athletic Club, not far away. We arrive shortly after 7:00 AM and quickly claim our warm-up courts. As soon as all players are ready to go I join Wyatt on the last court where he is scheduled to play Wisconsin's Robles, a loser to Andrews yesterday. Wyatt starts slowly, but breaks Robles in mid set. He then holds on to finish the set comfortably, but Robles retires at this point. Wisconsin's assistant then tells me that his shoulder is bothering him and they did not want to risk making it worse. I am disappointed that Wyatt did not have the chance to finish, but there is nothing I can say or do to change things. It is now time to see how our other players are doing.

The time is always right to do what is right.

Dr. Martin Luther King

I quickly spot Michael Moore and he looks great to me today. Michael is playing Michigan's Alex Petrone, a short, fast, and aggressive player who has a terrific backhand and a strong reputation as a good competitor. Because the courts are fast and Michael's timing seems to be clicking on all cylinders, Moore bludgeons his way to the first set 6-3. Petrone is an upper lineup player for Michigan and Michael's performance encourages me. Nonetheless, Petrone fights back to take the second. Petrone's backhand is clicking now and this presents trouble for Moore, who wants to dictate with his inside-out forehand, feeding right into Petrone's strength. Because this is a consolation match it will end in a "match tie-breaker" a longer version of the normal 7 point model. Michael fights his way to 9-6, one point away from victory, but Petrone fights back, taking the ball on the rise and brings the tally to 9-8 before finally succumbing in a 10-8 score. This should be good for Michael's confidence. Petrone's reputation as a strong competitor is well known. I have always believed that Michael could be a very good lower lineup player for us. This might be the jump- start we need. If a player like Michael takes the next step in his development, it will make my last season much more fun.

After a quick break for a snack we return to Michigan State's facility where I know Greg Andrews will be playing Ohio State's Hunter Callaghan, a tall, rangy player with lots of upside. Anyone from Ohio State will be tough, as former Buckeye player, now coach, Ty Tucker, has built a midwest powerhouse. Tucker has rapidly moved OSU to national prominence. He is both aggressive and highly knowledgeable and expects to win every match he plays. Tucker and Illinois's Brad Dancer have jockeyed for Big Ten prominence and both programs are fixtures in the nation's top ten. Still, this is a match I fully expect Andrews to win. Greg has worked harder than anyone on our team and only his self-doubt is keeping him from becoming an All American. However, as I walk into the facility I see him shaking hands with Callaghan, who is smiling. I can tell from his crestfallen expression that he has lost. This is doubly disappointing for me, as I had believed that Greg was ready to win or go very far in this event. More importantly, I know that he feels terrible about his performance and knows it is an opportunity lost. He and partner Spencer Talmadge are still alive in doubles so we must simply put this performance behind us and get ready for the doubles to begin. Many players would pout after a loss, but Greg quickly puts today's fiasco behind him. I believe that he has the ability to re-engage for the upcoming match and decide not to say anything to him.

~ Cross Court Reflection ~

One man with conviction is enough to overwhelm a hundred who have only opinions.

Winston Churchill

Life Lessons Taught by College Athletics

I believe very strongly in the value of intercollegiate athletics. I know the values it taught me and I have seen too many times what it can do for its adherents who commit to excellence. Life lessons abound in sports, but particularly so in tennis, an individual sport played in a team setting. Unlike other sports there is no one to block for you, set a screen for you, or pinch hit for you. You are truly on an island left to your own resources. How you handle adversity and perform under pressure can make the difference between whether or not your team wins, advances to the NCAA's, or wins a conference or national title. You call your own lines and essentially serve as your own referee. You control your own destiny, but also sometimes that of your teammates. Being the last player left on court with the match tied 3-3 is an intimidating experience, much like shooting a one - and one - foul shot with your team trailing by one point with no time left on the clock. Another analogy is kicking a field goal with time expired and trailing by two points. You must manage your body language, your strategy for winning, and execute at a level higher than that of your opponent. If this is not life learning then I don't know what is. I consider my own life lessons from sports to have been a major factor in whatever successes I have experienced. What did I learn? Let's see:

1 - Nobody wins every time. [*You can't always get your way.*]

2 - Hard work, well spent, definitely pays off. [*Improvement follows.*]

3 - It is not always all about you. [*This is why tennis in a team environment beats its individual version.*]

4 - The most important thing about failure is to get back up again. [*Recover from adversity. This is perhaps the single most important lesson tennis and sport teaches us. You are often going to find yourself down a set and a break, yet need to be able to overcome these circumstances to find a way to win. This mirrors life, where you are constantly challenged in similar ways.*]

5 - Don't judge a book by its cover. [*Some players and teams are better than you think. Having the prettiest warm-ups will not affect the outcome.*]

6 - Believe in yourself and carry yourself well, but don't show off. [*Having 10 rackets and a fancy, new polo shirt does not make you a better player.*]

7 - You can't get what you want without enabling others to get what they want. [*Empower your teammates and friends.*]

8 - Respect for others goes a long way. [*Don't be a show-off.*]

9 - Let your racket talk for you. [*Cockiness gets you nowhere.*]

10 - The respect you seek must be earned. [*Your money, car, Rolex, etc. can't help you.*]

11 - Most importantly, the earned success you achieve empowers you in other areas of life. [*You grow because of the confidence gained from overcoming adversities.*]

12 - Allow integrity and accountability to guide you. [*Resist the temptation to take what you have not earned. Tennis players call their own lines. Imagine baseball players calling their own balls and strikes. This makes our sport unique.*]

13 - Doing things the right way trumps bending the rules for personal convenience. [*Golf is perhaps an even better teacher here.*]

14 - Learning to handle and deal with pressure under fire might be sport's greatest legacy for life's success. [*Doctors, fighter pilots, lawyers, etc all have to make split second decisions that might affect life and /or death. What better way to learn this than being forced to change tactics or strategy in the middle of an important match with the team outcome on the line?*]

15 - Your attitude toward most things can be more important than you ability. [*"Optimism is going after Moby Dick in a rowboat. Chuztpah is taking the tartar sauce with you."......unknown*]

16 - Preparation is essential to success. [*Make sure that you have water, overgrip, an extra pair of socks, and a snack in your racketbag. Anticipate problems before they occur.*]

Certainly, there are many activities that can provide strong self-empowerment. I imagine that performing on stage with others, writing for the school paper knowing that your words will be read and discussed by your peers, and winning the science show or debate offer some of the same life lesson opportunities. My wife, Pat, was a member of the University of Richmond's debate team in college [along with her partner, former PGA Commissioner Tim Finchem] and her experience brought her many of the same satisfactions. I feel, though, that in our society, sports are a proven pathway to self-actualization and one's successes and failures are magnified. When I go back to Richmond I always call one of my college teammates and he contacts many of our tennis group and we meet for drinks and dinner. The stories get repeated, but never grow old. We are genuinely happy to see each other once again. There is a bond and a mutual respect forged from countless hours on the court [or field, etc.] that will always link us despite the miles and years apart. Within a few moments the tales begin and we are all once again twenty years old and can almost feel the same pressure to win. I can feel the closeness we enjoyed even though many years and miles have kept us apart. Most importantly, we immediately feel that hard earned respect for each other for the countless hours each of us took to push ourselves to a higher level. We have all failed and succeeded, won and lost, advanced and suffered elimination, and been both cheered and booed. Through it all this bond between athletes brings about a togetherness chiseled from balls hit, miles run, matches won and lost, and shared successes and failures.

You can't be afraid to show your scars.

Morgan Spurlock

It is in this environment that I have chosen to spend the last half-century of my life. Along with remembering the excitement of an unexpected win in a great environment I find that I take my greatest pleasure outside of family in seeing former players return as husbands, fathers, and successful members of their respective communities. It is especially rewarding to see them interact with each other in a manner exactly like what I described with my own friends. I know that years from now at one of our team reunions Greg will be kidded about today's loss, but even moreso, he will be cheered for what he did right after losing today. For Greg and doubles partner Spencer Talmadge upset two doubles teams that were considered favorites to win the tournament and advance to Flushing Meadows for the National Indoor Doubles.

They are an unlikely pair, Andrews and Talmadge, much like fire and ice. Greg is a fiery competitor who wears his emotions on his sleeves, while Spencer rarely speaks and is more prone to introspection. Nicknamed "the Bear" by teammates for the large frame and heft he carries with him, Talmadge has both power and touch combined with an uncanny feel for play around the net. Time after time over the next two days, the "Bear" fights off break points with thunderous 120 mph serves and pinches toward the net on each of Andrews' blistering forehand returns. I am especially excited to see Greg excel from his backhand side today on returns. We have encouraged Greg to hold his ground on that side and meet the ball earlier with a firm, compact two-handed backhand return. Today his efforts to do this come together and it is a beautiful thing to behold. He is stepping in on the backhand to take returns of difficult serves several feet inside the baseline. They run through the draw methodically to reach the final, only to lose a heartbreaker. This is an important development for our team. Doubles is a fickle part of our game. In forming teams coaches generally look for one steady player to pair with one who plays with a flourish, or, in the words of former USC coach Dick Leach, a "hammer and a wedge." On top of this there needs to be a chemistry between the two. We coaches try to make partners speak or touch rackets together after every point so that the player who just made a mistake doesn't feel his partner has lost faith in him. In this combination it is Andrews who must be the cheerleader because Talmadge communicates more with nods than words. This will be a difficult, but absolutely necessary task over which Greg needs to take ownership.

> *I left nothing in the locker room. That's something I can be proud of. I always gave 100%.*
>
> Lleyton Hewitt

At weekend's end we return to Notre Dame with both disappointments and some excitement with the weekend's results. There is but one more event for us to play, the William & Mary Invitational in Williamsbug, VA. Other than the Tribe, we will interact with teams from Harvard and Old Dominion. We have two weeks to prepare, knowing that all play will be indoors. There is a tremendous disconnect between schools from the sunbelt and those of us who suffer the perils of winter. From late October through mid-March we, by necessity, are forced to play indoors. In "the olden days" as my children refer to my college years[1962-66] colleges had a different layout for their academic year. Classes usually began the day after Labor Day and continued until Christmas vacation, after which everyone returned for a short week or two before beginning their exam period. Exams were followed by a few days off before the second semester began, normally around the beginning of February. Second semester generally had a spring break, and for most schools it came in late March. Northern schools all travelled south for their spring break trip, and played matches or practiced in the warmer weather, returning to a climate that allowed outdoor play. The school year went into early June for graduation and the NCAA Tennis Tournament was held from early to mid-June. That left all of April and May for outdoor play, enough time for a college season to unfold. Teams more or less played their way into shape during the spring trip and many of the matches played were counted as exhibitions.

Today that "old" system and schedule seems laughable. Schools begin in August and exams finish, for the most part, in December. The second semester begins in January and graduation generally takes place in mid to late May. The NCAA Championships run from mid-May through Memorial Day weekend. In order to avoid cramming 3-4 matches into each week, play begins in mid-January. Northern schools can't get outside until March, so the ITA National Team Indoors is held in mid-February. This keeps most play indoors until Team Indoors ends, at which point everybody tries to move outdoors. My philosophy was to save most of our allotted class-miss dates[Notre Dame has a very strict class-miss policy] and use them in late February and early March. With spring break built in we could fly south or to the west coast and play outdoors for nine consecutive days. Normally I would take the team south for the first two weekends after we returned from spring break. Figure Duke/North Carolina, Texas/Texas A&M, or USF/Florida State, for example. By the time April rolled around, and our playable weather with it, we had been playing outdoors for several weeks and could successfully navigate the transition from indoors to outdoors. Without doing it this way I felt we would acclimate to outdoor play over spring break, but then find ourselves back indoors needing another "acclimation" period when April arrived. This gave us the best chance for success.

---◦◦◦---

Success is simply a matter of luck. Ask any failure.

Earl Wilson

---◦◦◦---

As I mentioned earlier, indoor play contrasts with its outdoor counterpart because of the relative vacuum inside, allowing players to play farther up in the court, take more rally balls down the line, and, in general, play more aggressively. When we would move outdoors coaches would understand the learning curve and have their players put more air under the ball and change pace, etc., forcing us to adjust to tactics that were not as successful in our indoor arenas. Throw in the difference in temperature, wind, and sound distractions and you have the makings of, at best, inconsistent results, but such is the nature of college tennis. The ITA has been forced to regulate when a match moves indoors [50 degrees, wind over 20 knots] because each coach might have a different preference.

This forces me to tell the story of one of college tennis's worst fiascos. Several years ago Ohio State was scheduled to play a match at Baylor. The weather conditions were iffy, at best. It also involved the confrontation between two of college tennis's best and most strong willed coaches- Ty Tucker of Ohio State and Baylor's Matt Knoll. Ryan and I knew and respected both coaches. Matt had worked in our summer tennis camp while an assistant at Kansas and actually received the offer from Baylor while at our camp. Ty had played in Columbus for former Buckeye coach John Daly against us and had succeeded his mentor at the helm. Each inherited teams that needed rebuilding. Both had done phenomenal jobs. Ohio State has won the National Team Indoors and been an NCAA finalist while Baylor has won an NCAA championship and hosted the 2015 NCAAs. In any given year each figured to contend for national prominence. Since this match each has built a tremendous new indoor and outdoor facility. Now for the story.

Before leaving Columbus, Tucker had asked Knoll for an inclement weather plan. Baylor had no indoor courts in Waco, TX at the time, although they now have a great indoor facility. Tucker asked for the telephone number of the nearest indoor facility, but was told there was none. This is true, but there is, apparently, a four court facility slightly less than an hour's drive away. Since the forecast looked doubtful Tucker was hoping for an indoor backup plan. Knoll insisted that the plan was to be outdoors. Ohio State arrived to find bad weather, both cold and rainy, but by match day the fortunes had turned. The temperature was scheduled to reach 48 or 49 degrees, but the sun was out and there was little or no wind. Technically, Ohio State could escape play due to the ITA's 50 degree rule. It would take much too long to go through all of the machinations that took place, but when all was said and done the match was never played. There was a good crowd of hundreds of spectators present when Knoll had to walk to them and explain that the match was cancelled. Ohio State flew back to Columbus without playing the match. Depending on whom you ask the fault could lie with either coach, but the real villain was a simple lack of communication and the clash of two large egos that refused to back down. At present, each school has a great indoor facility, but then it was a different story. To me it appears that the athletic administrations at both schools needed to communicate and solve the problem, recognizing that the coaches had reached an impasse. There is no shortage of sport administrators in today's athletic departments.

I was sympathetic with Tucker because he was used to being able to move indoors, but I also understood Knoll's side of the story. In 2001 we had flown to Texas to play SMU and Baylor over one weekend. After beating SMU in Dallas we drove to Waco to take on the Bears. I awoke to 35-40 mph winds which remained constant all day. We could not change our flight for a one day later departure because of the costs involved and Notre Dame's stringent class-miss policy, yet in my entire playing and coaching career I had never tried to play in such conditions. I could not fault Baylor for not having an indoor backup. While Matt had been in residence long enough to build a nationally prominent team, the generosity of Baylor alum Mark Hurd had not yet come to sufficient fruition for the now-present Baylor indoor facility to become a reality. After speaking with my assistant, Billy Pate - now the Princeton coach - I decided to suck it up and play the match. It was an artistic fiasco with balls flying and rolling everywhere. One of the biggest challenges was avoiding stepping on an errant ball rolling over from another court. Anyone used to standing toe-to-toe and driving groundstrokes needed to change the game plan, as the ball changed direction in mid-flight, frequently taking a right or left turn as it crossed the net. In reality, the wind was so difficult that both teams suffered similarly, perhaps negating the Baylor home court advantage. Perhaps it was the luck of the Irish, but when the dust had cleared [no pun intended] Notre Dame's Aaron Talarico became a man that day and won the decisive third set as we nipped Baylor 4-3. I was rewarded for my courage. God, I had learned, must follow college tennis.

~ Cross Court Reflection ~

It does not matter how slowly you go as long as you do not stop.

Confucius

BAYLISS

Final Fall Event: The Tribe Invitational

As our fall season worked its way toward the final tournament remaining I could begin to see a blueprint for success in the coming spring. I had seen enough of our freshmen to know that we should be able to field a team that competed for a spot in the ITA top 25 rankings if several things came together. The freshmen offered new talent and enthusiasm. There was no question that Greg Andrews could develop into one of the country's better players sometime in the next year or two, but I hoped it would happen sooner, rather than later. Quentin Monaghan was going to be a star[he became an All American as a junior], but this year he was going to be a very solid mid-to-upper lineup player. Classmate Alex Lawson had big-time athletic ability and was ready now for doubles, but his singles, while inevitably going to be very good, was yet a work in progress. Losing Eric Schnurrenberger for the year was a blow, but Ryan Bandy now seemed ready to assume a singles role in addition to his doubles. Billy Pecor was healthier than the previous year and had the potential to be a game-changer for us. A healthy and motivated Pecor could beat anyone on the right day. Wyatt McCoy had added much needed punch and looked like a very tough out in the lower lineup. The leadership and continued improvement of Blas Moros was going to be a big plus, not to mention his improved aggressive play. Spencer Talmadge's doubles was close to very good and classmate Michael Moore appeared ready to break through in a singles role. With only one event remaining we journeyed to Williamsburg, VA for the Tribe Invitational. It will provide us with an opportunity to see what we might become.

This year we are going to run and shoot.
Next year we are going to run and score.

Abe Lemons

William & Mary's Peter Daub had long been a close friend and we had formed a pact to assist each other by comparing notes on our respective teams. Typically we would talk to each other after competing and share "insider information." Each of us would be very open as to how we would attack the other's players individually. We agreed never to share these insights with other coaches and I found Peter's insights into my own team invaluable. Playing in Williamsburg gave us the opportunity for live insights and comparisons, as we often commented to each other about what we saw while the match was still being played. I looked forward to this, to be able to view my own team through the eyes of another coach whose opinion I respected. Daub prided himself on his doubles acumen and his teams always demonstrated a sound knowledge of tactics and strategy. He believed in lots of movement from the net man and his teams closed tight on the net. It was more difficult to beat them indoors because of the difficulty in countering with angles and lobs. The W & M teams also communicated well and covered for each other without giving away an aggressive move in advance. They would be a challenge. Being in Williamsburg was special for me, as it was less than an hour's drive from my hometown, Richmond. It was where Pat and I had honeymooned and also the place where I won my own first-ever college dual match as a player. As if that was not sufficient reason to enjoy the trip, a group of my college teammates always drove in for a day and ate a meal with us. Add to this my friendship with Harvard's Dave Fish and I had the ingredients of an enjoyable weekend. Fish was a coach I admired and I very much looked forward to an insightful weekend of matches.

Matches began on Friday morning and we opened with Old Dominion, an up and coming team about which I knew very little. Their coach, Aloja Piric[now the head coach at Miami], was a graduate of the University of Richmond, my own alma mater and was doing a good job. No one knew it, but he would take over the reins for the Hurricanes in two years. Play was competitive and a couple of the matches proved interesting. One of the match-ups to catch my eye was that of Monaghan against ODU's Dante Terenzio. Terenzio had transferred from Louisville where we had beaten him by getting in on him and forcing him to pass from the backcourt. He was built like a fireplug, short, but muscular, and ran down everything. He played with lots of spunk and emotion in sharp contrast with Monaghan who normally kept his emotions to himself. Because Quentin lacked the instinct to attack, today's strategy needed to be different. I doubted that Terenzio had the fire-power to hurt Quentin sufficiently and thought we would win a war of attrition. The points were long, but Monaghan had the biggest weapon on the court, a two-handed backhand that he could hit with both power and disguise, keeping most rallies cross-court until a slightly shorter ball gave him the opportunity to step in and take the ball early down the line for a winner.

On another court, Greg Andrews won an easy first set, but things tightened in the second. For Greg, the determining factor was usually whether or not he could dictate play sufficiently with his rifle forehand and remain somewhat up in the court on back-hands without giving too much ground. He is the quintessential essence of what a college student-athlete should be: a dedicated worker and good team player who led primarily by example. He had come a long way since his freshman year and looked to be ready to become a prime time college player. Moros seemed to be in control and needed little coaching. I had learned a long time ago that it was equally important to know when NOT to add coaching into the mix as it was to know when to do it, so I left Blas alone and moved to another match where Pecor was in a dogfight. Bandy and Moore were in control and I decided to focus on Andrews's match.

Allow me to interject a story here that happened when our team was playing Illinois indoors in the evening at our place, as it illustrates the importance of knowing what to say in a tight match. Craig Tiley, now the tournament director of the Australian Open and a driving force in Australia's tennis resurgence, had built the Illini into a team that had ascended the national stage rapidly and forcefully. They played with lots of emotion and intensity. Our matches were always competitive. I chose this match to insert Eric Enloe, a junior who had steadily improved since his freshman year, even though I feared that he might be overwhelmed by the occasion. Sure enough, Eric lost the first set 6-1 and looked lost and scared. The overall team match was close and I simply did not have the time to remain on Eric's court and baby-sit him through the conflict. I counted on Eric's character to get him through what I planned and simply walked onto Eric's court as he dropped the first set. I stared at him and said "Eric, when I recruited you I thought you were a tough little guy. I was half right. You are a little guy." I then walked away, hoping my words would shock him into facing the competition more aggressively. I was right. Enloe exploded through his opponent and, as soon as he had finished, ran toward me to show me that he, indeed, was also a tough guy. He was visibly upset with me and said "Did this show you that I was a tough guy?" I nodded in assent just as he realized what I had done, making him so mad that he forgot about his earlier troubles and performance. He then added "Well, I'm glad you did that." Eric remains one of my most loyal and trusted alums to this day. It is important to know that I believed Eric could handle my critical remark. Using this tactic on the wrong player can be disastrous. Eric was a streetfighter.

If you want to compete in the jungle, don't do your training in a zoo.

Barry Buss

Matches in fall tournaments like this one offer an opportunity for a coach to suggest changing tactics in mid-match when necessary, as the stakes are far less than those in the heat of battle in a tightly fought dual match. Sometimes it is necessary to force a player to do something that is out of his comfort zone in order to win. It is much easier to see this while observing than it is while competing. This reminds me of a dual match we played against North Carolina in the mid-1990's in our indoor facility. At #6 singles Notre Dame's Brian Harris was locked in a war against UNC's Tony Thomas. The winner was going to determine the overall team outcome. Harris was filling in for the injured Steve Flanigan. It was his first important dual match. Brian was a big, strong aggressive baseline player whose backhand was as big and as good as there was in college tennis. Thomas was even bigger and had a huge forehand that he used to gain control of points and get to the net. As the match moved into the third set and its importance became obvious to all, the stakes were raised. In such moments, most players needed to stick to their strengths and stay in their comfort zone. It would be risky to require a change at this point.

Each player must accept the cards life deals to him or her; but once they are in hand, he or she must know how to play the cards in order to win the game.

Voltaire

As the match reached an outcome-determining third set tiebreaker Thomas had begun to chip and charge his way to the net whenever Harris missed a first serve, as the second went predictably to his backhand, making it easier to execute this change in strategy. UNC coach Sam Paul had wisely figured out a path to victory for Thomas. I knew what had to be done and immediately told Brian that, if he missed his first serve, he absolutely had to serve and volley on his second. Knowing that Thomas would be chipping and following it into the net necessitated this ploy. The problem: Brian hated to serve and volley and said to me "Coach, I have never served and volleyed on a big point in any match in my entire life. I just can't do it." I refused to back down and told him that there was no other option. This story, though, has a happy ending. Harris followed every second serve to the net and was able to put away some very easy balls. He won the decisive match and we beat Carolina that day 4-3. Harris had learned that he possessed a gear he had not known that he owned. He was able to change his natural and comfortable playing style to what was needed that day. Lesson learned.

It is difficult to free fools from the chains they revere.

Voltaire

I thought Greg had let down his guard a bit after a strong 6-1 first set and I was right. Now things got sticky as both players held serve with few break point opportunities presenting themselves. As the second set moved into a tiebreaker I became concerned as Greg began to press too much. He is wired pretty tightly and today things slipped away from him as he dropped the second set in a breaker and began the 10 point "match" tiebreaker which would take the place of a third set. Ryan and I had worked hard to find ways to help Greg relax in these situations, but today my words had little effect as he lost the "superbreaker," as we call it, 10-7 and shook hands. Pecor was giving a great effort, but made too many unforced errors and dropped the second set and the match. Moore, Moros, and McCoy all won their second sets and we had finished the singles. It was time for a lunch break and then to finish with some doubles. As we left the W & M indoor center I had learned a little bit more about my team and knew that I was about to learn even more over the next two days. We were making progress.

*Behold the turtle. He makes progress only
when he sticks his neck out.*

James Conant

Saturday found us ready to take on the weekend's biggest
challenge - Harvard. When I began my college coaching career
at Navy we were a member of the Eastern Intercollegiate Tennis
Association which included Army, Navy, and the eight Ivy League
schools.Each spring we played the other nine schools, alternating
home matches annually. Harvard had been coached then by the
venerable Jack Barnaby, a very well-known and respected coach. I
was impressed with the depth of his tennis knowledge and that he
still, in his sixties, cared very much about how his team performed.
I marvelled at how a man THAT old[Jack retired at 66] was still
very much into his coaching. The fact that I would soon turn 69
seemed irrelevant.

*Knowing what you need to do to improve
your life takes wisdom. Pushing yourself to
do it takes courage.*

Mel Robbins

One of Barnaby's best players in my early years when the
Crimson was always in the hunt for both the Eastern League and
Ivy titles was a quiet player with immaculate ground strokes who
would eventually become one of my best friends. You guessed
it; this is the same Dave Fish I mentioned earlier. I got to know
Dave during the summers when he coached the New England
junior players and brought them to Kalamazoo, MI for the National
Boys and 18's Junior Championships. One day we found ourselves
sitting next to each other watching one of the New England boys

play. Pleasantries were exchanged and we began to analyze matches until somehow we decided to leave and play some tennis. That began a routine in which Dave and I played tennis and ate some meals together at recruiting events almost daily, leading to a real friendship. When Dave took over at Harvard for Barnaby, we often compared Ivy League opponents in scouting exchanges. Eventually it was Dave, as I previously explained, who helped facilitate my becoming the teaching professional in summers at the Wellesley Country Club in the Boston suburbs which allowed me to stay in coaching and led to a three year stint at MIT just before taking my position at Notre Dame. Fish has also coached professionally, including a stint with ATP top ten player Tim Mayotte. Dave had remained humble, despite much success.

The trouble with most of us is that we would rather be ruined by praise than saved by criticism.

Norman Vincent Peale

There have been times when our friendship has become a hardship when our respective teams square off in competition. The players on both teams know we are close friends and rightfully fear that we might not be sufficiently competitive. Nothing could be farther from the truth. We have had some tremendous matches over the years, both during my Navy tenure and stay in South Bend. We frequently recruit the same players, yet have always been able to do so without giving anything away. I know that Fish says positive things about me to the recruits we both covet because they are quick to tell me about it. It is easy for me to reciprocate, as he does an extraordinary job developing his players' games and character. Today we are in for some great matches.

The first match begun involved #1 singles where our Greg Andrews was pitted against Harvard's Denis Nguyen. Nguyen is a smooth player who loves to take balls early, especially on his steady backhand, and use your pace against you. He can change direction in an instant and presents a big match-up problem for Greg indoors. Outdoors on slower courts Greg would be able to get the ball up on Nguyen's forehand and break it down. Indoors this is problematic, as the pace is quicker and allows Nguyen to play closer to the baseline, taking away the time Greg needs. It also makes it more difficult for either player to break serve, so any such break can present an insurmountable advantage. Sure enough, Greg seems nervous and edgy initially and goes down an early break before losing the set 6-2. Nguyen is doing just what I feared, standing in on Greg's forehand before it can get up and out of his strike zone. Greg's favorite play is his inside-out forehand which penetrates a right-hander's backhand, but this feeds right into Nguyen's strength. Both players hold through the second set and begin a hard fought tie-breaker which Greg wins, pulling even and forcing the dreaded "superbreaker." It is a war, taking almost twenty minutes before Andrews finally wins 11-9.

The other matches are almost as competitive and we take most of them. Moros , Bandy, Moore, and McCoy win in straight sets, while Pecor and Monaghan win super-breakers in place of third sets. As we head off to lunch I am satisfied that we played well, but have little anticipation that we are going to see the Crimson again down the road with bigger stakes and a different outcome. I exchange thoughts with Fish's very good assistant, Andrew Rueb. Rueb was a star at Harvard before playing professionally and turning to coaching as his career. Dave has his replacement in place, much as I have been able to do, and it guarantees a continued bright future for Harvard tennis. We have but one day remaining in our fall season and I want to make it good one. As we gather for our matches Sunday morning I realize that this marks my final fall season. The inevitable conclusion to a life spent coaching college tennis is not far down the road.

A champion is someone who gets up when he can't.

Jack Dempsey

Sunday's matches are almost anti-climactic, as the wear and tear of the two previous days has taken a few casualties. It is the last day of a long fall season and aches and pains seem a little more severe, especially since fall results have no carry-over value to the dual match season. Indoor play is much harder on the body, as it forces players to be up in the court more than outdoor play does. The balls are hit with more force and your body has to absorb greater punishment.Not surprisingly I see that a few of the players from other teams have scratched. Coach Daub puts out a revised schedule and play begins. Greg Andrews suddenly finds himself in yet another war, this time with talented Tribe senior Jamie Whiteford. An English import, Whiteford has a smooth and unrelenting forehand that finds creases just inside the lines and, today, he is too much for Andrews. Moros struggles mightily, but his years of experience in big-time matches barely gets him through W & M's Anton Andersson, a Swede with a heavy forehand and he ekes out the superbreaker 10-8. Pecor overpowers the Tribe's Ben Hoogland in straight sets. It is good to see Billy back on track, for he can be the difference between a good season and a great one. McCoy is all over the court, sliding as if he were on clay, as he bests the Tribe's Adrian Vodislav easily. Finally Monaghan loses only three games to Jon Banks and it is time to shower and head for the airport, but not before a stop at one of the great college town eateries, Paul's Deli, where in addition to great food you can look at the autographed photos of former Tribe greats, including former W & M head football coaches Lou Holtz and Buffalo Bills coach Marv Levy. As we arrive back on campus I note enthusiastically that I will not have to board an airplane for an entire month.

~ Cross Court Reflection ~

I have fought the good fight, I have finished the race, I have kept the faith.

2 Timothy:4:7

Workout at Roland Garros Stadium. Notre Dame players pose for a picture after practicing on the red clay at Roland Garros, the home of the French Open. First row; [l to r] Mike Sprouse, Ron Mencias, Jason Pun, Horst Dziura, and Jakub Pietrowski. Second row: Coach Bobby Bayliss, Steve Flanigan, JJ O'Brien, Brian Harris, Ryan Simme,. Taken by Bill Mountford. August, 1995.

Then 22 year old Bobby Bayliss serves and volleys in tournament play in 1967.
Photo courtesy of the Richmond Times Dispatch

CHAPTER FIVE

The Lull Before the Storm

I was smart enough to be naive enough not to know what I couldn't accomplish.

Kevin Plank, founder
of UnderArmour

Outside of the summer months, the only break in the playing and practice seasons comes in mid-November and finishes at December's end. Since the season requires most of our 144 days, we coaches are careful to end the fall season at this time. Of course, tennis activities do not stop entirely, as NCAA regulations allow for up to eight hours of work for each team. Two of these can involve skill instruction, leaving six for strength and conditioning. For the schools that offer a full strength and conditioning staff, many of us allow our strength coach to handle much of this work. Typically, the routines change in the weight room, adding more weight to build strength. Players, of course, can do other things on their own. Some enter tournaments, most practice daily on their own, and others take a step back to recover from almost six weeks of continuous practice and competition. In the early years of my career there were no restrictions on how much or often a coach could run practices and I honestly preferred that system. Because of our time limitations, many coaches try to squeeze too much into the six allotted weeks. I typically spaced things out, giving the team a full week off after regionals and adding long weekends when I felt they were needed. A very few coaches abused that system and brought about the current restrictions, which are backed with monitoring from the Compliance personnel present at every university today. It is normal practice for each school and sport to submit time logs weekly, notarizing the mandatory hours in tennis related activities for each player. I count on our players staying engaged and continuing their commitment to excellence, even though I am unable to enforce it. I also know that they need to make these decisions individually. As the saying goes "All work and no play makes Jack a dull boy."

Leadership is the ability to translate vision into reality.

Warren Bennis

For me, it is a mixed bag. While I am happy for a break, I find it frustrating when a player wants me to look at his serve, and I am forced to tell him that NCAA rules require that I am unable to help. The frustrating thing about most of the NCAA rules is that they are well intended. This year, knowing it is my last, I realize how much I am going to miss working with our young men, and I try to do all that I can to encourage their improvement. Back in my younger days, I frequently played sets with our team members. That practice became more of a doubles thing as I reached my forties, and as I hit fifty, I began to drill in ways that did not make the same physical demands. Now, at 69, I still get out on the court with our guys, but there is more feeding and less playing involved. When we hit with each other I establish patterns, such as cross-court rallies that don't require me to run for every ball. I still believe that a certain bonding takes place on the court that is difficult to replicate in off-court activities. While the days of being able to compete with our players are long gone, I find value in drilling with them. While I am now restricted to only two hours per week of skill instruction I cherish this time for individual and technical improvement. I have always gauged my effectiveness as a coach by my ability, or lack thereof, to hone the skills of those who are hungry for excellence. Improving biomechanics and adding strategic options to the arsenal of our players gives me a great sense of reward. The pride I feel when I see a graduating senior develop true all-court skills he lacked as a freshman keeps my blood pumping and my competitive fires stoked! The cookie-cutter approach that has overtaken our current game leaves players lacking in their ability to slice effectively and also to come forward and finish at the net. I realize that my job is to fill in the holes left by those in junior development and supply our guys with still-to-be-developed skills. Because of these NCAA restrictions, though, I find that I sometimes have time to catch up on administrative details that I have neglected. I get home earlier for dinner, something Pat appreciates. Being empty-nesters now, we are getting used to seeing more of each other. I can tell that she will be in for an adjustment period when I retire, as her routines will be impacted more than anything. I look forward to life's next chapter.

———◦———

A leader takes people where they want to go. A great leader takes people where they didn't necessarily want to go, but need to be.

Rosalynn Carter

———◦———

For most of my coaching career, my presence was needed at the National Junior Indoors, an event held over the Thanksgiving week in Dallas at the Brookhaven Country Club. Family life was important to us and I always stayed home for Thanksgiving dinner in the late afternoon before driving to the airport as dessert was served to catch the last possible flight to Dallas. Prior to the 1990's the "NCAA Signing Period" was in April. While coaches and players could commit verbally to each other, nothing could become formal until April when players signed the school's grant-in-aid form and its accompanying letter of intent. A little over twenty years ago the NCAA decided to offer an "Early Signing Period." For tennis and many other sports this arrived in November and schools and prospects could make their declarations and move on to other important things. For coaches, this ended the responsibility of having to call each prospect every week for fear of losing him through perceived inattentiveness. For prospects, they could enjoy their senior year of high school without the fear of a coach changing his/her mind and withdrawing an offer.

The National Indoors was quite important through the period in which there was no early signing, as it might be the last opportunity to see a player in action. There has always been a lot of "babysitting" at junior tournaments. By sitting and watching all, or most, of a player's match the coach was demonstrating his visible and transparent interest in said player. The dilemma created when more than one player was scheduled for play at the same time as other[s] forced decisions to be made in advance as to whom I wanted to see in action. In short, I frequently had to decide which players to watch based on my showing more interest in one player over another. Additionally I felt the need to know everything I could about as many players as possible, as it was not unusual to receive a call late in the game from someone expressing interest about whom I knew very little. Play began at most events as early as 8:00 AM and continued well into the night. I often felt, as I returned from a recruiting tournament, like I did in college when I had been cramming for exams, really mentally exhausted.

There is only one way to avoid criticism: do nothing, say nothing, and be nothing.

Aristotle

Sometime near 2000, the USTA eliminated the Thanksgiving-timed National Indoors and replaced it with the Winter Nationals which were held over the Christmas holiday. This meant flying to Phoenix on Dec. 26, as play typically began that day. Neither of these events was very family-friendly for coaches, but at least Phoenix offered sunshine and warm [sometimes] weather. Now we were critically watching the players we had already signed, in addition to those we would be more heavily recruiting the next year. At all of these events the coaches grew closer to each other, running out for meals together, sharing information, and spending time together in non-competitive situations. We compared notes and gossip. Which key players from other teams had suffered injuries or become academic casualties? How were our respective teams and players progressing? Who had the inside track on the next hot prospect? What information could we gain about a team coming up early on our schedule? Would there be a job opening at another university at season's end? Were any players transferring to another school? Other topics of conversation included family information, proposed NCAA rules [this took place in early January], and which teams had made statements in the fall. For most of us, the break from routine and rest had been terrific, but we were now only 2-3 weeks from opening the season and getting itchy. I vowed to relax as much as I could because I knew that our opening match usually took place in mid-January, and from that time through May I would be totally immersed in the details of running my program and navigating the emotional highs and lows that were unavoidable. The flight back from Phoenix marked the end of my Christmas vacation and signaled that I would be back in the bunker of competition sooner rather than later. It was not unusual to plan my first day's practice while airborne. I wanted to be ready ahead of time.

~ Cross Court Reflection ~

Success is not owned; it's leased.....and the rent is due every day.

JJ Watt

Old vs. New

Nobody ever reached her potential by
scattering herself in twenty different
directions. Reaching your
potential requires focus.

John Maxwell

Up until now, my retirement was not something that preyed
on me, but, coming back from Phoenix, the realization that the
coming five-month season would be my last grabbed me and did
not let go until it ended in May. This was my LAST Winter Nationals. Each trip to another campus would be my LAST such trip as
a college coach. March would bring about my LAST Blue Gray
National Tennis Classic. April would supply my LAST Big East
Conference championship. And, of course, in May I would coach
a team in the NCAA Championships for the LAST time. I became
reflective about this and wanted my LAST season to be a memorable one. I wanted to coach to the best of my ability in such a way
that all of our players remembered me as an engaged and dynamic
coach, not one who had "mailed it in" before the season began.
I wanted to enjoy every day and, of course, I wanted our team to
experience great success.

One of the things that I would be doing all spring was to
consolidate 26 years of belongings- scorebooks, ITA yearbooks,
recruiting notes and files, clothes and team uniforms, memorabilia
collected since my Navy days began with the 1970 season, and
various other things I had saved- for reasons long since forgot-
ten- and gradually remove them from my desk and office so that at

season's end Ryan could move into my desk and I could move into my new office. In doing this I had to be careful not to drift off into one of thousands of memories that popped up steadily all spring whenever I found an item that brought back a poignant memory. Perhaps the grandest of themes that crossed my mind involved all of the changes I had seen come to fruition in college tennis and how fortunate I was to have been able to be a part of it. I had really seen it all…..

What we have done for ourselves dies with us. What we have done for others and the world remains and is immortal.

Unknown

When I began coaching at Navy in 1969, tennis balls were all white. The metal [not plastic] cans containing them were opened with a key as you twisted it around the top, much like opening a can of sardines until the hissing sound told you to carefully pull open the top. Cans of balls had no plastic top, as now is the norm. On- court coaching in college matches was not allowed, although you could sometimes spot coaches whispering through the fence. For all of our matches in 1970 I wore a coat and tie, as did the opposing coach. The varsity courts at Navy [and all of the IVY League schools [except Pennsylvania] were clay courts. The only school with an indoor facility was Harvard, which had three clay courts in their Palmer-Dixon facility, a building with a curved roof to accommodate lobs. The courts were more than slippery, as it was difficult to monitor proper watering, and visiting teams left with bloody knees and elbows from falling down. There were no chairs on each court except for umpire chairs, if they existed. There were no chair umpires, and in the event of an argument, the home coach was the designated referee. Surprisingly, there were fewer disputes in that era and overall a better sense of sportsmanship. Perhaps today many coaches feel absolved of the responsibility to ensure that their players behave with integrity, allowing the officials to provide this oversight. Certainly, there are more disputes and disagreements.

Everyone played with wooden rackets, usually strung with gut. Most players had only two or three rackets, as strings did not break at anywhere the frequency of today's polyester strings, as the grid was much tighter in a 70 square inch head[most of today's frames run from 95 to 110 square inches], limiting the wear from cross and main strings rubbing against each other. Many players kept a smaller hand towel tucked partially into their shorts right where their hand would be to take care of a slippery grip. This took care of the constant delays we see today for a player to go to the towel behind the court. I remember using a rosin bag which I kept in my right pocket so that I could slip my hand there and make it immediately dry. Almost no one used sunscreen. All players wore white clothes. Many schools had the school color trimmed around the collar or sleeve, but almost as many wore Fred Perry or Lacoste shirts and shorts without any designation of school. A dual match was the best of three sets in singles[6 matches] and doubles following the singles[3]. We used regular scoring with no tie-breakers. It was not unusual for a match have a score like 7-9, 8-6, 10-8. Dual matches could take six hours, as one especially long singles match could hold up two doubles matches from starting if the participants played on different doubles teams. Teams did not travel with entourages. On site there were no SIDs[sports information directors], trainers, videographers, etc.

―――

The difference between the old ball player and the new ball player is the jersey. The old ball player cared about the name on the front [the team]. The new ball player cares about the name on the back [his own].

Steve Garvey

―――

There were no college rankings. Conferences were strictly geographical, which made more sense than today's system, which is based more on money and television contracts than anything else. Rivalries seemed more passionate. It would have been unthinkable then for schools like Texas and Texas A&M not to play each other, as happens today. The NCAA Championships rotated annually and included individual play only. The NCAA champion was determined by points earned as a result of winning individual matches. There was a very large[256 players with some byes] singles tournament as well as doubles[128 teams with byes]. No team could enter more than 4 players in singles and 2 teams in doubles. They did not have to be the same players. The academic calendar then, as noted earlier, ended in June. The NCAA Championships sometimes competed with Wimbledon for players, as it ended in mid-June. Former professional star and world top-ten player Barry MacKay once told me that he passed on the NCAA tournament to play Wimbledon in its place. Michigan's Coach Murphy was not pleased. There was no open tennis, as we know it today, so there was no conflict between amateur and professional status. The first open event took place at Wimbledon in 1968. It took a few years for open tennis to begin to resemble today's product. Some of the best players in the world played college tennis and played the tour events as amateurs during the summer. In the late 1960s UCLA featured Arthur Ashe and Charlie Pasarell, while USC boasted Stan Smith and Bob Lutz. These four were also the heart and soul of the US Davis Cup squad. All were among the world's top players while they were in college.

~ Cross Court Reflection ~

Get your eyes off where you've been and back on where you are going.

Billy Cox

1971 NCAA Tournament at Notre Dame

My first NCAA tournament took place in 1971 at, of all places, Notre Dame. My Navy team finished 21st there in a field that included Jimmy Connors [#3 at UCLA], Roscoe Tanner, Dick Stockton, Brian Gottfried, Harold Solomon, Eddie Gibbs, Freddie McNair, Sandy Mayer, and a couple of Northern Illinois players [Tim and Tom Gullickson] that not many people had heard of. All of these players made into the ATP top ten or won grand slam events after college. USC's Dennis Ralston and Rafael Osuna had won the Wimbledon men's doubles years earlier as freshmen. The individual nature of the championships carried drama lacking in today's individual NCAAs, as each individual victory added a point to the team total. The best teams were much better than today's and if Stanford's #4 upset UCLA's #1 in the round of 32, for example, the ramifications were huge. Large crowds cheering enthusiastically quickly gathered around a court on which a highly seeded player fell behind in a match which could impact the team standings. A second or third round meeting in the draw between the Stanford #2 and the UCLA #4 became great drama, as a team championship might be on the line.

My first ITA[then it was the ITCA-Intercollegiate Tennis Coaches Association] meeting lasted less than an hour. The most important function of the ITCA, it seemed, was to select the All-America team of 12 players. As a young coach I was just happy to be in the room and did not open my mouth. The most visible coaches: USC's George Toley, UCLA's Glenn Bassett, Stanford's Dick Gould, Trinity's Clarence Mabry, and Georgia's Dan Magill. The organization in no way resembled that of today, created by then-Princeton coach David Benjamin. There were no college grand slam events, no coaches conventions, no team and individual awards, and nothing near the cache' and awareness that today's ITA holds. As I look back on my early years I feel fortunate to have coached at a time when the three most important names in college tennis's history were also coaching. They were David Benjamin, who transformed the ITA - and college tennis - into the vibrant and dynamic organization we see today; Dick Gould, the greatest coach in the history of college tennis, who taught us all that excellence was not only possible, but expected; and Dan Magill, the greatest promoter of college tennis - and a pretty darn good coach himself. As I have already mentioned, it was Benjamin who essentially created today's ITA, adding team and individual rankings, the ITA Summer Circuit, all of the Grand Slam events, the many national and regional ITA awards, the ITA Coaches Convention, and even the very rules that govern us today. Gould taught us how to promote on our campuses, recruit the best players, ensure that our teams demonstrated good sportsmanship, and simply did everything the right way. Add Magill to the mix for his vision for college tennis and the NCAA Championships. He took a group of courts on the Georgia campus and built them into a tremendous facility that crowds 6,000 barking and screaming Bulldog fans into Henry Field Stadium and paints a tennis tapestry like no other. Ever the gentile Southern gentleman, Magill thought of every detail, from providing host sororities for each of the competing teams, to ensuring that the newspapers and other media outlets made the NCAAs bigger than other athletic events competing for your attention, be it the Atlanta Braves, the NBA playoffs, or anything else that could possibly take attention away from his tournament. He would even give you a personal tour of the ITA Hall of Fame, and proudly mention that he convinced Kenny Rogers to provide the funding for it. His former players remain intensely loyal to this day.

———⊸◦⊶———

The final test of a leader is that he leaves behind him, in other men, the will and the conviction to carry on.

Walter Lippman

———⊸◦⊶———

A further comparison of college tennis today with its forerunner during the early 1970's would be remiss without examining the coaches. Today's coaches are much better paid, and most competitive staffs include a full-time assistant and volunteer coach, as NCAA regulations allow only one paid assistant. The volunteer can earn an income from camps, private lessons, and clinics or racket stringing, but not be paid directly by the school.. Other assets today include teams' access to sports psychologists, dieticians, and pretty much anything that will positively affect performance, diet and massages included. Current teams travel better than their predecessors and eat at better restaurants. It was the norm in the sixties and seventies for an entire team to cram into a van and drive five or more hours to compete. On the way back a McDonald's meal might supply the evening's sustenance. Now, at least among 'Power Five" schools, most teams fly such distances and those that drive do so in a large bus where they can spread out for comfort, as the trickle-down money from the modern television contracts has, at last made its way to the Olympic sports. Technology has impacted team morale and spirit today, as compared to the 1960's and 1970's. Shortly after getting comfortable in his/her seat, today's player will often don headphones or open a laptop and be swept off to another world. Their predecessors had no such distractions and spent hours discussing the just-completed match, or other team issues. Better team morale was the by-product by necessity and better communication was the key.

Teams today benefit from the television and shoe/apparel contracts that are commonplace and related to football and basketball. "Power Five" schools have a significant competitive advantage due to the lucrative TV contracts of their respective conferences. Some college matches today are televised. The USTA, led by the imagination and persistence of former Penn State star Virgil Christian has led the way in an effort to see the sport garner more media attention. Coaches today have access to the athletic department's promotions group which assists in drawing larger crowds with advertising and give-aways. This was extremely rare during the seventies and eighties. Magill and Gould led the way for the rest of us. On a typical weekend when Stanford was scheduled to play USC and UCLA at home, Gould scheduled the #3-6 singles matches outdoors in the afternoon. Shortly thereafter the #1, #2, singles and doubles matches moved indoors where two carpet courts had been installed on the floor of Maples Pavilion, Stanford's basketball arena. Crowds of 7,000- 8,000 then watched the top two players duke it out to settle the outcome. It was not unusual for each of these teams to have ATP top 100 players on their respective squads. What a statement for college tennis that provided! It didn't hurt things that these same players would later battle deep into the later rounds of ATP events. Many soon-to-be professionals stayed all four years before joining the Tour.

Dan Magill wearing Notre Dame tennis shirt. Georgia fans will not believe this, but I was able to coerce college tennis's greatest promoter into posing in one of our team shirts. Rumor has it that Magill immediately took a shower.

MIT and a Hard Fought Match

Looking back like this brings an amazing memory to mind. It illustrates that even in DIII tennis, the matches are as hard-fought as those in DI. I left Navy in 1984 to become the Director of Tennis/Head Professional at the Wellesley Country Club as well as the men's tennis and squash coach at MIT. The logic behind the move was simple: we had four children, and the oldest, Jackie, was entering high school. I simply did not make enough money at Navy to be able to send each of them to the college of their choice. My goals at MIT were different. Instead of beating Army every year, I wanted MIT to contend for a Division III National Championship. I learned quickly that I was no less competitive, nor were the better DIII coaches, and began the task of building a nationally competitive team. On our spring break, I was able to schedule Navy [a trip down memory lane and also good competition], Washington College [one of the top DIII teams] and Swarthmore, another DIII power. The Washington College team was the fruit of the efforts of Dr. Fred Wyman, who put his heart and soul into their quest for excellence and would, in fact, win the DIII NCAAs a few years later. At that time only six teams made the NCAA tournament in DIII, so beating the "Sho'men" was the best hope for us to really make some noise.

Unless you try to do something beyond which have already mastered, you will never grow.

Ralph Waldo Emerson

The match began with a great level of play and an even higher level of competitiveness. This was every bit as competitive as any DI match, as the stakes were high and emotions were there for everyone to see. Players were flying around the court and cries of "Come on!" echoed after each seemingly impossible shot. All of the matches were tightly contested, so much so that when it was time for doubles the sky was beginning to darken and the score stood at 3-3. Accordingly, we immediately began the doubles, then in best-of-three set format, hoping for straight set finishes. At a certain point it became too dark to see. Washington had no lights or indoor courts at the time and the ability to finish with a team winner seemed impossible. Despite the inevitability of an unfinished match, players and coaches alike wanted desperately to find a way to see this great effort to a fair conclusion. I went over to Fred and made a half-hearted suggestion to have all of the spectators - there were hundreds in attendance - drive their cars in a circle surrounding the courts and leave their headlights on high beam. We agreed to try it. It worked - sort of! The lights were somewhat sufficient to see the ball and rallies from the baseline were possible, but when anyone hit a lob the ball immediately went into the great, black hole of the dark sky. No one could see the ball after it disappeared into the darkness, so players would have to wait for it to come into view, sometimes only recognizing its presence by the sound it made hitting the courts. So the strategy was obvious - lob the first ball possible and hope that it hit one of the opposing players as it came down. As ridiculous as this sounds, it was the best way to win. The keys to victory lay in being able to lob successfully.

I imagine that the spectators had to be laughing as the ridiculous scene played out, but both teams were competing ferociously. Unfortunately for us, Washington won the match, but I can recall it today like it was last week. Many years later Tim Gray, the men's coach at Bradley University at the time, drove to South Bend to observe the workout of a local player I had been coaching. After we finished hitting Tim and I caught up and began talking about humorous former experiences in coaching. Guess what? Tim had played for Washington that day and we had a blast conjuring up memories from that experience, both agreeing that it was truly the most surrealistic thing in tennis either of us had experienced. The tennis world seems to have no bounds. Coaching college tennis might be many things, but boring is not one of them.

~ Cross Court Reflection ~

Laughter is the jam on the toast

of life.

Diane Johnson

Answering the Bell

Too many people overvalue what they are not and undervalue what they are.

Malcolm Forbes

When I arrived at Notre Dame, it did not take me long to realize the importance of the practices that came just before we opened the season. We began the season with a routine that had our players arrive the week before classes began in January. Our players took up residence in Ivy Court, a hotel within walking distance to our indoor facility. I assigned roommates and practices began, using all six of our indoor courts. We went at it hard, twice per day and for a week. In the mornings we focused on technique and drilling, while the afternoon sessions were all about competitive play, be it singles or doubles. Mornings typically included lots of transition work; approach/pass, defending with the slice backhand, and finishing at the net were among the things that took the greatest chunks of time. Attacking the second serve was also a favorite theme of mine and I could not ask someone to risk it in a tight match if I was not confident in its successful execution. In the afternoons we played lots of sets and by the week's end our guys were sick of facing each other and excited to get the opportunity to face off against someone from an opposing team. This opening week of practice gave me the chance to push hard when I needed to and to relax a bit when tempers began to flare. There were no classes yet, therefore no homework, no tests, and no academic stress. Most of all I loved watching our players become a team, and that is what almost always happened during the opening week of practice. Our guys were rooming with different teammates and getting to know even more than they had about each other. One of the highlights was a home-cooked meal at our house. My wife, Pat, cooked "spaghetti to die for" and our guys ate more in that evening than perhaps any other during the season.

Pat's contribution to our season was no small thing. She felt like the adopted mother of each of our players. She wanted to know as much as possible about all of them. She had gluten-free food for Greg Andrews and Blas Moros [also dairy free]. To any reader who is entertaining a career in coaching I have the following advice: marry a great woman, because you will need her at various times during the season - when the team underperforms, after a difficult loss, or when you begin to doubt yourself. Pat has always been my greatest asset. I still remember waiting in the anteroom for my interview to become the head coach at Navy as a 23 year old who desperately wanted the job, but had no clue about its demands and responsibilities. Pat and I were just back from our honeymoon and were holding hands when the Navy director of athletics, Capt. J. O. "Bo" Coppedge asked me to come in and meet the Naval Academy's Athletic Board of Control, a group of officers and faculty as well as successful people from outside the Naval Academy. This group would decide if I were to be offered the position. It seems odd now, but Pat got up with me and we walked in together, still holding hands, as if she were part of the interview. The all-male Board must have been somewhat taken aback, but no one asked her to leave, so she joined me in my interview for the next 90 minutes. Capt. Coppedge swore through my entire career that he would never have hired me if Pat had not joined me in that interview. I witnessed more than a few divorces among my friends in the coaching profession and to this day realize that Pat deserves much of the credit for any successes I have had in my career.

Having established how important a spouse can be, let me tell you that there are times you do not want to say the wrong thing. In 1972 our Navy team had flown to Colorado Springs to play the Air Force Academy, certainly an important match for me as I began my career. Pat was pregnant with Rob, our second child, but he was not scheduled to arrive for five more weeks. Beating Air

Force in Colorado Springs was a difficult assignment, as we played on clay courts and Air Force had fast hard courts, not to mention close to 6,000 feet of altitude that made it next to impossible to lob. Their guys closed in on the net and we really had our hands full through a very difficult and hard fought 5-4 victory that left me as excited as I was out of breath. After the match I called home to give Pat the good news, only to learn that she had gone into labor and was in the hospital preparing to prematurely give birth. I called the hospital and was patched through to the labor room, and she answered the phone. I was happy to learn that she was doing well, and Rob's birth was imminent. At that point, I said something like "That's great, Pat. Now let me tell you about the match today." Big mistake!!! Don't ever do that! I realized that I had not used very good judgment and spent the rest of the conversation trying to ensure that I would have a place to sleep when I returned.

To all prospective coaches: learn from your mistakes! If my telephone conversation from Colorado Springs had not sunk in, I made yet another error in judgment twenty years later in 1992. Our team had just beaten - in consecutive days - #7 Mississippi State, #3 Georgia [in Athens], and #1 USC - and would play Stanford the next day for the national championship. Was I excited? You bet your #*@!! I had forgotten that our daughter, Jackie, would graduate the next day from Notre Dame. Our plan was for me to fly back for that and to be there to share the day with her, as the odds against our advancing this far in the tournament were astronomically high. As I called Pat to give her the fantastic news that we had won, she asked if this meant that I would not be able to get back for Jackie's graduation. Of course not, I replied, reminding Pat that we were in the NCAA final, and I needed to be there to coach my team. She was obviously disappointed and told me that. My reply was something like "Don't spoil this for me. It is the greatest day of my life!" Wrong answer again!!! She said that she believed that weddings, births, and graduations might, in fact, comprise the greatest days of my life. I had done it again. I must say that I was able to talk with her later that evening and dig myself at least part of the way out of the 50-foot hole I had dug earlier. Words matter. We coaches do stupid things. Enough said.....

Off and Running ~ The Season Begins!

*Leadership does not always wear
the harness of compromise.*

Woodrow Wilson

January in South Bend means several things to me: cold weather, snow, and the beginning of a new season. Pre-season two-a-day practices were over. It was time to begin the season. There was tangible excitement in the air. This was a time when optimism runs high and our players could not wait to begin and compete against someone wearing colors other than our blue and gold. It was time to see if many of the things we worked on during the fall had become ingrained or whether we had to go back and regroup in certain areas. Classes had begun Jan. 15. Our guys had settled into the routine of attending class and then coming to practice. It was now time to see how good we could be. Our opening match pitted our squad against Marquette, coached by Steve Rodecap. I knew we could expect them to be aggressive, play pretty good doubles, and fight, but I expected to win, especially at home.

In the last two practices, we focused on poaching in our doubles combinations, and I felt we were ready. Finding the best possible doubles combinations was important for several reasons. The first is to maximize your strengths and mask your weaknesses. We had two players who volleyed especially well and were not afraid to poach [cut across on the return, gambling to cut it off and put the ball away]. I needed to place them with players who re-turned serve well and were a little passive at net in order to provide the balance and punch needed. Greg Andrews, our best singles player, had been dragged into college doubles kicking and screaming. He had a great forehand and returned serve pretty well, but lacked natural aggressive instincts at the net. Spencer Talmadge was his opposite. He had great doubles instincts and moved early and often at the net, giving him the ability to cash in on Greg's returns. This seemed like a no-brainer, but there was one slight problem. One of them had to become a vocal leader, and they were both pretty quiet. Ryan and I spoke with Greg and asked him to assume this role, even though he was a year younger. Getting Spencer [the "Bear"] to say more than a few words took him out of his comfort zone. We also wanted tangible communication after every point, as each of them tended to look disappointed after any miscue. Our rule was to either speak, bump a fist, or touch rackets after every point to keep them both upbeat.

A freshman, Alex Lawson, had great doubles instincts. He was athletic, anxious to move, and always seemed to be in the right place on a doubles court. I believed he could become an All American in time. He proved me right by reaching the NCAA semi-finals in doubles as a senior before embarking on a professional career. Billy Pecor, on the other hand, had tons of firepower from the baseline and could take the racket out of your hands on his returns, but was a reluctant volleyer. Billy was also pretty quiet by nature, but could hit a backhand through a brick wall. Because Alex was outgoing and emotional instinctively, we solved a similar problem by pairing them at #2. We were a bit uncertain about #3 doubles and decided to open with Ryan Bandy, a junior who had worked his way up the ladder over his three years and looked like he could help us in both singles and doubles. We partnered him with Matt Dooley, another junior who had a well-rounded game, but had been inconsistent in the past, as he appeared ready for this role and had worked hard to earn it.

As the doubles began, I could see that we would win the doubles point because we took charge at #1 and #3 immediately. We won both matches 8-2 and #2 did not finish, as the point was clinched. College tennis was in turmoil about whether or not to end the remaining doubles after the point was clinched. Many argued that the air had been let out of the building when the point was concluded and fans would grow bored waiting for a meaningless conclusion in the final doubles. This debate would continue for years, but for now we had decided to play it this way-ending the competition as the point clinched. There is a five minute break between doubles and singles. Typically, both teams retreat to a quiet place and quickly go over the singles match-ups. While doubles differs greatly from singles, it is possible for the doubles players to pass on observations to singles opponents as to how to read the serve or any obvious tendencies or weaknesses. The coach who wins the doubles point starts the singles knowing he only needs to split the singles to win the match, while the other coach needs to find four singles wins for a path to victory.

In matters of style, swim with the current. In matters of principle, stand like a rock.

Thomas Jefferson

My confidence in our team was justified, as we swept all six singles, but not without some hiccups along the way. Marquette had a very strong #1 player in Danil Mamalat, a guy who could be creative and hit with power from the baseline and had a very good forehand. Greg was tested, but won 4 and 4 [tennis vernacular for 6-4, 6-4] because he was quicker than Mamalat and able to handle his offensive salvos. Blas Moros, Quintin Monaghan, and Bandy all won in straight sets, as did Pecor, after squeaking through a first set tie-breaker. Wyatt McCoy, on the other hand, won a third set super-breaker, after dropping the first set. Wyatt is as quick as anyone in college tennis, but relies too much on his defensive speed to get him out of trouble. He cannot continue to allow opponents to take charge and needs to initiate some offense himself. This will be his challenge for the season and it will determine whether or not he can help take us to elite status.

210

With a win in hand, our guys go to grab a quick bite to eat before returning for an evening match to face Western Illinois, a team coached by former Notre Dame #1 Chris Kane. Kane is a familiar face to me as I remember recruiting him for my Navy team in the 1970's. Chris took a scholarship to Notre Dame and played #1 singles. After a stellar college career Chris became an attorney and had a successful practice, but missed tennis. He recently took over the reins at Western Illinois and called me in the fall to see if we could play. Our schedule was full, but I agreed to "double up" to play WIU. We expected a relatively easy match and that is pretty much what happened. This enabled me to get Dooley and Michael Frederica into the singles and both won in straight sets. One of the frustrating things about coaching college tennis is that once a match begins there is no way to substitute another player. In sports like football, basketball, and soccer, a coach can reward a hard- working player with some playing time after the team builds a big lead. If things go south, he can always re-insert the starter to restore order, but the player who got into the game will feel justly rewarded. In tennis there are no substitutions. With a limited number of playing dates available and a challenging schedule, I find it difficult to be able to adequately reward our non-starters with opportunities to show what they can do. I remember my own college days and how frustrating it was as a basketball bench warmer who found it difficult to score from where I was sitting. Today, Michael and Matt can go back to their dorms and discuss their matches. They will work even harder in the coming days because of this positive reinforcement and their other teammates who did not get to play will know that their own chances will come. The coach who is inattentive to team morale and chemistry is looking for trouble as the season progresses. The softer portion of our schedule was over. The matches would now get tougher.

Anyone can hold the helm while the sea is calm.

Pubilius Syrus

Our next match came quickly, as Northwestern arrived to play us only three days later. These two schools had a great deal in common. Both had very high admissions standards and were ranked academically among the top twenty universities in the US. Less than 120 miles separated our campuses and we recruited many of the same players. Because of this I felt some extra importance was in play in this match. The "Cats" coach was Arvid Swan. Arvid was a friend and someone who had played against us in his Michigan days as an undergrad. I felt, and still do, that he was one of the better coaches in the country and that his team was sneaking in here below the radar. I knew the match would be tough, as it usually was. Nonetheless, I thought we could win.

This match was a war from the get-go. Northwestern played very intelligent doubles. At #1 they had Spencer Wolf, someone we had recruited and a great ball-striker from both sides, paired with an Israeli, Fedor Baev. They were aggressive and led 7-6 after the point ended. At #2 Sid Balaji and Raleigh Smith formed an unlikely, yet outstanding pair. Balaji was a poor volleyer and his backhand was vulnerable, but he had a howitzer for a forehand that could knock the racket out of your hands and a serve that clocked in at about 130 mph. He played the deuce court and ran around every backhand to crush forehands. Our team, Lawson and Pecor, needed to make a very high percentage of first serves to keep Balaji from getting forehands. We did not execute well in this regard. Smith was a great complement to Balaji, as he was very consistent returning and made almost no errors. When Balaji served he stood almost on the center service line in the deuce court and all of the way over in the ad court, thus ensuring that he would be hitting most balls as forehands. He did not serve and volley, something that is no longer a big surprise in college tennis today. They broke us once and served out the match to win 8-5. Balaji's serves and forehands were too big for us to handle and Smith's backhand returns were "money." In the last game at 30-all Balaji missed his first serve and Alex ran around to crush a forehand, giving us break point. They won the next point, giving us as a no-ad break point. Normally without thinking I would want Billy to receive, as his ability to crush returns is the best on our team, but since Alex had successfully run around and won the previous deuce point I expected them to spin in a medium-paced first serve to avoid a repeat sequence. As I told Alex to take the return[in no-ad scoring, the receiving team has its choice for the return], Billy became very upset, not understanding my reasons and perhaps thinking I had lost faith in his abilities. I relented and he took the return, but missed and the match ended. I knew that a private discussion was needed, as his reaction hurt our team. The difficult thing about on-court coaching in college is that you have almost no time to explain things and your player needs to trust your reasoning. I have to remember that our guys are not robots and feelings are easy to damage. Similarly, they need to trust me in the moment.

Having lost the doubles point, we began singles play and the competition was ferocious. We have a decent crowd and they are making plenty of noise. College tennis desperately wants to increase its relevance on campus and one of the ways to do this is to draw large crowds. At some of the venues we play- Illinois, North Carolina, Texas, Louisville, etc.- the crowds can get pretty rowdy and it is up to the host coach[that would be me tonight] to ensure that there are no inappropriate and personal comments or chants aimed at the visiting team. Given that some of the crowd will not be familiar with tennis etiquette, it is a lot to ask for me to be coaching and monitoring our crowd and a dilemma for our sport. Yet if we turn spectators away, they will not return, so this is truly a delicate balancing act, and one that screams today for attention.

Three matches finished in straight sets, albeit close ones. Blas Moros took out Smith 7-5, 7-5 and I am proud of him, as Raleigh Smith is a tough competitor and very smart player. Ryan Bandy recovered from an early break to beat Mihir Kumar 7-5,6-3. Kumar is a guy we really wanted in the recruiting process. He has great instincts around the net, something not developed in many of today's junior players. He has an explosive forehand, but doesn't like to come over his backhand. The solution: get in on that backhand. Bandy agrees and turns the match around by pressuring Kumar to hit passing shots. Seeing this begin to work, I now move to Monaghan's court where Balaji looks simply too strong for Quentin, leaving the match tied at 2-2 as third sets began at #1,#4, and #5. Whichever team won two of these would walk away with the victory. The tension was building and everyone felt it. Alex Pasareanu's all court skills took out Pecor while Andrews' forehand was too much for Wolf. We stood now tied at 3-3 with the match clearly in the hands of Wyatt McCoy. Chris Jackman, his opponent, is a senior who has been there before and his aggressiveness was the deciding factor, as he won the match for Northwestern 3-6, 6-0,6-4. Wyatt's speed and defensive skills were overmatched today. He is going to have to play up in the court and attack at least some of the time if we are going to achieve much. He will not want to hear this, but without adding more punch to his forehand and overall game he will encounter some rough sledding ahead. This was a tough loss, as we had won the previous eight against the Wildcats. There is little time to cry about it, as we leave in two days for the ITA Kick-off Weekend. While I begin to feel sorry for myself, I am reminded of the words of former ND football coach Lou Holtz, who often said "Don't tell me about your problems. 90% of the people you know don't care and the other 10% are glad you have them."

~ Cross Court Reflection ~

I cannot give you the formula for success, but I can give you the formula for failure which is: Try to please everybody.

Herbert Swope

ITA Kick-Off Weekend

They call it coaching, but it's leading.
You do not just tell them - you
show them the reasons.

Vince Lombardi

The ITA created the National Team Indoors for the top twenty teams in the 1980's. Every coach wants to see his/her team at Team Indoors, but the field is highly selective and was based on overall ranking and geographic representation. Not too many years ago the ITA Board of Directors and Operating Committee discussed this problem. SMU's Carl Neufeld offered an interesting solution which was adopted and has been a godsend for competitive programs. The ITA has a draft in June to select the field of 60 teams. The top 15 ranked teams will serve as hosts for four- team events that send the winners to the Team Indoors. The 16th team is the host university. There are 15 #1 seeds and a like number of #2, #3, and #4 seeds that travel to those qualifying events. As one of the #2 seeds[teams that finished last year ranked between #16-32] I chose to take our squad to Oklahoma. John Roddick's Sooners were on the move. In a relatively short time he had taken them from non-NCAA Tournament status to the elite eight just two seasons ago. While I respected what John had done, I knew that we had beaten them a year ago in this same event at the University of Illinois. I was hoping that our squad would remember that 4-0 victory and go into the anticipated re-match with some confidence. As I watched the draft play out online last summer I saw that we would play Harvard first with the winner taking on the OU/Mem-

215

phis winner, likely to be Oklahoma. Memphis was no slouch either, and in May would make the NCAA Sweet 16, but I am getting ahead of myself. I need to remember my own advice and enjoy the journey.

———⊷∘⊶———

It is the journey that matters. Learning is more important than the test. Practice well and the games will take care of themselves.

Tony Dungy

———⊷∘⊶———

One of the things that can drive a coach crazy is how his team handles the college, or ITA, rankings. We understand, all too well, that the best example of your ranking was described by William Shakespeare in the expression "much ado about nothing." Our rankings come out weekly during the season and can interfere with a team's performance. Rankings evolved for purely promotional purposes and have virtually no relation to how well a team is going to play. Thinking about your ranking is 'outcome oriented' and can set you up for a poor performance. Performances are best handled through 'process goals.' Because we are ranked higher than Harvard and handled them in the fall, I worry that our players will enter the match with a false sense of security and, when things become competitive, as inevitably they always do, our players will not embrace the competition as the challenge that it is and will instead see it as a threat. I warn our players about focusing on the right things frequently. Our ranking is certainly not on that list. Nobody wants to 'defend' anything and typically the higher ranked team feels this need. We all compete better when we are in 'attack' mode.

A good example of this occurred in April, 2002. We were having a very good spring and had seen our ranking climb into the middle of the top ten. The next opponent was Michigan, a talented team that had been bitten by the injury bug and had badly under-achieved. As we sat down for our pre-game meal at our hotel, our #1 player, Javier Taborga, joined us with a smile on his face. He had just checked the ITA rankings and seen that our ranking had climbed to #4 and announced this to the team. I was ready to strangle him! That is the last thing a coach wants his players to ponder before a match and I immediately told our guys to forget about the ranking and prepare for the Wolverines, who now had regained the services of all of their players, healthy for the first time all year. Ranked #43, Michigan, on paper, looked like an easy win, but I knew better. Unfortunately, I was correct and we dropped a 4-3 heartbreaker that day in Ann Arbor. The three hour ride back to South Bend seemed to take eight hours. Our players finally understood why it was important to ignore a team's ranking and instead focus on competing well, controlling those things over which we had control. When we later faced them again, in the first round of the NCAA tournament, we defeated them 4-0. Another lesson learned.

Today, Harvard is coached by the veteran and well-liked Dave Fish, one of my closest friends and someone with whom I shared many confidences. If ever there was a perfect marriage it is Fish and Harvard, his alma mater. Our friendship went back to my Navy days and led to my accepting the tennis professional position in summers at Boston's Wellesley Country Club, due largely to his recommendation. Our teams had played only a few times. Both of us had difficulties with the natural contrast between friend and foe. While Harvard was the best team on the east coast, I expected to beat them. I knew that they were very well coached, as Harvard assistant Andrew Reub was an outstanding complement to Dave. I remember recruiting Reub, but knew he was likely to end up at Harvard. We were healthy and optimistic when we arrived in Norman. I saw Dave at the site and he informed me that his top player would not play against us due to an injury. My confidence soared, and I began to anticipate Sunday's final against Oklahoma. Big mistake!

From the moment the match began, I sensed that we were in trouble. In sports in general, and certainly in college tennis, there seems to be extra pressure when you play someone whom you respect but is ranked below you. You focus on the expectations of others, and that is never a good thing. Expectations can really play with minds. I believe that our guys felt pressure because they knew Harvard was a man short and we were expected to win. Harvard played like they were using house money and competed far better than I had anticipated. Not having a full roster took pressure off their shoulders. In a match eerily similar to the Northwestern contest just three days earlier, we found ourselves locked in another 3-3 tie with all hopes riding once again on Wyatt McCoy. Harvard had taken the doubles point from us and put us on our heels. The Oklahoma courts were arranged with three courts on each side of their indoor facility, just like our own. It makes the most sense for each coach to take one side, so you are not running back and forth. Ryan had Greg, Quentin, and Wyatt, while I had Blas, Billy, and Ryan Bandy, who won quickly in straight sets. Blas was not as aggressive as he normally is from the ground and lost in straight sets to Alex Steinroder, an outstanding freshman. Billy played Casey McMaster, a 6'6" freshman whom we had recruited seriously and who could not really hurt Billy from the backcourt. McMaster was quite good moving forward and difficult to pass when he could get in on us. Therefore, Billy needed to get into the net and force Casey to pass, but once again he showed a reluctance to move forward. The best way to keep someone off the net is to get there first yourself. Billy looked downtrodden the entire match and never really asserted himself. He was playing not to lose, rather than to win in a match he should have won, as McMaster looked injured and, in fact, played only in doubles for the rest of the season. As disappointed as I was with the results on my side I quickly raced to the other courts where Wyatt was once more in a tight three setter with Nicholas Mahlangu. Both players were giving it their all. Wyatt appeared to have better skills, but once more was in defensive mode, allowing himself to be pushed around. He reached match point, but was afraid to pull the trigger and take the initiative, wanting Mahlangu to lose rather than trying to win. Once more Wyatt's reluctance to be more aggressive cost him and he lost 4-6, 7-6,7-5. This needs to become a point of emphasis for him as we move forward into the meat of the season. As someone who served and volleyed almost all of the time when I was playing, it was baffling to me that I could not pass on some aggressiveness to our guys. They certainly had the talent to assert themselves more often.

————⊙————

Talent sets the floor. Character sets the ceiling.

Bill Belichick

————⊙————

As I shook hands with Dave afterwards, he could see that I was devastated and offered words of encouragement, but the well-intended remarks fell on deaf ears. I had fully expected to be 4-0 at this point with a chance to make it to Team Indoors if we beat Oklahoma the next day. Not only that, but I had watched some of Memphis's match earlier and felt that they were better than Harvard. This would be borne out at season's end when they reached the "Sweet 16" at Illinois. This is the point where I am going to try to tell you what a coach feels in vulnerable moments like this one. Logic simply has no place in this discussion. Not only was I crushed and disappointed, but I really felt numb and very heavy. I had no appetite and simply did not want to talk to anyone. Losing can do funny things to you. I knew that this was my final year and I had really wanted to go out in style. The team I had felt was a top 25 squad now looked to me like even making the NCAA tournament might be a stretch for them. Knowing this I tried my best to put a positive spin on things to keep the team from feeling my pain, but I doubt that I succeeded. The funny thing about sports is that there is no gray. Everything is black or white. You win or you lose.

~ Cross Court Reflection ~

There is no try.

Yoda

Bouncing Back and Faith Restored

The next morning, I awoke feeling slightly better but quite resigned to the beating I expected to be administered by Memphis, a team almost entirely made up of international players. They had looked pretty good to me against Oklahoma. They had some big hitters and played with lots of emotion. Their coach, Paul Goebel, had done a very good job with them. As we passed coming into the Oklahoma indoor facility, I told him as much. I have to believe that he expected to win. The funny thing about sports is that you simply never know what to expect. We had a good warm-up and began the doubles holding our own. Our #3 doubles team, Bandy-Dooley, who yesterday could not have hit the water while standing on the beach, jumped out quickly and cruised to an 8-1 win. Yesterday they [Dooley and Bandy] had lost 8-0 to Harvard. Go figure!

When you look at a scorebook and peruse the scores, you have no clue as to what really happened without being there. In reality, that 8-1 win at third doubles put tremendous pressure on both of Memphis's other two teams. We only had to split the doubles to claim the point; they needed both. In fact, both matches went to 8-6 and Lawson-Pecor clinched it for us. Winning that doubles point brought us back from the near-dead and breathed vibrant life into all of us. Pecor, who yesterday had been hanging his head with a 'woe-is-me' look, came out vocal and firing and was one of the first to finish in a 7-5,6-1 thrashing. He looked like an ATP professional. McCoy, who had just lost two third set heartbreakers, dropped only five games and looked like a completely different player in a 6-2,6-3 victory. Thank God for the resilience and short memories of youth! Monaghan clinched it for us, as he downed the highly ranked former ITF junior player, Lukas Vrnak 7-6,6-2 by keeping the ball deep enough to avoid Vrnak's offensive salvos and just out of his strike zone, something necessary against great ball strikers. The other three matches were stopped to allow Oklahoma and Harvard to prepare for their battle, but all were close. Moros had just split sets with Brit Joe Salisbury and Andrews was even in the third with Connor Glennon. Michael Moore had subbed in at #6 for Bandy, who was injured in the doubles, and was trailing 6-7,2-1. While he had not won, he had stayed alive in a close contest, putting even more pressure on the Memphis players. We had done it! As I contemplated the rest of our schedule I knew we were capable of some good things. I could wait a few days before cutting my wrists. I could feel the self-imposed pressure lift from my shoulders. I had worried myself sick for no reason. It was not the first time this had happened and would not be the last.

Don't spend time beating on a wall hoping to change it into a door.

Coco Chanel

As I indicated earlier, it is nearly impossible for me to explain the mood swings that a coach endures. I walked into the Oklahoma indoor facility this morning looking and feeling like someone on suicide watch. I left the facility with a song in my throat and love in my heart. How can this be? I am close to my 69th birthday, hopefully old enough to have developed a healthy sense of perspective. I am retiring at the season's end. How can someone who appears to be normal [me] allow such swings of emotion to control himself? I have absolutely no answers for those questions because logic does not seem to be involved. This is the roller coaster of emotions with which I have lived for 44 years as a head coach. In most of those years there were no incentive clauses in my contract. I have always had the loving wife and family waiting for me at home, yet there seems to be some achievement-driven force that mandates that I measure up to my own personal standards that I simply MUST meet. Is my need for approval that off-kilter? It is not simply result-based, as there have been matches my team played in which we played well, but lost that did not bother me. Similarly, we have won at times and I have reacted with disappointment when the team did not reach the standard I had set. Keep this in mind, as we may come back to it later.

We now had six days to get ready for a very good Duke team. Duke became a consistent top 10-15 team in the early 1990's when Jay Lapidus took over. A former ATP top 30 player in his own right, Lapidus had recruited well, as he had much to sell - good weather, a great academic standing, terrific facilities, a national name, and a great conference, which he quickly began to dominate until Brian Boland's explosive arrival at Virginia. For twenty plus seasons the Blue Devils had been outstanding. Lapidus had retired several years ago and was replaced by his more-than-able assistant, Ramsey Smith. Ramsey's pedigree was impeccable, as his father, Stan Smith, was a former Wimbledon and US Open champion and world #1 player. His mother, Margie, had also been a very good player at Princeton. Stan's performance in Davis Cup play against Romania remains to me the single most courageous achievement in US tennis history, slightly above that of Don Budge in 1938. There is no greater advocate for college tennis than Stan, who still values his USC experience under ITA Hall of Fame coach George Toley. I have gotten to know Stan pretty well through both the recruiting process and his work with the ITA. I had recruited Ramsey and his brother Trevor, but lost out on both. As the warm-ups began I congratulated Ramsey for a strong start to the season while we exchanged lineups. I realized that we were an underdog, but knew that our home courts at the Eck Tennis Pavilion had inspired us to upsets of many outstanding teams over the years. Their top player Henrique Cunha had been ranked as high as #1 in the college ranks and would be a tough out. At #3, Michael Redlicki was a big and very talented freshman who hit powerful groundstrokes and could be overwhelming when his serve was consistent. He had won the US Nationals in Kalamazoo in the 16-and-under category just two years ago, giving me an idea of how talented this Duke team can be. The Blue Devils looked like a top ten team. Additionally, Ramsey's influence would encourage great sportsmanship. Today's match would be interesting.

While the not-quite champs complain about officials, or field conditions, bad coaching decisions, or cheating opponents, champions get back to work. They take care of their own house: show up early, stay late, focus on the process, get 1% better each day.

John O'Sullivan

The match began with a hard fought doubles point, as we split the top two matches, but lost a squeaker at #3 8-6, giving Duke the momentum it needed for singles. Nonetheless we were pretty competitive. I can see that Duke's #2, Fred Saba, has an improved forehand and is coming forward more than I expected. We have beaten him in the past and I thought Blas could do it today, but Saba also is more aggressive than a year ago and wins in two tough sets. When Wyatt also goes down in consecutive sets, we are in a big hole, but fighting hard. Pecor wins the second set from Chris Mengel, a player we recruited hard several years ago. Mengel and Billy both are better on the backhand, but Mengel is the better mover. This one will not finish today. Bandy wins the second set by putting more air under the ball, as Jason Tahir can flat out drill his groundies as well as anyone in college. We need to vary the pace, spins, and depth of our shots today. Exchanging bullets with him is a doomed plan. At #1, Greg is playing as well as he can, but Cunha is just a little bit better. Both have massive forehands, but Cunha is a lefty, which takes away Greg's inside-out forehand and he falls in a real battle 6-4,6-4. Greg has always put pressure on himself, and today is no different. Getting him to relax has been problematic. He has worked very hard and now deserves to be ranked among the nation's elite players. We had agreed ahead of time to stop when the match is clinched, as Duke has a flight to catch. Quentin also was unable to finish, having battled Redlicki to the hilt, losing a first set tie-breaker 13-11. He led 3-2 in the second when play was suspended. The final score of 4-0 does little justice to the fact that we were in a position to possibly win all of the unfinished matches. I shake Ramsey's hand and wish him well. He is just the type of young coach for whom I would want my own son to play. He grew up with a great role model and it shows.

After the match we assemble in my office, as always, to examine what we did well and where we need to show improvement. I can see the disappointment in the faces of our players. I remind them that the day is not finished, as we will play IUPUI at 6 PM. While we missed an opportunity today, I saw some good things and believe we can still make an impact nationally if we clean up a few areas needing improvement. The evening match is predictably an easy one and I sit out Billy, Ryan, and Quentin, as all are nursing nagging injuries. This gives me a chance to play Michael Moore, Matt Dooley, and Michael Fredericka at nos. 4,5, and 6. Dooley and Moros are forced into third sets, but we sweep all of the matches. We are now 4-3 with a trip to East Lansing, MI next up.

On the Road

It is hard for even the best players
to continually commit actions to
helpful process point after point,
because we all have a mind that
is easily distracted.

Anthony Ross

As we prepare for Michigan State, I am as concerned about adjusting to the Spartan's indoor courts as I am for competing against their players. Having been there for several days during Regionals will help us adjust. My record against Michigan State is 25-1. I lost to them in my first year at Notre Dame, 1988. Despite this one-sided ledger I know that history has shown that our squad has struggled in matches there and barely come out with wins on numerous occasions. In 1993 I took a top ten[and NCAA elite eight] team into East Lansing feeling pretty confident, enough so that I left our All American Chuck Coleman out of the lineup. The NCAA has strict limits on the number of team and individual contests we could play and, knowing that I was returning 5 of 6 starters from an NCAA runner-up squad, I allowed some of our guys to enter extra events in the fall, knowing that each of them would be required to miss one contest. This match was one that I planned to use accordingly. I could not have predicted that we would lose our top returning player for the season when another All American, Andy Zurcher, severed a tendon in his wrist over Christmas vacation and missed his entire senior year. I also could not have predicted that Michigan State coach Gene Orlando would have his team playing at such a high level that evening. Even though it was 20 years earlier, the memory of that match was still strongly etched in my mind and the fear I felt watching our All American, Will Forsyth play for all the marbles in the third set against MSU's own All American, Mashiska Washington[brother of Michigan's Malavai Washington, a Wimbledon semi-finalist] was still palpable. Fortunately for us, Will settled down to play a controlling third set and clinch the win. I admired the way Will took over in the third set and dominated play with his explosive forehand. He had become a great college player by putting in the extra work required. Not everyone is similarly motivated.

───◦○◦───

The time will come when winter will ask you what you have been doing all summer.

Henry Clay

───◦○◦───

There were other examples, too, of close calls in East Lansing. In 1996, our #6, Andy Chmura fought off two match points at 5-2, 40-15 in the third set to come back and clinch another 4-3 battle. We also won 4-3 decisions in East Lansing in 1999, 2003, 2005, and 2008, so I was not taking the Spartans lightly. In fact the 2003 decision came down to a third set tie-breaker won by our Luis Haddock in a remarkable display of poise with everything hanging in the balance. Luis is now Dr. Haddock and proved to be one of Puerto Rico's most successful Davis Cup players. I have tried to figure out what seemed to bother us there, but never really came up with a legitimate answer. The lights are a bit dimmer than ours. The courts in the MSU indoor tennis center were normally pretty slick and fast, so we always used lots of just-opened balls in practices leading up to this match. I also felt that the officials were a little too interested in seeing the home team win, at times. In fact, as I returned from a trip to the bathroom in that 1993 match and the score 3-2 in matches in our favor, I passed the officials whose matches had finished and overheard one of them say, "We need to win both of these matches if we expect to win tonight." I commented, tongue in cheek, "Now you didn't really mean WE, did you?" The crowd also sat lower than normal there and some of our guys had trouble picking up the ball as the Spartans served on one side of the building. Whatever it was, I was expecting a tough match and made certain that our players were ready.

Right on cue, the doubles came down to #3, as we split the top two. At 7-6 on our advantage Matt Dooley hit a beautiful topspin backhand lob for a winner that clinched the doubles point. That was a huge momentum builder and we took it to them from there, winning 5 of the 6 singles. Billy Pecor had a tough evening and lost in straight sets, but our other guys won relatively easily in straight sets. The slick courts did not give Billy the time he needed to set up for his shots. Andrews led the way with a 6-2, 6-2 spanking of the Spartans' reliable Drew Lied. We had avoided one of the potential potholes on our schedule. I was personally touched as Michigan State coach Gene Orlando had the PA announcer read out a lengthy tribute to me during the introductions. He then presented me with a beautiful memento which now hangs in my office at home. It was as appreciated as it was unexpected. Next up....the Kentucky Wildcats in Lexington, KY.

~ Cross Court Reflection ~

The only thing that really matters in life is your relationships with other people.

George E. Valiant

A Close One in Lexington

Dennis Emery has done an extraordinary job coaching at Kentucky. While he is an opponent he is also a friend. He arrived at a place that celebrated basketball, but placed little value in the sport of tennis. The facilities he inherited were poor, at best. The SEC had become perhaps the strongest conference in the country, benefitting from the efforts of Georgia's Dan Magill and his very able successor Manny Diaz, LSU's Jerry Simmons, Tennessee's Mike DePalmer, Florida's Ian Duvenhage, and the successful recruiting efforts abroad by both Missippi's Billy Chadwick and his arch rival from Mississippi State, Andy Jackson. Add South Carolina's head coach, Kent DeMars, and you have the strongest conference in the country during the 1990's and early 2000's. Magill, DePalmer, and Simmons had retired, but the efforts of this group had taken the balance of power in the collegiate ranks away from the west coast[USC, UCLA, Stanford], as the SEC was truly the deepest conference in the country. Emery walked into a situation where no one seemed to care and rolled up his sleeves and went to work. His vision for Kentucky tennis was far different. Gradually he fund-raised millions and built a first class facility. He talked the USTA into bringing the National Interscholastics to campus every June. He worked with the ITF to begin an ITF event that would ensure that many of the world's top junior international players would play his event. Not stopping there he again fund-raised money to host his own professional event in the summers, a Challenger level tournament which delivered a high level of professional tennis to Lexington, increasing local interest in the sport. He also used his talents to organize the community to bring the ITA National Team Indoor Championships to nearby Louisville, knowing that, as the host school, his team would always be included in that elite event. Additionally he changed the surface of his indoor courts to mirror the lightning paced courts in Louisville which allowed his team the best chance to defeat one or two of the best teams there almost every year. His is a story which simply does not get told enough. He had not only boarded the SEC train of excellence, but was riding in first class. He had indeed won the conference championship to show that he more than belonged. His teams played with an abandon and aggressiveness that left no room for doubt.

A mind troubled by doubt cannot focus on the course to victory.

Arthur Golden

For years I have enjoyed exchanging views and stories with Dennis. Today, he told me another in the long line of unique things that seem to only happen in the SEC, the "wild west" of college tennis. He brought up Mike DePalmer, the now retired, but formerly charismatic coach at Tennessee. DePalmer had, in 1992, played and lost to Kentucky four times[dual matches, tournaments, etc.] before meeting them again in the SEC tournament. In one highly competitive match DePalmer began ranting at the official, who had rendered several decisions that favored Kentucky. With the team match still in the balance DePalmer began screaming at the official. He yelled, loud enough for all to hear "What do we have to do to win a point here? You have taken every decision from us, so here is everything else." DePalmer then took out his wallet and laid it on the umpire's chair, followed by his watch, his change, and his car keys. As he walked away from the surprised official, he turned and began taking off his shirt, yelling. "Here. You might as well take the shirt off my back, too!" As the match ended with yet another Kentucky victory, DePalmer and his assistant, Bill Henry, got the attention of Emery by waving white towels, indicating their surrender. Hang around Emery long enough and he is always good for stories like that one.

Last year's Kentucky team reached the "elite eight" at the NCAA's, and Dennis had accepted an administrator's position as an assistant athletic director. He had also seen that his protege, Cedrick Kaufman, would be his successor. It certainly seemed different to me without Dennis coaching, but Cedrick was a great choice and this year's Wildcats were one of the best teams we would play all year, ranked #7 on the day we played. Our matches had a long history of being extremely close and hard-fought. The first five or six all ended in 4-3 wins for the home team. Today's was no exception. The doubles was fiercely contested, as once again we split the top two, leaving everything on the inexperienced shoulders of Bandy and Dooley. Perhaps buoyed by their strong showing in East Lansing, the duo handled a strong #3 team, Anthony Rossi and Beck Pennington by an 8-5 count, as the freshman Pennington struggled near the end of the pro set. The Wildcats were simply too strong at #1, as Frenchman Tom Jomby's 130 mph serve made for easy service holds. He dominated the court, as we tried to make Jomby's partner, diminutive Kevin Lai beat us, but Jomby was everywhere and his ball was so big that we were frequently lucky to get it back in play, let alone control it. His inside-out backhand return in the deuce court lived in the opposite alley and we were challenged to hold every game we served. They took a hard fought pro set 8-6. At #2 we more than held our own, as Pecor lashed out with several laser-like backhand returns and Lawson moved freely around the net. This one went to Notre Dame 8-5, evening the score. That left everything in the hands, once again, of Bandy-Dooley, as just mentioned. They played with the presence of seniors and we entered singles with a 1-0 lead.

If you are looking for a sign from the universe and don't see one, consider it a sign that what you really need is to look inside yourself.

Lori Deschene

Now I thought we had a fighting chance, and an upset of Kentucky on their home courts would resonate throughout the world of college tennis. This team had finished in the final eight a year ago and returned most of its star power. A win here would certainly impress the NCAA tennis committee and improve our draw in that event. The singles were going to be interesting. One of the difficulties in playing indoors at Kentucky is that the Wildcats have only four indoor courts. After the doubles ends, players nos. 1-4 take the courts to play their matches, leaving nos. 5 and 6 waiting for matches to conclude and courts to open. This is not my first rodeo, and I have been here many times, but these players have not. It is the first such trip for McCoy and Bandy, who play at #5 and #6 today. They are going to have to wait for two matches to finish. This means eating something while waiting and taking dynamic stretches and warming up without hitting a ball during the matches so that, when they go on court they will be ready after the customary five minute warm-up. Depending on how things go in the other matches, either McCoy or Bandy could be playing for the whole shooting match, and that can be a heavy load for an inexperienced player to carry. As the match begins I take nos. 1 and 2, while Ryan will monitor 3 and 4. Determining which coach handles which player can take some heady thinking, as it is important for the chemistry to be compatible during the match.

Immediately I can see that Greg has his hands full with Rossi at #1. The Kentucky All American is a talented player who competes very well. He hits a big ball and can hurt you from both sides. This means that Greg has to be careful when running around his backhand to get his favorite shot, the inside-out forehand. Rossi is serving big and quickly establishes control of a very well-played match. Greg has chances, but loses a hard fought first set 6-4. On court #2 Jomby is serving extremely well - no surprise here- and lacing forehands to the corners. Blas has few answers, but refuses to concede anything despite clearly being uncomfortable with both the speed of the court and the pace of the 6'5" Frenchman's ball. I am afraid that he will be overpowered here and, unfortunately, I am right.

Things are going better on Ryan's two courts. Both Quentin and Billy win first sets to paint a brighter picture for us. Quentin gets very few style points, but is ingrained with an absolute will to avoid giving his opponent free points and to ensure that he has to earn every single point. His forehand has improved and is not leaving the ball short today. His consistency prevails and he wins the first set 6-4. Billy, as I have noted, has the power of world class players off the ground and overwhelms Juan Pablo Murra 6-3. When Billy is "on" and playing with confidence he is very difficult to beat and today is one of his better days. His backhand is ripping through the court with pace that Murra can't handle and, even though he drops a second set in a tiebreaker, Billy resumes his pin-point bombardment to take the third in yet another tie-breaker. Quentin holds on against Alejandro Gomez in another tie-breaker. Gomez plays hot and cold and with only two speeds- fast and faster. Today Quentin simply makes him earn more points than he is able to produce. 7-6 Irish. We now lead 3-2 as the 5 and 6 players take the court.

While I am happy to be leading 3-2 against the nation's #7 ranked team, I know that winning either of these last two matches will be difficult. Unfortunately, I am correct in my assessment. McCoy's challenge is Charles Minc, a good mover who also makes you earn everything and it is Minc who has just enough offense to win in straight sets. Bandy's is the last match to begin and he knows that he is playing for all the marbles. His opponent at #6 is Grant Roberts, a native Kentuckian whose record is a strong one. Roberts, unlike some of the other Wildcats, doesn't overpower you, but he has a good all-court game and plays intelligent, percentage tennis. He is left-handed and today our own lack of lefties with whom Ryan can practice is apparent. Bandy can't generate enough offense and falls in straight sets 6-3, 6-0. This was a difficult situation for him and his inexperience shows. Roberts will go through the SEC season with almost no blemishes on his record and his experience is clearly the difference. Being a lefty is normally a good thing. The fact that we have only one such player on our team has limited Ryan's exposure to left-handers and made this match even more difficult. He drops the deciding match, but the lessons learned today will bear fruit in matches yet to be played. He will simply have to let go of today and get ready for the next match.

━━━━━◦◦◦━━━━━

Hold fast, for if dreams die, life is a broken-winged bird that cannot fly.

Langson Hughes

━━━━━◦◦◦━━━━━

At the conclusion of the match, we meet briefly with Don Ralph and Chuck Stevens, two members of Notre Dame's 1959 NCAA Championship team who live sufficiently nearby that they make almost all of our matches here in Lexington. Since I first arrived in South Bend I am continually impressed with the loyalty of our Notre Dame alumni. We have tennis reunions every other year and many alums from earlier eras return to renew old friendships. I am reminded how fortunate I am to have spent most of my life in either Annapolis or South Bend and to have enjoyed the company of such loyal and successful alumni. Notre Dame has the largest collection of alumni clubs in higher education and, at times, it can be problematic to successfully navigate between preparing our team for the next day's match and handling the wonderful requests from alumni to take us to dinner, etc. We should all have such problems.

The six-hour bus ride back to "the Bend" always seems longer after a loss. Our managers have done their jobs well and, as we board the bus for the drive back home, each of us is handed the meal that the managers have picked up for us. The bus is predictably quiet. On only a few occasions after losses have I heard some chuckling in the rear of the bus. I have rarely had to intervene and for that I am grateful. Team culture is an important piece of what determines success. Call me "old school"- and you won't get much argument from our players there - but I believe that even if one of our players has played his best match of the year and won, he needs to be respectful of the others and hold his good feelings inside with some degree of silence. Because tennis at the college level is both a team and individual sport it is important that the team always take priority over individual success or failure. It is a lesson many have to learn after they arrive, as their previous tennis experience has primarily been an individual one.

~ Cross Court Reflection ~

There are no wrong turns, only unexpected paths.

Mark Nepo

Why College Sports?

There is nothing noble about being superior to some person. The true nobility is being superior to your previous self.

Ernest Hemingway

This is as good a time as any to explain my fifty year love affair with college sports. I believe that I learned more life lessons from sports than from anything else, save the guidance given me by my parents. I grew up loving and valuing sports above most everything. As a basketball player in high school and college[only one year] the toughest and most important lessons were handed to me daily. I learned humility through my performances. I clearly learned that you advance best through hard work, sacrifice, and discipline. I learned that sometimes you are not given what you deserve. I also learned that success shared is far more enjoyable than its individual counterpart. I learned that when you become too boastful you sometimes get knocked down. I learned that everyone is important, not just the stars. Once in a college basketball game I offered my own shoes to our high scorer, as he had forgotten to pack his own. Our coach, Lewis Mills, went through the normal "coach" reaction at first, telling me that it was his responsibility to bring his own shoes, but when I insisted, he shouted in relief "That is what makes sports such a great thing. Thanks, Bobby!"

When I entered the world of collegiate sports, tennis coaches were not as well paid as they are today. There were no "dealer" or "courtesy" cars for most non-revenue coaches. Budgets were smaller and hotel accommodations not nearly as nice as the norm today. Some of the coaches were very knowledgeable, but not all were experts. Facilities were nowhere near what we see today. Not all college tennis players received all of their equipment at no cost….in fact, most needed to supply at least some of what they used. I strung every one of the rackets that I used as a college player. Today most college players do not even know how to string a racket. In my one year spent coaching high school tennis I inherited a really good high school team, one that would win the Virginia High School championship and beat several college teams in matches, including beating Penn State at our school 6-3. Yet there was no budget for nice uniforms and lots of extra practice balls. I organized a "work day" and all of our players went out into the community and performed chores for which they were paid, with the money pooled for uniforms, balls, etc. Many of our players came from upper economic backgrounds, but I made sure that each did the work, rather than have their parents pay their share. What it brought us was was great team chemistry and bigger crowds. Starters and bench players alike rang doorbells and performed chores for the neighborhood. They raked leaves, cut grass, and did whatever was asked. The results: great camaraderie, great team results, and lasting relationships. Several of those young men played #1 for their college team and one, Richard McKee, was an NCAA finalist. And we wore nice uniforms because of their efforts.

On the friendly fields of strife are sown the seeds that on later fields will bear the fruits of victory.

General Douglas McCarthur
on the role of college sports

Many college players today are spoiled, but I really don't have to tell you that. They perform community service, but frequently with a photographer taking their pictures and publicity negating the potential life lessons learned. It is an honor to represent your college or university...a sacred honor. I believe that I mentioned Lou Holtz's comments about current athletes.... "They used to want to know their responsibilities and obligations. Now they want to know their rights and privileges." Make no mistake about it. College professors are in a position to teach life lessons and some do. One of the professors here at Notre Dame, Dr. Steve Fredland, greatly affected and influenced the life of my own son, Brendan, encouraging him to pursue success in his music career. However, a coach spends several hours each day with his squad. He travels with them. He eats meals with them. He simply has a greater opportunity to effect change on the life of an 18-22 year old man or woman. My point is a simple one. None of us in a non-revenue sport is going to generate appreciable revenue for the athletic coffers, but each of us is in a position to impart valuable life lessons. If winning at any and all costs is one of those lessons, that coach has forfeited his or her right to continue coaching, in my opinion.

While many of today's coaches have better technical preparation, a few are in this for the wrong reasons. We need a wake-up call. While winning is important - and I believe that it is - we should be doing more. If we don't heed this advice I truly believe that what we have now will all go away. Campuses are mostly land-locked and many schools are looking for a reason to drop sports, particularly in today's Title IX world. That bank of tennis courts would also make room for a nice academic or student activities building. The University of Texas recently demolished one of the truly great tennis stadiums in the country, the Penick-Allison Tennis Center, making room for another building. The tennis team's new indoor headquarters are now farther from campus, creating a logistics problem for coaches, players, and fans. Because Texas's coaches have kept their respective teams consistently in the rankings and do things the right way, and have been successful on the courts, the sport has not faced elimination, but on other campuses, tennis has not been as fortunate. Bill Scholl, the well-respected athletic director at Marquette, reversed a previous decision and saved tennis there when it appeared to be on the chopping block. A program that consistently produces leaders and proud alumni is far less likely to face elimination.

As sports are eliminated more frequently today, sometimes as an unintended consequence of Title IX, I feel colleges are making a big mistake. The ITA deserves credit for acting immediately as news of any possible elimination of tennis on a college campus is released. On several occasions, the actions of the ITA saved college tennis on those campuses. David Benjamin jumped on this early and Tim Russell has continued his proactive policies to not only save, but to grow our sport. The best example of this is the decision made by Arizona State to bring back men's tennis, prodded and encouraged by the ITA and a courageous director of athletics Ray Anderson. My own feelings on this are that as coaches, we need to lead exemplary careers and provide examples for our employers to view and appreciate. Behaving inappropriately during matches, pulling scholarships from deserving players, looking the other way when a player misbehaves all provide reasons to question the relevance of tennis on that particular campus. Certainly it is easy for me to preach about this now that I have retired and am no longer on the firing line where my character is laid bare during the heat of competition, but it is something in which I have always believed deeply. End of sermon because I suspect that I am preaching to the choir here.

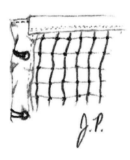

Next up ~ The Michigan Wolverines

If at first you do succeed, try to hide your astonishment.

Henry F. Banks

Despite our recent loss to Kentucky, I know that our guys will bounce back quickly, for our next opponent is Michigan. Notre Dame and Michigan are natural geographic and athletic rivals and the electricity in the air can be felt by spectators and players alike. When I arrived in South Bend, the Wolverines were clicking on all cylinders. In my first year Michigan reached the NCAA Final Four, and held match points on LSU to advance to the championship match. Their lineup was loaded. Former NCAA singles runner-up Danny Goldberg played #2 and future Wimbledon semi-finalist Mal Washington was at #3. At that time we were not at all competitive with Michigan, but that changed quickly. Since losing my first match to the Wolverines 8-1 in 1989, we have taken 18 of the next 24, but it took a 7-6 in the third set tie- breaker to defeat them a year ago in Ann Arbor and I know all too well that a similarly close match awaits us today, as they are ranked #21, some eight spots above us in the most recent ITA poll. In last year's match our senior, Sam Keeton, broke serve to go up 5-3 in the final set and try to serve it out, but was quickly broken himself and it took some gutty shotmaking for Sam to clinch the win in a 7-5 third set breaker. Michigan coach Bruce Berque has recruited another strong team, led by All American Evan King, a very athletic left-hander whom we recruited hard, and one of the best players in college today. Thank goodness we are at home in the friendly confines of the Eck Tennis Pavilion.

The doubles begins well for us, as Pecor and Lawson are razor sharp in the return game and coast to an 8-4 win. Both of the other remaining matches, however are very close and we inexplicably find ways to lose both in tie-breakers, 8-6 at #1 and 10-8 at #3. We held match points in both, so the quick journey to my office for the five minute pre-singles scouting discussion is uncomfortable. I am visibly upset and our players know it. We now will have to take four of the six singles. This is made more difficult by the fact that King is a clear favorite to beat Greg Andrews at #1. As we leave the office to begin singles I sense a calm confidence from our guys and I realize that all is not lost....yet. Andrews is predictably overpowered by King in the first set 6-2. Not much hope here, I think, as King's lefty serve has Greg tied in knots. Yet we somehow win all of the other first sets. Moros is matched up against Maryland transfer Vlad Stephan, a 6' 5" European with a big serve and dominant forehand. Blas, though, is determined tonight and understands that Stephan cannot cover court as well as he and takes balls early, limiting Stephan's ability to step around his backhand for forehands. This formula, playing the ball on the rise, works well and soon Blas is forcing Stephan to move corner to corner without time to load up on his forehand, as the distance Blas's ball travels is reduced. It is a courageous showing by Moros, who quickly evens the match score at 1-1, losing only four games.

People who do not understand the dynamics of a dual match will not see how important this quick win was to our team. By getting on the board quickly we have eliminated Michigan's emotional doubles win and put the pressure right back on them. Miraculously we go up a set in all but #1 and show Michigan that we are not going away. Quentin follows his script and forces scrappy Alex Petrone to play some high, off-speed forehands, something he prefers not to do. "Q" is moving well and in this match gives spectators a quick peek at the form that will take him to the NCAA semi-finals as a junior. His combination of consistency coupled with his ability to change direction effectively on his backhand will carry the day, Just after closing out the first set, though, his ball begins to fall short and the scrappy Petrone crushes him in the second set 6-1. Showing the poise of a veteran, Monaghan reverses course promptly with more aggressiveness and takes a 6-2 third set, giving us a 2-1 lead. McCoy puts his recent problems behind him and frustrates Shaun Bernstein with his speed and uncanny ability to counter, making get after seemingly impossible get and forcing Bernstein to play shots closer and closer to the lines. The strategy works and McCoy delivers 6-2,7-5, giving us a 3-1 lead. Wyatt is moving like a gazelle today and it is impressive to see.

Life is about moving and change. And when things stop doing that they are dead.

Twyla Tharp

Remarkably, Andrews is able to climb back into his match with King, something that takes pressure off our other players. What has worked is taking the ball out wide with power and sufficient pace to limit King's ability to hurt him. On changeovers, Greg is upbeat and senses his opportunity. Even though he comes up short, Greg's grabbing the second set has changed the dynamic of the match, for Michigan has counted on a decisive win at #1 and the rest of King's teammates understand that since that match is now in play there is more pressure on each of them to deliver a win. Bandy, a 6-4 first set winner, now is in a hole against New Zealander Barrett Franks. The key here was to take advantage of Bandy's superior movement and force the slower Franks to cover an equal amount of court. This worked well in the first set, but beginning in the second, with new balls [the ITA rules now require a new can of balls at the beginning of each set] Franks has been able to play a bigger game and now controls the match. Bandy simply can't replicate Franks' pace and falls 4-6,6-2,6-1. The updated score is now 3-2 overall and, King regains his confidence to down a determined and scrappy Andrews. Three all! Anybody's match!

This places the match in the hands of Pecor, who is battling Michigan's Michael Zhu. Zhu is short and very quick. He loves pace and is at his worst playing someone who can run down his balls and change pace. This formula normally causes Zhu's forehand to de-rail, as his backhand is rock solid. Pecor, though, was not built to play the likes of Zhu. Billy prefers to slug it out and challenge his opponent to match his power and shot-making ability. This is a real challenge for Billy, but he plays today with fierce determination. It is now strength against strength and the ball is humming as it flies across the net. He wins the first set but drops a tie-breaker in the second. There are ebbs and flows, but Pecor suddenly reaches match point on Zhu's serve at 5-4 in the third. Zhu misses his first serve and I hold my breath. The best play here is to roll a high return up to Zhu's forehand, but Billy will have none of that. Stepping into the court he hits a backhand as hard as one can be hit and screams in joy throwing his racket high in the air as the ball lands just inside both lines in the corner. Notre Dame 4, Michigan 3! Our players run onto the court to embrace Billy and a celebration begins as several hundred fans scream their approval. I am especially happy for Billy, as his parents are here in the gallery, and can now celebrate with him. I am glad that we allowed him to play his game at the biggest moments of the match [see quote below]. It is moments like this that make our sport so unique and enjoyable. I feel a sense of relief as we move to the next challenge. The Michigan-Notre Dame rivalry in all sports is special, so this one needs to be savored.

~ Cross Court Reflection ~

It is easier to reel in a rebel than prod a pansie.

John C. Officer

The Big Picture

Our win over Michigan holds larger implications. At the end of the season the NCAA Tennis Committee, of which I will soon become a member, meets in Indianapolis in May to determine the fate of the 64 teams that comprise the NCAA Men's Tennis Championships. This group will decide which teams travel to each of the 16 host events. The NCAA has directed this committee to make every attempt to minimize the number of flights in order to minimize costs. While this appears to be logical, the downside of this policy means that unless we are one of the 16 host schools chosen by merit and ranking, we will likely end up in Columbus, OH or - less likely - Champaign, IL. Both Ohio State and Illinois are among the nation's elite teams. Each has played in the NCAA Championship match and both venues hold true home court advantage. Ohio State, though, currently holds the record for consecutive home court wins at well over 200. Going to Columbus to finish my career is not high on my list of things to do. Because of the NCAA policy that no teams from the same conference should meet until after the first two rounds, this makes it more than probable that we will be sent to Columbus unless we boost our ranking into the top 24. Today's win will move us to #25. Guess whom we play next? Yep, the Ohio State Buckeyes in Columbus.

In keeping with my policy to play the most challenging schedule possible, we have played Ohio State every year in my Notre Dame tenure. While my regular season record against them stands at 15-10, wins have been tough to come by recently against the Buckeyes. For example when we beat Ohio State in 2006 by a 5-2 score here in the Eck, it was the only regular season loss the Buckeyes suffered. The reason in two words - Ty Tucker. The former Buckeye All American has made his team a championship contender every year and has done one of the great jobs of all time in college tennis history. Tucker is a ferocious competitor who hates losing more than anything. He has built great facilities, both indoor and outdoor. His work ethic is without peer. His ability to impart winning tactics and strategy in matches is among the best. I have enjoyed exchanging scouting opinions with him on college players, teams, and coaches. There is a definite chip on his shoulder on match day. Most coaches agree that it is difficult to get favorable calls from umpires in Columbus. Ty wanders the sidelines looking like a bouncer from a bar, constantly worrying, frequently without reason. In short, you are never going to catch Tucker or his team overconfident or asleep at the switch. He routinely wears his sweat pants rolled halfway up both legs. Perhaps he is trying to make you think he is a country bumpkin, but nobody falls for that act...he has simply had too much success to make you overconfident. It is readily apparent that this guy knows his stuff! He anticipates problems and is extraordinarily efficient at recognizing when a shift in strategy or tactics is needed. While some coaches are fearful of ruffling the feathers of their players in big moments, Tucker is quick to see what is needed and act upon it.

One of the tests of leadership is to recognize a problem before it becomes an emergency.

Arnold Glascow

Our team arrives with some positive momentum. Our last two matches saw us lose 4-3 on the road to #7 Kentucky and beat #21 Michigan. We are healthy. We are upbeat. But we are in Ty's house and we both know it. Our match begins with an unexpected tribute to me from the PA announcer. I am touched. Tucker doesn't miss much. Nonetheless, we are steamrolled in doubles. Tucker has done a unique and unusual job coaching college doubles. His teams use different formations designed to maximize their talents and minimize yours. He is the first college coach to find situations where his team frequently doesn't serve and volley and it seems to work well. They do many things well, particularly using left-handed servers to hammer the "T" in the deuce court with the net man poaching frequently. They never miss from the "2 back" formation. They are able to volley short against the same formation, something few teams do well. It is fun to match wits with him in matches, as he barks out changes in tactics. My problem is that it is not fun when you lose. And that is exactly what happens today. The doubles are not contested at a high level. We end each of the pro sets trailing by two service breaks. As singles begin I have the same feeling of deja vu that I felt two years ago in this same building.

The singles matches are closer, but with the same results. Quentin has multiple match points against the nation's #2 player, Peter Kobelt, but loses a 14-12 tie-breaker for the third set. Kobelt is 6' 8", but moves extremely well and serves at 135 mph. Greg plays hard against Blaz Rola, but is overpowered. Next year at this time Rola will be in the main draw at the Australian Open, as he reaches the top 100 in ATP Tour play. You get my drift. We are simply overmatched. Pecor plays another good match, but Chris Diaz is too consistent for him in a 6-4,6-4 battle, in a great match-up for OSU. Diaz moves like a small gazelle, darting all over the court. Every ball seems to come back. He overcomes an inability to hit his forehand with great pace by displaying extraordinary control and rarely makes an unforced error. It is very difficult to beat Diaz without coming forward and volleying well. Michael Moore fills in at #6 for Bandy, who is injured. Moore wins the first, but falls 6-3 in the third. This one is going to be tough to steal, despite our dreams.

We dream to give ourselves hope. To stop dreaming, well, that's like saying you can never change your fate.

Amy Tan

245

Blas and Wyatt similarly have their hands full and cannot win a set, but each is giving his all. Soon the Buckeyes are celebrating their trillionth consecutive home court win and I am shaking hands with a smiling Tucker. The bus ride home takes a predictable five hours. It is easy to see why some of our guys do better in the classroom than others. Greg is the first to open a book for study. He will graduate next year with a 3.9 GPA in Accounting, probably the most difficult major in the Mendoza School of Business. He will win the prestigious ITA Arthur Ashe award, given nationally to the college tennis player who best exemplifies the virtues of leadership and sportsmanship. It is an award that our Chuck Coleman and Mike Sprouse won in 1993 and 1995. I find that I learn a great deal about our players on airplanes and busses. I find it easy to predict which players will be ultra-successful as alumni. Established habits go a long way toward determining one's future successes. At some point during the drive we have a brief meeting to go over the next matches and itinerary for spring break, just to be certain that we are all on the same page. While it is never fun to lose, I realize that we are holding our own and with Wisconsin and top ten Illinois on the horizon we need to stay focused and upbeat. We are just about halfway through the season. If we are to make a move we need to do it soon.

The next few days pass quickly and it is on to play Wisconsin. As we drive into Madison, WI I can see why it is a popular choice for students. In addition to being home to a terrific university, it is also the state capitol. Large lakes offer swimming and boating in summers and a large number of shops and restaurants are fun to browse. In my first years at Notre Dame, Wisconsin was a top 25 team and we had exciting matches with them. As the Badgers' fortunes dropped, fiery Greg Van Emburgh was hired to rejuvenate the program. Within a few years Van Emburgh took them to the NCAA Sweet Sixteen, but many of that group have graduated or transferred and Greg has some young faces with yet-to-be-proven potential. The Nielsen Indoor Tennis Stadium is a wonderful facility and includes twelve indoor courts. It has been the home of the ITA Women's Team Indoors for many years. Nielsen has undergone a recent face- lift and now sports bright clean walls and new lights. It will not take much to adjust to conditions here. We follow a typical itinerary on this trip, getting to Madison in time to practice the evening prior to our match and once again the next morning.

I have great respect for Van Emburgh's ability to have his team play good doubles. A former Wimbledon semi-finalist in doubles himself, Greg coaches an aggressive style that encourages poaching and they go to our weaknesses right away. Andrews and Talmadge start us off well at #1 and win 8-6, but both tandems at #2 and #3 fall behind early and struggle early. We lose both to give the Badgers a 1-0 lead. I do not hold back my frustrations as we meet to go over the singles scouting notes. As a coach, I try not to use profanity in front of our players, saving it for an occasion when it might jolt them into a greater sense of urgency. Today is such a day. I hope the message is received. Fortunately, the singles provide a different story. Andrews handles 6'5" Billy Bertha, whose serve is formidable, but lack of speed is an advantage Andrews can exploit. Greg's quickness disarms Bertha, and keeps him from setting up for his big forehand. Greg follows a familiar pattern: look for the first forehand opportunity and attack Bertha's movement, preferably to the backhand. It works, and Greg is the first to finish, tying the team match at 1-1. Only Moros and Pecor drop first sets and we quickly take control, winning nos. 2, 5, and 6 in straight sets. Moros recovers and wins the next two to give us a fifth point. Pecor is giving his all, but makes more errors today than in recent matches and succumbs 6-2,6-0. Next week is midterm week and Billy has been up late preparing. It shows. Hopefully he can get things together quickly, as we have the Fighting Illini in four days. We will need him at his best to beat Illinois. The four hour bus ride home is smooth and uneventful. I know that our guys are focused on Tuesday's match with Illinois.

~ Cross Court Reflection ~

Coaching is an everyday event, not something we do at practice, or game days, or in a season. It is all year.

Bo Schembechler

Irish duo returns to campus. Notre Dame All Americans Javier Taborga and Casey Smith pose for a shot with their coach. They came back to see Notre Dame beat USC in football on October 12, 2019. Javier Taborga is on the left, Coach Bayliss is center, Casey Smith is on the right. *Photo by Sue Molnar.*

Craig Tiley Builds a Champion

~

Brad Dancer Continues the Quest for Excellence

When I arrived at Notre Dame, Illinois was at, or near, the bottom of the Big Ten. The 1993 team, though, had a new coach. No one in the midwest had heard much about Craig Tiley, but before the native South African left Champign-Urbanna to become CEO of Tennis Australia and the tournament director of the Australian Open, his name had become a household word. Tiley methodically built a great program, amassed spectacular fan support, and brought in alumni contributions that led to a new 12 court outdoor stadium that would one day host the NCAA Tennis Championships. Shortly after being named the Illinois coach, Tiley called me to introduce himself and asked for a meeting so he could pick my brain. Having been in the same position only six years earlier I agreed to sit down and discuss what he might be able to do at Illinois. I was thoroughly impressed. Tiley took notes as we discussed my own path at Notre Dame and we continued for two or three hours. I knew right away that this guy would be a difference-maker, and boy was I right! It took a few years, but Tiley quickly built a top ten team and Notre Dame-Illinois became a great rivalry. We had endured some great battles with them and I was sorry to see him go.

This, of course, is my segue to one of the best road matches our team ever played. Tiley's Illini had just won the ITA National Team Indoors and ascended to college tennis' #1 ranking in 2002. They would win the NCAAs the next year with a loaded roster. We played them just over a week after their National Team Indoors coronation in early March. The forecast for Champaign was mixed, with the possibility of rain looming. This would, of course be bad news, as Illinois was a much better indoor team. Tiley had recruited a number of players who would make their marks in professional tennis. Most were big and all played an aggressive style. Full of serve-and-volleyers, the Illini almost never lost the doubles point and then came at you with a powerful lineup that took no prisoners. Amer Delic at #1 would later become an ATP Top 50 player. Their nos. 2-5 would all go on to play professionally, experiencing differing degrees of success. The word on the street was "Never play Illinois indoors when there is a chance to get them outside."

Tiley told me the forecast was for rain, so I agreed to begin indoors, meaning that the entire match would finish there. It was always problematic as a road team to have to move indoors once a match had begun. We were no slouch that year, either, coming into the match ranked #6. The doubles was ferocious. Our #1 team of Javier Taborga and Casey Smith topped Delic and Michael Calkins 8-5, holding the only break of serve in the match. Then things got very interesting. Michael Kosta and Nathan Zeder finally edged out our own Aaron Talarico and Brent D'Amico 8-6, leaving the match in the hands of our talented, but up-and-down team of James Malhame-Ashok Raju. Both teams sported classic serve-and-volley styles and they went at it tooth and nail. Predictably it was decided by a tie-breaker which remained deadlocked at 6-6 until we held and broke on successive points to take the breaker and begin singles up one point. The overflow crowd was stunned[as, perhaps, was I], but grew louder and more supportive of their team.

—◦—

You don't win games on optimism. You win games on preparation.

Monte Clark

—◦—

The Illini pulled back even as Kosta downed our Luis Haddock in an unpredictably one-sided score of 6-1,6-3, but we soon jumped ahead as our flamboyant lefty, Taborga, took out the future NCAA singles champion[next year] and soon-to-be-ATP professional Delic in straight sets 6-2,6-4. We would play the Illini two more times this year and Taborga would win both against Delic. I simply did not see this one coming. All of the other matches went the distance and finished in third sets. This match went on for hours with both teams appearing to hold advantages. Our Andrew Laflin recovered from a disastrous first set[1-6] to topple big-serving lefty Nathan Zeder 6-3 in the third, while Matt Scott lost a heartbreaker 6-3,3-6,7-5 to hard-hitting Michael Calkins. We still clung to a narrow 3-2 lead in matches with just two remaining. Only one would be required for the win. At this point we were in a great position to clinch, with Casey Smith holding a 6-1 lead in the second set tie-breaker and holding five TEAM match points. Then things became surreal. Aaron Talarico dropped a 6-3,2-6,6-4 decision to Phil Stoldt, temporarily tying the match at three. However, after losing, Talarico threw his racket toward his equipment bag and was called for a code violation by the umpire.

This created an unheard-of dilemma. As Casey prepared to serve holding a 6-1 lead in the breaker, Referee Linda Hinshaw stopped play. The umpires convened. I was flabbergasted. Nobody stops a match at team match point for a meeting! Casey looked very confused. What the heck was going on? After a short conference, Linda ruled that Aaron's code violation needed to be applied to Casey's match, as it was the only match left. I disagreed, as code violations are supposed to go to the next highest match, but only to begin the next game - not to interfere with the current one. Once the decision had been rendered, however, I thought it important to resume play, as Casey still held match point on his own serve at 6-2 and held four match points in all. Surely he would win one of those four! I don't have to tell you what happened next. We lost all four match points and the second set. All of a sudden the upset of the year in college tennis was quickly fading.

Somehow Casey composed himself and played valiantly in the third, gaining a 5-1 lead in the final set. As I finally relaxed to enjoy the seemingly inevitable finish, things began to once again unravel. Casey's lead shrunk from 5-1 to 5-4, as our entire team looked on. I stood with my assistant, Billy Pate, now head coach at Princeton. My hope was that, since it was Casey's serve he could stem the tide and serve it out. After Casey lost the first two points I turned to Billy and told him that I couldn't look anymore. Feeling like I might throw up, I turned my back and began to walk away after Casey fell behind 0-30 while serving. I glanced his way to see him win the next point, but continued to walk away, superstitiously refusing to re-kindle hope. At 30-30 I stopped, almost afraid to look. The next point gave him a 40-30 advantage and yet another TEAM match point. Casey finished the match with a screaming winner and I almost jumped into Billy's arms as our team began to celebrate. It was a short ride home that night, as the tires of the bus seemed never to touch the ground.

Now back to our match with Illinois in 2013. After Tiley left to take over tennis in Australia, the Illini hired Brad Dancer. I had recruited Brad and gotten to know his family. He was both energetic and likeable. His energy was non-stop, as he hopped from court to court, barking instructions to his players, looking like the television commercial's Energizer Bunny. More importantly, he had continued the tradition of Tiley-coached teams and had recently made his own way to an NCAA final. This particular Illini team had just dropped out of the top ten, but at #13 still provided us with both a threat and plenty of incentive. Oddly enough, during Dancer's tenure we had always beaten them here and always lost there. Our matches were always dogfights. In the previous year's contest in Champaign we held match points in numerous matches, yet somehow frittered them away and lost.

———◦◦◦———

Others can stop you temporarily, but only you can do it permanently.

Bob Moawad

———◦◦◦———

I expected yet another close match and was not disappointed. We won at #2 and #3 doubles without great difficulty as Pecor had regained some of his swagger. He and Lawson seemed in control the entire time and took the pro-set 8-5. With Bandy still nursing an injury we had moved Monaghan into third doubles with Dooley. The chemistry was good, as Dooley provided the punch around the net and Monaghan the consistency from the backcourt. Down at third doubles, Quentin's still-developing net play was less problematic. As a senior he would reach the NCAA semi-finals with Lawson, but no one could imagine that just yet. The singles were, predictably, very close. Only two matches finished in straight sets. Andrews continued his consistent and aggressive play, downing Jared Hiltzik, one of the country's better players 6-4,6-4, while Michael Moore again subbed in for the injured Bandy and defeated steady Bruno Abdelnour 6-4,6-3. This gave us a 3-0 lead, but it was difficult to see which of the remaining matches might provide us the fourth point. Now it was time for me to show why I was receiving those big bucks [?]. The matches seesawed back and forth. Big serving Stephen Hoh won a tie-breaker from Monaghan to take the first, only to see Quentin jump back with a 6-1 victory in the second. Moros held on for a 6-4 first set over the solid Tim Kopinski 6-4, but began to experience some pain from a nagging hip flexor injury and dropped the second 7-5. I was especially proud of Pecor, as he fought back from a 6-2 first set loss to squeak out a gutty breaker in the second 7-6. This was certainly anybody's match.

The prize for guts and scrappiness went to McCoy who, it appeared, lacked the firepower to stay with big hitting Farris Gosea. Somehow, though, Wyatt hung in there and made athletic get after get, running down balls sufficiently to frustrate Gosea and skillfully countering his less-than needed efforts to come to the net. The match finished in yet another tie-breaker. Pecor once again finished the match for us, having barely survived a second set breaker with scrappy Ross Guignon. It was a re-match of his earlier loss at Regionals. With guns predictably blazing he overpowered the scrappy lefty in a decisive third set 6-1, avenging his earlier fall loss . With a clinching 4-1 lead we decided to stop play to give Illinois a chance to drive back earlier and our guys to rest. We were in the middle of mid-term exams this week and would leave for spring break in two days. Brad Dancer came over to congratulate us on our performance, no doubt masking his own mixed feelings. I feel his pain, but am very happy with this win which will move us to #22 as we fly down to Montgomery for the Blue Gray National Classic in Montgomery, AL. I will sleep much better tonight.

~ Cross Court Reflection ~

You don't lead by hitting people over the head. That's assault, not leadership.

President Dwight D. Eisenhower

254

Zurcher receives Dan Magill Award. Notre Dame All American Andy Zurcher received the Dan Magill Award given annually to the most outstanding senior in college tennis. David DiLucia received the same award two years earlier. Taken in Dallas, Texas, June 1994. He is shown with his coach, Bobby Bayliss and parents.

Team USA at the gold medal presentation for tennis at the 1991 World University Games in Sheffield, England. L to R: Angela Farley, Karen Wilson, Vimal Patel, Brett Hansen-Dent, Mark Booras, Susan Gilchrist, Erica Cutler, Angela Lattiere, Bobby Bayliss. *Photo courtesy of USTA.*

CHAPTER SIX

Spring Break and Beyond

If you are going to achieve excellence in big things, develop the habit in little matters. Excellence is not an exception. It is a prevailing attitude.

Colin Powell

One of the things I have tried to do over my career is to plan an attractive scenario for our guys during the spring break. At Notre Dame the timing could not be better, as mid-term exams have finished and we really need to come up for air. The grind of a dual match season combined with a difficult academic load leaves most teams exhausted. Add to this a warm climate, particularly if a beach is nearby, and morale soars. If you compete in the northeast or midwest you are tired of shoveling snow and ....oh so happy to finally feel the sun's warm rays beating down on your face. We have gone from Florida to California over most of these breaks and each time I find them welcome. For an indoor team there is the added incentive of making the adjustment from indoor play to outdoors.

My favorite place to visit on spring break is the La Jolla Beach and Tennis Club in San Diego. When you walk into the club you are immediately taken back in time, as pictures of Pancho

Gonzales, Jack Kramer, Don Budge, Stan Smith and other past greats are prominently displayed. They serve as a reminder of the club's significant roles in tennis history. It is located right on the Pacific Ocean and beach. The rooms have kitchens and we would typically have breakfast and lunch there, cutting costs and encouraging more bonding. The club hosted the Pacific Coast Doubles every year during the first weekend in March. We would typically arrive on Wednesday evening late and practice the next day- our only exposure outdoors before we competed. The format was a coach's dream. Not only did many of the best college teams participate- USC, UCLA, Stanford, CAL-Berkeley, and Pepperdine always seemed to be there- but non- college players, professionals, and top juniors also played. This meant that the results did not count in the college rankings, Furthermore, if your team competed against a non-college team coaching was not allowed, meaning that I had the day off at times. When the doubles tournament concluded we would continue to stay there for practice and perhaps drive to LA for an end-of-the-week match with UCLA or USC. Those were tremendous spring breaks.

When match schedules allow [they did not this year], I have tried various "tricks" to get our team ready for the not-so-subtle differences in playing styles that fresh outdoor tennis provided. Some years I have used ear plugs for practice and in others we have practiced with less-than-lively balls to prepare the players for the slower speed and more patient shot selection required by a team making this adjustment. The ear plugs block sound. Playing indoors you experience near perfect conditions, allowing more aggressive shotmaking. One of the first things I notice outdoors is that your hearing is not nearly as clear. There are distractions and competing noises: wind, traffic, birds, etc., none of which are present indoors. Additionally the air is heavier and you soon realize that you had been playing in a relative vacuum. Because the sound of both your own shots and those of the opponent no longer echo clearly, your ability to use your sense of sound is deterred. Your best shots come back more frequently and you have to resist the common instinct to simply hit the ball harder or aim it closer to the lines. Because your own shots do not "echo" off your racket, there is a false impression that you are not hitting with sufficient power. This encourages you to hit a bigger ball and usually results in unnecessary unforced errors. Add to this the strategic difference of being able to play tighter to the baseline indoors and it is clear that adjustments need to be made. Experience has shown me that to make the adjustment fully it might take as much as two weeks for this transition to gel. It will be important for me to once again remind our players of how to properly adjust to the new conditions.

Seniors reminisce after earning a trip to the "Sweet Sixteen" in 2007. Barry King, Coach Bobby Bayliss, Stephen Bass, and Ryan Keckley pose immediately after 4-0 victory over Wisconsin in the round of 32.

The Blue Gray National Classic

With an eye on our budget constraints, I have elected to return to the Blue Gray National Tennis Classic this year after missing it last year. It falls during this break and takes place in Montgomery, AL. Shortly after I arrived at Notre Dame I tried my best to secure an invitation to this event. It was an extremely strong tournament at that time, featuring the likes of Southern Cal, Georgia, Duke, Mississippi, Mississippi State, Florida, Texas A&M, Texas, South Carolina, Arizona State, Alabama, Auburn, and many other prominent teams. My third team, even though ranked in the top twenty, was not given an invitation, but we received one the next year and participated in 1991, defeating #20 Mississippi State, #6 South Carolina, and losing to #8 Arizona State. The team winners were presented blazers by Palm Beach and watches by Seiko, in addition to a USTA Gold Ball. We won the event for the first time in 1993 beating #19 New Mexico, #6 Mississippi State, #8 Florida, and #7 Alabama. I still have my watch and blazer, although the latter fits me a bit too tightly now.

I have arranged to fly to Birmingham and drive to Tuscaloosa where newly named head coach, George Husack, has generously agreed to allow us to practice on their courts. George replaces Billy Pate, my popular former assistant who has moved on to Princeton. After several days we will then make the two hour trek to Montgomery. A dilemma faces me. While we desperately need as much outdoor play as possible to be ready for the tournament Friday, I also realise that our players have just run through a gauntlet of difficult matches and are beaten up and tired. My decision is to practice for only an hour and one-half, but to do it twice daily. Experience has taught me that having to adjust each time you play outdoors counts for more than practicing only once, but for longer hours. We will see soon enough if I am correct. One of the highlights of being in "T-town" [Tuscaloosa] is a meal at Dreamland, where the ribs and barbecue are simply world-famous, so we make this one of our stops. Our guys are predictably impressed and will ask to return as often as possible. We also watch the Alabama women's team, coached by Jenny Mainz, take on the LSU Tigers coached by newly married Julia Scaringe Sell. Julia was our women's assistant for several years before beginning her employment in Baton Rouge. She has married Mike Sell, one of the greatest competitors we ever faced and they are coaching the team together.

DiLucia at Wimbledon. Notre Dame All American David DiLucia in action against #4 seed Jonas Bjorkman. This photo hangs in Coach Bobby Bayliss's office. Its inscription reads "Bullet, your guidance and inspiration have been a gift. Keep the boys focused on that NCAA title............Your former #1, David DiLucia."

A Trip Back to 1994 ~
The Irish Host the NCAAs

Seeing Mike reminds me of one of the truly memorable college matches I have ever seen. We were chosen to host the 1994 NCAA Championships and I am still proud of the effort made by our athletic department to make it an exceptional event. Missy Conboy, our Associate Athletic Director was the tournament director and left no stone unturned. The pride I felt seeing the event come together was enormous. The biggest reason the NCAA decided to rotate the event after a 17 year stint in Athens was the exceptional home court advantage enjoyed by host Georgia. Our first challenge was to ensure that we qualified for the tournament by winning the regional qualifier, now known as the first and second rounds. We had graduated five seniors from the previous year's team, but needed to produce another strong team for this to happen. It loomed over our team the entire season.

When the draw was announced I saw that our likely second round opponent would be Minnesota. The Dave Geatz-coached Gophers had beaten us in South Bend earlier in the season 5-2, so this was going to present a challenge. Not only that, but our first round opponent was Michigan, a team that edged us in Ann Arbor only a month earlier. After beating the Wolverines 4-0 we were ready for Minnesota and knew it would be a nasty fight. It certainly was. With the match tied at 3-3 our freshman Ryan Simme served-and-volleyed on match point at 5-4 in the third set and stuck a swinging volley into the corner to give us the win. This meant that our appearance in the round of 16 was guaranteed. Being able to make the field in this event took the financial pressure off my shoulders. Notre Dame had put up a $50,000[more than six figures in today's dollars] guarantee to land the NCAAs. We drew 2,000 noisy and energetic fans to open the event the next week and locked into a real battle with Georgia. I will spare you the details, but nobody left disappointed in the drama they observed that day. Cutting to the chase, the match stood tied at 3-3 just as our #1 player, Andy Zurcher, began the third set, which would decide the entire shooting match. Zurcher looked tired against Mike Sell, the ultimate Bulldog, known for his competitiveness. He fell behind 5-0 to Sell, and the disappointment hung in the air like a low-hanging cloud.

Suddenly, though, Zurcher began to win games. He held serve and miraculously broke Sell to bring the score to 5-2. Our crowd began to go wild, chanting "Let's Go Irish!" between points, as our leprechaun mascot ran from one section of bleachers to the next. On the changeover, Zurcher confided to me that he was cramping so that I would know. He was gulping down Gatorade and eating bananas, but the cramping became worse and visibly noticeable. Somehow, though, Andy found ways to stay in the match and incredibly evened the score at 5-5. The noise was deafening and the drama at the highest level possible. Inevitably Andy's cramping reached the point where he could no longer run. He then was unable to change grips to execute his shots. At match point, he fell to the ground, unable to move at all for Sell's shot. Mike, in fact, had to climb over the net to reach Andy and shake his hand, ever the sportsman. Andy was immediately taken to the medical facilities where he was administered saline via IVs. Even though we lost, that match remains on my all-time highlight reel. People still ask me about it today.

After four days of practice on the Alabama courts, we drove to Montgomery, one of my favorite towns. The Blue Gray Classic had been begun by Jack Bushman, the consummate Southern gentleman who really put on a show. He brought the community together and for four consecutive days, Lagoon Park was teeming with excitement, outstanding tennis, and lots of drama. We had been to the event for twenty consecutive years. The tournament had changed and now hosted eight women's teams along with a similar number from the men's side. As I pulled into Lagoon Park I immediately spotted Boise State's Greg Patton who came over to give me a big hug. "We've got you again, brother," yelled Patton, perhaps the country's most exuberant and highly motivated coach. "Oh no" I replied. "Another long 4-3 knock-down" I countered. We had played many times and seemingly every match went right down to the wire, as the last remaining match settled the outcome. In fact, in 2006 it had all come down to a third set breaker, as Stephen Bass edged out Luke Shields for the win that put us in the finals.

I will always remember my first trip to Boise where we played Greg's team. He is VERY involved in the community and one of the best promoters in our sport. After practicing at the Boise State facility we returned to our hotel to shower before having dinner. I turned on the local news and- believe it or not- there was Greg doing the sports show and rallying fans to come out to our match the next day. I thought it was "neat" that he had the energy to do so much for his team. The next morning as I rose I again turned on the television in my room and the local weather forecast was beginning. Yes, you guessed it, Greg was doing the weather and ended his forecast with an invitation for fans to attend our match. This guy is amazing, I thought.

After practicing in Montgomery at Lagoon Park, we drove our players to the private housing that had, over the years, become a second home to many Notre Dame players. I had driven to the Montgomery airport to pick up my wife, Pat. She had heard me talk about the Blue Gray, but never experienced it. Now she would know its charm. Jack Bushman passed away several years ago and the Blue Gray is now more than ably chaired by Paul Winn, an Alabama native and a true and another charming Southern gentleman. The banquet was entertaining, as always, and I was asked to speak and gave a short talk about why the Blue Gray had become my favorite event. Immediately thereafter Wayne Bryan took over and provided the evening's entertainment. Bryan is the father of ATP and Grand Slam pro tennis stars Bob and Mike Bryan and is college tennis's greatest champion. He kept everyone in stitches with his many stories and all left with full bellies and new hoodies provided by the Blue Gray committee. It was now time to play.

—◦—

Happiness is active participation in something that brings fulfillment.

Tom Morris

—◦—

The next morning as we warmed up to play Troy, I had a chance to catch up with their coach, Eric Hayes. Eric had been in college tennis for some time and had served a stint as head coach at NC State. He seemed to enjoy his new position, but talked openly to me about its challenges. I mentioned earlier the divide in most college sports. As the "Power Five" conferences [ACC, SEC, Big Ten, Big Twelve, and PAC Ten] were able to negotiate the big TV contracts for its member schools, the cupboard was bare for most everyone else. TV contracts for the Power Five conferences began above the twenty million dollar mark per school and for some were approaching the forty million dollar range. This meant that each school began the year with millions of dollars before any tickets were sold or other TV games had been added. Some of that money trickled down to non-revenue sports. Shoe and apparel contracts added to the sum and also gave packages to its schools that provided for all shoe and clothing needs. Simply looking around the field at a tournament like this and it was easy to see which schools were part of the Power Five, as the players had great looking uniforms, warm-ups, etc. Our current contract with adidas[note-there are no capital letters in adidas] allowed us to furnish each of our players with tennis shoes, running shoes, and trainers for each player, not to mention performance apparel, cold weather apparel, and more. Notre Dame then signed an incredible deal with UnderArmour. I think back to my college days and remember how often I practiced and competed with adhesive tape covering the hole in my shoe from serving. Our uniforms were simple and inexpensive when compared to what is available to these teams today.

Count your age by friends, not years. Count your life by smiles, not fears.

John Lennon

Our match with Troy was quick and uneventful, as we lost only one set and finished in less than two hours. We would be fresh the next day. That is important in a multi-day event like this one. By day three the team with the easiest path to that point might have an advantage over one less fortunate. After checking in with the tournament referee, Scott Dillon, it was time to take our guys to lunch. Scott is an old friend and has been running the Blue Gray and assisting with the NCAA championships for many years. On a trip to North Carolina to play UNC and Duke, Scott had invited our team to dinner at his home. The relationships formed over many years mean a lot to me and I am glad to see Scott in good spirits. Ryan and I drop the players for lunch and immediately head back to Lagoon Park because the next day's opponent, Boise State, is playing and I have not seen them this year. It will be good to scout this match, as Boise State has several new players with whom I am not familiar.

Greg Patton Takes Tennis to Idaho

The Boise State tennis story is an interesting one. Coach Greg Patton had made his reputation building a top ten team at UC Irvine. California born and bred, Patton was as happy as he was entrenched at UCI where he built top ten teams, but the Los Angeles riots and strife in LA forced him to consider relocating, as he had a young family. He had called me then to brainstorm what might be his best course of action. He mentioned that he had been approached by Boise State, but was not particularly excited, primarily because he knew little about Idaho, except for its potato production. I mentioned that we had friends who had moved to Boise and loved it. Greg then decided that it was worth a look. Not only did Greg take the job, but he built the Broncos into a top fifteen team before leaving to become one of the USTA's national coaches and working to develop top American talent to enter the professional ranks. He realised, though, that he missed college coaching and was able to return to Boise when an opening occurred. He is the most positively motivated coach in college tennis, and possibly the world. His teams are loud and voice their enthusiasm continually throughout the matches they play["That's a break on court four, Broncos!"]. I knew that tomorrow's match would be a barn-burner. We would need to do whatever it would take to win this one.

If you can't fly, then run. If you can't run, then walk. If you can't walk, then crawl, but whatever you do, you have to keep moving forward.

Martin Luther King

267

Saturday's match was no disappointment if you were looking for excitement. We began by taking the doubles point and a quick 1-0 lead and, as the singles began, I was pretty optimistic about our chances. Little did I know how tight things would get. When the dust began to clear and only one singles match remained, the score was knotted at 3-3 as Greg Andrews began his third set against the nation's #25 ranked Andrew Bettles, an Englishman. We were playing without Wyatt McCoy, who had injured his right wrist and could not hit forehands. We college coaches do not control our own fates and I had learned that Wyatt had played in an intramural hockey game just prior to our leaving. He had been checked into the boards and twisted his wrist. Wyatt at first acted as if the wrist would heal quickly, as he did not want me or his teammates to know how the injury happened, but word eventually trickled down to me. All coaches assume that their players will exercise good judgement, but we are frequently disappointed. Every year when I address the team I make it a point to emphasize that there is no room for poor judgement when it comes to common sense. Alcohol is a frequent culprit and I make myself clear in the first meeting of the year when I let them know that there will be consequences for such transgressions. In fact, I usually repeat the same line. "If you do anything to inhibit your performance [usually this refers to alcohol] or embarrass our program or the university I will[at this point I express a pregnant pause]......Kill You!!" Now our players probably understand that murder is not a likely punishment, but I use the phrase to signify its seriousness. A sharp expression can carry much weight.

If I had eight hours to chop down a tree, I'd spend six hours sharpening my axe.

Abraham Lincoln

Back to our match. Blas plays brilliantly and dispatches his Boise opponent in straight sets 6-4,6-3. Billy Pecor has shown up today and fights ferociously after dropping the first set to give us team point #3. Surely we can win just one of the remaining matches, I believe. However usually reliable Quentin has his hands full today with Nathan Sereke who plays pretty far back in the court. While Quentin has very steady groundstrokes, his inability to punish with his forehand is too much to overcome and he falls 6-3,6-3. Michael Moore fills in for Wyatt and finds himself locked in with a mirror image of himself. Both players are a step slow, but have explosive forehands. Thomas Teinrero, his opponent, is weaker on the backhand, but very committed to hitting everything with his forehand. I point out to Michael that he needs to look for opportunities to take his backhand early and change direction, hitting it down the line, but he lacks confidence in his ability to execute this pattern. Immediately I face the dilemma of directing him to do the right thing[take the backhand down the line] when I know it is not what he wants to do. There is no simple answer here and this is where I need to call on my years of experience. I explain the situation, but leave the final decision in Michael's hands. Knowing he will attend medical school the next year I remind him that this is certainly less stressful than what he will face using his scalpel in surgery. Michael reminds me that he does not plan on becoming a surgeon. I have picked the wrong analogy and it costs Michael who falls in straight sets.

On the next court Ryan Bandy is locked in a battle with Garrett Patton, Greg's son. I have known Garrett, or "G-Man" as many call him, for many years. While I thought this match-up favored us I can see that Patton's ball is too heavy for Ryan and he similarly falls 6-4, 6-2. The match draws even and all eyes follow the Andrews-Bettles match between the two #1 players. The level is high on their court. Both men would run through the fence to retrieve the next ball. Both have bigger and better forehands. Both prefer playing back in the court to better give themselves the chance to play forehands. By now darkness has arrived and we will finish under the lights. To me it is clear that whichever player cuts in to take time away from his opponent, even a small amount, will win. Andrews had lost the first set, but wins the second, so I am hoping his momentum will carry him. Alas, that will not be the case, as Bettles is simply a small fraction better and wins a nail-biter 4-6,7-5,6-4. Greg is crushed. His parents are in the crowd and they are quick to offer consolation, but Greg unfairly feels that he has lost the match for us. Being involved in the last match to finish in a 4-3 battle places too much pressure on any player, but this is what all of us imagine as we practice. I quickly tell Greg how proud I am of his effort, but the look in his eyes gives away his disappointment. I know that we are going to need Greg tomorrow, so I remind him that he will have the chance tomorrow to overcome his disappointment. This also has personal ramifications for Greg, as Bettles has a strong national ranking and Greg needs wins like this to ensure his presence in the NCAA singles field.

This one will hurt for awhile, not simply because we lost, but because Boise's schedule doesn't always give them great opportunities to play good teams at home, where upsets are most likely to occur. Therefore today's loss might drop us farther in the polls than it should. We need to maximize every opportunity going forward because I know that a ranking in the #29-32 range at NCAA time will send us to Columbus for the first two rounds of the NCAA tournament. Ty Tucker's Buckeyes have a home match winning streak of well over 200 consecutive matches. Not many teams leave Columbus with a "W."

———⊙∞⊙———

It is our choices that show what we are, far more than our abilities.

JK Rowling

———⊙∞⊙———

As Scarlett O'Hara said in "Gone With The Wind" …."Tomorrow is another day." And indeed it is. While the disappointment of last evening's finish still hangs over us it is my job and Ryan's to see that our guys have left that disappointment far behind us. Because Ryan is such a highly motivated coach I never really have to worry about our team not being ready to play. Another opportunity presents itself to us in #29 Cornell, a team that hopes to win the Ivy League. They have a young and aggressive coach who has big plans for the Big Red. Silvio Tanasoiu has injected competitiveness into his squad and I take them seriously because of this season's good start. Unlike yesterday, we drop the doubles point, dropping 8-6 matches at #1 and #2. We were just beginning a tie-breaker at #3, but that match is stopped as soon as the doubles point is decided. We are in for a battle.

Andrews get us off to a good start with a straight set bashing of Cornell's Venkat Iyer 6-2, 6-2. Iyer served big in doubles, but as the singles match unfolds it is apparent that he is not moving well. An injury, perhaps? Who knows? As I said, the third consecutive day of play in an event usually takes a toll on at least a few of the teams. Greg is not feeling sorry for anyone today and is the first to finish. The match score evens at 1-1. Monaghan looks like he has his hands full with British born Sam Fleck and drops the first set 6-4, but I know Quentin will bounce back. Fleck is ultra-steady. He does not possess big weapons, so I urge Quentin to be patient, but ready to pull the trigger on any short ball. Moros is all over Alex Sidney at #3 and finishes just after Andrews 6-1,6-3. Blas looks as good as he has been all year. Pecor today has shown up with all guns blazing and simply overpowers Quock-Daniel Nguyen 6-1,6-1. When the stars align correctly for Billy he can be untouchable. Few college players possess his clean power and today it is on full display for all in the enthusiastic crowd to see. These fans know their tennis and it is always a pleasure to play in front of them, especially if you are not playing hosts Alabama and Auburn.

Quickly we move to a 3-1 lead. Only one more match needed to clinch. While Monaghan fights back to lead Fleck 4-2 in the second set, he will not finish today because Moore has overpowered Lefty Jason Luu 6-2,1-6,6-1, a significant win for Michael. Both players have markedly better forehands and, because of the lefty-righty battle, both play on the same side of the court, doing everything to get forehands. Normally this might favor Luu, as he is quicker than Michael, but Moore has better resolve today and is able to sneak into the net a few key times when he stretches Luu out wide on his weaker backhand side. That, or at least the threat of it, is the difference today, as our record improves to 10-6. I am disappointed that Bandy doesn't get to finish today, as he was only a few points away, leading 7-5,6-5. He is growing in both confidence and his ability to play solid all-court tennis. I believe that he will be a key player for us down the stretch. We win the match 4-1.

As we make the two hour drive from Montgomery to the Atlanta airport, something I have done more than twenty times with our team, I find myself fighting off the pangs of nostalgia. The Blue Gray Classic has been good to us over the years. We have won the event several times and lost in the finals in a similar number of contests, and those victories occurred when the Blue Gray had a much stronger field, boasting as many as five top ten teams. I realize that this might be my last trip to Montgomery and know that I will miss the friendships and excitement of past years. Fortunately for us, there is a direct flight from Atlanta to South Bend and we arrive on schedule, signaling the end of spring break. Next up, the #1 ranked and defending national champions of USC.

~ Cross Court Reflection ~

My motivation is always the same, being #1 or #5, so that's the truth. And my goal is the same - to be happy playing. It is to enjoy the game and improve always.

Rafael Nadal

Down The Stretch

Great minds discuss ideas; average minds discuss events; small minds discuss people.

Eleanor Roosevelt

It is always special to take on the nation's #1 team. We certainly have done this many times, but were able to emerge victorious only twice. The first occasion couldn't have been better timed, as we beat #1 USC in Athens, Ga in the NCAA semi-finals to give us the opportunity to compete for a national championship on the last day of the season. Not only did we win, but clinched the match 5-1 in singles, not even having to play doubles at all. The second such win was just as sweet, but more dramatic, beating the Fighting Illini in Champaign-Urbanna 4-3 in very dramatic fashion right after they had captured the National Team Indoors. Today's match with the USC Trojans presents a more than formidable challenge because the men of Troy are on an incredible roll, having won four consecutive NCAA championships, something only previously happening to Dick Gould's Stanford Cardinal. The Trojans are coached by Peter Smith. Smith and Virginia's Brian Boland have owned men's college tennis and have occupied rarified air for the better part of a decade.

When Peter called me to request this match a year ago I was very flattered. It is indeed special to host the defending NCAA champions and, while I hold no realistic illusions of an upset, I am convinced that we can be competitive and am excited for the opportunity that this presents. It has been very gratifying to see the growth in Peter Smith. I have encouraged both him and Boland to take ownership of our college game and the ITA. When the ITA Board of Directors passed the new format[no-ad scoring with matches stopped when clinched] it was important for the top coaches to climb onboard to help end the bickering that ensued. Peter and Manny Diaz of Georgia were among the first prominent coaches to encourage others to get on the train. We had been advised by athletic directors to make changes which would bring match times below the three hour threshold. The ITA Board had seen a number of colleges drop men's tennis, an unintended consequence of Title IX, and knew that this new format gave us the best chance to thrive. Nonetheless there were the usual nay-sayers, many of them from the women's side, whose complaining was weakening our sport. Peter made a difference in this battle.

Smith was taking a chance scheduling this match, as the temperatures in March in South Bend frequently would dictate that the match be played indoors. There are plenty of coaches who refuse to put their teams in challenging positions, fearful that an avoidable loss might hurt their ranking or NCAA seeding. The best coaches, however, realize that they must challenge their teams and players in order to guarantee future successes when it most mattered. It requires both vision and courage to deliberately throw obstacles in the path of one's team to ensure its growth and future readiness for similar challenges. The last thing a coach wants is to send his team into post-season play without it being challenged. The NCAA's newly announced policy that teams below the .500 mark would not be given at-large entry into the NCAA tournament despite a ranking that would normally guarantee selection was yet another reason to avoid unnecessary losses. The Trojans, of course, had no indoor courts, as the California climate rendered them unnecessary.

I arranged a tour of the football stadium for Smith's team and he texted me a photo of his team gathered around the famous "Play Like A Champion Today" sign that all Notre Dame football players touched as they made their way from the locker room to the field. Peter then came to my office and gave me a very pretty pen that he had purchased for me as a memento for my final season as a coach. We coaches are sentimental. I still have that pen in my desk today and treasure it, just as I treasure the inscribed office - magnifying glass given me by Dave Fish on HIS [not my] 50th birthday. I truly value my relationships with other coaches.

We're born alone, live alone, and die alone. Only through our love and friendship can we create the illusion for a moment that we're not alone.

Orson Welles

As our match began I appreciated the way the USC players took charge in doubles. I have said before that singles more accurately reflects recruiting while doubles reflects coaching. There is some truth to this, as most doubles in the junior ranks is not taken seriously enough. The Trojans won at #2 and #3, clinching the point. We trailed 6-7 while serving at #1, but could not finish. When singles began I thought we might have some chances. Three of the six matches went to third sets. Andrews gave a great effort, splitting the first two sets, only to lose to Emilio Gomez in a 10-8 tie-breaker for the third set. Gomez fought off match points and was not afraid to go for his shots at key times. Bandy dropped the first set to Johnny Wang, but came back to win 1-6, 6-3, 6-3 to put us on the board. Yannick Hanfmann's backhand and overall pace off the ground proved to be too good for Moros in his third set. On top of that, Blas had irritated a nagging hip flexor injury which would never quite go away for the rest of the year. While Monaghan and Moore were unable to win, each pushed his Trojan counterpart to a tie-breaker. We were still playing without Wyatt McCoy and I was hoping to get some better news about him from our athletic trainer, Tony Sutton, soon. It was now time to move outdoors, although rain and falling temperatures were always a part of every college tennis coach's life. We would need confidence to successfully navigate the remaining portion of our schedule.

~ Cross Court Reflection ~

Confidence doesn't come when you have all the answers, but it comes when you are ready to face all the questions.

Michael Josephson

US Team in Tokyo for "Dream Match" against Japanese All Stars.
In 2003, I was selected to lead a US/ITA Collegiate All Star team to
play the Japanese All Stars. It was a great experience. We were led
by Amer Delic and Amber Liu and won both matches in a modified
format much like World Team Tennis employs today. David Benjamin
oversaw the event and Ann Lebedeff coached our women. That is JP
Fruterro holding the American flag.

BAYLISS'
LAST STAND

THE BULLET

CHAPTER SEVEN

Nearing the Finish Line

*What you GET by achieving your goals is
not as important as what you BECOME
by achieving your goals.*

Goethe

With spring break behind us I realize that there remains
only one month of regular season play. The loss to Boise State has
been costly. This week's ITA rankings show that we have slipped
from #22 to #27. Thinking ahead, my mind is constantly focused
on the practical ramifications awaiting our results, i.e. where our
ranking will place us in the NCAA tournament. The NCAA committee tries to keep teams in appropriate pods. I want to avoid the
#29-32 pod, which will certainly send us to Columbus and Ohio
State's record of well over 200 consecutive home victories. This
weekend will take us to Williamsburg to face Coach Peter Daub's
Tribe team. I anticipate warmer weather in Virginia and believe
that our nine days spent in Alabama has prepared us for outdoor
play.

Left - Bobby Bayliss holds t-shirt designed for his last home match – the 2013 Big
East Tennis Championships. Team captain Blas Moros had the shirts made for
each player and handed them out immediately before play began. Notre Dame
defeated Louisville 4-0. *Photo courtesy of Pat Bayliss.*

The flight to Richmond is uneventful and we will have adequate time to adjust to the William and Mary courts. There is a surprising forecast for chilly weather when we arrive, so we practice in the Tribe's beautiful McCormack-Nagelsen Indoor center, a gift from the sports icon Mark McCormack. McCormack was the first real agent in the world of sports, beginning in the 1950's with his partnership with Arnold Palmer and culminating in the formation of IMG which represents Bjorn Borg, among many great tennis players and celebrities and even includes the Vatican. This brings back memories of Brian Kalbas and his ultra-successful run as the head women's tennis coach at William and Mary.

In the fall of 1993 I received a call from Millie West, the SWA[senior women's administrator] at W&M. They were searching for the right coach to lead them into the next millennium. Millie read a list of candidates to me and asked me to rate them in order of preference. I asked her if she wanted only names from her list or, if I could do better, should I suggest someone else. She told me that she, of course, wanted the best possible candidate. I then told her that she could not possibly do better than Brian Kalbas, my former player, team captain, and current assistant coach. Millie was skeptical, noting Brian's age[25] and relative inexperience. She explained that tennis was W&M's flagship women's sport and they needed a "home run." After haggling a bit I made a suggestion to her. I told her that I would pay for Brian's airfare and, if he was not hired, W&M would owe me nothing, but if they hired him they would need to reimburse me. She agreed and I went to find Brian to tell him the news, as he had begun a search to take over his own program. "No way!" Brian said. "Why would I want to become a women's coach?"

I explained to Brian that I felt this was a perfect opportunity and, since he had just finished a three year stint ending in an NCAA runner-up finish, he would not have to re-establish himself on the men's side, should an opportunity subsequently come his way. I convinced him to at least take the visit, as the experience of an interview would be helpful to him in the future. As you might guess, Brian hit the home run I mentioned and he was named the new head coach at William and Mary within a few weeks. History shows that Brian wasted no time and within a few years he took W&M to its highest-ever ranking and an NCAA elite eight appearance. He was named ITA National Coach of the Year. He now plies his trade in Chapel Hill, NC and has taken the Tar Heels to a runner-up NCAA finish and has won the National Team Indoors three times. Here is yet another instance of the pupil surpassing the teacher. As our team enters the tennis center Brian's pictures and other tributes are visible and I feel a small sense of pride.

The only way to do great work is to love what you do. If you haven't found it yet, keep looking. Don't settle.

Steve Jobs

The William and Mary courts are a bit faster than I remembered and also have some cushion to them. While this makes them user-friendly for your feet, an adjustment is required, as balls hit with underspin slide a bit more and you need to get up to the ball quickly. While such differences are small, a player needs to adapt quickly or find himself out of position on some of his shots. Our guys are aided by their appearance here in the fall and they take little time to settle in comfortably. As the match nears, one of our players hands me today's program and I am once again touched to see my picture on its cover with an appropriate tribute to my career and coming retirement. Peter Daub is obviously behind this and I walk over to thank him.

Any fuzzy and warm feelings I have are quickly shattered, as the doubles point begins and the Tribe comes out with guns blazing. Daub takes great pride in his ability to coach doubles and it is evident today. He has always excelled here and his teams are aggressive, moving across the net to poach any return that hangs in the middle. The net men on each court are ready for anything and begin the points on serve closing in tightly on the net, almost inviting us to lob. In my playing era most returners could easily lift a "bump" lob return of serve over the head of the net man to solve this problem, but in today's tennis most players use a two-handed backhand for returns. This makes the offensive lob more difficult on the return, particularly on first serves. They take big cuts at second serve returns and soon we find ourselves down a break on court #1. Ryan hustles over to handle that court and I now focus on #2 and #3. His doubles acumen is very high, so it is easy for me to focus on my two courts, as we can share responsibilities on court #2. All three matches are hotly contested. Pecor and Lawson lock in early on returns and come close to breaking serve in each of the first several games, but coming close brings you nothing except in horseshoes or hand grenades. Bandy and Dooley break early and look in control. Soon we grab #2 8-6 while we drop #1 9-7. All eyes shift to court #3 where Ryan Bandy serves it out for yet another 8-6 victory. We take a quick 1-0 lead.

Nothing diminishes anxiety faster than action.

Walter Anderson

As the singles begin I am pretty confident and find that confidence rewarded. While two of the matches require a third set, we decisively take #1, #2, and #5, losing only seven games in all. We also grab #3, 6-1,6-4. Greg Andrews' forehand takes control over Anton Andersson and he wins the last nine consecutive games 6-2,6-0. Monaghan is far too steady for Aaron Chaffee and his result is a similar 6-2, 6-1 win. Michael Moore pastes Scott Huang in another route 6-2,6-0. While I of course want each of our other players to win, it is difficult to explain how much more relaxed I am with the team victory guaranteed. When the match outcome is still in doubt, I find myself checking and re-checking the large electric scoreboard to monitor our progress on the courts out of my vision, even though I have no control there. However, as soon as we nail down the clinching point I am much better in my focus. I am able to spend pretty much all of my time on my courts [the layout of courts in the McCormack-Nagelsen Tennis Center has courts 1,3, and 5 together, while nos. 2,4, and 6 are adjacent, but out of my visual range.] Ryan, on the other hand has his hands full, as both #4 and #6 go to third set super-breakers. Alex Lawson has filled in for Ryan Bandy and, while he has all of the shots needed in his repertoire, the connection from doubles remains difficult for him. His instincts are geared to doubles and he never seems quite sure of what to do in singles. He drops the breaker 10-7, but Pecor turns on the jets and wins somewhat comfortably in his overtime period. Billy is learning to stay "in the moment." Mission accomplished.

Learn from the past, set vivid, detailed goals for the future, and live in the only moment of time over which you have any control.

Dennis Whaitley

Once again we head to Paul's Deli for lunch and are accompanied by my college teammates who have driven from Richmond to see my team perform. Sandy Tucker, Bill Schutt, Butch Cohen, and John McGinty are in attendance and I can sit with them and catch up on hometown gossip. Although Schutt played at Davidson against us in college, we count him as one of us, as we all played our formative tennis at Richmond's Byrd Park. The bond between teammates is a special one and I truly enjoy the fellowship. I attended the French open with Tucker in 2006 and we also took in the Australian Open in 2018. One of my great regrets is that I was unable to get Notre Dame to move its campus to Richmond where I could see these guys more often. Whenever we get together it seems that we are somehow magically transported back in time. We feel and act like we are somehow 20 years old once again. When you have shared so many experiences together there is no room for pretense. We have all seen each other in embarrassing situations, in good times and bad. This could mean having seen one another whiff overhead smashes, double fault on break point, and do foolish, immature social things while in the process of growing up. This is truly one of the great things about competitive athletics. The bond between teammates is as close to unbreakable as it gets, topped only by family. As we get into our vehicles to drive back to the Richmond airport I wave goodbye once again. Left unsaid is "until next time." Next up for us is Ball State, much closer to home in Muncie, IN.

~ Cross Court Reflection ~

It is amazing what you can accomplish if you don't care who gets the credit.

Harry Truman

Changes in College Sports

As we drive to Muncie to play Ball State I find myself pondering the changes in college athletics since my own college days. As I mentioned earlier, the influence of television and money in college sports has shaped a different playing field. When I landed in South Bend in 1987 Ball State was one of the nation's top 25 teams. The Cardinals' coach, Bill Richards, had built a powerhouse squad with predominantly players from the midwest by combining an extraordinary work ethic with an unusually effective blend of his competitiveness and tennis acumen. The Cardinals have always played "blue collar" tennis under Richards. They asked for and gave no quarter. It was hard not to admire what Richards had created and his team beat my first Notre Dame team soundly in our first meeting in 1988. They continued to be highly competitive for several more years. In fact my 1992 team, the NCAA runner-up, was fortunate to defeat Ball State 6-3 in a hard fought match that saw us win two of the matches by 7-6 third set scores. Our own David DiLucia, the nation's #1 singles player, had to fight off a match point in the second set. These guys had been really good in the late 1980's and early 1990's.

The college landscape changed, though, about this time. The schools that now comprise the "Power Five" began to reap great sums of money through the television of football and the margin between them and those less fortunate grew bigger. Add to this mix apparel and shoe contracts and an "arms race" in the construction of athletic facilities and you have the ingredients needed to take away the opportunities that had heretofore been spread pretty evenly. As various TV networks began to bid for the rights from the larger conferences, heretofore unexpected dollars moved those conferences, now called the "Power Five" into positions of prominence. Add to this a large influx of international athletes and the landscape changed enormously. Soon it was much more difficult for a great coach like Bill Richards to attract the talent to keep up with the big boys. This process has continued into the present where almost no school outside of the "Power Five" can compete evenly. To be sure, there are a few notable exceptions aided by geography and climate[Pepperdine and San Diego, now coached by our own Ryan Keckley, are examples], but in most sports what I have described holds true. When you add in 30 to 40 million dollars per year that each school receives from networks with whom its conference partners.......that will buy a lot of tennis rackets, etc.

A successful man is one who can lay a firm foundation with the bricks others have thrown at him.

David Brinkley

What I have just described is something Bill Richards and I have discussed many times and it is sad to observe today. The plight of the mid-major schools today makes meaningful competition between the more powerfully aligned schools and those less fortunate almost impossible. I truly admire what Coach Richards has done at Ball State and remind my team to expect a difficult match from a well-coached team that will give its all. That is exactly what happens today. The doubles is very close, as Ball State takes #1 8-6 and we control #2 in an 8-3 effort. Everything comes down to #3 and it is a hard fight, but Bandy and Dooley show why they have had so much recent success with an 8-6 victory to clinch the point. I can see the disappointment on Richards' face, as he knows that we are both more talented and deeper than his team in singles.

Armed with the doubles point our guys play a strong match and we take all of the singles in straight sets. Michael Moore, playing in place of the injured Ryan Bandy, struggles a bit, but wins 7-6,7-5. I am impressed with the big forehand of Ball State's Cliff Morrison at #1, but Greg takes a back seat to no one in the forehand department and his superior movement is the difference, 6-3,6-4. Monaghan, Moros, Pecor, and the recently-healed Wyatt McCoy all win comfortably. Richards and I exchange comments about what each of us observed as the match concludes. I am careful to listen to him, as he remains one of college tennis's more knowledgeable coaches. Surprisingly, I am able to spend a few moments with Ball State[and now Marquette] athletic director, Bill Scholl and his Associate AD, Brian Hardin. Bill served ably as as associate AD at Notre Dame and was very open and helpful to our tennis needs. Brian was our sport administrator during that time. It has been a good move for both and I feel that it will not be the last. Each is on a fast track to significance in the world of college sports. Only a few years will find both of them in AD positions at Marquette and Drake, respectively.

Happiness is not the absence of problems, but the ability to deal with them.

Steve Maraboli

Next up on our schedule is SMU, a dangerous team that I respect immensely. The Mustangs are coached by an old friend, Carl Neufeld. I first met Carl when I moved to Notre Dame, as he was the first coach to call me about scheduling. I admired the job he did at Northern Illinois University, but really grew to respect him when he became an assistant at USC where he played a major role in building the Trojan team that won NCAA titles in 1991, 1993, and 1994. When the position opened at SMU and he was appointed head coach I figured that this was a team to watch. He took over for tennis legend Dennis Ralston and wasted little time recruiting strong players and blending a group of both American and international players into a final four squad in 2000. In the years since, SMU has twice torn down its varsity tennis facility to build a new one. They now have one of the truly elite set-ups in college tennis. Carl also worked with me when he was at USC to begin the series of fall dual matches between Notre Dame and USC the evening before the football games which produced sellout crowds and some electric tennis. He is ably assisted by Kyle Spencer, a former USC All American and until recently the head coach at Maryland until the Terps dropped men's tennis. We would need to be ready for this one.

Neufeld is a keen student of doubles and I knew that SMU would press us here. I also was dealing with a new and unanticipated problem in our doubles lineup. Greg Andrews and Spencer Talmadge had played #1 doubles for us all year. They were, it seemed, the perfect combination: one of the country's better singles players and competitors[Andrews] and a doubles specialist whose ability to be in the right place and put the ball away at net[Talmadge]. One of the keys to successful doubles at the college level is to combine the talents available into a real "team." We had done that with these two. The other problem was to ensure that both players liked and inspired confidence in each other. I talked earlier about how we wanted each player to acknowledge, or speak to, the other after every point. Both players were quiet by nature, but Spencer could, at times, take silence to new heights. During the course of any college season it is normal to see partners lose their mutual cohesiveness and revert to a state of poor communication. That is exactly what seems to be the problem with this pair. The answer can be as simple as making them more aware of the need for constant mutual reinforcement, but sometimes it is necessary to break them apart and begin again with new teams. Doubles teams at the college level sometimes have a short shelf-life. When either partner loses confidence in the other, results quickly suffer. Chemistry is all-important here.

Because Lawson-Pecor had become a better team, I decided to move them up to #1. I felt that Spencer's skills were sufficient to combine him with Ryan Bandy and see what they could do at #2. It looked promising. That also meant moving Andrews down to #3 with Matt Dooley. Many college #1 singles players would have

balked at having to move from #1 to #3,even in doubles, but Greg
seemed energized. Never as comfortable at #1 due to functional,
but less-than-extraordinary volleying skills, Greg made himself
at home at #3 where he felt he would be the best tennis player on
the court. It worked…...and not a day too soon. We had an entirely
new doubles lineup, free of the entanglements and frustrations that
a long college season can bring.

—◦○◦—

*Failure is not the problem. It is our reluc-
tance to try, our attempts to avoid it and
smother it, and our unwillingness to learn
from it.*

Chad Stoloff

—◦○◦—

Armed with new combinations and the uncertainty of what
to expect, we began the doubles with SMU anxious to see where
we stood. Changing doubles a few weeks before the NCAAs was
risky, but I thought we had done the right thing. At #1 Pecor and
Lawson were a bit anxious, it seemed, but put up a good fight before dropping a one-break pro set 8-5. Andrews responded just as I
had hoped, acting like he owned the court and dominating long rallies with his howitzer forehand. They scrapped out an 8-6 set over
Perez-Lammon, as all eyes turned to #2 where Talmadge seemed
energized and Bandy provided the needed steadiness as the match
moved to the decisive tie-breaker which they won 7-5. As the
favored team, it was important never to allow the visiting team to
win the doubles point and give them a reason to believe.

The singles was easier than anticipated. Monaghan and
Moros took their opponents apart, losing only six games between
them. Monaghan was becoming accustomed to playing at #2 and
Moros was handling a nagging injury well. A hip flexor injury can
be painful and limiting, and many take a long time to heal. We
now looked strong at the top of our lineup. Bandy, recently fully

recovered, moved well and "routined" Nate Lammons 6-3,6-3. It was good to get him back. Ryan had developed into a very strong #6 for us after beginning the fall out of the singles rotation. He will be a strength for us when NCAA play begins. McCoy, now seemingly fully healed, made short work of Eduardo Razetto 6-3,6-2. With the match clinched, both Pecor and Andrews were forced into match super-breakers and each won comfortably. Another hurdle conquered. It was good to avoid any long matches today, as we have the South Florida Bulls scheduled for tomorrow. Any anxiety our guys felt has been erased with this performance today and tomorrow beckons.

———

Every tomorrow has two handles. We can take hold of it with the handle of anxiety or the handle of faith.

Henry Ward Beecher

———

The South Florida match is an easy one for us to want to play, as one year ago in the conference semi-finals we lost to the Bulls in Tampa in a five hour marathon 4-3, costing us an opportunity to play for the Big East title the next day. We held team match points which we squandered that day and the heat and humidity were beyond oppressive, not to mention the enthusiastic crowd support. None of us has forgotten. I will not need a motivational speech to capture our guys' attention. This match will be in South Bend and the change in venue is significant. In Tampa, not only do we face humidity and higher temperatures, but USF simply plays much better at home, buoyed by the many Latino chants of "Ole!" from its enthusiastic crowd which includes a distinct Hispanic element. This year's team has a new coach, as veteran Don Barr, a very successful and likeable coach of many seasons has retired, beating me to the punch. In his place is a young and highly motivated Matt Hill and he brings tons of energy to the job. It is obvious that he is not afraid of hard work.

Chop your own wood and it will warm you twice.

Henry Ford

It is immediately easy to see that Matt Hill will be successful. I first met him when he served as the volunteer assistant coach at Alabama. His energy level is visible to all as his team begins to warm up prior to the match. I envision a successful career for Matt. He has beaten cancer and is ready for life's next chapter. He will do well in our sport. In a few short years he will take over the reins at the newly re-instituted Arizona State program.

Today is special because it is the final regular season home match for our team and it has been designated as "Senior Day." Our seniors, Michael Moore, Spencer Talmadge, and Blas Moros will be honored just prior to our match and the trio seem genuinely excited. Our Sports Promotions staff has brought out enlarged cardboard cut-out "big heads" of the three to pass out to our crowd for recognition and to build enthusiasm, but I am more than surprised to see that they have included "big heads" of me, as well. They explain to me that I am, in a way, also graduating with the seniors, as it is also my own final home regular season match. Our PA announcer, Bob Buckley, whom we affectionately call the "voice of Notre Dame Tennis" carefully reads from a script of the highlights of each of the seniors and finishes with some kind remarks about me, as well. It is time to play.

You must have a larger than average ego to be in the pilot seat.

Erika Armstrong

I mentioned earlier that in our match a year ago in Tampa the USF team played well in front of its home crowd. It is entirely natural for this to happen. The players are used to the surface, the wind currents, and the playing background. Additionally they will respond positively to the cheers of their own fans. Today, though, there is an added element to our own home court advantage. Because of the day's unseasonably cold temperatures our match will be moved indoors. Not only will we have the earlier mentioned advantages, but USF rarely plays indoors. Because of the warm year-round climate it makes little sense for indoor courts to be built in Florida and only Florida State, in Florida's panhandle, has them.

Nearly all men can stand adversity, but if you want to test a man's character, give him power.

Abraham Lincoln

As previously explained, the ball travels faster indoors, as there is no wind resistance in the relative vacuum. Not only does this force "outdoor" teams to recover more quickly and get ready for the next shot, but it rewards the player who can play the ball early on the rise. Many players from warmer climates tend to play farther behind the baseline because they have more time to run down the opponent's shot, as well as the tendency of today's players to try to run around backhands to get forehands. This style leads to "working" the ball around the court patiently while trying to wear down the opponent and count on attrition to play a factor in the match. Longer rallies, heavy topspin, and greater height and "heaviness" become the norm. This rarely works indoors, as "quick strike" tennis takes over and the player who anticipates the short ball best and plays closer to the baseline has a distinct advantage in taking away the opponent's time. Coming to the net works better indoors also, as the ceiling dictates that high, defensive lobs are much less effective. Many of the biggest upsets in college tennis occur when indoor and outdoor teams clash, particularly early in the season. As I observe the South Florida players warming up it is easy to note the difference in where they stand relative to that of my own team. We are closer to the baseline instinctively, while the Bulls hang back just a bit more. That difference may influence today's outcome.

USF is clearly better outdoors and looks uncomfortable at times in the early going. We jump on them quickly in the doubles and our newly adopted doubles lineup takes charge immediately. We take #3 first, as Greg Andrews looks like a new puppy in the lower slot, running around to take forehands at every opportunity. Result: 8-3. Bandy and Talmadge have really adjusted well to each other and also take control early, holding serve without facing a break point throughout to win 8-5. Only at #1 do the Bulls have much of a chance, as their top player, Oliver Pramming adjusts quickly, but Pecor-Lawson hang on for a 9-7 win there. Our solid play continues in singles. While several of the first sets are close we manage to win them all and I realize that we are in full control. We are indeed in our own comfort zone today.

Life begins at the end of your comfort zone.

Neale Donald Walsh

Andrews is all over the court in the singles, ripping forehands past Pramming and keeping him pinned to the deep left corner of the court. He wins 6-4,6-2. Monaghan settles into a comfortable rhythm and makes Gonzales Muniz work for every point. He wins 7-5,6-2. I now begin to see the beginnings of a player who will later become an NCAA singles title contender. Moros puts his all-court skills together and moves Guillermo De Vilchez from corner to corner, finishing with a well-played 7-6,6-4 victory. Pecor starts with a bang and dictates play throughout his 6-2,6-4 win. Billy can be very imposing when his shots are clicking. His ball not only has great pace, but carries a "heaviness" with it that further pushes Federico Sabogal back to an uncomfortable place on the court. He reverses last year's painful loss to Sabogal. When Billy is "on," I rarely have to pay much attention to his match. Today provides another such example of this. Michael Moore, peeking up in the bleachers to see his smiling "big head" bouncing up and down is challenged in the first set, but sneaks it out in a tie-breaker and wins in straight sets. The last match to finish is Wyatt McCoy and it is a classic. Matched against the strong backhand of Ravi Patel, Wyatt can no longer depend on his own backhand to dominate the cross-court rallies. He will need to change direction more often today and be willing to take a few chances offensively. Both players have exceptional backhands and both are very fast. The rallies are long and intensely fought, sometimes tallying 30 and 40 shots. They split sets and begin a "match tie-breaker"[first to 10, win by two]. Wyatt might be the fastest player I have ever coached, but he needs to step in and take a few balls early to best utilize his speed. Old habits die hard and today Ravi Patel is simply too much for him, 5-7,7-6, 1-0. There is defensive and offensive speed. Ryan needs to add the latter to his repertoire. Close, but no cigar.

After the match ends Matt Hill approaches me and says some very flattering things about me and my career. He and I know that we could meet yet again back here in the Big East tournament in two weeks. If so, today's match was a great dress rehearsal for our guys. Pat comes out of the crowd to offer congratulations and I quickly think back to her many years of holding the fort for me. I am indeed fortunate to have her as a best friend and life partner. I always appreciate her kind words.

Kind words can be short and sweet, but their effect can be endless.

Mother Theresa

It is not yet time to go home because we have a second match yet to play. The Butler Bulldogs have come from Indianapolis to play the second half of a doubleheader and new coach Parker Ross is eager to take his team to the next level. We both know that our squad will be too much for them, but nobody became great by ducking good competition. Ross wants to ensure his team's readiness for the upcoming conference tournament, as the winner will gain an NCAA berth. For me, the biggest problem involves whom to play in our lineup. After checking with our squad I decide to sit Moros, McCoy, and Bandy in singles. This will give others a chance to get into a match while Moros can rest his continuingly painful and persistent hip flexor injury. McCoy needs the rest as well, as he played a three hour singles match earlier. It is time to throw Alex Lawson back into a singles match, as I know that he will eventually become a strong presence there for us....but not just yet.

The singles goes pretty much as anticipated. We win five of the six in straight sets with relatively little difficulty. Michael Frederica jumps right into the fray, looking as though he has been a starter all year, winning easily. He has always had a terrific backhand, but now is showing signs that his forehand may become more reliable. I always enjoy seeing how one of our squad members who has not been a regular in the lineup handles this new responsibility. Tonight Michael maximizes his opportunity. It has been a long three years sitting on the sidelines and he does not want to waste tonight's chance to show what he can do. Lawson, though, is still having difficulty connecting the dots in singles, as opposed to the way he walks on a doubles court acting like he owns it. I have spoken with his parents about this, as his mother is a tennis professional and they agree with the dilemma. Tonight he is forced into a match tie-breaker in place of a third set and he wins it comfortably. It is an important first step for him. In post-season play[conference and NCAA] we are restricted to an active roster of only eight players. Most of this season we have played nine, as Lawson, Talmadge, and Dooley play only in doubles roles. It does not take a genius to see the problem I will face in two weeks. One of these players will not be allowed to play due to the NCAA's restriction limiting teams to eight. In fact, one of the things of which I am most proud of during my three years on the NCAA Tennis Committee, served right after my retirement, is leading the charge to change the number of allotted players to nine. While this is a problem I cannot run from, I decide to put it on hold and enjoy my own "senior day" just a little bit more. We have just one more regular season match left to play and it will be an important one.

———

Don't let what you cannot do interfere with what you can do.

John Wooden

———

Notre Dame joined the Big East Conference in 1995 and we immediately found ourselves in a natural rivalry with Miami. The Irish vs. Hurricanes rivalry has been well documented in the ESPN "30 for 30" film entitled "Catholics vs. Convicts." Both schools battled for national titles in football during the late 1980's and early 1990's. History shows that Notre Dame broke off the series because it had become far too contentious. Miami has never forgiven Notre Dame for that and the folks from Coral Gables have long memories. When we joined the conference the Hurricanes had just changed tennis coaches and the cupboard was a bare one for new coach Rodney Harmon. Fortunately for me, Rodney and I were old friends, having both grown up in Richmond. I have as much respect for Rodney as I do for anyone in tennis. His career is a distinguished one. As an ATP player he had some great wins in a career cut short by several surgeries. As a teacher/coach he has headed up USTA Player Development for American tennis and has worked with many of the world's best players. Whoever has occupied this post regularly has to suffer the stinging criticism of those who disagree with its decisions or policies. Harmon handled the position extremely well and has many friends all over the tennis world.

Having a strong relationship with Harmon helped me as we joined his conference. It also helped that he inherited a team with very limited talent. In fact, one of his players had acquired the nickname "Bicycle" because he had lost some matches 6-0, 6-0 [zeroes = wheels]. We were able to easily handle the Hurricanes in 1996, but by the next year Rodney had built a powerhouse and our matches became much tougher for us to win. He then moved to the USTA position mentioned earlier and was replaced by another outstanding coach, Jay Berger, himself a former ATP top ten player. We had some great battles and often both teams were in, or near, the top ten. My point is that there always existed a strong rivalry for us in conference play. When Miami left to join the ACC it did not take long for another strong rivalry to develop between our squad and new addition Louisville, as the Cardinals slid into Miami's position as our biggest Big East rival. Most years one of these teams took home the conference crown, with occasional resistance from South Florida.

A New Rival Emerges

My point here is that our next - and final - regular season match was in Louisville against the Cardinals. Coach Rex Ecarma had built a strong team that had, on occasion, made it into the nation's top twenty and our matches had been hotly contested. They were especially tough at home, where their newly resurfaced courts were slower than ours and a legitimate cause for concern. Getting the team up for Louisville was not difficult, and, in fact, I found it necessary to downplay the rivalry and treat the match as just another along the way. By now it was difficult for me not to become very reflective about the impending end of my coaching career. At each stop during the season I found myself reminiscing about previous matches played at each venue and the memories that every one of them evoked. I wanted this to be all business and to save my reflections for later when I could afford the time, but telling your heart what to do has never been a strength of mine. I saw ghosts sneaking onto courts and memories cascaded through my thoughts. There were few stops along the way that failed to move me. "Enough" I would tell myself and force a return to the task at hand. I have always been a sentimental and reflective person and I want to savor all of the great memories. Retirement may beckon, but I realize that there is still much to do before it arrives.

Life is too short to drink the house wine.

Helen Thomas

This day was no different and we needed to be at our best. As we took the court, everyone knew the score. We needed to win

today to secure the top seed in next week's Big East Championships, Notre Dame's last appearance in this event before joining
the ACC. This would mean that the loser would likely have to face
South Florida in the semi-finals of the Big East, while the winner would not. Incentive was not a problem. The match began in
an unusual manner. After winning the toss and serving first on all
three courts we jumped out of the blocks quickly, breaking serve
at both #1 and #3, while giving up a service break at #2. Normally
it is easier to hold serve in the initial games because the balls are
brand new and more difficult to return. The pattern continued, particularly at #1 and #3, as Pecor and Lawson started off on fire. Both
players can be streaky and fortunately for us they were streaky
good. Lawson served bullets and Pecor hit returns with abandon....
all the way through the match. The 8-1 score reflects our dominance and the same result came through for us once again at #3, as
Andrews-Dooley battered Simich-Brown by the same 8-1 score.
Oddly enough, the new combination of Talmadge-Bandy was not
able to pull it out and lost 8-5. Somehow, though, I felt that had
the other matches been closer we would have made a comeback.
No matter.....when offered the chance to start off with the doubles
point in hand I will always take it. Notre Dame leads 1-0.

*The successful warrior is the average man--
with lazer-like focus.*

Bruce Lee

The singles match-ups presented us with some intriguing
dynamics. Andrews took on Sebastien Stiefelmeyer. Both players were very good off the ground. Greg hit a slightly bigger and
more dynamic ball, while Stiefelmeyer had the stronger backhand.
He liked to play up in the court and, theoretically, this could take
away some of Greg's time and limit his ability to run around and
get forehands. He also had the ability to change direction on his
backhand, occasionally ripping a winner down the line. The contrast would be interesting to follow. Which player could force his

style on the other? Stiefelmeyer had been ranked #1 in the country earlier in the season on the strength of a terrific Fall. Pecor, on the other hand, was taking on Michael Lippens, a player with a very big and heavy forehand, so there would be plenty of firepower on court #4. Monaghan was paired against Albert Wagner, a player who could dominate by hitting big groundies. Quentin would need to keep everything deep and try to move Wagner, who looked to be a step slower than he. The other matches held similar challenges for us. Louisville's court layout paired off players in groups of two. Ryan would start out on courts 3 and 4, as those matches looked challenging for our guys. I would focus on #1 and #2 and we would wait to see how much we would be needed in McCoy's and Bandy's matches at #5/6.

Almost immediately Pecor fell behind and dropped the first set 6-1, while Moros similarly went down an early break. I would need Ryan to stay on those two courts, most likely for the entire day. His ability to analyze and pass on strategic and tactical advice is one of the things that separates him from other good coaches. While many are quite knowledgeable, few have his ability to couch that knowledge into "just the right" phrase that connects the dots for players in the heat of battle.

———⚬———

There's zero per cent correlation between being the best talker and having the best ideas.

Susan Cain

———⚬———

Fortunately we won all four of the remaining first sets as the match settled in. Greg's matchup with Stiefelmeyer was intriguing. The Louisville sophomore was diagonally cutting into the court on all backhands, hoping to get an opportunity to attack the net. Greg countered by noticing that Stiefelmeyer came forward just a bit too hard which made him vulnerable to an offensive lob and countered with that play. This worked well and Greg eventually got his hands on a forehand which he would play high and heavy back to the Stiefelmeyer forehand. This usually gave him control of the point. Today's level was high and the difference lay in Greg's ability to maintain this level throughout. He won 6-4, 6-1. The pressure on the Cardinals was increasing. Monaghan figured out quickly that Wagner was a far better attacking player than defender and amped up his own groundies to gain an advantage in the rallies. He also noticed that whenever Wagner came to the net he dumped his volleys short, so an adjustment here took care of that problem, as Quentin moved up in the court after hitting some dipping passes, forcing Wagner to volley deep or be very precise when dumping his volleys short. The result: Monaghan in straight sets 6-3,6-3. We were clearly in control.

Wyatt McCoy looks to be playing one of his better matches today. His speed disarms Alex Gornet, an attacking all-court player who likes to come to the net. We had recruited Alex and I liked him. His game had improved, I noticed, as I felt myself saying "another one who got away." Wyatt's ability to counter, however, is on full display and he takes the first set 6-2. Next to him, Bandy is in a dogfight with Van Damrongski. It can go either way, but he scratches and claws his way to the first set 7-5. Suddenly, and from apparently nowhere, Pecor roars back to life. He wins the second set decisively 6-1, an abrupt turnaround from the pasting he received by the same score in the first. As I have said before when Billy gets it rolling there is little that most opponents can do and he bagels Lippens in the third set 6-0. Almost immediately thereafter Andrews and Monaghan close out their matches in strong fashion, while Moros, clearly hampered by his hip flexor injury loses 6-4,6-2. We have clinched the match and lead 4-1. I relax with the knowledge that all Louisville can do is make the final score appear closer. We split the two remaining matches and leave with a solid 5-2 victory. It will make the five hour bus ride home seem like only two. An obstacle in our path has been converted into an opportunity.

~ Cross Court Reflection ~

Opportunity is missed by most people because it is dressed in overalls and looks like work.

Thomas Edison

20th Reunion of the 1992 NCAA Finalist Team. It was special to be with these guys again. Kneeling[l to r] Brian Kalbas, Horst Dziura, Tad Eckert, Tim Kalbas, and Chris Wojtalik. Standing: Andy Zurcher, Ryan Wenger, Bill Mountford, Ron Rosas, Bobby Bayliss, David DiLucia, Chuck Coleman, Walter Dolhare, Will Forsyth, and Paul Odland. Photo taken just before the Notre Dame football game on the 50 yard line by Mike Bennett.

Big East Championships

Boy, this year has gone by quickly! It is hard to believe that all remaining in my coaching career is our conference championship and the NCAA tournament. I am especially fortunate that, as luck would have it, this year's Big East will be hosted at Notre Dame. A quick look at the week's weather forecast shows that there is a strong likelihood that much of the play will be indoors, as temperatures will struggle to rise above 50. There are inherent advantages to being the top seed. One is that our scheduled matches will receive priority in when they are played. We will not have to wait around until others finish. Nonetheless, we can't count on our regular season's success to win this tournament and must once again prove ourselves. Conference championships are an important part of any coach's resume, just as is his/her won-loss record.

I mention won-loss record because of an interesting thing I observed just before my second year at Notre Dame. As the 1989 tennis media guide arrived, I took some time to thumb through it and found myself looking at some interesting history. Our team finished 17-13 in my inaugural year and right there, in black and white was a comparison of the records and winning percentage of each coach. There was my picture, aligned with all of Notre Dame's previous coaches. The cumulative record of each was listed, along with his winning percentage. I noticed also that in the early years of the program there was no coach. That era, nine seasons in all, was entitled "Coachless years," and the winning percentage for that period was .567. In contrast, my own record at Notre Dame also included my percentage. Yes, it was .567. So much for the importance of a good coach!

You can't build a reputation on what you are going to do.

Henry Ford.

While seeded #1, we need to focus on the task at hand. First up for us in this year's Big East is St. John's. Their coach, Eric Rebuhne, wears his heart on his sleeve. His passion for his team and what he wants them to do is readily apparent. He is full of energy and routinely races from court to court, barking out instructions to his players in a loud voice that carries throughout our building. Yes, I said building, which means that once again we are forced indoors due to cool temperatures. While perhaps every team's greatest home court advantage is on their own indoor courts, I realize that we need to get some matches played out-doors because we are more than likely to be playing our NCAA match[es] outside. Nonetheless we must take care of today's task before looking ahead. I have great respect for Rebhune, who has taken a previously weaker program and made them into a solid team that might be able to beat us in one or two spots in our lineup. Their top player, Vlasko Vladinov, has had some impres-sive wins and will be a tough out for Greg. A year ago in Tampa, he beat our Casey Watt at #1 in this tournament. They are always well prepared and I remind our team of the importance of not only winning, but doing so in as timely a manner as possible, as each team will play on three consecutive days. If we allow matches to creep into third sets when they could have been clinched earlier we might pay a price in Sunday's final. Sometimes the freshest team is the best one in a multi-day event like this one.

We should be taught not to wait for inspira-tion to start a thing. Action always generates inspiration. Inspiration seldom generates action.

Frank Tibolt

Monaghan, Moros, and McCoy come out of the blocks quickly after we begin the singles. We won the doubles point in good fashion by garnering #1 and #3 before Andrews-Talmadge could finish, after leading 6-4. Bandy has a tender shoulder and will skip today's match. Fortunately for us he will not be missed today. Things go pretty much as expected in singles play. Only Greg loses a set, and he was ahead in the third when play is stopped. Michael Moore fills in admirably for Bandy and was leading 6-4, 4-2 when we clinched. Survive and advance, as the saying goes and we will live to fight another battle tomorrow. In post-season play all matches will stop when one team clinches the match. This helps in scheduling and will be the rule in NCAA play, as well.

The Golden Eagles of Marquette are our semi-final opponent and I recall the earlier match we played in January, knowing that January seems a lifetime ago. I know that Steve Rodecap will have them ready. At #1, Danil Mamalat can be very good at times. He is a lefty whose shotmaking can be troubling for anyone. Greg, though, remembers Mamalat and jumps to an early lead, never to look back 6-3,6-1. Our other players follow the same script and only Pecor and Moros have any real difficulty, with Blas dropping the first set 7-5. Blas is still operating at below 100% of his capacity, and I am hoping he can feel better tomorrow. He is a four year starter and we need his experience if we are going to make much of a dent in post -season play. Billy, on the other hand, is still searching for day-to-day consistency and drops his match to Cameron Teherani 6-4,6-3. He has always lacked the ability to temper his game and make adjustments when he is not "on." Nonetheless, we find ourselves in yet another Big East final and my thoughts take me back to 2003 when we played in one of the most unusual set of circumstances I can remember.

It is better to light a candle than to curse the darkness.

Eleanor Roosevelt

Our 2003 team will always hold a special place in my heart. I have only had one losing season in my 44 years as a head coach, and it ended in the most frustrating experience of my career. This is a story worth telling. Our 2002 team was quite good. We played most of the season in the ITA top ten, peaking at #4 in April. We started nine players regularly in either singles or doubles and six of them graduated. Anticipating this I had a strong recruiting class signed featuring Shannon Buck and Sergey Leonuk. I expected both to compete with returnees Luis Haddock, Brent D'Amico,and Matt Scott for the top spots in our lineup. We would be young, but probably remain among the nation's top 20-25 teams, I believed. There is an old expression - "Man plans and God laughs." 2003 translated that expression perfectly for me.

I received a call from Shannon very late in the spring of 2002 telling me that, although he had signed with Notre Dame, he had changed his mind and would attend the Air Force Academy. Boy, was that a blow to our team! Having a Naval Academy background I appreciated his desire to attend Air Force, but unlike many other schools, Notre Dame would not allow me to try to replace Shannon, as the incoming class was set in stone. Shannon qualified for and played in the 2003 NCAA tournament playing #1 for Air Force, so that will illustrate what his loss meant. Later in the year I learned that Leonuk, a native of Russia who had been an Orange Bowl quarter-finalist, had become an academic casualty, ineligible for the spring semester, leaving us without two of our anticipated top players. We faced the 2003 season without either. Not only were we lacking our normal level of talent, but we lost five or six matches by 4-3 scores. In several we had held team match points, including a very narrow 4-3 decision to top ten Texas.

Fast forward to the 2003 Big East Tennis Championships. Our team was ranked too low to receive an at-large NCAA bid. Our record of making the NCAA's stretched back to consecutive seasons beginning in 1991. In fact, as I close out my career I am proud of qualifying for the Tournament in 22 of my last 23 seasons. Yep, you guessed it. 2003 is the missing link. The stakes were set and the bar was high. We had to win this Big East, as all conference winners received automatic bids. In the semi-finals we had to play a VA Tech team that was positioned to receive an at-large bid. The match was scheduled for Saturday, but it rained all day and night in Miami. The tournament committee decided to play both semis and finals on Sunday, as the NCAA draw was to be made the next day, Monday. Our match was scheduled for 7:00 AM. We packed all of our bags and left our hotel at 5:30 AM, arriving at the courts before 6:00. We arrived to find no opponent. The VA Tech representative must have failed to explain the start time to its coach, as they arrived late. We warmed up, but the committee decided to put the women's semi-finals on, as they were there and ready to play. VA Tech arrived just before 7:00 and it became obvious that they had not been given the correct time, so we had to wait, even though the Notre Dame and Miami women's teams were already assured of an NCAA bid due to their rankings.

There are defeats more triumphant than victories.

Michael D. Montaigne

Sparing you the details, I will recount that we began our match with VA Tech around 9:00 AM and battled as though our post-season lives depended on it. They, in fact, did. Our guys played by far the best match of the season and, when the dust had cleared, had beaten Tech, a team ranked in the twenties, 4-3 in a five hour plus war. We were given 45 minutes by the committee to eat and return to play Miami for the title and NCAA bid. No shower, no clothes change, and a rushed lunch. We began the final and played like a team possessed. We began with singles to save time and won four first sets and led in each of those second sets. We were going to do the impossible........and then it rained. The committee convened while our Associate AD, Missy Conboy, called our AD Kevin White to ask permission to stay and play when the rain allowed. He gave her his assent. We were going to be able to finish. I must add that this meant new hotels, flights, and lots of extra expense. I became a huge Kevin White fan that day, as the adjusted costs were quite significant.

At that moment the committee re-convened and spent perhaps ten minutes in conference. They came out to render their decision. The tournament was cancelled. There would be no 2003 Big East champion. Host Miami, as the highest remaining seed, would be given the automatic bid. We were denied the chance to play our way in. We were told that the committee had checked the weather forecast carefully and had been advised that the rain would not stop. As we drove to the airport 45 minutes later we watched as the sun broke through the clouds. We could have played that match and still today I get very upset whenever it is brought up. I remain as proud of that team - the only one in a 23 year period not to make the NCAA tournament- as I am of the one that defeated #7, #3, and #1 on consecutive days to reach the 1992 finals.

Sorry to digress, but any mention of "Big East," in any context, evokes those painful memories for me. Back to 2013 and a different final. As I explained, the spirited conference rivalry with Louisville was once again a reality. This title, especially since we were hosting and I was retiring, was one I wanted. I am not sure that I remember a match when our team played as near to its potential as this one in 2013. I am always wary of having to play a good team twice in the same season after having won the first time. Certainly we knew them well and they similarly were not expect-ing any surprises. It should have been tight. It was not!

As we began the warm up, I sensed something special in our guys. Our captain, Blas Moros, had purchased some very sharp looking long sleeve t- shirts with "Bayliss's Last Stand" emblazoned across the back and distributed them to everyone. We warmed up crisply. I could feel the confidence permeating through-out our Eck Tennis Pavilion. My wife Pat walked around to get every player to sign a shirt Blas had given her for me. Anticipation hung lightly in the air.

I cannot remember any match I have seen or in which my team competed that a doubles point was so decisive. We broke serve immediately on all three courts. Everywhere I looked a Notre Dame player was crushing a return or pounding an overhead smash. The doubles point took 34 minutes to play. We won #1 and #2 convincingly and held a 7-2,40-30 lead[match point] at #3 when the point was clinched. I doubt that Louisville had anticipated this kind of start. Certainly, I had not. As we met to go over the brief scouting report before singles play I was afraid something might happen to change the obvious momentum we had established.

I was wrong. Nothing was going to get in the way today. We had a large and enthusiastic crowd that wanted to be a part of things and that helped enormously. The Andrews-Stiefelmeyer marquee match was played at a very high level. Ryan Bandy, who had last week lost to Van Dambrongsri, took him to the woodshed 6-3,6-1. Moros, who had lost in straight sets a week ago to Chris Simich, edged out a tight first set in a breaker 7-6 with an ace on set point and was at 1-1 when we clinched the match. Andrews and Monaghan took care of the rest of the heavy lifting, both in straight sets. If I had to finish my home match career in a better way, I don't think I could imagine one. A couple of the Louisville players walked over to congratulate me which I appreciated. Stiefelmeyer is as nice a person as I have encountered in coaching. We had done it and I was as relieved as I was excited. I relaxed for the first time in a week and tried to take in the post-match awards and commentary as if I were a spectator. Next year I would be. There was one item left on our agenda - the NCAA Tournament. We would learn our destination and opponent in a few days. Until then I believe that the smile on my face never left it.

~ Cross Court Reflection ~

Coming together is a beginning.
Keeping together is progress.
Working together is success.

Henry Ford

Bayliss Family on the 50 yard line at Notre Dame Stadium. Here are the most important people in my life. This day celebrated my retirement immediately before Notre Dame kicked off to Oklahoma. Front row: Julia Petrozzi, Gabriel Petrozzi, and DeLaney Bayliss. Back row: Annie Bayliss [pregnant with Roman], Pablo Petrozzi, Jackie Petrozzi, Alex Petrozzi, Patrick Bayliss, Pat Bayliss, Bobby Bayliss, Rob Bayliss, Brendan Bayliss, Sam Bayliss, and Amy Bayliss. September 2013. *Photo courtesy of Mike Bennett.*

2013 NCAA Tournament

Success is neither magical nor mysterious.
Success is the natural consequence of
applying basic fundamentals.

Jim Rohn

The NCAA tournament is the prize jewel at the end of the yellow brick road. It is what all players and coaches anticipate more than anything else. For many coaches, it is the mark by which they are judged. Knowing that this year's tournament will be my last makes it even more special for me. Prior to 1977 the NCAA tournament champion was determined by winning the most matches in the combined singles and doubles tournaments. It was not a team event. That all changed in 1977 when the nation's top sixteen teams fought it out in Athens, GA. The new format was an instant hit and then grew to include the top twenty teams, remaining that way until 1994, when Notre Dame hosted the final site and round of 16 and 64 teams joined in the fray to reach South Bend.

I remember that 1994 Championship like it was yesterday. Missy Conboy did an extraordinary job as tournament director. The weather was fantastic, only raining briefly on the second day of the singles and doubles individual event. As soon as we were awarded the tournament I asked Lou Holtz to be the speaker at the team banquet. He agreed and gave perhaps the best motivational speech I have ever heard. Afterwards most of the teams lined up to have their pictures taken with Lou. Our round of 16 match with Georgia was a 4-3 classic. Our Andy Zurcher recovered from a 5-0 deficit in the third set, only to lose 7-5 as he went into full body cramps. USC won the team title, its third in a four year period. I was so proud of Notre Dame and all that we had done to make the event special. Our AD Dick Rosenthal put all of his weight behind our efforts and it remains one of the best examples of a university and its tennis community coming together to create an event all will remember for many years.

The first two teams I coached at Notre Dame simply were not good enough to qualify for the-then 20 team NCAA's. However, my 1990 team was perhaps the most improved college team in the country with a 24-3 record and #16 ranking that I felt would more than qualify us for selection. Boy, was I wrong! The NCAA Tennis Committee handled selections and each of the nation's eight geographic regions would have representation. This meant that a few of the teams selected were, accordingly, not as good as some that were not selected. I felt that our ranking was sufficiently high to guarantee that we would be among those chosen. The selection committee was then composed entirely of coaches, one for each of the eight regions. That year's committee was chaired by Kansas's Scott Perelman who was assisted by Tennessee's Mike DePalmer. Other than ranking there were other criteria for the committee to use in selection, such as strength of schedule, impact wins and bad losses, late season results, and a few others. Being the new kid on the block, I had difficulty getting ranked teams to play us, as we had never been ranked and yet our outstanding freshman class aided by sophomore David DiLucia made us a potential loss for many top 25 teams. We had tried to get into the Blue Gray, but our acceptance there was a year away. We entered the Corpus Christi Invitational and there had beaten Oklahoma, #13 Duke, and #8 TCU before losing to #3 Pepperdine 5-4. I was counting on that showing to guarantee us a place in the draw.

I received calls immediately after the selections were announced from two members of the committee. Each called to apologize for the decision and told me, in confidence, what had happened. Two or three committee members had influenced any who were neutral and had used their influence to ensure that we were not selected. Having since served on the NCAA Tennis Committee I am very aware that everything that takes place is held in strict confidence. There was no appeal. We were denied entry. Our season was over. Ranked #16 with a 24-3 record was not enough. We were all dressed up, but with no place to go. This decision and that of the Big East in 2003 have lived with me every day since each occurred. I remember having to tell our team about being left out of the 1990 tournament and I can still see the pain and disbelief on their faces. However, there is a happy ending here. Almost all of those players were part of our 1991 team that won its first round NCAA match against Kansas and also the team that made the 1992 run to the finals. Being left out made us a tougher and more determined team. We all learned something that day and going forward we were unquestionably better for having gone through the experience.

As the NCAA Tournament evolved over time, it now includes 64 teams. The top 16 teams now each host a first and second round site. The 16 winners of each of those sites advance to the final site that begins with the round of 16 and concludes with the championship match. Immediately thereafter the 64 player singles and 32 team doubles events begin, but have no effect on the team event. Reputations are forged based on NCAA success. Coaches are fired, sometimes, for not making the tournament or, at a more elite level, for not advancing far enough.

My reason for going back to tell the story of our non-selection is to try to put the NCAA tournament into context for those who have not been involved with it. We all call it, simply, "the tournament" and never have to clarify it for one another. We are often judged by our tournament performances. Many coaches have performance incentives written into their contracts, and most use the NCAA tournament as their basis for financial rewards. It is the light at the end of the tunnel and the reward for all of the hard work put in during the season. Being left out was extremely difficult to take.

~ Cross Court Reflection ~

Getting over a painful experience is a lot like crossing over the monkey bars. You have to let go at some point in order to move forward.

Unknown

Big Ben welcomes Notre Dame tennis to London. Jakub Pietrowski, Steve Flanigan, JJ O'Brien, Ron Mencias, Coach Bayliss, Horst Dziura, Jason Pun, Ryan Simme, and Brian Harris take in the sights and sounds of London. August, 1995. *Photo by Pat Bayliss.*

Coach Bobby Bayliss and Mike Sprouse at the West Side Tennis Club in Forest Hills, NY. On August 25, 1995 Sprouse received the ITA's Arthur Ashe Award for leadership and sportsmanship. *Photo courtesy of Intercollegiate Tennis Association.*

CHAPTER EIGHT

For All of the Marbles

You don't buy heart at the supermarket.

Mike Ditka

Coming off such a strong finish in the Big East Championships I had every reason to believe that our guys were ready to play their best tennis in the NCAAs. We swept the awards given, by a vote of the coaches, at the tournament's end as Greg was named "Most Outstanding Player," I received the "Coach of the Year" award, and Quentin was named "Rookie of the Year." While individual awards are nice, I have never gotten caught up in thinking about them, especially the "Coach of the Year" awards. Almost any of us would gladly trade this one for a team title. I am happy for Greg and Quentin, but I also believe that each of them feels the same way. Since we won the conference title there is no reason for comparisons. I want our guys to enjoy this celebratory feeling for a day and then get down to the business of preparing for the NCAAs. While our ranking would get us into the tournament as an at-large entry, now that will not be necessary, as the winners of each NCAA conference are automatic entries. We will gather to watch the selection show on television, as we always do. Once we know where we are headed and whom we play it will not be difficult to hone in on preparing to play our best tennis. This is where I believe that our character will carry us.

When wealth is lost, nothing is lost. When health is lost, something is lost. When character is lost, all is lost.

The Reverend Billy Graham

I have a positive feeling about our team. We have shown growth and improvement during the season. Chemistry continues to develop and team relationships are better than at any time all season. In order for us to make much of a dent in the NCAA draw I knew that several things needed to happen as the year unfolded. First, we needed to solidify our doubles lineup. In beating Louisville we lost only 8 games in the three doubles matches. It is hard to ask for more than that. Seeing the chemistry between Greg and Matt at third doubles and watching how easily Ryan blended with Spencer at #2 gave me a great deal of confidence. Billy and Alex could beat or lose to most #1 teams, so I knew we would not be giving away any of the slots while battling for the all-important doubles point. On top of that, Ryan Bandy's development at #6 where he had built a strong record highlighted by his 3 set victory over USC's Johnny Wang, told me that we could play with anyone there. Things were looking up. I felt pretty excited about my last hurrah as a college coach. Clearly this group is not as talented as those I have had that finished in the top ten, but they seem to be peaking at the right time. Most coaches are simply seeking for their teams to perform in the biggest matches at a level commensurate with their respective abilities. I can live with being beaten by someone more talented as long as we give a maximum effort and play to the limits of our potential. We are more cohesive than our last few teams and you can achieve pretty darn good things when everyone cares more about team than themselves.

Life only demands from you the strength you possess. Only one thing is possible - not to have run away.

Dag Hammarskjold

Most people are familiar with the basketball scene in which each team assembles in front of a big-screen television to learn whether they have been selected for "the big dance" and their venue and first round opponent. This happens in college tennis, as well. As we watched the television screen I had a strong feeling that we would be going to Columbus. It would be our fourth trip there in a five year period and this bothered me, not just because Ohio State was a very tough out at home, but because after a long season of play, nobody wants to go back to a place so familiar. This was the NATIONAL tournament, not a regional one. We had already played our Midwest ITA Singles and Doubles Championship there, not to mention having taken on the Buckeyes in Columbus during the regular season. What the student-athlete experience cried out for was an airplane ticket to some part of the country where we had not travelled. I had voiced my thoughts to the NCAA committee more than once and, while I believed they understood, I knew their hands were somewhat tied, as a recent rule made it impossible for teams from the same conference to meet before the third round. To me, it seems like the move to regionalize play much more than in the past has been a move by athletic directors and presidents to cut costs by forcing teams within a 400 mile radius to drive to their respective matches. In an era where the student-athlete experience is supposedly highly valued, almost all coaches and players oppose this policy, but as Abraham Lincoln once told his cabinet who had advised him negatively: "Gentlemen, the 'ayes' have it." For all of the Big Ten teams this meant a free pass away from Ohio State. For us it meant the strong likelihood that we would once again be greeted by Uncle Ty. There are other teams that share our fate. San Diego, now coached by our former player Ryan Keckley, almost always ends up at either USC or UCLA for the same reason, among others. Each of us has imagined a best-case scenario for our squads.

Almost on cue the television confirms my belief and I learn that we will indeed travel to Champaign [IL] on a path that runs through Ohio State and Tucker's Buckeyes. Interestingly, though, our first round opponent will be the University of Washington, coached by former ATP star Matt Anger. Anger has done a good job in Seattle. Many thought he was a likely successor to Dick Leach at USC, his alma mater, but Peter Smith has taken out a mortgage there in Trojanland while Matt seems very content with life in Seattle. While our team would prefer a different venue they seem energized by the prospect of playing the Huskies. They know almost nothing about them and it is my job - and Ryan's - to immediately gather as much scouting information as we can to best prepare our guys for the upcoming battle. The next day will be busy. There are hotels to book, practice times to reserve, and restaurants to find. Everything happens very quickly. It will be tricky and take some maturity from our players. Exams begin in six days and we will need to leave for Columbus on the Wednesday of exam week. Notre Dame takes this very seriously and each of our players will need to arrange to have his exams finished by early Wednesday afternoon. We have addressed this all year, encouraging each of them to stay ahead in their academic responsibilities. It seems very difficult, but somehow, someway our guys are always able to meet with their professors and work out a time to fit all exams into a three day period. In 2006 we had three players who had to take their last exam - at Texas A&M - in the morning before our match against the Aggies. It was not what I would have wanted, but once the decision was made we simply took care of the details. One of the players who took the exam, Eric Langenkamp, played one of his better matches of the season and was a key to our upsetting A&M in Tim Cass's last college match, sending us to Palo Alto for the round of sixteen.

Just as I begin to feel that things have fallen into place I receive the terrible news that Ryan Bandy had been rushed to the emergency room for an appendectomy. The surgery is successful, but he will not be available for the NCAAs. Now I need to think on my feet and figure out how to minimize his loss. He seems comfortable when Pat and I visit him in the hospital. He has gotten assistance from our office of Academic Services. A new and workable exam schedule will be made for him when he is ready. I am glad to know that there are no issues and that he will be "back in the saddle" pretty quickly. I will need to adjust the lineup I sent in to the NCAA committee and try to see how we can best overcome a pretty big blow. Fortunately, Michael Moore has been called into action at several key times. As I look at Washington's lineup I firmly believe that Michael will be able to win for us at #6, but filling in the gap left by Bandy's absence will be more difficult in doubles, as I am only allowed to make a straight line substitution. Due to the NCAA's policy limiting the active roster to eight players, freshman Alex Lawson will need to play the #6 singles position if anyone else is sick or injured. Alex is a terrific athlete, but has very little singles experience and I am counting on winning at #6. Interestingly, one thing that I accomplished when appointed to the NCAA committee several months later was to expand the travel roster to accommodate nine players.

One of my responsibilities now is to arrange for transportation and housing. Ohio State has e-mailed the information I will need. The Hilton in downtown Columbus is the official hotel. Anthony Travel will arrange a bus and driver for the trip. With these details out of the way we can focus on preparing each player to be ready for his best performance. While the stress of compacting exams into a short period will take a toll, I don't want to hear a single negative comment and make that known. There are reasons and extenuating circumstances for poor performance. Excuses are not allowed. I have always admired the creed of the great Australian tennis dynasty of the 1960's and 70's. It read simply "If you are hurt, you don't play. If you play, you are not hurt." It is yet another of sport's lessons that follows us into the real world. There is no room for excuses.

Realize that if you have time to whine and complain about something, you have time to do something about it.

Anthony D'Angelo

Ryan has done a great job getting everything ready to travel. Rackets have been strung. We have plenty of overgrip and extra clothing, etc. If we lose it will not be because we left something behind. I can see how his attention to detail will serve him well next year and beyond as a head coach. Now if we could only slip him into the lineup. A presence like his would guarantee a positive outcome. I am always thinking ahead.

Ryan's last college dual match took place at UCLA. As one of the last #2[#29-32] seeds we were flown to Los Angeles and had beaten New Mexico State in the first round. UCLA was ranked #1 or #2, so an upset did not seem likely to many, but it almost happened that day in 2000. We lost the doubles point, but Casey Smith and Andrew Laflin won for us at #3 and #6. Aaron Talarico was up a set and a break and looked like the likely winner at #5. Ryan was deadlocked and on serve late in the third set. His opponent held serve and Ryan was serving at either 4-5 or 5-6 in the final set. The game was close and somehow he found himself down a break point - and team - match point. After just missing on his first serve he noticed the opponent cheating slightly over trying to get a forehand and courageously decided to take a big chance. He went for the "T" ace down the middle and it was narrowly called out. Game, set, and match UCLA. Potentially the biggest upset in NCAA history narrowly averted. Ryan was, understandably devastated. He shook hands and slowly made his way to the bench.

It is NCAA policy for the media coordinator to allow up to five minutes after a match's completion for the coach to meet with his players and give them a little time to compose themselves before facing questions. Accordingly I was approached and asked to bring Ryan with me to the media tent. As we walked that way I could not help but see that he was sobbing uncontrollably. The UCLA official understood and agreed to give him a little more time, but it was just not going to happen. You had to know Ryan, but I understood perfectly. He had just lost what appeared to be the likely final point in an incredible team effort in his final collegiate dual match and he simply had nothing left emotionally in the tank. That day, the NCAA wisely abandoned its interview policy and gave him a pass, leaving me to handle all questions. It was the right thing to do. To this day it is the only time I have had a player unable to talk to the media after a match. The scene still stays fresh with me. It is a simple example of his commitment and loyalty. It is why he will be a Hall of Fame coach someday. He gets it. He cares.

There isn't much thrill in success unless one has been close to failure.

William Feather

Back to Columbus. On the five hour drive there was little conversation. Everyone fell immediately to sleep, the result of having six days of exams compacted into three. It was what all of them needed. While it can be argued that having to compete so near to the grind and exhaustion of exams put us at a competitive disadvantage, I chose to view things differently. With the pressure of exams now over, we had nothing except tennis over which to worry. The relief of finishing that last exam is empowering. The weight of the world has suddenly slipped off your shoulders. This is what we coaches must learn to do - find ways to turn a negative into a positive. Nonetheless, it is difficult to explain to someone who has not had the experience, how sudden and gut-wrenching it is to be so emotionally engaged in a tremendous battle, only to see it immediately end as the match is clenched on another court.

323

~ Cross Court Reflection ~

You can never cross the ocean unless you have the courage to lose sight of the shore.

Christopher Columbus

Notre Dame tennis celebrated on billboards. It took some getting used to for me to adjust to seeing my name on a billboard.

Practice in Columbus

As we pull into the parking lot for the Ohio State courts, I realize that this could be my last team match as a college coach. While there are some snippets of sentimentality, my focus is on the importance of ensuring that we have a great practice. I am hoping that the surface is close enough to our own that adjustments will be simple and, accordingly, spirits will be high. I have some genuine concerns. Blas Moros has been struggling with a hip flexor that just doesn't seem to heal and he is also battling the aftereffects of pneumonia. He has been cleared to play, but his ability to be in good form throughout a long, tough match has to be in question. Billy played poorly here last year and we need him to be firing on all cylinders. Knowing how hard Billy competes, I hope he is not putting any extra pressure on himself. While I like Michael Moore's chances as he fills in for Bandy, this will be his first-ever NCAA match. I feel good about the status of our other players and know that they all want to win this one for each other. Keeping a positive approach is now a necessity. I don't have to remind them that it was on these same courts one year ago that we beat a pretty good Vanderbilt team in the first round.

We send the players to practice on the courts on which they are likely to play on Saturday. There is a slight chance of rain then, so we will need to use both the indoor and outdoor courts tomorrow. Experience has taught me that a player will compete with much less anxiety if he has spent some time on the court on which he will compete. The Ohio State outdoor courts are in a straight line of six with plenty of elevated bleacher seats behind each. There is a row of four behind them which will allow others to practice or warm up after doubles play begins. Since Moore and McCoy are not involved in doubles play they will be able to finish a warm-up just before beginning their singles. This will be helpful, as they will not have to walk onto the court cold to begin play. One thing Ryan and I need to decide is which of us will coach the #1, #3, and #5 matches, as the other will take #2, #4, and #6. This can be an important decision, as some players might prefer a certain coaching style.

College tennis is one of the few venues to allow on-court coaching in the sport of tennis. I remember when this was first allowed during the early 1970's. There was a real learning curve to be mastered. Heretofore, on- court coaching was only allowed in Davis Cup and Fed Cup play at the professional level. There is an art to knowing when to say something and when to remain silent and there are no written rules and no available user's manual. I explained earlier that when a player is tight or beginning to feel pressure there are two emotions that remove those fears: laughter and anger. It is easy enough to anger a player and more difficult to make him find humor in a pressure situation, but it can be done. While there is risk involved in this, I would rather try to affect a change to a deteriorating situation than sit idly by. Fear demands action. Allow me to tell a couple of enlightening stories that illustrate this.

At Navy in the early 1970's, we prepared to play state rival Maryland, the ACC champion and a team loaded with talent. Their #1 was John Lucas…..yes, THAT John Lucas, All American basketball player, future #1 pick in the draft, and NBA superstar. John was also an All American tennis player and had been a top five junior in USTA play while only playing tennis a few months of the year. I had recruited him ,but found that becoming an admiral was not in his immediate plans. I knew we would have a big crowd to see John play and scheduled the match at a local indoor club at night to accommodate lots of spectators. Right on cue a large crowd arrived for a spectacular evening of tennis. We played very well and our own #1, Mark Jee, played an inspired match, taking Lucas to a third set. Both players held serve to 5-5, at which time Mark played a little cautiously and dropped his serve. Lucas was 6' 4", lightning-quick, and was serving rockets. It appeared the die was cast. Unless I could draw Mark out of his shell emotionally his fate seemed sealed. I knelt down on one knee and looked at Mark. I was facing the crowd and they could see my every move, but could not hear me, as the noise from other courts and spectators drowned out my words. I tried to think of how I could make him laugh. I looked at Mark and said "Mark, look at me and nod your head enthusiastically." He seemed understandably confused but followed my request. I repeated the words and he likewise again nodded his head positively. At this point he had to be really confused, as he was hoping for pearls of wisdom, not some idiotic exercise. Finally I stared him down and told him to make a fist with one hand and to pound that fist into the open palm of the other hand. He did so. I then stood up and got close to him to say "Mark, you're in a heck of a jam here and I don't have any answers for you, but these spectators have been watching me and they believe- from your aggressive gestures- that I just gave you some very sage advice. Now, if you don't break serve they will not blame me!" Mark suddenly caught my drift and began to laugh….and I could see the tension slip away. In fact, he played a terrific game and broke serve, only to lose in a third set breaker.

The one thing that great coaches have in common is the ability to discern the different ways to motivate each guy.

Seth Davis

I can quickly give you an example in which I made a player mad at me, hoping that he would forget his fears and take out his anger on the opponent. In one case it backfired and cost our team in a big way. In 1975 our Navy team played a strong Princeton team that was on its way to the Ivy League title. We had a plebe[freshman] playing at #6, Buddy Robinson. A former #1 ranked junior in the East, Buddy had a big, aggressive all-court game. One of his strengths was his serve, a delivery that included both power and a variety of elusive spins. When Buddy was "on" he could beat almost anyone in the country at #6. His opponent that day was Princeton's John Hayes, a tall, hard-hitting player who would go on to some success on the ATP Tour after graduation. As the match began I could see that Buddy was not playing with his usual confidence. He consistently was missing his big first serve, giving Hayes predictable looks at his second delivery. Hayes began to win almost all such points, requiring me to ask Buddy to back off a bit and raise his first serve percentage. After communicating that message to him, I grew impatient as he continued to blast away and have to deal with Hayes's ability to attack his second serve. My mistake here is that I assumed that Buddy understood that by instructing him to "make more first serves" Buddy understood that he needed to add more spin for control. Big mistake on my part. I had failed to tell him how to raise his percentage of first serves. By saying "More first serves" without adding "Use more spin," all my insistence on raising his first serve percentage was doing was making him try too hard and causing a predictable "paralysis by analysis." I finally lost it and screamed "Buddy, you must make more first serves!" At that point Buddy looked at me, confused and with tears in his eyes, and said "Coach, I'm trying!" His voice was cracking. My insensitivity had him on the brink of tears. It was an important learning moment for me, and one that radically expanded my ability to see that my message was understood. I now frequently ask players to repeat what I have told them before moving to another court on a change-over, giving them the chance to ask for clarification.

A more positive example of using emotion to free up a tight player occurred in 1993 when our team reached the final of the Blue Gray Classic in Montgomery, AL. We had beaten #5 Mississippi State and #7 Florida on consecutive days and faced #8 Alabama in the final. The match was close, but the freshman I had inserted at #6 was getting clobbered early. Once again, I could see that it was a case of nerves. Knowing that Mike Sprouse was one of the more determined players I had ever coached, I believed that angering him was the right thing to do. At the end of a quick first set in which Mike had won only one game I joined him at courtside and threatened him, saying that he might never play another match if this continued. He looked up at me with great emotion. I knew that he wanted to hit me, but he kept quiet and got up to resume play. Less that 45 minutes later and with a decisive win in hand, he stormed over to me, but before I could explain my actions it dawned on him that I was simply trying to take his focus away from the outcome and guide it elsewhere, perhaps on what he might do to me when things finished. Once again, I had pushed the right button, but I realize that there is some luck involved. You don't take that kind of risk unless you are convinced that nothing else will work. And you have to be pretty confident that the player you throw under the bus will have the presence of mind to understand afterwards and will not only forgive you, but appreciate your willingness to take a great risk to right the ship.

One more quick story to illustrate how on court coaching might work, even when your message is misunderstood. In 2010 we locked horns with a very good and highly ranked Texas A&M team in an evening match in our indoor facility. One of the more difficult match-ups for us involved our own Stephen Havens and A&M's Austin Krajicek. Krajicek had won the US National juniors in Kalamazoo and would move, after college, to a successful ATP career that saw him break the top 100. He was a solid player who could serve and volley as well as construct points effectively from the backcourt. Neither player was blessed with great speed, but both could hurt you when given the opportunity. Havens was as good a natural ball-striker as there was at the collegiate level. Stephen played very well and somehow found himself as the last match remaining with the team score tied at 3-3. His match would determine the team winner. As the third set moved to a conclusion Stephen found himself serving for the match at 5-4, 40-0. He held three team match points. Certainly he would win one of them.

Actually, he played all three points timidly to move the score to deuce. When ahead, I observed, he played not to lose. When behind, he played aggressively. The next four points saw him win the deuce point with strong, aggressive play. However on each of those ad points[team match points four and five] he shrunk competitively and simply could not convert, playing guardedly, rather than playing to win. After fighting off yet another break point he once again held team match point number six. With no time or opportunity to discuss the issue with Stephen we told him to move all the way wide on the ad side, next to the doubles alley, as he lined up to serve, as far as the rules allowed, to force Krajicek to similarly move wide to cover the angle he had created. The thinking was that this would force Krajicek to have to win the point, as Stephen had been far too conservative on his own opportunities. It also changed the dynamic in the ad court, giving Krajicek a different look. I assumed Stephen might hit an aggressive serve out wide and then look for the opening and a big forehand, as he could be very creative off the ground. Instead, I groaned, as he simply rolled in a slow serve right to Krajicek's strike zone forehand, a "bunny." It was so easy - as I gasped - that Krajicek was forced to go for a down-the-line winner. Stephen had challenged his manhood. Fortunately Krajicek missed by one inch. Game, set, and match to Notre Dame. We were extremely lucky. Sometimes things do not play out as you drew them up. It was not executed as I had hoped, but - hey - I'll take it. There are times when it is better to be lucky than good.

Truth is not only stranger than fiction, it is more interesting.

William Randolph

Our first practice on the Ohio State courts went smoothly enough. I tried to see if anyone looked out of sorts. Adjusting to a new surface can be problematic, but we have another day's practice to become comfortable and, as I observe, I don't see anyone struggling. I think that we will be ready on Saturday. We work hard for almost two hours and I call for a halt. I understand that many of the guys will want to continue, but I know from experience that several days of limited sleep can be the precursor to an injury. Their bodies need rest as much as anything. The mood on the bus is upbeat, as I expected. With exams now behind them and an exciting challenge ahead, our players are finally beginning to let off some steam. Good-natured jokes were flying through the bus. A great dinner and full night's sleep will provide an even better team practice tomorrow. I continue to hammer home an emphasis on process, rather than outcome. Most players compete much better after adopting this approach to competition. New England Patriots coach Bill Belichick's famous mantra of "Just do your job" is yet another well-known way to emphasize process over outcome.

Success is not final; failure is not fatal. It is the courage to continue that counts.

Winston Churchill

Another good night of sleep finds us feeling good about our ability to be comfortable on the Buckeye courts. We practice today on both the indoor and outdoor facilities, as there is a chance for rain tomorrow. We are able to go over the expected Washington lineup with our guys to give them an idea of what to expect. We have played Washington several times during my Notre Dame tenure. I know that Anger will have his team ready to go. In looking at the match-ups I realize that this looks to be a very close match, perhaps another 4-3. With our regular, full lineup we would be a favorite, but we no longer have that luxury. After dropping the team at the hotel following practice Ryan and I head back to the courts for the mandatory NCAA meeting to go over lineups. After some discussion both teams' lineups were approved and after a few housekeeping issues we were dismissed and headed to join the team for what could be our last dinner together. We have chosen an Italian eatery recommended by several Ohio State officials.

The dinner was terrific and spirits ran high. I felt that we were in a good mental state. I wished that Ryan Bandy were available, but am very confident that Michael Moore would be able to handle Nicolas Kamisar, the man we anticipated would be playing at #6. Much of a team's success depended on - at times - the type of matchups the opposing lineup presented. Each player has a distinct playing style and that style frequently has greater success against a particular type of player. Big hitters, for instance, had difficulties against steady counterpunches who could keep their groundstrokes sufficiently deep in the court and cover court well. Aggressive baseliners normally did not like playing all court players who could get to the net. One person's pie might be another's poison. Moore hit sufficiently big off the ground that he could dominate many steady counter-punchers, and we felt good about the matchup. Moore had also begun to follow some of his offensive salvos forward to the net where he could often finish with an easy volley. If he couldn't hit Kamisar off the court I thought he could finish him off at the net. It is nice to have the ability to use a different tactic when one fails you.

When it is obvious that goals cannot be reached, don't adjust the goals, but adjust the action steps.

Confucius

Dinner concluded, we drove back to our hotel for a final meeting and a good night's rest. Ours was the first of the day's two matches and we seemed upbeat and ready to play well. I ran over our scouting reports with Ryan and we came up with a plan for who would handle which matches tomorrow. I am a notoriously poor sleeper the night before a big match and this evening was no exception. I can't speak for all other coaches, but I have always found myself going over last minute details, comparing earlier match results, and simply worrying about things over which I had no control. Would it rain? Did I prefer playing inside or out? How tight were the match officials going to be with regard to foot-faults, etc.? Nevertheless, this seemed absurd to me. I had already announced my retirement. The result of tomorrow's match was not going to affect me next year in recruiting. The prevailing thought in my mind was that one thing I would not miss about coaching was the needless worry that was always THERE. I still vividly remember how I had felt at Navy after each successful Army Navy match. I was always relieved and elated. The team was excited about achieving the season's biggest goal. I would join the team on our bus back to Annapolis and join in some of the highjinx and jokes with our guys for a few minutes and slowly allow our success to sink in and relax. Yet, somehow after about 15 minutes of comfort, my thoughts inevitably turned to….. "We lose #3 and #5. Who does Army lose? Who do they have coming in? How do they match up with our newcomers? Etc. Etc." I was already playing next year's match in my mind. I simply could not even enjoy what we had just achieved. Welcome, again, to my world!

It is not what you look at that matters. It is what you see.

Henry David Thoreau

Before going to bed I remind myself to write down some things that I might need to say the next day as we are playing. This might include reminders of an opponent's playing tendencies, but it also includes examples from each player's past of instances when he was down and came back to victory. When things are tense and the breaks seem to be going toward your opponent, it is helpful to pull out a memory of a similar situation in which you turned things around successfully. While I should be able to remember such things, I sometimes find that the heat of battle impedes my ability for quick recall. A quick glance at my notes allows me to refocus and, hopefully, supply the much-needed insightful anecdote of overcoming an obstacle which might fit tomorrow's circumstances.

"Last Hurrah"

Pressure can burst a pipe or pressure can make a diamond.

Robert Horry

Morning arrives, and with it the hope of a new day. As I shower and dress for breakfast I am not surprised to find that I am both excited and nervous, for this seems to always be the case. In my 44th year as a collegiate head coach, it seems as though I am still trying to prove something to myself. I will finish my career never knowing what it feels like to approach a dual match as just something next on the to-do list. We are always competing, always comparing ourselves to others, and always wanting just a little bit more. At my age one would think I should worry more about gaining entrance to heaven than which team will advance to the next round in the NCAAs, because I doubt that God will be impressed with a potential win today. As someone once said "There is a fine line between genius and stupidity."

After organizing everything, I head down to the team breakfast and learn that Michael Moore has been up all night, sick with apparent food poisoning. This news hits me with the force of a bull. Michael soon appears, looking green and frail. "I think it was the clams" he says, referring to last evening's dinner. He tells me that he is weak, but hopes to feel better. Somehow I know better, as he eats almost nothing for breakfast. It dawns on me that we are going to put a freshman into his first-ever meaningful singles match, as the NCAA mandated eight player limit gives us no wiggle-room. Alex Lawson will need to be Michael's replacement and I realize the enormity of his task. The advantage I expected at that position has evaporated in an instant. Michael wants to see how he feels as match time nears, but I am extremely doubtful that he will be ready to go. While this is certainly a difficult obstacle, I need to instill in our team a sense of belief that I do not share.

We are not retreating. We are advancing in another direction!

General Douglas MacArthur

I remind myself that this could be a teaching moment and that I am a teacher first and coach second…..or rather that they are, in fact, one and the same. I know that in the past we have many times overcome similar obstacles and found a hero in our midst. I quietly hope that Alex is up to the task he will likely face.

We meet in the lobby. The air is charged with excitement. While we are going into this short-handed, our players seem un-fazed and ready for yet another challenge. As we climb on the bus I search the face of each of our guys and am impressed with the resolve I find there. Today there is little chatter as we ride to the courts. I am convinced we will play hard today and hope that it is enough. The drive to the courts is a short one. I remind the team to keep Michael's illness a secret, for if he does play, it will not be on a full tank and we do not want to give this information to Washington, as it could determine how they choose to play. He has had next to nothing to eat this morning and is also missing most of last evening's nourishment. As we take our assigned courts I ask Michael to use one of the back courts so that he can take his time and let me know how he feels. He will not play doubles, so we will have almost an extra hour before announcing a change. It is important that Washington see him out there so they will not have much time to prepare for Alex, if he is thrust into the lineup. We begin a spirited doubles warm-up. Ryan has taken ownership of this for several years. He has a routine of serves, returns, volleys, poaches, and some one-up, one-back play that covers everything an opponent can throw at us. I remind our guys that today presents an opportunity and there are no excuses.

We go over the lineups with each team, pointing out serving targets for each of the Washington players and reinforcing which ones to attack when they are at the net and also when both are back. If one of the doubles players on a team is weaker than the other I frequently have yelled out "Mixed doubles!" as a quick reminder to focus on the weaker target. As we follow the strains of the national anthem I once again remind myself to appear calm, whether or not I actually feel it. Game on!

Our best chance in doubles today comes at #3, where Greg Andrews is paired with Quentin Monaghan. Neither is a great volleyer yet, but both return well. Quentin seems to make all of his returns and Greg can be lethal there. His forehand will be the biggest weapon on the court. In our submitted lineup we had Ryan Bandy with Talmadge at #2, but due to the NCAA limit of eight active roster players we are forced to move Wyatt into doubles with Spencer. We normally would have come up with different pairings, but when our final lineup was submitted ten days ago it had Bandy with Talmadge at #2, a position at which I believed we could win. My fear is that Wyatt's lack of doubles exposure and attackable second serve will leave us vulnerable here. At #1 we are potentially very good, but have been inconsistent. As I shake hands with Matt Anger I know that this doubles point will be an important one and hope we are up to the task. If we take the doubles point I am confident we can win the match.

It does not take long to see an emerging pattern in the doubles. As expected, Greg and Quentin come out of the blocks quickly and are ALL OVER Washington's Victor Farkas and Max Manthou. They go up an early break and roll from there. They will win 8-3, but I have seen enough to know I need not worry about #3. As Clemson's Chuck Kriese likes to say "Put a fork in them. They are done!" At the same time it is hard not to see how difficult it will be for us to win at #2. Emmett Egger and Jeff Hawke are in control. I remember Egger from his days in junior tennis where he was a very good shotmaker. His talents are on full display for all to see. Wyatt has played almost no doubles for us and looks uncomfortable. Spencer will need to be at his best, and that is hard to do when playing with someone for the first time. Spencer's quiet demeanor makes it tough for Wyatt to feel any encouragement. When picking teams I have always believed that each doubles team needs to have a vocal leader. Neither of our players can handle this role, and it shows. McCoy's serve is a liability in doubles where his blinding speed is of little use to him. Doubles is more a game of execution, while singles can be a game of imagination. The Huskies will take this one 8-4.

This leaves the doubles point in the hands of Billy and Alex. When the stars line up well for Pecor, he can be overpowering. His laser-like returns can be difficult to handle, but today they seem to come and go, despite his good intentions. Alex has done well for a freshman in a key doubles role and shows moments of brilliance, as he darts across for successful poaches and leaps for well-disguised lobs. As a senior he will become an All American, but today our duo is slightly out of sorts. Marton Bots and Kyle McMorrow are simply too good. They are well coached and seem to move around the net at just the right times to keep us on defense. They serve it out for an 8-3 win. Doubles point to Washington. They lead 1-0.

Lots of people want to ride with you in the limo, but what you want is someone who will take the bus with you when the limo breaks down.

Oprah Winfrey

As the doubles conclude, I sprint [For me it was a sprint. Others said I was walking fast.] to the back courts to find Michael

Moore to see if he feels he can play. He seems unsure. He says he wants to play, but fears he might not be strong enough to finish. I leave the decision to him, but he tells me he is unsure. That is enough for me. I can't put him out there to possibly determine today's outcome unless he gives me a reason. Decision made. Alex Lawson will play in his first real college singles match. I rush to tell him to get ready and then rush to Coach Anger so that he knows. There are only five minutes between doubles and singles and he has the right to know promptly. I leave the last minute review of scouting information to Ryan so that I can handle these responsibilities, as well as notify the referee. It is time for the singles to begin and we need four of the six to win. It is going to be a challenge. Anger has also made a lineup change, inserting Nicolas Kamisar into the singles lineup, something he did frequently during the year. We were expecting this move, so no surprise here. Kamisar is a battler who makes his opponent work for each point. Alex has the tools needed, but lacks experience in singles. I am asking a lot from this 18 year old. He has never been in a place like this before and will need as much encouragement as he can get.

You can become a winner only if you are willing to walk out to the edge.

Damon Runyon

Surveying the action I see several interesting matches taking shape. At #1, Greg takes on Kyle McMorrow, a tall, lanky contrast to Greg's compactness. McMorrow has had an outstanding year and is in position to clinch an All American spot at season's end. The contrast in styles is readily apparent. McMorrow hits a flat, clean ball, while Greg's forehand is loaded with topspin and its shape and heaviness is not apparent until you engage him in a meaningful rally. McMorrow has the better serve and will hit his share of aces, but Greg's all court movement and the heft of his groundies lead me to believe that he will win a majority of the long rallies. Both players favor their forehands, so perhaps a good play for Greg will be to begin the point going out to the forehand in order to move McMorrow out wide in order to get to his backhand. Three years before, in a story I told earlier, Greg came back from a service break down late in the third set to clinch a first round victory for us. Regardless of the outcome I know that today's fans are in for a treat today at #1 singles.

Navy players on hand for Bayliss's Notre Dame retirement. I was thrilled to see five of my Navy players join Notre Dame to honor me. In order, here are (l to r) Bill Mountford '83, Bayly Taff, '84, Franz Wagner '86, Mike Spanos '87, and Gene Miller '79. Gene became my godfather when I joined the Catholic Church.

Comparing the Matchups

The courts at Ohio State are set up so that #1 and #2 are in the middle and the other matches branch out from there. This gives spectators a good chance to see the top two matches. It has worked out for me to take #1, #3, and #5 today, while Ryan has #2, #4, and #6. This puts Blas Moros on my side. I have never coached a player with better intentions than Blas. He has done everything asked of him. He arrived with solid groundstrokes, but little or no understanding of how or when to get to the net. In his methodical growth he took on this and other challenges and has become a strong #3 for us. Today, though, he will be challenged. He is coming off pneumonia and, while cleared to play by our medical staff, will not be at full strength. We are hoping for a quick match because there is a finite limit to how long he can go. His opponent, Max Manthou, is just what we did not want the doctor to order. Manthou is a counter-puncher who is best in long rallies and wants to keep his opponent out on the court as long as possible. Grinders are tough to beat when your fitness is not at an optimum level. It is not a matchup I like, although I have learned never to count Blas out. We will see what the tennis gods have planned for us, as it is rarely possible to predict the way a match will play out.

Some days you're a bug. Some days you're a windshield.

Price Cobb

My last responsibility today will be Wyatt McCoy at #5. His opponent, Viktor Farkas, is a better attacker than a defender.

He has a better forehand and, when he has time to set up, can hurt you from that side. His second serve is attackable, but he has the ability to move it around. This appears to be a classic case of an attacking all court player vs. a counter-puncher[Wyatt]. McCoy has had an up-and-down year, mostly due to injuries, but has beaten some very good players, like Illinois's Faris Gosea. If you attack Wyatt prematurely and come in behind a so-so approach shot, he will absolutely undress you. In addition to greyhound-like speed, Wyatt has an uncanny knack for making you finish at the net with a ball below your knees, something most college players prefer to avoid like the plague. This one will be tough for us, but well worth the price of admission. All three of the matches for which I will bear responsibility are going to be interesting and close.

The other three matches, nos. 2, 4, and 6, are in Ryan's hands today. At #2 Quentin, a freshman, will face Marton Bots, a big, strong senior with a dominant forehand who tries to play right on top of the baseline and take the ball early, preferably with his forehand. Generally when we play this type of player the best recipe for success is to keep the ball deep to avoid his moving up in the court and mix up the pace and spins of the ball to keep him from getting a good rhythm. This seems right out of central casting for Quentin, whose patience and ability to sustain long rallies is a strength. It will be a war in which strength will be pitted against strength, senior against freshman.

Next on Ryan's dance card will be Billy Pecor's match against Emmett Egger. These two were high-level junior players and both have plenty of firepower. Nobody hits a bigger ball than Billy, but consistency is his challenge. Egger has had a somewhat disappointing year, but is capable of beating almost anyone when he plays well. I believe that this is a coin flip. Fans watching here will see some great shotmaking today. I look for a match long on shot-making and short on patience, as both players have the ability to hurt you from anywhere on the court. Common sense and calmness will be important ingredients today.

⬥

Common sense is wisdom with its sleeves rolled up.

Kyle Farnsworth

⬥

Ryan's last responsibility will be to get Alex Lawson through his match with Kamisar. On paper this looks like a favorable matchup, as Kamisar is a grinder, a player who keeps the ball in play and counts on you to make a mistake. If this were being played as a practice match I believe that Alex has the game to win, but it is not a practice match. It is, in fact, the biggest match of our season and Alex's inexperience is the question mark of the day. It is asking a great deal for someone who has never played a meaningful college singles match to win in this scenario. Nonetheless, if Alex plays with poise he has the game to be able to pull this off. He will need positive thinking today.

⬥

My center is giving way, my right is in retreat; situation excellent. I shall attack!

Ferdinand Foch

⬥

The singles matches begin and the atmosphere surrounding the courts bleeds with excitement. There is something about NCAA play….perhaps its finality….that coaxes the best from its competitors. Should we lose, this will be the last time this group will ever compete together as a team. For our seniors it will be their last match in a Notre Dame uniform. While no one brings this up it hangs heavily in the air. Today players will lay out and dive for balls on on a very hard surface that they might previously have let go past them. None of us wants things to end here, today. I know that effort will be at peak levels and settle in to see what I can pick up to pass on to those on courts 1, 3, and 5. I will not really be in much of a position to see what is happening on courts 2, 4, and 6, but know that Ryan is more than capable of determining what to say to Monaghan, Pecor, and Lawson. Match analysis is one of his strong suits.

There are lots of different approaches to on-court coaching. Some coaches become very involved, barking out instructions as the match progresses. Others try to remain calm, hoping that they display a confident air that reinforces the player's confidence. I have changed my approach over time and now carry a small legal-type binder that includes the scouting information and tendencies of each opponent, with a plan best suited to our player's abilities. On a blank page I write down things that I feel I need to remind each player as I observe play. On change-overs I move to the bench and try to give the player my thoughts. I learned long ago that this information needs to be simple and concise, for while he is listening to me, there are countless thoughts, elevated heart rates, and unlimited raging emotions running through the mind of each 19-to-21 year old player. Long sentences and too much information will simply not be absorbed in the limited amount of time available on change-overs. After I pass on my thoughts I ask the player to tell me what I just said. This forces them to listen, when the last thing in their comfort zone is a pep talk from me. For some, the advice is technical and/or strategic ["You must get in on his backhand!!" or "Be sure to keep your left arm up longer on your serve. You are rushing it again!!"] For others it is emotive and has nothing to do with strategy ["You are carrying yourself like a loser. I want to see better body language immediately. He is scared to death of what you can do. Focus on your breathing….in through the nose and out through the mouth. Now go get him!!"] It is necessary to know what your player is feeling when you talk to him on changeovers.

True mentors necessarily take the time to listen to, and understand, the person they are mentoring.

Bill Patton

Once I have told a player anything I write it down if it is not already on my pad and place a check mark beside it. This is my reminder that I have already passed on this particular piece of information. If I have to repeat it I draw a line through the check. One more repetition has me circle the check, indicating that he has been told this three times. It is my own code and way of keeping track of what I have passed on and what, if anything else, needs to be said. If my advice is being ignored - sometimes for good reason - I will want to know why. Also included will be something of motivational value, for instance a reminder of a big win the player had earlier against a similar style player, or anything else to reinforce confidence.

There is a fine line between giving a player too much information and supplying too little. I have tried to learn by trial and error. I frequently ignore one of my players if I see that he is winning and playing with confidence, as I can only be at one place at a time and try to go where I am most needed and where my advice will make a difference in the match. In other words, don't spend too much time waiting for me to drop in on your court when you are either winning or trailing 6-0, 5-0.

As I survey the scene and follow the scores I begin to feel that "my" players- those on courts 1, 3, and 5 all are playing well and will have chances to win. Ohio State has a large electronic scoreboard which allows spectators [and coaches] to see what has happened on each court. On Ryan's courts, Quentin alone appears to have a reasonable chance to win unless things change quickly. Clearly there will be little room for error on courts 1, 2, 3, and 5. We will need each of them to win today, as Billy and Alex have dropped their respective first sets.

Wyatt has begun his match with more aggressiveness than he has shown of late and is not allowing Jeff Hawke to push him around. He wins the first set 6-4 and looks to be in control. His ability to dig himself out of trouble is amazing at times. Hawke is doing what many of McCoy's opponents have done-trying to place the ball too close to the lines - anything to keep the ball from continuing to come back. This inevitably results in unforced errors. It is frustrating enough to miss when an opponent has dictated play, but Wyatt can force you into errors even when you are controlling the point. His passing shots are the best on our team. He can hit through you off the backhand side, but relies on his forehand to dip his passes, forcing you to volley up and that next ball is where he passes you cleanly. I remind him on each changeover to play as aggressively as possible and not to sit on his one set lead. I think he is in control and will win. Time to move to the next court.

As I move to court #3 and focus there I can see that Blas is doing all of the right things and playing as well as could possibly be expected from someone just released from the Notre Dame Student Health Center. He has won the first set 6-2 by establishing position on top of the baseline off the ground and methodically closing out points at the net. I feel great pride, knowing that when Blas arrived at Notre Dame he would venture to the net only to spin his racket for serve and to shake hands at the end of a match. He has embraced all- court tennis and now knows when to dart in and when to hold position for one more ball. It is apparent to me that he has very little energy and it will be a Herculean task for him to be able to finish off Manthou, whose ability to extend the points is going to have a cumulative effect sooner or later. I just hope it is later. Playing guys like this is like dying of a thousand paper cuts, rather than one single knockout punch. Manthou looks like he would literally run through a wall to win the point. This will test Blas like perhaps no other match he has played. He also knows that if he loses it will likely be his last outing wearing the interlocking "ND." He has left a legacy of doing things the right way. I want so very much for him to win his match today. I am reminded of what a great privilege it is to work with men of great character like Blas Moros.

The ultimate measure of a man's worth is not where he stands in moments of comfort and convenience, but where he stands at times of challenge and controversy.

Martin Luther King, Jr.

On the court adjacent to Blas, Greg Andrews is laying everything on the line for us. It has been gratifying to see Greg expand his skill set and embrace the importance of closing in to take balls out of the air to finish points. His forehand is truly one of the great shots in all of college tennis and he depended on it to end points when he arrived. This allowed the opponent to get away with floating high, defensive shots on the run to extend points and forced Greg to hit smaller targets resulting in unnecessary errors. As he followed more balls in towards the net he found the opponent making more unforced errors from the backcourt and his game grew by leaps and bounds. Add great character and effort to his resume and a 3.9 GPA and you have the model student-athlete we are all seeking. Nonetheless, Greg has his hands full today. Kyle McMorrow is an All American with a booming serve and a forehand close to Greg's in velocity. McMorrow is tall, handsome, and a very good player. The first set is razor-close, but Greg ekes out a 7-5 win and readies himself for the second. Greg is almost too respectful to me on change-overs and I fear that he might, at times, prefer not to take the advice I pass on for fear of appearing unappreciative. One day I want to tell him to lob short and rush the net, just to see if he will finally tell me to leave him alone. I will not do that today, though. Save that line for the Buckeyes tomorrow….if there is a tomorrow for us.

The level on court #1 is high and spectators crowd in to get a better view of the exchange of nuclear forehands. I can see that McMorrow is not used to seeing his own salvos returned even harder and the two players put on quite a show. Back and forth they go and it is Greg's ability to draw McMorrow out to his right to open the court that allows him to find the weaker backhand side that eventually gives him a slight edge. The applause- sprinkled in with some 'ooh's' and 'ahh's'- is the reward for these two warriors, as their battle continues. As I stand between courts #1 and #3 watching both Greg and Blas I am reminded just how lucky I have been to spend my life among great young people with high motivation levels. I have never once regretted my choice of vocations and I wonder how many of my friends can say the same thing.

They deem me mad, for I will not sell my days for gold. I deem them mad, for they think my days have a price.

Kahlil Gibran

A quick look at the scoreboard restores my attention. Both Billy and Alex have dropped the first set and Quentin is locked deep into a tie-breaker on court #2. If we lose all three the match is over despite the fact that we might win at 1, 3, and 5. The doubles point looms large now. In the little that I have been able to see of Lawson it appears that he at least held his own until 4-4 in the first set and then made unforced errors when it mattered most. I have put him in a difficult position and understand that the poise Alex needs will come eventually, but not during my tenure. He is a terrific athlete, but lacks the experience and exposure that junior players from California, Florida, and the South have when they step on a college campus. Three years later, as a senior, Alex will clinch the match in an upset win against #1 ranked North Carolina and become an All American, but this is 2013, not 2016. Alex holds on well until each set reaches 4-4, but at that point his lack of experience becomes all too apparent and errors creep into the mix. He needs to add more consistency when the sets near an end. He can't continue to do the same thing.

Staying the same means going backwards.

Roger Federer

I know that I can't allow myself to worry about the other three matches and move quickly to McCoy's court. His quickness and ability to counterpunch has broken Hawke down. In point after point Wyatt runs down a well hit approach and passes him cleanly. I have seen this movie before and know what is coming. Soon Hawke begins to miss from the backcourt, trying too hard to hurt McCoy, forcing plays that simply are not there and doubting his ability to outlast the sophomore in long rallies. McCoy closes it out 6-4, 6-2 and we are on the board. Match tied 1-1. We need three more "W"s to advance.

Blas is really laboring in his match. He played a courageous first set and stayed sharp throughout, as he won 6-1 with intelligent, aggressive play. As the second set began I could see the aftereffects of his illness, as he began to take more time between points and was breathing heavily. When healthy, he has a better game and, I believe, would take this one in straight sets, but he looks like it might be asking too much of him to count on winning his match today. I have told him to stop if necessary, but quitting is not in his vocabulary. I know he is going to do everything within his diminished capabilities today, but wonder if it can be enough.

As I look on the adjacent court I am encouraged by Greg's ability to control many of the points off the ground. He has saved his best effort for when we need it most. The pattern he is running with the most success is taking his forehand deep and inside-out to McMorrow's backhand. If McMorrow leaves the ball anywhere near the middle of the court Greg is able to finish with an inside-in forehand. While McMorrow is considerably taller and has terrific groundies, Greg's ball has a heaviness that few at the college level can replicate. He is able to continue to hold his own in the rallies, although both players are going to feel today's match for a while, as the pace in the rallies is closer to what I normally see in professional tennis. If he can just hold on, things are going to get interesting. He clearly hits the heavier ball between the two. It is this very physicality that will likely prove the difference.

The dynamic of a dual match in tennis is like no other sport. Effectively, we have six different one-on-one matches taking place simultaneously. Each has its own pace, its own separate challenges, and its own dynamics, yet all affect the outcome equally. In most sports the coach can focus on the team's offense or defense and all rally around his plan. He can substitute when necessary. In tennis each player has his own different plan of attack and a coach really needs to focus on what is happening on every court. This can be difficult when all matches are in play together. Each has its own ebbs and flows, unrelated to the others. It is important for me to be in a position where I am most needed, be it for moral support or for strategic and tactical advice, so at times I need to cut my losses in a particular match, leaving that player alone to fend for himself while moving to a different court, much as an Army medic might do on the battlefield. Obviously, substitutions are not allowed. When Ryan was playing for us, for example, I frequently passed him on a changeover and asked "Is everything ok? Any questions for me?" knowing that he was likely to win without my assistance. Ditto for David DiLucia. Some players are what we coaches call 'high maintenance,' in that they really require you to spend extra time with them. Others could not care less if you are there. They are singlemindedly focused on the task before them. I need to know which matches require my presence so I can best utilize my analytical and motivational skills where they can do the most good. And if my absence hurts some feelings I can't let it deter me.

Care about people's approval and you will be their prisoner.

Lao Tzu

Before long both Pecor and Lawson are at the net, shaking hands, having lost. The disappointment on Billy's face demonstrates how much he wanted to win. I have never questioned his effort or intentions. We now trail 3-1, but Greg is nearing the finish line. One massive forehand after another finally brings him to match point. Thirty seconds later, he, too, is shaking hands and we have closed the gap. It is now 3-2 and Blas has courageously taken the fight right at Manthou. After dropping the second set 6-1, he now finds himself up a break and close to victory, leading 5-3 in a match I did not believe he could finish. Quentin has also won the second set and is beginning a third. Things are looking up. There just might be a way for us to take this thing!

Now back to Moros as he aggressively finds ways to get in on Manthou and puts yet another volley away. He reaches match point and finally finishes to even the match at 3-3 in an unbelievable display of courage. All heads turn to court #2 where Quentin breaks in the second game of the third set to forge ahead 2-0. The path to victory is there and I can smell the finish line, but now another obstacle rears its ugly head. Leading 2-0 in the final set and serving at 30-0, Quentin clearly has all of the momentum. Bots looks tired and the match seems to be slipping away from him, but suddenly rain comes from nowhere and the match is suspended right there. What bad luck….. just as Monaghan had taken control and momentum. We huddle in the hospitality tent for a decision. With dark skies and an ominous later forecast staring us in the face I want to move the match inside before Bots has time to rest and regroup. He is breathing hard and Quentin is clearly the fresher of the two. Nonetheless, NCAA policy is to give the weather an opportunity to allow an outdoor finish. Ryan feels Quentin will win, whatever the decision. Moving indoors will give Bots a better chance to create offensive opportunities, so I hope for a quick change in the weather, as Quentin will need to step up his own offense if we move indoors.

And Then Came the Rain…

The decision has finally been made. We will move the match inside. Our party gathers its gear and enters the bus, as the Ohio State indoor facility is perhaps a ten minute drive away. I feel for Quentin, who sits alone, contemplating the enormity of the task ahead of him, much like a pitcher in the dugout nursing a no-hitter. Everyone gives him plenty of space. Because I have not spent any time on his court I need to leave any advice to Ryan. My mind races as I try to think of something funny to relax him, but nothing clicks for me and I, too, leave Quentin to his own thoughts, not wanting to do anything to diminish the momentum he has built. Like everyone else I allow Quentin some privacy and hope that he can pick up right where he left the match. Clearly, though, he feels the responsibility on his shoulders.

So much of handling sports is about handling pressure.

Tim Tebow

As the bus arrives and we exit it for the indoor courts, I walk beside Quentin and pass on a few words. "Thank goodness it is you who are in this position, and not several others" I hear myself say, hoping to inspire him with some much-needed confidence, but I am not even sure it registers. Quentin is quiet, but this is nothing new. He has never been much of a talker. I want Ryan to continue to coach him now, as he alone has seen the previous portion of the match and will know best what to say. I will back off in a supporting role only, realizing that it would be selfish for me

351

to stick my nose in a place it doesn't belong. I note that it is appropriate for Ryan to handle this, as he is about to assume control of everything in a few weeks. While I might want to take control now I realise it should clearly be Ryan who finishes this match with "Q," as he affectionately calls Monaghan. Because I have not followed the previous action, this decision is the correct one. I will later regret not interacting on one specific issue.

The players are given a few minutes to warm up and play begins. The tension hangs in the air. The Ohio State players and coaches sneak in to watch, as they will play the winner tomorrow. With a 30-0 lead Quentin holds serve. I have to like our chances, up a break and 3-0 ahead in the final set, but now things get tricky. Quentin plays several good points and has a break point. I am absolutely positive that a 4-0 lead will allow him to finish Bots and move us into the second round. As Bots serves, down a break point, I anxiously await the apparent end of the game, but it is now Bots who raises his game and stops the bleeding with a hold of serve. 3-1 Irish.

There are no magic plays. You win based on effort, unmet focus, and being brilliant at the little details.

Steve Kerr

Pressure in sports, but specifically in tennis, is a funny thing. One would think that forging ahead gives a competitor unlimited confidence, and sometimes it does. Frequently, though, being ahead places more responsibility on the competitor. He then plays more to protect his lead than to increase it and can lose his aggressiveness and creativity. He thinks of percentages rather than of aggressive risks, sometimes allowing conservatism to take the place of aggressive action, failing to continue with the strategy that pushed him into the lead. And in a team sport, like college tennis, he will feel terrible about letting down his teammates when he had the benefit of a lead. He feels alone on an island. There is nobody to block for him, pinch-hit, or set a screen. All responsibility now falls on his shoulders. Correspondingly, the player who trails plays with a sense of desperation, of knowing that he has to wrestle the lead away from his opponent and, to do this, he must take chances rather than to "play safe." If there is one thing that I would want to have known better it is how to coach a player nursing a lead. Certainly we can say "keep doing what you are doing" or, as 'Dandy' Don Meredith used to say "Dance with the girl who brung ya." That seems simple, but it doesn't always apply. The chances you took to regain the lead now seem to defy the percentages as you attempt to hold on to that lead. Unquestionably, a different dynamic is now in play. This is a time when I might try to use anger or humor, but the fact is that I don't know which buttons to push with Quentin and I have not spent any time on his court today. Additionally, there is no one in whom I would have greater confidence for this assignment than Ryan. I am now a highly interested spectator and it is not fun. Like everyone else, I can only watch and hope, feeling somewhat helpless.

<hr>

No one plays this or any game perfectly. It's the guy who recovers from his mistakes who wins.

Phil Jackson

<hr>

Quiet by nature, Monaghan is a hard guy to read. The first sign of nerves shows itself as the official calls several foot-faults when he serves at 3-1. It is easy to see, as he moves his left, or front, foot slightly forward, no doubt ignited by nerves, touching the line. It costs him points, but more importantly gives Bots, who had looked as though he were done, some looks at Quentin's second serve, allowing him to regain some of the aggressiveness he showed earlier. Before long Bots has broken back. I will always regret my decision to stay in the background at this point. As regards this situation I know that, rather than try not to move his foot and think about the serving motion, Quentin should simply move back six or eight inches and continue to serve normally, but since I have not been coaching him in this match I am afraid it might look like a last gasp and desperate measure for me to come running over to the court and engage him. I am confident that Ryan has advised him as I would, but wonder if another voice might force him to face this fear. The appearance of calm is important, I decide, but it is the wrong decision. The foot -faults continue and before long the tables have turned. History records that Monaghan lost six consecutive games, but I will always take responsibility for this match. In my heart of hearts I know that I failed Quentin by failing to pass on what I believed might work. It is a tough way to go out.

As the match ends Quentin is crushed. He feels that he has let his teammates down. Fortunately for "Q" there is an extended happy ending. His next three years are marked by success after success. He reaches the NCAA semi-finals in singles as a junior and in doubles as a senior, the best NCAA showings by a Notre Dame player in that event in over a half-century. His banner designating two-time All American status hangs proudly on the wall in our Eck Tennis Pavilion for all to see. Who knows, hopefully the loss in May, 2013 may have steeled his determination and helped him to continually strive for the excellence he displayed over and over again. Nonetheless, my inaction, or decision not to add my own input stays with me and will always be a source of regret. My job is to pass on needed information and I failed one of our players when he needed me most. There are no 'do-overs' in coaching and my sense of responsibility forces me to look squarely in the mirror and accept this failing. Don't get me wrong. I did not have to remove all sharp objects from my home and office, but I will always feel some responsibility. Quentin's subsequent great successes on the court have provided ample balm for my wounded pride. Perhaps this match might have helped spur Quentin on to later greatness. I am always looking for the silver lining in this cloud.

—◦◦◦—

When the Lord closes a door, somewhere he opens a window.

Mother Superior to Maria Von
Trapp["Sound of Music"]

—◦◦◦—

The finality of a loss in the NCAA tournament is difficult to describe. All year long coaches and teammates have scratched and clawed for the right to extend the season to another day and opportunity. Suddenly, in the blink of an eye, it is all gone. There is no more tomorrow. Your season is over, done, finito! Seniors know that the end has arrived, but somehow, someway, we are never ready for it. For the last four years there has always been another day, another match, another season, but there is no more "Survive and Advance" mantra to follow. There is a hollowness that can't be put to words. Teammates look at each other as if to say "What do we do now? I haven't read this script before." All energies have been focused on the task at hand. All year long there has been an answer to "What's next?" because there has always been a next match. There is no precedent for what has just happened for our players. We haven't discussed this scenario because to do so would be to admit that losing this match had been a possibility and that could have raised an awareness of doubt. Having been all the way to the NCAA finals in a losing effort, I can tell you that it felt remarkably similar, even at that moment. The inevitability has arrived as we all stand looking at each other. It is one of the worst feelings in sports. Despite the fact that I have lost over 300 matches in my career, words are hard to find now. I have never gotten used to losing. Perspective is nowhere to be found.

—◦◦◦—

Whoever said 'It's not whether you won or lost that counts' probably lost.

Martina Navratilova

—◦◦◦—

My first action is to congratulate Matt Anger on the win. After a few kind remarks exchanged we part ways to gather our respective teams. I always make it a point to thank the umpires and officials and remind our guys to do that as well, especially after a loss. We then gather our gear and get on the bus to go back to the hotel. Because of the late checkout I will attempt to avoid being charged for an extra day. I ask our manager to get a dinner order to go for each of our players to allow us to leave earlier. This will allow our players to make travel plans, etc. When they have showered, packed, and checked out of their rooms each player will have a warm meal of his choice waiting for him on the bus. This process is not fun and it has not gotten any easier. I know there will be ample time on the bus to thank our seniors and also to gather the returning players to talk about next year, but suddenly I realize that this is no longer my team and that chore will be Ryan's. I am now - at this moment - the FORMER coach of Notre Dame men's tennis. I spend considerable time on the bus trying to write down a few things to say that will send the team off with an optimistic mantra, but despite my efforts I come up short with a suitable message. Explaining my emotions after a losing effort to someone who hasn't been in my shoes is like asking my wife to explain what childbirth must feel like to me.

The finality of an NCAA loss, and sometimes even a win, is something for which you are never ready. You are locked in an emotionally charged contest, using everything at your disposal to help your team "survive and advance" to the next round. Emotions run high. Your focus is all-encompassing. Suddenly a winning shot is hit, the crowd roars, and the players in front of you are shaking hands while some of the others look on with blank expressions on their faces. Then it hits you. The match….and your season….. is over. Your players look to you to see what to do. It is not something you have discussed or thought much about. Probably the last thing you should do to prepare is to rehearse a speech to be given after a loss. If you have lost, you must gather the players and find something to say to them as well as deciding what else needs to be done. For nine months, everything has been built toward winning this match and suddenly, in the blink of an eye it all goes away.

In this case I first need to get back to the hotel and settle the arrangements there. We need to eat. All players will need a shower. Transportation needs to be confirmed....or changed. It seems that I was never issued the manual entitled "Great Speeches For Losing Occasions." In fact, there might not be such a speech.

If you have suddenly won the second round match and are playing away from home, an enormous burden is thrust upon you. In 2006 our team was sent to College Station, TX where we beat Ivy League champion Brown in the first round to advance to play Texas A&M in the second round. It was a hard fought match with the usual number of ebbs and flows, but suddenly Ryan Keckley, our # 5 player, found himself at match point. As he pounded an aggressive second serve return and won the match on the next shot, the crowd erupted. We had beaten the Aggies and their Hall of Fame coach, Tim Cass, in an unexpected upset. We would be going to Stanford for the "sweet sixteen." As our players celebrated and then dunked me with the water remaining in a large cooler in the familiar scene known to all, I realised that I had much to do. We drove to eat and while we waited in line for food I had to call the NCAA travel agency to arrange for our flights, secure hotel rooms, rent cars, and all that accompanies team travel because we would be leaving in only three days. It happens in an instant and you need to think on your feet. Somehow I was able to pull it off that evening and finally relax and privately celebrate being the only team in a decade to beat A&M in College Station in the NCAA second round. It happens quickly and you need to be ready for it.

———⚬⚬———

Live as if you were to die tomorrow. Learn as if you were to live forever.

John Wooden

———⚬⚬———

As I enter my hotel room and see that tomorrow's uniform is already laid out, the reality hit me that I will not need it after all. Certainly there are things left to do. We have Greg entered in the

NCAA singles championship. There remains some preparation for that and a few other odds and ends, but it hits me like a sledgehammer that my career as a coach is effectively over. There is no worrying about next year, no planning for the upcoming schedule, and no need to advise each player on how to best use the summer months to grow his game. While I know what I will be doing for the foreseeable future and understand that it is time to get on with life's next chapter, I feel strangely lost. There is no user's manual for this situation, either. Although the individual NCAAs in Champaign will be something to which to look forward - I will be enshrined in the ITA Collegiate Tennis Hall of Fame - none of that grabs my attention. For 44 years I have done one thing- coach college tennis- and I simply can't believe that this day has finally arrived. Although there are things about my job that I will not miss- recruiting and the logistics of team travel come immediately to mind - I realize how much I love what I have been doing and how fortunate I have been to enjoy this sometimes crazy profession with all its ups and downs.

The ride back to South Bend is quiet and uneventful. Our guys are subdued, as they expected to be playing Ohio State tomorrow. Perhaps the seniors are feeling some of what I feel, a combination of nostalgia and uncertainty. We arrive on campus late in the evening and it is then that I try to say something of substance to all of our players. I thank them for their many sacrifices and remind them that I will gladly provide letters of recommendation and even some advice, if needed. They know that I will be around in a different capacity, so perhaps they are less sentimental than I. More than anything I realize that I feel inadequate for not having prepared a moving speech that captures my emotions and understand once more that there is no list of instructions for this occasion. All of my focus has been on the next match, knowing that there would be time after that to properly express myself.

The Day After

How lucky I am to have something that
makes saying goodbye so hard.

Winnie the Pooh

Having arrived quite late, I awoke at home the next morning much later than expected and see it is after 10:00 AM. I very rarely am able to sleep in, even if I need the rest. Suddenly it hits me that I don't have to rush into work. Normally if I awaken prematurely the day's tasks make it impossible to go back to sleep, so rather than toss and turn I simply get up to begin my day. Today, though, I awoke and went back to sleep twice, a very unusual occurrence. Pat and I enjoy a leisurely breakfast and I decide that I am going to go to the Farmer's Market to shop for some food. As the morning turned into afternoon I had a nagging feeling that something was amiss and it finally dawned on me that not having the next match, the next season, and the next recruiting class in the back of my mind was very liberating. It dawns on me that I can spend more time with Pat, and this brings a smile to my face. While it is indeed early into this process I now begin to understand that my life really will go on and that there is much to which I can look forward. There will, in fact, be life after coaching. I remember the comment of Texas basketball coach Abe Lemons after his career ended. He mused "The trouble with retirement is that you never get a day off." Although it still hurts to think back on yesterday's loss I can comprehend that many of the aftereffects of the loss - how it might affect recruiting or the perception of our team heading into the future- hold no significance for me. It is a feeling of relaxation. "I can get used to this," I think.

359

The tragedy of life is not so much what we suffer, but what we miss.

Thomas Carlisle

There is indeed much to anticipate. In just over a week will be my Hall of Fame induction in Champaign, IL at the NCAAs. In June Notre Dame will host a retirement dinner/ceremony that will prove to be as memorable as it is enjoyable. Over the summer Pat and I have rented a home in Virginia Beach big enough to handle all of our children and grandchildren and both of my brothers will join us there in a wonderful reunion. I do not know it yet, but Ryan and Missy Conboy have been planning a fall reunion of former team members and it will be something I remember for the rest of my life, as all of our kids and grandkids will be here to share it with us, along with almost 100 former players, many coming from long distances. Slowly the sense of responsibility for each season has drifted away and I am discovering the emotional freedom that it brings. There is much more to come, although I don't quite know it yet.

~ Cross Court Reflection ~

The moment of victory is much too short to live for that and nothing else.

Martina Navratilova

Bobby Bayliss addresses the crowd in Athens, Georgia. Immediately after the 1992 team championship match ended, there was a brief opportunity to address the crowd and thank them for their support. With the notable exception of the Georgia match, I felt that they were cheering for us and appreciated it.

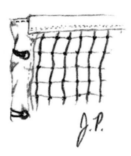

Notre Dame Men's Tennis team at Guinness Factory, August, 2006. One of the highlights of our foreign tour in 2006 was our visit to the Guinness Factory and the veritable history lesson one receives there covering Ireland's past. L to R: Brandon Pierpont, Santiago Montoya, Barry King, Brett Helgeson, Ryan Keckley, Stephen Bass, Eric Langenkamp, "Bubba" Akvlediani, Sheeva Parbhu, Coach Bayliss. *Photo courtesy of Pat Bayliss.*

CHAPTER NINE

On To Champaign ~ a Career in Conclusion

A trophy carries dust ~
Memories last forever.

Mary Lou Retton

While I know that I have coached my last dual tennis match, I realize that there is much for me to grasp and even more to celebrate. I have not died, but I am clearly beginning life's next chapter and am no longer buying green bananas. In golf terms, I am playing the back nine. More recently, I now find myself looking quickly through the obituaries in our local newspaper each morning. Interestingly, I find myself keeping score, something typical of my competitive nature. I notice, daily, how many of the departed are older than I and how many are younger. As long as the younger group is smaller than the older one, I feel somewhat reassured that my number is not ready to be called. Lately, though, the score has become closer and it serves as a reminder of my own mortality. When I look at the wrinkles on my hands, among other places, it is as though I do not recognize that they are mine. Still, though, I feel like I am in my thirties.

A few housekeeping chores remain from this 2013 season, the first of which is to provide assistance for Greg Andrews who has qualified for the NCAA singles championship. It is at this event- the NCAA Championships- that both the individual and team elements are best observed on full display. After the first and second rounds have been played on the home courts of the top 16 teams, all winners advance to the final site, this year in Champaign-Urbanna, IL. Both men's and women's teams combine to make the event a true tennis lover's dream come true. Because of the number of teams present, men's teams will play on the first and third days while women's teams will compete on the second and fourth days, thus advancing the four remaining teams from each gender to the semi-finals. These matches are played on Monday and Tuesday and conclude with a champion from the ranks of each gender. On Wednesday singles play begins with doubles added the next day. The finals conclude on the following Monday, Memorial Day. As I walk away from this event I do so knowing that I have given my all, from those formative days at Thomas Jefferson High School right through my years at Notre Dame. Quitting has never been an option.

Most people give up just when they are about to achieve success. They quit on the one yard line. They give up at the last minute of the game one foot from a winning touchdown.

Ross Perot

One of the highlights of the NCAAs is the ITA Hall OF Fame induction ceremonies, normally held on the evening the singles championship begins. I have attended almost every one of these occasions and have many memories of them. I have heard some dramatic and heart-rending speeches and have learned a great deal about our sport's collegiate heritage by listening to what many legends of our profession have passed on to audiences. This occasion, though, is special for me, as I am one of the inductees, along with fellow coaches Dennis Emery and John Peterson, as well as players Paul Goldstein, Harold Solomon, and Kelly Jones. Recent USTA president Alan Schwartz has entered as a "contributor." Pat joins me here and her sister Bridget accompanies her, as well as my daughter Jackie and son Brendan. It will be a special and happy evening for me to carry in my memory.

Success does not lead to happiness. Happiness leads to success.

Peter Smith, USC

But first things first. Greg Andrews has drawn Jeremy Efferding of Texas A & M as his first round opponent. Efferding is ranked among the nation's top 20 players and he has a solid all-around game accentuated by great movement. He will be a challenge. I have decided to have Ryan stay on court with Greg to begin his head coaching tenure. I will watch from the sidelines and I will be able to sneak out to Ryan to offer suggestions if needed. Virginia has won its first team NCAA championship and did so in dramatic fashion yesterday. They were down team match point to UCLA. As the UCLA player approached the net to finish the point with a volley, he inadvertently touched the net with his toe. As the large crowd burst into applause for UCLA, assuming the Bruins had won, the umpire announced that the point had instead been won by Virginia's Mitchell Frank, causing a big stir. Frank then methodically rode that momentum and good fortune to victory. It will be talked about for years. I was standing next to Virginia AD Craig Littlepage when the incident occurred and joked with him that it might keep UVA coach Brian Boland out of a padded cell. He agreed.

As Greg's match begins I find myself suddenly and unexpectedly sandwiched between two unexpected guests and former players. Andy Zurcher and Mike Sprouse have flown in for tonight's festivities and I could not be happier. They act as though they had just dropped by to see Greg play, but Andy has flown in from Denver and Mike has driven both down from Chicago. I am thrilled to see them both and humbled that they took the time and effort to be here for the Hall of Fame ceremonies. Greg's match begins as expected. His forehand is the biggest weapon on the court, but Efferding's speed helps to neutralize Greg's advantage somewhat. As the match proceeds it is clear that Greg will decide the outcome, despite Efferding's ability to neutralize with well-placed sliced backhands. I can visualize the drill we did so often in which I forced Greg to sneak in at just the right time to put away a backhand volley down the line. He is moving forward just enough to keep Efferding from floating "gets" back to get out of trouble. Creating the threat is the key here. Greg's baseline dominance forces the Aggie to do more off the ground than he would like, causing a few unforced errors. This is as well as Greg has played all year! A clear pattern emerges: after a rally Greg is able to step around for a heavy inside-out forehand and guardedly sneak in to pick off the Efferding sliced backhand response, firmly putting that ball away with a crisp volley. This is clearly a match Greg would not have won earlier in the year and the hard work that he has put in pays off in spades. As I have said earlier, my greatest rewards come in seeing a player "buy in" and, in match play, successfully adopt and execute a strategy that was previously out of his comfort zone.

Somewhere behind the athlete you've become and the hours of practice and the coaches who have pushed you is a little girl who fell in love with the game and never looked back!

Mia Hamm

With the first set in hand Greg's confidence grows and soon he is shaking hands with a 6-4, 6-4 victory over a very good player.

His smile coming off the court tells the whole story. This guy has now arrived. He just might be ready to do some damage here in Champaign. Zurcher and Sprouse are quick to congratulate him and Greg is obviously pleased. He has heard the stories that these two former players made popular over the years due to their courage and determination. Give me six like these two and we will win an NCAA title. Ryan is equally pleased, as he has had the most to do with Greg's growth. It is difficult to believe that only 40 months earlier Greg began his Notre Dame career with four straight losses. As the old Virginia Slims mantra rang, "You've come a long way, baby!" Next up will be Southern Cal's star Ray Sarmiento, someone who will play professionally after graduation and a threat to go far in this event. Now, though, I must get ready for my Hall of Fame evening and all that it entails.

~ Cross Court Reflection ~

A bad attitude is like a flat tire.
You can't get anywhere until you
change it.

Michael Josephson

In Retrospection

Our souls are not hungry for fame, comfort, wealth, or power. Our souls are hungry for meaning, for the sense that we have figured out how to live so that our lives matter, so that the world will be at least a little bit different for our having passed through it.

Harold Kushner

I am finding that I waste little time looking back and questioning decisions I made in good faith, whether they be in recruiting, scheduling, personnel, or team dynamics. I do, however, wonder how things might have turned out had I decided on inaction as a plan. Fighting harder for a recruit, either by offering a larger scholarship, or trying to assert myself more aggressively in the recruiting process are the type of things that always offer idle speculation and occasionally cause me to think 'what if?' Hindsight is always seen through 20/20 vision and is never wrong. Recruits that got away, plays run in matches from the bench, and scheduling decisions perpetually offer opportunities to allow one's mind to run rampant and need to be avoided. Clearly, I wish that I had seen the warning signs on the horizon sooner so that I could have made different decisions in a number of areas, but I am comfortable that, given the information available to me at the time, I made sincere and honest efforts to build my program in a manner in which I can take pride. Circumstances have changed exponentially since I began in Annapolis in 1969. NCAA overreach in regulations, political correctness, the smothering advent of social media, the increasing litigious nature of our society, Title IX, the breakdown of the family, 'helicopter parenting', and an unsustainable arms race for facility expansion, have all taken on a heretofore unforseen importance and have left their marks on college athletics.

The moment a coach's thought process steers him/her towards a course that conflicts with the best interest and welfare of the players it has become time to recalculate things and return to core goals. It is much too easy to think it is all about YOU. Your won-loss record, your NCAA finish, your ranking, and the desired significance of your legacy simply DO NOT MATTER in any rational final analysis. Altogether too often I found myself thinking about our issues as though they were only important as they related to me. That is when I needed a rest and I promised myself never to let those thoughts guide me. When you walk away you want to be able to look in the mirror and say to yourself "Well done, good and faithful servant." The wins meld together, as do many of the losses and become barely rememberable. What might stay with you are the times you neglected to pat a player on the back when he needed a pick-me-up after a sincere, but losing, effort.

The people you meet along the way and the relationships you form are the things you will remember most and become the most important parts of your career. I have attended too many retirement dinners and hall of fame inductions not to notice that those honored almost uniformly take the time to make their close relationships the priority in their remarks. I have never heard any-one say "I should have spent more time at the office." I began my career like many, hoping to be accepted and respected by my peers. I believed that this was best accomplished through my won-loss record, team's ranking, NCAA finish, tournaments and coach-of-the-year awards won, etc.- all quantifiable things - rather than my involvement with people. Fortunately, I can now look back and know that, somehow, the message filtered through. I believe that I did pay attention to the lives of my players and my relationships. Nevertheless, I understand the lure of championships and matches we failed to win.

2013 ITA Hall of Fame Class Inducted at the University of Illinois. The ITA Hall of Fame class was composed of [l to r] John Peterson, Alan Schwartz, Harold Solomon, Paul Goldstein, Kelly Jones, Dennis Emery, and Bobby Bayliss.

An Evening to Remember

The dream begins, most of the time, with a teacher who believes in you, who tugs and pushes and leads you to the next plateau, sometimes poking you with a sharp stick called truth.

Dan Rather

"Can this really be happening?" I ask myself as I meet Pat, shower, and get dressed for the evening's festivities. I have been to virtually all of these ITA Hall of Fame dinners since they began in the 1980's and have thoroughly enjoyed them all. Typically, they run late and speeches are long, but I would not miss one and have many great memories of them. For instance when James Wadley of Oklahoma State was inducted his remarks were laced with humor. He described how he once called a professor to protest an "F" given to his star player, Pat Harrison [father of ATP star Ryan Harrison], indicating that an "F" did not reflect the true scope of Harrison's work. The professor agreed, telling Wadley "I agree with you coach, but "F" is the lowest grade I can give him."

My class includes players Harold Solomon[Rice], Kelly Jones[Pepperdine], and Paul Goldstein[Stanford]. All were stars on the ATP Tour - Solomon a top ten player, Jones more renowned for his doubles prowess, and Goldstein, a chameleon-type player who almost never lost in the college ranks and could adapt his game to do whatever was needed to win like no other in my memory. Alan Schwartz, former Yale star who became USTA president and impacted worldwide tennis with his leadership was another to be inducted. Two other coaches joined me, John Peterson, who won more national junior college titles than anyone in history, and Dennis Emery, the coach who placed a floundering Kentucky program on his back and recruited, built facilities, and willed the Wildcats to a place among the nation's elite through sheer hard work and determination. I am honored to be in their company.

The interesting thing about coaching is that you have to trouble the comfortable and comfort the troubled.

Ric Charlesworth

Pat and I are accompanied by her sister Bridget, who is joining her to perform musically in a couple of days at a conference at Notre Dame. I pity Bridget for having to sit through an evening of speeches and platitudes when she knows only one of the honorees. Each of the recipients is fitted with the ITA Hall of Fame blazer, similar in style and color to those given the Master's winners in golf. While mine almost fits, I regret not having requested a slightly larger size. Egos keep us from prudent decisions, at times, and I hope no one notices that my coat is just a bit too tight to button, as we pose for pictures. Eating in airports and fast food places has made me an unlikely candidate for a swimsuit model. During the reception I am able to speak briefly with those who came to support me, including players from Navy and Notre Dame, professors, and parents. Tony DiLucia has flown in from Philadelphia for the occasion and his presence blows me away. He will catch a 6:00 AM flight the next morning and I let him know how much his efforts to be here mean to me. I introduced his son David in 2008 when he was similarly inducted to the ITA Hall of Fame at the NCAAs in Tulsa and was honored by the opportunity to do so.

As the evening begins I listen with awe to the achievements of my fellow inductees, wondering how I have been selected to join them.

———◦◦◦———

A group becomes a team when each member is sure enough of himself and his contributions to praise the skills of others.

Norman Shidle

———◦◦◦———

After many speeches, much laughter, and some very impactful stories, it is finally my turn, as I am the last to be honored. This brings back a memory from 2002 when I was similarly enshrined in the athletic hall of fame of the University of Richmond, my alma mater, and my first such honor. I was given no instructions and therefore assumed that I would not be asked to speak. As the formal festivities began, the Athletic Director, Jim Miller, asked me if my remarks were ready, as I was the first to speak. Horrified, I grabbed a napkin and began jotting down some emergency remarks that I hoped would not show my lack of preparation. I knew that it would be appropriate to begin with humility and was deciding whether to go with…"I am humbled to be here" or….."It is humbling to be here." At exactly that moment Jim asked me to lead off and I stumbled to the dais and somehow uttered "I am absolutely HUMILIATED to be here with you today!" Somehow 'humbled' had become 'humiliated' and I did not even know what I had said. The rest of my remarks are a blur to me, yet somehow as I finished I asked if I had really used the word 'humiliated.'

Tonight I have asked Dave Fish, the extraordinary Harvard coach to introduce me. He has found an old "fake news" press release that I issued on the occasion of my 300th loss. Its point was to throw some humor on statistical milestones. Although written three years earlier, it still evokes some laughter.

373

Bayliss Joins Vaunted 300 Club:

Notre Dame's Bobby Bayliss has achieved a career milestone- his 300th career loss. "I never would have dreamed that this could have been possible" said Bayliss, in the middle of his 41st season as a collegiate head coach." I have so many former players and coaches to thank for their parts in this achievement. It would be impossible to list them all, but I want them to know that I remember each and every one." The Irish dropped a 7-0 decision to Duke in Durham last weekend to cement the record. "If it had to happen, a 7-0 shutout seems appropriate."

"This could not have happened without the assistance of assistant coaches like Billy Pate and Todd Doebler. And let's not forget Ryan[Sachire, current assistant]. He was right by my side Sunday to make it all possible. Bayliss also agreed that much of the credit should go to former players, most of whom shall remain unnamed except for Navy's Bill Mountford. He also wants to claim much of the credit for himself. "Face it, there aren't many coaches around who could have amassed a record like this" mused the follicly challenged giant in his profession. "Gould, Basset, Leach, and even Fish at Harvard fall short of what I have been able to do. I think Dave Benjamin left Princeton because he knew he could never match this."

Former US Naval Academy athletic director, J. O. Coppedge agreed with the accolades, adding "I knew when we hired Bobby that something like this could become a possibility, but I had no idea it would happen so quickly. I am justifiably proud of him." Former West Point adversary Paul Assaiante chimed in: "We just set the record for consecutive wins in collegiate sport at 221 here at Trinity in squash, but Bobby's achievement puts mine to shame." Notre Dame Sports Information Director John Heisler noted, "We have 7 Heisman Trophy winners and 11 national football championships, but they pale in comparison to what Bobby has just achieved. And he's not yet through. We can only speculate as to what might yet be possible."

Dave added many flattering comments afterwards, but everyone had gotten a good laugh and had seen that I am never afraid of self-deprecating humor. As I rose for my own remarks I was overcome with emotion as I looked at Pat, Jackie, and Brendan and quietly thanked Pat for her role in my career. Not only did she run the household, keep up with all of the children's responsibilities, and pay our bills, but she was an exemplary wife and partner. As I often joked to others, I had "outkicked my coverage" in convincing her to marry me. To be able to come home to her after a weekend's loss that was eating away at me has been my salvation, as I have always felt fortunate to know that her unconditional love was my greatest gift. My comments are blurred now, but I well remember standing at the podium and not quite believing this had all come true. Soon the evening had ended and I stayed awake much of the night re-living many of the matches and memories from 1969 through the current 2013 season. It would not be the last such evening spent tripping down memory lane.

Relationships with people are what it's all about. You have to make players realize that you care about them.

Greg Popovich

I realize how blessed I was to spend much of my career at Notre Dame. There are few universities that allow you to become the best you can be while still incorporating an atmosphere in which you feel an awesome responsibility to do the right thing all the time. Yes, we coaches enjoy tremendous resources, but all the while understand that we are but one small thread in a much greater tapestry. Every academic year in South Bend, we begin with a Catholic mass attended by the entire athletic department and celebrated by the president of the university. It provides a fitting perspective for us to remember our place in the greater hierarchy of Notre Dame. I also know that my formative years at Navy provided me with the tools to use when I arrived here. I kept my eyes and ears open at both places, for there was much to learn. Seeing how some of my colleagues handled media issues taught me to anticipate trick questions. I will always remember the question asked Lou Holtz after his team had miraculously snatched victory from the jaws of defeat in East Lansing, MI. A reporter asked how such a narrow escape had been possible, intimating that Holtz's team had a large edge in talent and that the game should not have even been that close. Without batting an eye, Lou looked the reporter squarely in the eye and replied "You know, I was wondering about that myself, but I just learned the answer." "What is it?" queried the reporter. Holtz's answer "They give scholarships, too!" was the quick reply. It was hard to beat Lou in one-liners.

—◦—

If you want to be really good, you don't have a lot of choices because it takes what it takes.

Nick Saban

—◦—

Not long after I returned from the NCAA Championships, Notre Dame had a retirement dinner for me geared primarily to its own staff and the local tennis community. My two brothers and their wives flew in for the occasion, as did coaches like Peter Daub, Bill Richards, and Billy Pate. It was held in the most beautiful of venues, the large press box in Notre Dame Stadium with the field fully lighted and the football scoreboard offering congratulations. Missy Conboy handled everything and left nothing to chance. The next day there was a similar ceremony in our Eck Tennis Pavilion that brought together the local tennis community.

—∘∘—

*It is not because things are difficult that we
do not dare. It is because we do not dare
that they are difficult.*

Seneca

—∘∘—

Throughout all of it, there was a surreal feeling that I find hard to explain, even today." Is this it?" I found myself asking. It was time to take a deep breath, swallow hard, and realize that there would be no more wins, no more losses, no more recruiting trips, and no more sleepless nights before a big match. While some of the memories might fade I am surprised to report that most remain, but without anguish and anxiety attached to them. What remain indelible are the relationships. Someone who has played for you, has scratched and clawed over and over to seek victory for the team, simply becomes absorbed into your own DNA. Try as you might, you cannot forget them, nor will you want to do so. It is the gift of coaching and it is wonderful. It is what has allowed us to commit so much of ourselves to others.

~ Cross Court Reflection ~

Life is amazing. And then it's awful. And then it's amazing again. And in between the amazing and the awful it's ordinary and mundane and routine. Breathe in the amazing, hold on through the awful, and relax and exhale during the ordinary. That's just living. Heart-breaking, soul-healing, amazing, awful, and ordinary life. And it's breathtakingly beautiful.

L. R. Knost

Another Look Back

*One moment of courage can change
your day. One day can change
your life. And one life can
change the world.*

Mel Robbins

    The day was spectacular. Seventy-eight degrees, with a slight cooling wind and a sky as blue as the water surrounding the Greek Islands, with white, puffy clouds adding just the right touch of contrast. As I took in the surreal surroundings it had finally registered on me that my 44 year career as a college tennis coach had come full circle and no more victories or defeats would follow. I, along with my family-my own kids and grandchildren- was being honored at the fifty yard line in Notre Dame Stadium in front of almost 81,000 fans who, while anxious for the kick-off of the Notre Dame vs. Oklahoma game, took a moment to lift me right out of my shoes with their applause following PA announcer John Thompson's listing of my career highlights. With Pat, my wife of 45 years beside me, I glanced left and right to see my entire family and almost 100 former players, including five from Navy, who had flown or driven in for the occasion, cheering for us. I realized that all of the efforts, late hours, bus and airplane trips, and time spent agonizing over internal team matters had not been in vain. At that same moment I realized that our players were not only cheering for me, but also for each other, celebrating the hard work, long practices, difficult matches in boisterous and hostile environments, and the challenge of having balanced their athletic and academic lives while here on campus. Yes, it had all been worth every sacrifice. Suddenly the former players were all twenty years old once again, laughing and kidding each other, evoking names of former opponents or girl friends alike, ribbing each other about former conquests and losses. It was a moment in time that I will always remember and cherish.

———⟞⟐⟝———

You've always had the power, my dear. You just had to learn it for yourself.

Glynda, 'The Wizard of Oz'

———⟞⟐⟝———

As the National Anthem was played I found myself engaged in a silent prayer of thanksgiving for once again being allowed to be a part of the lives of all surrounding me. Coaching is akin to parenthood in the bonds and emotions that hold us together. I still remember the first match I coached - a 5-4 Navy loss - like it was yesterday. I can feel the March chill of an Annapolis spring, picture the freshly rolled clay courts, and remember the team's training meal - roast beef, baked potato, green beans, and toast with butter and honey. My, have times changed! I even remember my own first college dual match, the opponent, and the score in 1964. We have learned much from each other, these men and I, and something tells me that the education will continue. My chest literally swells with the joy of this occasion. To be surrounded by so many that I know and love is truly a blessing I did not see coming. This entire weekend has been a surprise kept from me by Pat and Ryan. I learned about it only a couple of days ago.

———⟞⟐⟝———

It matters not what someone is born, but what they grow to be.

JRR Tolkein

———⟞⟐⟝———

At the game's end we were taken to the Joyce Center's Club Naimoli for a mass celebrated by former player and current priest and Notre Dame professor Sean McGraw, after which all partook of a delicious dinner followed by flattering comments and gifts bestowed. McGraw is a handsome and charismatic guy and shows that he can think on his feet. Nearing the end of mass, someone breaks wind loudly. As everyone looks nervously around, McGraw blurts out "It appears that the Holy Spirit has spoken. It is time for dinner." Everyone laughs and embarrassment is avoided. McGraw and friend Lou Delfra were David DiLucia's roommates during his senior year. Both Sean and Lou became priests. When David is asked how he missed the cut, he frequently indicates that he was waiting for the waiver of his celibacy vow. Most players took a turn at the microphone, passing on memories, flattering and/ or funny remarks, and before you knew it the hour was late and it was time to retire for the evening. Armed with gifts, a ND cruise taking Pat and me from Athens, Greece, to Turkey, Santorini, to Sicily, to various stops along the Italian coast including Rome and Florence, to Nice and Marseilles, and ending in Barcelona, and a 2014 trip to London and Wimbledon courtesy of Scott Malpass, I was simply overwhelmed and had to hold back tears. Despite the beautiful and wonderful gifts it was the time together with family and former players that brought out the most emotion from me. I had died and been given a short glimpse of heaven….and boy, was it amazing! And you know what? It continues every day!

If you're searching for the one person who could change your life, look in the mirror!

Mel Robbins

I have searched for some common threads typical throughout my career. Here are a few:

1 - There is no excuse for not working hard to make something happen.

2 - There is no reason to tolerate unethical behavior.

3 - You must try to be fair to all, but always with the team's[or group's] best interest in mind.

4 - Always know that your players are watching you. How you treat them, your opponents, your family, and those who cannot help you in any way will influence how they handle similar situations in their own lives.

5 - Understand that you are part of a large and extended family. My recent bout with cancer and prostate surgery forced me to face many challenges. One of the most rewarding parts of the experience was the outpouring of support from former players, coaches, and friends made in the coaching profession.

6 - Never dwell on any decision that was made in good faith, but turned out to be the wrong one. All we can do is our best.

7 - Those around you will not care how much you know until they know how much you care.

8 - Giving less than your best effort is never a good thing.

9 - Trust and respect from those you know is more highly valued than their admiration. That will come anyway because of how you have lived.

10 - Never be afraid to let those you love and admire know how you feel. It is never a mistake to do so.

Everybody makes mistakes. That's why they put erasers on pencils.

Tommy La Sorda

I recently received an e-mail from Trinity's Paul Assaiante that included the final words of Steve Jobs, the acclaimed founder of Apple and all of its technological wonders. It was yet another reminder that the path I had chosen had been the correct one for me. As he lay dying in the hospital, Jobs' thoughts were not on his latest or most famous creation, but on incomplete relationships. He said:

> "I reached the pinnacle of success in the business world. In others' eyes, my life is the epitome of success…
>
> However, aside from work, I have little joy. In the end, wealth is only a fact of life that I am accustomed to….
>
> At this moment, lying in my sick bed and recalling my whole life, I realize that all of the recognition and wealth that I took so much pride in have paled and become meaningless in the face of impending death.
>
> In the darkness I look at the green lights from the life supporting machines and hear the humming mechanical sounds, and I can feel the breath of God and of death drawing closer….
>
> Now I know when we have accumulated sufficient wealth to last our lifetime, we should pursue other matters that are unrelated to wealth…{They] should be something that is more important. Perhaps relationships, perhaps art, perhaps a dream from younger days….
>
> Non-stop pursuing of wealth will only turn a person into a twisted being, just like me. God gave us the senses to feel the love in everyone's heart, not the illusions brought about by wealth…
>
> The wealth I have won in my life I cannot bring with me. What I can bring is only the memories precipitated by love. That's the true riches that will follow you, accompanying you to give you strength and light to go on. Love can travel a thousand miles. Life has no limit. Go where you want to go. Reach the height you want to reach. It is all in your heart and your hands……

What is the most expensive bed in the world? -
"sick bed."

You can employ someone to drive the car for you,
make money for you, but you cannot have someone
bear sickness for you…

Material things can be found, but there is one thing
that can never be found when it is lost - "Life.".....

When a person goes into the operating room, he will
realize that there is one book that he has yet to fin-
ish- "Book of Healthy Life.".....

Whichever stage we are at right now, with time, we
will face the day when the curtain comes down….

Treasure love for your family, love your spouse,
love your friends…

Treat yourself well. Cherish others…."

My journey continues, yet in a different vehicle. The sun
still comes up each morning and sets in the evenings. While there
is no longer the same sense of urgency to complete many of the
tasks in my life, I find that this is a good thing. There remain
more mountains to climb and even a few dragons left to slay. I am
comforted by the knowledge that the pace is a bit less hurried and
anxiety no longer rents unlimited space in my mind. I joke with my
friends when I tell them that the only bad thing about retirement
is that you never get a day off. There is much left to do and even
more joy remains in the doing of it. Tie-breakers and third sets no
longer hold sway over me and relaxation comes easier and for longer periods of time. Whenever I want, I can air-brush the memory
of an inspirational match played long ago into my thoughts. More
than anything I have the comfort and support of the love of my life
and children and grandchildren that I know I am more than fortunate to have. In addition, I am fully aware that whatever I do moving forward will have the support of so many of the lives I have
been so fortunate to share. I have learned a great deal from family,
players, and coaches alike and there is a world out there waiting for

me to share it. When I awake each morning I take a quiet moment to thank God for the blessing of yet another day and realize that I can't wait to begin again once more. Thank you for sharing some of my experiences with me.

~ Cross Court Reflection ~

It is not what we eat, but what we digest, that makes us strong; it is not what we gain, but what we save, that makes us rich; it is not what we read, but what we remember, that makes us learned; and not what we profess, but what we practice, that gives us integrity.

Michael Josephson

BAYLISS

Members of the Notre Dame women's tennis team gather for post-season cookout at the Bayliss home shortly after the season ended in May, 2019. Front row, left to right: Zoe Taylor, Zoe Spence, Brooke Boda. Second row: Rachel Chong, Julia Lilien, Cameron Corse. Top row: Maeve Koscielski, Coach Bayliss, Coach Alison Silverio, Bess Waldrum, Ally Bojczuk. *Photo courtesy of Pat Bayliss.*

CHAPTER TEN

Epilogue: Never Saw This Coming…
An Unexpected Opportunity!

One athlete of character can change a team.
One team of character can change a school.
A school of character can change
an entire community.

Pat Nickell

Fast forward to February 21, 2019. I had retired for good and hung up my whistle the previous July. Now I am going to see what real retirement feels like. You know what? It is pretty darn good. I now attend the matches here as a spectator. While I consider myself an avid fan, as I like both coaching staffs, and enjoy watching our teams compete, I now find it much easier to walk away from a loss without the bitter sense of disappointment I felt as a head coach. Both teams, our men's and women's, have begun their seasons. In fact, I was able to see our men play in the ITA National Indoors which was held in Chicago this year. Having two of our children living in Chicago has its advantages. I watched the men play against both UCLA and Columbia the previous weekend and had driven today to the Eck Tennis Pavilion to pass on my observations to Ryan Sachire. On my way to his office I passed the office of the women's tennis coach Alison Silverio and waved to her through the window. She came out to say hello and asked me to stop in before I left, as she had something she wanted to discuss with me.

After passing on my thoughts to Ryan I walked over to Alison's office to see what she might want. She had only recently taken over the program, replacing Jay Louderback, who wanted to spend more time near his family in Kansas. Alison came with outstanding credentials, having taken a relatively average Oregon team into the nation's top 25 in only two short years. She had energy and enthusiasm and was liked by all. Clearly, she was a coach with great potential. When I entered, she asked me to have a seat. What I did not know was that her own assistant had just left suddenly and she was caught in a very unfortunate situation, trying to find a replacement at a very inopportune time. She came right to the point, letting me know the importance of finding someone immediately. Then Alison looked me squarely in the eye and said "Is there any way you would consider filling in until the season ends? We will try to work around your schedule. Perhaps you could miss some of the trips if you already have conflicting plans. I know that this is the last thing you were expecting, but it would mean a great deal if you would think this over."

I swallowed hard. While I had coached a woman who played professionally when I lived in Boston, I had zero experience coaching a women's team and wondered if that alone should disqualify me. I asked her to give me a moment to think about her offer. On one hand, I had become comfortable with my new retirement status. On the other hand, I tried to put myself in her shoes. She really was in a terrible bind. I then told her that I could not make a decision without first running it by Pat. She had dealt with my extremely difficult travel schedule for 44 years and we finally had become accustomed to having more quality time together. I then asked her "When is the next match?" Her answer: "We play Clemson tomorrow." We talked more about what she wanted and how I might be able to fit this in. I knew that she needed to know something, so I told her that I would certainly like to help and would immediately commit to being with her for tomorrow's match and Sunday's[against #25 Syracuse] as well. This would buy both of us a few days for me to ponder and for her to reach out to other potential candidates, if necessary. I left the Eck and returned home to discuss the offer with Pat. I called Alison to let her know that I could fill in as requested, with one or two potential conflicts that I would try to resolve. I was back in the saddle, albeit in a different role.

When the Clemson team came into the Eck to practice the next day I walked over to greet their coach, Nancy Harris, and told her that I would be coaching against her that afternoon. She could not have been nicer. I also told Alison that she should feel free to use me as it best worked for her. I wanted her to know that I had no problem if she wanted to move me to a different court at any time during the match. I understood that she obviously knew the players much better than I and that my ego was not going to present a problem. I expected there to be a learning curve for me to better understand our players. I also understood that it would take some time for the players to become accustomed to my way of handling things and what expectations I might have. As the players began to arrive for the pre-match warm-up, I nodded to each, not knowing what to say. Alison called them all together to formally announce that I would be joining the team. I told them that it initially might be confusing if I asked them to attempt something tactically that they were uncomfortable trying. For that reason, I wanted them to feel free to let me know their feelings. Most of all, I wanted this to be fun for them.

A good coach can change a game. A great coach can change a life.

Davor Dekaris

As the match began, and the doubles commenced I began with the #3 team, Ally Bojcjuk and Zoe Taylor. The Clemson team was scrappy, but I could see that we were better around the net.

I encouraged each of our players to poach, cutting in toward the middle at an angle, allowing us the best chance for success. I was surprised to see them attempt whatever I suggested without complaint. I was impressed with our players' communication during the points and liked their doubles IQ. We comfortably won the match 6-2. While I doubt that my presence on the court had much to do with the outcome, it was good to get a "W" in my first opportunity. Fortunately our #2 team, Zoe Spence and Brooke Boda, also won, giving us the doubles point. It was 1-0, Irish. During the 5 minute break between doubles and singles, Alison went over the Clemson players and made certain that there were no unanswered questions. I kept my mouth shut and tried to stay out of the way.

As the singles matches began Alison asked me to start on the west side of the building with numbers 1, 3, and 5. I kept my notepad handy and began to jot down tendencies, strengths, and weaknesses, as I saw them. I moved from court to court, trying to let each of our players know that I was in their corner. Rather than bark out commands that had not been well thought out, I kept my remarks brief and positive. I needed to get to know our players before I asked them to leave their respective comfort zones. Just as I was getting comfortable with each court, Alison came over and asked me to move to courts 2, 4, and 6. As I took my place there I saw Cameron Course shaking hands with her opponent who had been injured and had to default. We now led 2-0. My two remaining courts held Maeve Koscielski [6] and Ally Bojczuk [2]. I had known Maeve's father, Paul, since his playing days at Texas, where he played #1 as a senior. Maeve was a solid groundstroker who played good percentage tennis, but today she was struggling to find a happy medium between being steady and aggressive. She was getting pushed around from the baseline by her opponent's heavy and penetrating ball, but when she tried to add more punch, she began to make too many errors. Maeve had a fairly big take-back on her forehead which sometimes made her a whisker late contacting the ball. Her backhand was more compact and she had no difficulty there, usually cutting in aggressively. In fairness, her opponent, Alex Angyalosy, was pretty good and, as I said, hit a bigger ball, so

Maeve found herself on defense. I trotted down to try to help, but by the time I arrived the die was cast. I was not able to right the ship and felt bad that I had not helped. You need to pass on information promptly in a match, before lost confidence makes an adjustment ineffective. As they shook hands, the team match began to heat up, as the top 3 matches went into third sets. Notre Dame was slightly ahead, but this one looked to be going down to the wire.

This left Ally Bojczuk as the only player left on my side of the Eck. I found her easy to talk with and she seemed open to suggestions. The overall team match had reached a point where we led 3-2 with both remaining matches in the third sets. Not knowing what was happening on the other side, I felt that we needed to grab Ally's match in order to clinch. Clemson's player, Fernanda Navarro, was a lefty with a big forehand and good serve. Her backhand was very steady, but almost always hit with underspin. While she could slice and approach effectively, I doubted that she could come over it and pass well, so I encouraged Ally to chip and charge to that side on Navarro's second serve. This was working well, but her wide lefty serve in the ad court was swinging Ally out of position. It became a chess match until suddenly Ally had a match point in the third set tiebreaker. Navarro missed her first serve and, without warning, I told Ally to move all the way over in the ad court, even beyond the doubles alley. She looked at me incredulously, but, to her credit, followed my directions. Her exaggerated court position was literally daring Navarro to try to hit the "T" with her second delivery, something I had noticed bothered most lefties. As Navarro looked up to hit her second serve, she seemed bothered by Ally's position off the court. As she began her motion, I felt the play would work. Sure enough, she hit the second serve into the bottom of the net, handing us the match. Game, set, and match to Notre Dame; we had beaten the Tigers! Ally was stunned, but then pointed at me and yelled "Awesome!" She then ran to me to give me a high five before shaking hands. I was as happy as she. I had gained some "street cred" and been able to help us win. "This could be fun," I thought.

What is the ultimate quantification of success? For me it's not how much time you spend doing what you love. It's how little time you spend doing what you hate.

Casey Neistat

With a day off before we take on #25 Syracuse, I am able to relax and finish another good book I am reading. I usually have several of them going at once and enjoy reading now more than ever. Sunday finds me anxious for our match, but, oddly, not nervous. The Orange of Syracuse play all their home matches indoors, so they are more than ready for the friendly confines of the Eck. Watching them prepare, I am impressed with their ball-striking ability. I also wish it were above 50 degrees, because predominantly indoor teams are used to the ball being right where they expect it to be. These same teams struggle when first moving outside, as the conditions don't allow that same comfort hitting the ball. The doubles begin and it is clear that Syracuse wants to be aggressive. They go for their returns and hit freely through the court from the two-back position. Before long they capture the doubles point. I stay with our #3 team, but the 6-2 loss we take lets me know that I need to do a better job from the bench. I am still learning the tendencies of our players. The singles matches are evenly split, leaving us on the short end of a 4-3 score. We won at nos. 2, 3, and 5. Ally follows her Friday victory with another 3 set win. Now that I have seen her again I can appreciate her passion for excellence. She runs for everything, is not afraid to come forward, and likes to compete. The biggest problem I see for her is improving her serve. She lets the ball drop too low, all while failing to elevate her hand and arm on the toss. This gets more problematic when the match gets close. The result: fewer free first serve points and a second serve that crosses the net wearing a smiley face. It is something I will discuss with her and I believe it can be fixed. Our other winners today are Cameron Corse at #4 and Brooke Boda at #5.

Cameron has good genes for tennis. Her parents both played on NCAA championship teams at Stanford. She has a laser-like backhand, great athleticism, a strong serve, and is not afraid to come forward. Her forehand carried too much spin a year ago, but it has improved. Her fearlessness as a competitor makes her fun to coach. The other winner, Brooke Boda, came to Notre Dame with a high ranking and great expectations. She, unfortunately, has had some significant injuries. She will become a success story for us this year, as she is able to play in almost all of our matches. She is an extraordinary ball-striker who can hurt you off both sides. Playing lower in the lineup this year, she will win some big matches and demonstrates a toughness that I did not see a year ago. Boda and Corse will win often for us this year. While we lost 4-3 today, we won three 3 setters and that might bode well for us down the road. I like the way our girls compete. We don't play again for five days, and in Chapel Hill, NC.

2002 Notre Dame team at the National Team Indoor Championships, Univ. of Washington Press Box, Seattle Washington. (L to R) Brent D'Amico, Luis Haddock, Casey Smith, Javier Taborga, Aaron Talarico, Coach Bobby Bayliss, Ashok Raju, Coach Billy Pate, and Bo Rottenborn.

Next Up...the Tar Heels and the Wolfpack

Appreciate what's good about this moment.
Don't always think that you're on a
permanent journey. Skip
and enjoy the view.

Allain de Botton

      This is a trip that I always enjoy. My men's teams always used to play both Duke and UNC together. Sometimes we won both. Sometimes we lost both. Sometimes we split them. But I always knew two things: both teams were good and they would compete at a high level. This weekend the ACC schedulers have us playing both the Tar Heels of UNC and the Wolfpack of NC State. It is no easy trip, as Brian Kalbas once again has his UNC women ranked #1 in the country, having just won the ITA National Team Indoors, for a third time. State is no gimme either, ringing in at #11. We will need to be on our toes for both. I have already told you how much I believe in Kalbas. He is knowledgeable, he competes hard, he is fair, and he cares about his players. Today is special for me because he and I sit together on #3 doubles, as Alison and Tyler Thompson, his assistant, handle nos. 1 and 2. Unexpectedly we are able to win the third doubles match, but to little avail, as UNC takes both #1 and #2 to clinch the point. I have become comfortable coaching Ally and Zoe Taylor. They have tremendous chemistry together, barking out "Yours!" and "Mine!" like they were sisters. Zoe "walked on" at Notre Dame without a scholarship, but she is in the process of earning one now. She poaches fearlessly and is quite comfortable at the net and it is fun watching them operate. In women's tennis it is difficult to recruit quality "walk-ons" because women's teams are allowed 8 scholarships. By the time all of the scholarships are handed out, the quality of what remains is much smaller than on the men's side. I need to give Jay Louderback credit for seeing Zoe's potential.

The Heels have an awesome lineup. All three of their top players are ranked in the nation's top six. That is a lot of firepower and it is backed up by other talented players. We are simply outgunned today, but not before Zoe Spence pulls off a major upset, beating the nation's #6 ranked player 6-4, 6-4. Zoe is deceptively good. At about 5'3" and perhaps 100 pounds dripping wet with her sweats on, Zoe looks like a little girl who wandered in and is lost. However, this little girl has a razor sharp two-handed backhand that she can hit with power and accuracy to all corners of the court. She NEVER quits and frequently runs down balls that surprise everyone. Many opponents get frustrated and try to hit closer to the lines, but then begin to miss. At times Zoe's second serve looks like it could be timed by an hourglass, rather than a radar gun, and players frequently overhit and make errors. You get the picture. Although we lose today, Zoe gives her teammates reason for hope. I speak briefly with Brian before leaving and wish him luck. He won't need too much of it. We now need to focus on the #11 ranked Wolfpack of NC State. Getting rattled by this loss is not going to help us.

75% of success is staying calm and not losing your nerve. The rest you figure out, but once you lose your calm, everything else starts falling apart fast.

Sam Kass

As we enter the NC State outdoor facility the next day for practice, I am impressed. There is a sea of red- the Wolfpack's chief color- and it looks terrific. Our girls spread out and begin to warm up. We will practice here and indoors today, as tomorrow's forecast is iffy. I have been impressed by Alison's sense of structure in practices. She dictates what will happen and sticks to her schedule. I'll bet she was an amazing team captain as a player. As we move indoors, she changes a few things and we go through a programmed routine. Towards the end of our practice I get the nicest of surprises.

Just as our players are doing a cool -down stretch, the men's team from the University of Pennsylvania walks into the facility, led by none other than David DiLucia. David wanted to give college coaching a try and was able to arrange a position under David Geatz in his hometown of Philadelphia. He comes over and gives me a big hug and I introduce him to our players. They spend 10-15 minutes comparing Notre Dame notes and getting to know him. It is a nice ending to our practice. Penn will play NC State on Monday and they are just beginning their spring break. This also gives me a chance to exchange words with Geatz. We battled through many tough matches when he coached Minnesota.

Another Close One

As we drive to the NC State courts it begins to rain. Glad that we took the time to move indoors yesterday, I anticipate little problems adjusting to the new surface. The biggest adjustment will be for the #5 and #6 players today. Because State has only four indoor courts, the 5-6 players will begin their matches on the first available courts as the 1-4 matches conclude. I am familiar with this, as Kentucky has the same layout and my teams played there every other year. Today will require the last two players to stay relaxed during the early round and eat something at an appropriate time to give them sufficient energy for the later match.

Surprisingly, we jump on State and take the doubles point by winning at numbers 2-3. I stayed with Ally and Zoe Taylor as they fought valiantly to clinch the point in a tiebreaker 7-3. Once again our players cut off balls at the net and outhustled their opponents at every opportunity. Cam and Bess Waldrum took charge early and stayed the course for a 7-5 win. Once again, we lead 1-0. As singles began I felt that we had a great chance for an upset. The level was high on all courts. We played hard and very well, but at the end of the day we had lost 5-2, losing 3 matches in third sets and another 7-6, 7-6. As a coach, I could not fault the effort or our competitiveness. It simply was not to be. This is but one of several close losses we experienced, any one of which, if reversed, would make a big difference to us at NCAA selection time. My best take was that we had played very well, and with a home match next up would grow from this experience.

I was right. The Louisville Cardinals were next on the schedule and we were ready to go. There was no letdown. Alison tweaked the doubles, moving Cam and Bess to #1. They responded with a 6-2 win, allowing Ally and Zoe Taylor to clinch things for us 6-4. In singles we won all three of our 3 setters and won going away 7-0. Today I sat on Bess's court early. She has the size, power, and racket skills to become an elite player. Concentration seems to be an issue. Today she experienced difficulty returning the serves of Raven Neely. She called me over on a changeover and we discussed this. She indicated that it was Neely's pace that was bothering her. I simply suggested that she move back a few feet to give herself more time to read the ball. We agreed that if Neely picked up on this, she would likely serve wide to take advantage of the angles that Bess would be allowing. It was a pretty simple adjustment and should not have worked as well as it did, but Neely never indicated that she noticed the change in return position. Sometimes even obvious changes can bring success. Zoe Spence, Cam, and Brooke won their third sets and we shut down the Cardinals 7-0.

Notre Dame Team visits Wimbledon, 1995. (L to R) Brian Harris, Steve Flanigan, John J. O'Brien, Coach Bobby Bayliss, Mike Sprouse, Jason Pun, Ron Mencias, Jakub Pietrowski, Horst Dziura, and Ryan Simme.

Spring Break ~ Never a Bad Thing!

When considering the consequences of little things, you realize there are no little things.

Brad Stevens

One of the things I negotiated with Alison prior to agreeing to become her assistant was that I would stay here in South Bend at the beginning of spring break. I would miss our match against Iowa at the new USTA Tennis Center in Orlando, but I would meet the team in Miami before we played the Hurricanes. Alison felt confident that we could handle that match. Boy, was she right. The 7-0 win over the Hawkeyes put our players in a better frame of mind. I met the team at our hotel in Miami, close to the Neil Schiff Tennis Center. We had a couple of days to practice before playing and, predictably, spirits were high. I was able to meet the team on Wednesday, two days before our Friday match. As we began to practice, I felt like the courts were waving at me. My teams had played over 30 matches on these courts and many had been memorable. The Big East Championships were held here for close to a decade and we played Miami here on alternate years during that time as well. The crowds here for many of our matches had been among the most active we had faced. Notre Dame and Miami broke off a contentious football rivalry in the early 1990's because it had gotten ugly. The Miami fans had not forgotten that and had been a factor in some close matches, but by now that seemed forgotten. While they cheered avidly, there was not the vitriol that I remembered.

The Hurricanes jumped on us early in doubles. I was again on court #3 and could not see much of the action on numbers 1 and 2.The courts at Miami are laid out in two groups of four, with walkways between the middle of each. For spectator friendly viewing, my court was out of the site line for viewing, so my visibility was very limited. I doubt that I could have helped much, as Miami was firing on all cylinders on each court. Before you could recite the Lord's Prayer both #1 and #2 had been claimed by the home team and our #3 match was called as we trailed 5-3. Match protocol had changed over the years, and the prevailing thought was that once the doubles point was clinched there was no point in finishing a "dead" match that would not affect the overall score. We had also decided to limit the time between singles and doubles to five minutes in order to keep the action flowing and keep the crowd from straying away. It seems to be a better plan.

As singles began, I found myself on courts 5-6, squarely behind nos.1-4. With only two matches to oversee, I should be able to zero in on just what needed to be done. Brooke was playing Ulyana Shirokova, an aggressive baseliner who hit a heavy ball. She was bigger and stronger, so I began to encourage Brooke to take the ball earlier and take some of Shirokova's time away. It began to work. I also tried to get her to come forward in better balance. Coaches overuse the term "split-step" in teaching players how to approach the net. I explained to Brooke that, rather than stop to see where the passing shot was going, she should use the term "assess" as she came forward, never really stopping. Then she would close on the net, but do so while in balance. This seemed to help her. I was especially pleased that she was making a sincere effort to adopt what I was telling her. My experience coaching men was different. It was difficult to get them to buy in during competition, and it was important to have worked on something in practice for it to be successfully applied in match conditions. More often than not, many of the men I had coached over the years might assent to my advice, only to return to exactly what they were doing before. In the heat of battle, the male ego can take over, making it difficult to absorb constructive criticism. I found myself admiring the sincere effort that Brooke was exerting. She wears her heart on her sleeve, and it is sometimes easy to read her emotions. While it can be advantageous to hide your emotions from your opponent, Boda is not afraid that you might guess her feelings. All of her focus goes into the point. She ekes out a difficult first set 6-4. Because her opponent is hitting a bigger ball, many of the spectators felt she was winning. Now it is important to maintain the momentum she has worked so hard to build.

On court #6, Zoe Taylor is having a more difficult time. I was concerned about Zoe's ability to quickly adapt to outdoor play. She is an imposing player, tall and aggressive. She hits a bigger ball from the forehand side, but her backhand is deceptive. I have been encouraging her to use more of her core as she hits the ball and she has also been receptive to constructive criticism. Unlike Brooke, who had great success in the juniors, Zoe is a late bloomer, and it will not surprise me to see her become quite good before she graduates. Today, though, Zoe is struggling. She can't generate any positive momentum and is making errors today that I have not seen before. She gets steamrolled in a quick first set 6-1. During the break between sets I try to emphasize a greater use of her legs and it seems to help. The second set is better, but serving at 3-4, she misses two close groundstrokes and is broken. Never a quitter, she breaks back to get back on serve. On the changeover I applaud her effort and encourage her once more, but her serve deserts her and soon she is shaking hands with an opponent who competed very well. For aggressive players like Zoe, it sometimes takes a few extra days to make the adjustment to outdoor play. She can bounce back, I believe.

Back on #5, Boda has begun to miss and seems confused. Because Shirakova hits a bigger ball, Brooke has fallen into the trap of initially trying to equal her pace, but begins to miss by small margins. This time my advice is simple. Hit out, I tell her, but aim for bigger targets, not so close to the lines. It is simple, to be sure, but it seems to work. I have frequently given out very basic advice in a critical situation, but dressed it up to appear more sophisticated. My model here is the classic Walt Disney story of Dumbo, the flying elephant, who suddenly and inexplicably, lost his ability to fly because he lost his "magic feather." He felt that without it he had lost his ability to fly. His mother, rather than explain to him that the feather had nothing to do with his flying, simply found another feather and convinced him that it was indeed the original one. Dumbo then resumed flying, and the circus was saved. Back in my Navy coaching days, we had a plebe [freshman] playing in an important match. He was quite good and had built a 6-2, 5-4 lead, but at that moment called nervously for me to rush over to his court. "I'm serving for the match. What should I do?" I looked at him and realized that he was having a momentary panic attack. Rather than berate him for such a stupid question, I gave him the same "feather" that Dumbo had used to regain his ability to fly. I looked him squarely in the eye and said, in a serious tone, "Here's what will work. Hit all groundstrokes cross court until you get a short ball. Then take that ball down the line and follow it into the net." For those of you who do not play tennis, this was advice I might expect to pass on to an eight year old....very basic. In that situation, though, it worked. I had given the Navy player his "feather," and he used it to secure a very good win. Brooke had her "feather" when I told her to hit for bigger, safer targets away from the lines. She was able to use this again to get her out of trouble.

Brooke's match put us on the board, but we needed three more to win. Having completed "my" matches, I walked over to the #1-4 courts to join a highly competitive match where Ally had won [giving us a second point] and both Bess and Cam were still fighting hard. Watching both, I felt that we were going to be a much better team in a year. Bess is a strong player who hits with power, but needs to line up for her shots better, taking small adjustment steps. Many of her errors are the result of simply not being in good position to hit the ball. For some players, this can indicate a lack of effort, but in Bess's case it is more about concentration. My advice to her has been simple: "Put the ball on the tee," I tell her, indicating that the key to consistency is lining up the shot much like a young baseball player would use a tee, as in "Tee ball." Cam also has a chance to become a great college player. She is athletic, has great tennis genes, exhibits solid basic fundamentals, and seems to thrive on competition. I think it might be wise to dare her to do great things, counting on her competitiveness to fill any gaps needed. Telling her she CANNOT do something just might make her want to do even more. She is fun to be around and I am going to follow her career with interest. Unfortunately, both players come up a little short today. While we lost 5-2, I see things differently. We left two points out there that could have been ours. Miami has been a consistent round of sixteen team, and we scared them today on their courts. We are not far from becoming a good team.

After dinner, Alison likes to meet with each player to discuss what happened on the court and what might be done to improve things. She has me sit in and allows me the freedom to add anything I feel is important. I should probably have done more of this. I realize that I am not too old to keep the learning process going. We have an early wake-up call tomorrow morning, so remarks are brief and to the point. It is beginning to sink in that I am in a position to make a difference.

I am convinced that it is not the fear of death, of our lives ending, that haunts our sleep so much as the fear ………that as far as the world is concerned, we might as well never have lived.

Harold Kushner

I don't care where you live, 5:30 AM is early. I struggle out of the bed and quickly grab a shower and dress. Within 10 minutes we arrive at the Miami airport and begin the check-in process. While Miami and Tallahassee are located in the same state, they could not be farther apart and our flight touches ground with most of our party still asleep. I know this city well, as our men's team has played Florida State on a regular basis. Dwayne Hultquist, the Seminoles' men's coach, has had good teams for years. We grab lunch and check in to the hotel before heading to the courts to practice. I recall that I was here a year ago, as Javier Taborga, a 2007

Notre Dame alum and All American flew me - at his expense - to see our men play both Florida State and Miami. In an unusual circumstance, our men are also here and we practice just as they are finishing. Both teams will play the Seminoles tomorrow at noon. This is an unusual occurrence, as normally the ACC schedules each school's men's and women's teams to play where one is home and the other away, to accommodate inclement weather possibility. Florida State has 12 championship courts with seating, as well as indoor back-up, so every contingency is covered. Each school has a travel partner and matches are typically played on Friday-Sunday. It works well, although, as conferences continue to expand, geography and logistics have become more challenging. I have alluded to this earlier. It is a shame to see long-time geographic rivalries go away. I doubt that anyone could have imagined a time when Texas and Texas A&M did not play each other. Money sometimes trumps common sense in today's college athletics world.

The morning brings good news. The possibility of rain has subsided, so we can stick to our schedule. Our players warm up well and I feel optimistic. Smart money today might call for an upset of the #22 Seminoles, particularly after we take #1 and #2 doubles to lead 1-0 as singles begins. Unfortunately, the singles do not go our way and smart money is once again wrong. While Zoe Spence, Ally, and Cam play well, fight hard, and have chances to win, it is not our day. Maeve Koscielski is getting another shot at #6 today, but falls short in straight sets, despite a great effort. I am disappointed for her, as she has handled not playing a lot very well. Her answer to losing a starting lineup spot has been simply to work harder, without complaint. It has not gone unnoticed. I always felt that removing a player from his spot in our lineup was the most difficult thing I had to do, but as I mentioned earlier, tennis teaches life lessons. Maeve has taken her "lemons" and made lemonade from them. She has demonstrated high character. While our team showers I am able to walk over to the other side and catch the end of our men's match. It is painful to watch, as it all comes down to a third set tiebreaker, which we lose. I feel for Ryan. He has a very good team which has been decimated by injuries. He has played with as many as four of his six starters out of the lineup, something that never happened to me. Predictably, the team's record has suffered and what looked to be a breakout season for him has his team battling for one of the last NCAA spots. Hopefully he will get his players back in time for a stretch run. He runs a great program and it would be a shame to miss "the tournament."

I watched the match from the bleachers, sitting around some avid FSU fans. I began talking with a few of them and one mentioned the name Richard McKee to me. Boy did that strike home! In my first paid coaching job, at Thomas Jefferson High School in Richmond, our best player was Richard McKee. They were one and the same. I asked one of the ladies sitting with me to email me Richard's contact info and gave her my card. She boasted that Richard was the best tennis pro in the world. I believe her. Richard became an All American at North Carolina, where he reached the NCAA finals in doubles with Freddie McNair, a French Open doubles winner. Richard remains one of the elite players I have ever coached. I was able to connect with him when we returned and we had a long and enjoyable conversation over the phone.

~ Cross Court Reflection ~

Heart beats muscle when muscle doesn't hustle.

Jon Gordon

Home Cooking is Usually Better

Next up for us is Wake Forest. The Demon Deacons come into our match at #17. One of the great, yet challenging things about the ACC is that it is the country's best and deepest conference. The fastest way to a higher ranking is to have the opportunity to play highly ranked teams at home, where the crowd is pulling for you and the surface and visual background is familiar to your players. The flip side of this is that beating strong teams is not an easy task. We have been close to wins over a number of teams that would have boosted us in the rankings, but moral victories do not factor into the ITA computer. The doubles begins well for us, as we are initially even or ahead on all courts. From my seat on the #3 doubles match I can see clearly what is going on. We break early on court three and complete the set with a 6-3 victory, but #1 and #2 are very close. I hope that having won one of the three creates added pressure, but the Deacons hold serve on both courts to clinch the point and take that all-important lead into singles play. Things get really interesting there. While Zoe Spence uses her quickness to extend many of the rallies, it is not quite enough tonight and she drops a closer-than-the-score contest to Emma Davis. Zoe has improved markedly during my somewhat brief tenure, but just a little more firepower in her arsenal would boost her considerably. Next year she will likely win many of these same close contests.

Numbers 2-5 all end up in third sets, with Brooke, Ally and Cam taking the initial sets. Three first sets in hand following a win in doubles is normally enough to get you a win at home, but once more, I watch several matches slip away. Brooke holds on for our second point, but Ally and Cam each fall 6-4 in the third set. The disappointment on our players' faces is there for all to see. We have played better tennis than our near .500 record would indicate. We need an impact win with only four matches remaining. Neither the computer nor the NCAA selection committee reward style points. Whatever needs to happen needs to happen soon. We have #3 Duke and last year's NCAA final four team, Georgia Tech here in two days. There is no place to hide in the ACC.

Most things that are worthwhile are difficult, and your willingness to work through those difficulties will set you apart from the competition.

Nick Saban

One of the most enjoyable parts of my jumping on board to help coach our women has been the chance to run into so many old friends. Today's opponent, Georgia Tech, is coached by Rodney Harmon, an old friend and one of the best liked people in the tennis industry. His team is young, but talented. Last year they reached the NCAA final four. As I mentioned earlier, Rodney is from Richmond and he became a great player, reaching the US Open quarterfinals while still in college at SMU, playing for tennis legend Dennis Ralston. Whenever we are around others I try to work into the conversation the fact that for the entire time I lived in Richmond, I was a better player than he. He then spoils my self-praise by letting everyone know that he was nine years old when I moved. Today's forecast is "iffy," with a 40% chance for rain. Harmon's team is much better outdoors. So what happens? The rain stays away. We will play outdoors. There were times when I felt like I could empathize with the emotions of Gen. Eisenhower as D Day approached. The weather sometimes decides your matches for you.

Today's doubles are an enormous disappointment. We drop both #1 and #2 by 6-1 scores. We will need to get things together in singles. We do just that. All but one of our singles are hotly contested. Uncharacteristically, Zoe Spence gets hammered 6-2, 6-1 by Kenya Jones, the #12 ranked player in college tennis. I was with numbers 2, 4, and 6 on the north bank of courts and could not see much of her match, but it is unusual for Zoe to be beaten this badly. The problem with playing #1 singles is that you never get an easy match. At some point it catches up to you and you can experience a day like this. Fortunately, Zoe is a great competitor and will bounce back. Ally looks out of sorts in her first set, losing 6-1 to Nami Otsuka, whose groundstrokes are too much for her. I point out to her on a changeover that Otsuka is not following her penetrating groundies to finish at the net. I emphasize that Ally needs to float some balls back when out of position and force Otsuka to take them out of the air, something she seemed hesitant to do. She listens. It works. Now we have a real tennis match. Ally has her chances, but falls in the breaker 7-3. Her second serve deserted her when it was most needed. Cam plays one of her better matches, winning in straight sets by getting in behind her more forceful groundstrokes in a 6-4,6-2 win. Bess is hitting with authority, but misses just a little too often and falls 6-4, 7-5 to Gia Cohen. Brooke and Zoe Taylor are locked in and playing well. They will split their matches, as Brooke drops two extremely close sets and, with the match now clinched, Zoe T wins the third by a 6-2 score. I feel for our players. The effort was there today, but the execution was just a bit off. With #3 Duke next in two days there is no time to feel sorry for ourselves. As Lou Holtz used to say….."Don't feel sorry for yourself or tell me your problems. 90% of the people you know don't care and the other 10% are glad you have them." Lou could cut right to the chase.

Sunday arrives quickly, and with it, the Blue Devils. As head coach Jamie Ashworth walks into our facility, it reminds me of an earlier era when I was recruiting him as a player. Jamie has become very successful at Duke. His wife, Caylan, played #1 for Notre Dame. O, the resiliency of youth! We have shown up today against the nation's #3 team and it is a war! After dropping the doubles point, we come out guns blazing in most of the matches. We are able to win three of the first five to finish, as Cam rips Ellyse Hamlin at #3, 6-2,6-3 and Brooke and Zoe T deliver wins for us as well. This leaves the match in the hands of the two #1 players, Zoe having won the second set 6-0 over Maria Mateas. Mateas has sported a WTA ranking of #300 in the world and is considered likely to be successful as a professional when she graduates. I think about the past missed opportunities and feel great pride in our team for putting themselves in this position to beat a great team. They are demonstrating that they deserve the name "Fighting Irish." Mateas catches fire, though, and wins the final set 6-2. Zoe looks crestfallen, but shakes the hand of Mateas as we move to Alison's office and a quick meeting. I feel for her as much as I do for our players. We have come so close, so many times, only to drop a heartbreaker like this one. There is not much to say in our meeting. We all knew what we signed up for when we made the decision to be a part of Notre Dame.

Nobody hunts small deer.

Tomi Lahern

April is the month in college tennis where you can set your destiny. Important late season matches followed by conference tournaments. We fly to Charlottesville, home of the Virginia Cavaliers, listed at #20 in the current ITA rankings. This is as close to home as it gets for me. Richmond is about 50 miles east. I played here after college when the Virginia State Men's Championships moved west from Richmond. It is nice to be close to home. One of my college teammates and a very close friend, John McGinty, has called and will attend tonight's match played in the UVA Boar's Head Sports Complex. John once coined one of the great nicknames for himself. Noting that the box scores always listed results as 'Jones d. Smith, 6-3,6-3', John made the mistake of calling himself "d McGinty,"[pronounced Dee McGinty] hinting that he has suffered his share of losses. The name has stuck and we never let him forget it. It will be special to see him here tonight.

Brian Boland awakened a sleeping giant when he took the reins here in the early 2000's. He wasted no time building a powerhouse team and, before leaving to take over the USTA High Performance Coaching program, had won three NCAA titles. I met Brian in the late 1990's when he became the head coach at Indiana State. He called to ask me if he could drive to South Bend to "pick your brain." I agreed and he asked me for the time I usually came to work. I indicated something like 9:00 AM. He was waiting for me the next day at 9:00, having left Terre Haute at "zero dark thirty" for the five hour drive to meet me. I knew then that he would be both successful and special. When he took over at UVA he insisted on an annual meeting between Virginia and Notre Dame. We had played some terrific 4-3 matches and I had enjoyed watching his success. The Cavaliers' women's team was following in his foot-steps and building a winner. The "Hoos" now ranked #20 in the country.

There was a good crowd to greet us and we responded by winning all three doubles, as two of them finished simultaneously. Game on! The singles were hotly contested and four of them went to a third set. While the score indicated a 5-2 loss, we were oh so close to winning. Cam took out a strong Vivian Glozman 7-5, 7-5. Glozman was reluctant to follow her strong groundies to the net to finish, and Cam adjusted well, competing as well as I had seen her. Brooke played very well, but Chloe Gullickson was launch-ing howitzers from the baseline that eventually became too good to return. Every other match lost went to a third set and we had opportunities to win all of them. Once again, the 5-2 score did not begin to indicate the toughness our players demonstrated. I was, once again, very proud of them and knew that they deserved better.

After breakfast we all piled into our rental cars for the two plus hour drive to Blacksburg. Once again memories surfaced for me from our Big East days competing against Virginia Tech. In our outdoor practice on Saturday, spirits were remarkably high, as I compared them to my many men's teams that tried to overcome adversity. While mentally contrasting my experience coaching our women's team with that of coaching men, I had begun to form some conclusions. There were differences between the men and women, obviously, but they were not what I had expected. What I have discerned from my brief foray into coaching a women's team:

410

1 - Women are easier to coach than men. There is no male ego to get in the way of accepting advice.

2 - Women are more appreciative than men of what you are trying to do for them. At least in my experience, they frequently thanked me after we had finished a drill or practice exercise.

3 - Women are more likely to be willing to accept coaching in the heat of competition than men. I have earlier listed several examples of asking a player to try a different tactic in a critical time in competition. In similar situations, most males were reluctant to try what I suggested.

4 - Women are more concerned about team chemistry than men. They are more comfortable in team settings when they all get along.

5 - Women recover faster from a loss than men. Conversely, they show more emotion immediately after a loss.

6 - Women are more sensitive and take things more personally. I found it more difficult to successfully use anger or laughter as motivational tools.

This is not to say that coaching one sex is BETTER than another, but from my brief sojourn into coaching college women in tennis, I think it is important to understand and work within the parameters that I established. Certainly, I have no claims to "expert" status on this subject. My experience is based purely on a three month period when I served as a coach at Notre Dame. I must admit that more than one former player called me to caution me NOT to tell the same jokes or use the same tactics to motivate, once the word got out that I was working as Alison's assistant.

We had a good practice on the Hokies' courts. While there was a chance for rain, it appeared we would get the match in outdoors. We had a nice dinner and then went over thoughts about tomorrow's match. I thought we were in a good place and would play a good match. It was time to put up or shut up. Any chance at all of NCAA selection mandated that we win this one.

As we warmed up I once again felt good about our chances. Ally had a bad cold, but wanted to play and I thought she had the determination to play through it. She was too important to us to leave out. Oddly, she and Zoe T struggled in doubles. They had been such a strong team all year and it seemed odd for them to be just a bit off. On the bright side, though, Brooke and Bess won at #3 and Cam and Zoe Spence served it out at #1. Notre Dame 1, VA Tech 0.

The singles came easier and we won in straight sets at numbers 1, 2, and 5. Brooke was a warrior, winning 6-1,6-1. Cam followed suit over Nika Kozar 6-2,6-4, rallying late in the second. Zoe Spence continued to show her growth as a player, beating Natalie Novotna 6-4,6-1 and Ally came back to win a third set 7-5 for the final point, enduring a few coughing fits. Losses at #5 and #6 didn't hurt us, but hopefully won't be an indicator of anything moving forward. In Bess's case, "putting the ball on the tee" was needed and playing outdoors again could have been the problem. She, like other players who play a big game, can look like Serena Williams on some days, but needs her timing to be working to be effective.

Our final match presented me with an impossible dilemma. I had long ago promised to attend the retirement dinner\celebration for Dave Fish, my close friend and Harvard coach for almost forty years. Pat and I had booked flights long before I accepted this position. Before I began coaching again I explained to Alison that our last regular season match would be one at which I could not be present. She was great about it. Now, though, I felt conflicted. I had grown much closer to these players than I thought possible. I felt their pain after a loss and I especially felt for Alison, a coach who was doing everything she could to build a program the right way, only to have to deal with more than her share of bad luck. I wanted them to be successful. Our ranking had slipped below what I felt the magic number needed to be for selection into the NCAA tournament. Our last match of the regular season was against Boston College, a team that had just beaten Miami 4-3. Any chance we had for selection mandated that we beat BC. I knew that BC would come here highly motivated. Many of the students there had also applied to Notre Dame, where the admissions process was more stringent. This led to the unfortunate nickname that stuck, to an extent, of "Backup College," as students of both schools engaged in lighthearted fun against one another. Both were Catholic schools and rivalries had long existed in football and hockey. We needed this match, and I was going to miss it to be, in of all places -- Boston.

There is a happy ending here, fortunately. I did, in fact, miss the match, but we won it 4-0. Even the unfinished matches saw us winning and indicated how well we played. Pat and I had a wonderful weekend, staying with old friends in Boston and I thoroughly enjoyed Fish's celebration. Dave even picked me up and drove me to and from the event. It was more than wonderful to see him showered with praise. Before leaving South Bend, I had left a note to the team with Alison for her to read to them. I also followed the match online. Almost immediately after the match ended my cell phone rang and it was Alison and the very happy team calling to let me know they had won. It was a much-appreciated gesture, as I had been quite concerned and feeling guilty about not being there for them. I was genuinely excited for each of the players and very much appreciated their understanding of my dilemma. It looked like our hard work was beginning to pay off.

~ Cross Court Reflection ~

Hard work isn't punishment. Hard work is the price of admission for the opportunity to reach excellence.

Jay Bilas

The ACC Tournament and Then the Wait

I had missed being in the ACC Tournament in my head coaching career. The decision to join, which I wholeheartedly embraced, came as I was retiring, so Ryan Sachire's first year coaching became Notre Dame's year of entry. Our coaches had nice things to say about how the event was run, so I was looking forward to our trip to Cary, NC. I came away even more impressed with the way the ACC does things than I expected. We arrived, grabbed some lunch, and went straight to practice. Seeing so many of my friends in the coaching community was fun for me and I was excited to see how our team would perform. We had a play-in match with Pittsburgh, but first there were some medical issues. Both Ally and Bess had some sort of flu or upper respiratory illness and had been in the student health center prior to departure. Both were running fevers and coughing up phlegm. Our trainer determined that neither could play if they were still running fevers, so there was some anxiety in our camp. Lineups need to be submitted in advance and only straight line substitutions are permitted in doubles. We would have to wait and see if they were on the mend before putting out a lineup. The next day came and both had shown some improvement. The trainer indicated neither could play both singles and doubles, so we improvised for our match with Pitt, using Bess, who seemed more sick, in doubles and Ally, who insisted she was fine, to play singles. Maeve and Rachel Chong would move into the #5 and 6 singles slots. Rachel would play with Brooke at #2 doubles, while Maeve teamed together at #3 with Zoe T. It wasn't pretty, but somehow we found a way. Rachel, who had been a starter since her freshman year, had missed the entire season with nagging pain in her wrist. It had gotten better and she was now medically cleared, but with virtually no match experience, it would be tough for her.

As doubles began, it became apparent that Cam and Zoe were going to win at #1, but both other combinations came out of the blocks slowly. Rachel, after really struggling early, hit some big shots, and we recovered from match point down to clinch the point 7-5. Third doubles was locked in a tiebreaker and did not finish. Irish 1-0. Singles began immediately. Zoe Spence, now among the nation's top 60 players, had an uncharacteristically bad day, winning only three games. This evened the match at 1-1, but Rachel picked up the pace and sprinted to a straight set win, as did Brooke, who seemed to play her best in our biggest matches. Ally, despite coughing through the match, somehow clinched things for us. Cam and Maeve did not finish. As the match concluded it was impossible not to see the tremendous show of emotion by the Pittsburgh players and coaches. Pitt had made the decision to drop the women's tennis program earlier in the year, so for ALL of the Pitt players, it was their last match...ever! It was difficult not to share in their grief. It also affirmed once more to me how important tennis was to these players. Pitt had dropped men's tennis years before.

The theme of post-season play is "Survive and advance!" and we had done just that. Tomorrow, though, would bring a rematch with Virginia, and we would need to be at our best. After consulting with the trainers we returned to the hotel to shower and eat. We would need to be at our best tomorrow. We were encouraged by the memory of our earlier close loss to the Hoos. It would take an even better effort tomorrow.

There was reason for optimism as we began the doubles, as we had swept them in our earlier meeting, but man plans and God laughs. With improvised teams we were never in it and went down quickly to give UVA the point. Now things get interesting. We are clearly in the top four matches, but will need them all if we are to advance. Cam takes the first set and Zoe breaks into a lead. Ally, after dropping the first, quickly wins the second. Brooke once again is locked into a war with Chloe Gullickson, but drops an

11-9 tiebreaker. We drop # 5 and 6. Zoe T is also sick and it shows. Maeve led in the first, but lost it in a breaker. Ally shows her competitiveness and loses only three games in the second and third sets, putting us on the board. I am pretty sure that Cam can also win in three, but suddenly it all ends: it's Virginia with Gullickson hitting yet another big backhand winner.

Suddenly, in the blink of an eye, our season looks to be over. Our ranking will likely leave us out of the NCAA tournament. We shake hands with the Virginia players and coaches. I feel for Alison, who has had to endure more than she should. After the players have gathered their equipment and checked with the trainers, we head back to the hotel and dinner. For the seniors, this is unchartered emotional territory. Consider this: you train, practice, and play tennis non-stop for many years in order to earn a scholarship or admissions bump to the [hopefully] perfect college. Then you make lifelong friends with teammates; practice, travel, and compete with them for another four years. It is all you know. Now, immediately, your world has changed. You know that you may not see these friends again for years, or maybe never. Life is suddenly very confusing. You now realize how much these relationships have meant to you. Oh, there is much ahead about which to be excited, but will you ever replicate these feelings and relationships? I am now 75 years of age and I exchanged emails with three of my college teammates today. It is indeed a lot to absorb.

Several Days Later

It is a beautiful afternoon here in South Bend. I am once again retired; no longer a tennis coach. I move the charcoal briquets around in my Weber grill and, as if on command, several cars drive up to our house and the members of our women's team walk up to the deck to greet me. In perhaps my last official duty, Pat and I have invited the team to our home for a cookout to celebrate the season. As I welcome them and introduce them to Pat, I realize how much I will miss them. We have travelled, practiced, competed, and eaten meals together. They have been kind enough to allow me into their lives. It has been an unexpected pleasure for me. While I am a little bit sad, I also realize that I will be able to watch most of them compete in the coming year.....and the next. When I watch those matches, I will know what each is feeling because it is what I do. I will feel their pain and joy. I will cheer when they win and empathize with them when they lose. Again, it is what I do. I am a teacher. Most of all, I am a coach.

~ Cross Court Reflection ~

Coaching is by far the best profession you could ever be in. You have a chance to be significant.

Lou Holtz

Bayliss Family at Virginia Beach, 2018: Left to right: Sara and Patrick Bayliss, Sam Bayliss, Amy and Rob Bayliss, Delaney Bayliss, Bobby and Pat Bayliss, Brendan and Annie Bayliss, Roman, Nola, and Jackson Bayliss, Alexandra Petrozzi, Jackie and Pablo Petrozzi, Julia Petrozzi, Gabriel Petrozzi. *Photo by Thomas Gorman Photography.*